Argument Licensing and Agreement

Oxford Studies in Comparative Syntax

Richard Kayne, General Editor

ARGUMENT LICENSING AND AGREEMENT

Claire Halpert

OXFORD
UNIVERSITY PRESS

OXFORD
UNIVERSITY PRESS

Oxford University Press is a department of the University of
Oxford. It furthers the University's objective of excellence in research,
scholarship, and education by publishing worldwide.

Oxford   New York
Auckland   Cape Town   Dar es Salaam   Hong Kong   Karachi
Kuala Lumpur   Madrid   Melbourne   Mexico City   Nairobi
New Delhi   Shanghai   Taipei   Toronto

With offices in
Argentina   Austria   Brazil   Chile   Czech Republic   France   Greece
Guatemala   Hungary   Italy   Japan   Poland   Portugal   Singapore
South Korea   Switzerland   Thailand   Turkey   Ukraine   Vietnam

Oxford is a registered trade mark of Oxford University Press
in the UK and in certain other countries.

Published in the United States of America by
Oxford University Press
198 Madison Avenue, New York, NY 10016

© Oxford University Press 2016

Cataloging-in-Publication Data is on file at the Library of Congress.

Library of Congress Cataloging-in-Publication Data
Halpert, Claire.
Argument licensing and agreement / Claire Halpert.
    pages cm. – (Oxford Studies in Comparative Syntax)
Includes bibliographical references and index.
ISBN 978-0-19-025648-7 (pbk. : alk. paper) – ISBN 978-0-19-025647-0 (hardcover : alk.
paper)   1. Zulu language–Grammar, Comparative–Bantu.   2. Bantu language–Grammar,
Comparative–Zulu.   3. Zulu language–Syntax.   4. Zulu language–Agreement.   I. Title.
PL8842.H35 2015
496′.39865–dc23
2015008116

ISBN 978-0-19-025647-0 (hbk);   ISBN 978-0-19-025648-7 (pbk)

9 8 7 6 5 4 3 2 1
Printed in the United States of America
on acid-free paper

for Dan

CONTENTS

LIST OF TABLES

ACKNOWLEDGMENTS

(0) umuntu   ng- umuntu   nga-bantu
     AUG.1person COP- AUG.1person NGA.AUG-2people
     'A person is a person because of people.'   (*Zulu proverb*)

As I do throughout this book, I rely on Zulu here to help me illustrate my point. I am extremely grateful to all of those who have supported me as I have worked to speak and research the Zulu language. There are too many to name here, but I am grateful to my teachers—Sandra Sanneh, Mary Gordon, and Nelson Ntshangase—and to those who welcomed me into their homes and communities and shared with me their friendship and grammaticality judgments. I am particularly indebted to Zoliswa Mali, Doctor Katamzi, and Michael Bongani Langa in Boston; to the entire Katamzi family (Jama!) in Umlazi Township, with whom I stayed while conducting large portions of this research; to the University of KwaZulu-Natal, Howard College, Linguistics Department; and to Percival Mthuli Buthelezi, Mpho Dlamini, and Monwabisi Mhlophe, whose patience and insights helped to push this research in new directions. This book also owes a huge debt to the many people who shared their time, wisdom, encouragement, and linguistic expertise with me in order to make this project come together. Foremost among them are David Pesetsky, Norvin Richards, and Sabine Iatridou, who helped these ideas grow from their infancy. The work of Leston Buell, Jochen Zeller, and Michael Diercks has also had a profound impact on the research in this book; I've learned a lot from their papers and from our conversations over the years; their thoughtful suggestions on my research has helped shape the path of my investigation from the start.

I've also benefited greatly from from feedback and discussion with many other people—too numerous for an exhaustive list—including Enoch Aboh, Nikki Adams, Alya Asarina, Mark Baker, Bronwyn Bjorkman, Vicki Carstens, Lisa Cheng, Jessica Coon, Laura Downing, Larry Hyman, Richard Kayne, Hrayr Khanjian, Langa Khumalo, Ruth Kramer, Nancy Kula, Lutz Marten, Jean-Philippe Marcotte, Juvenal Ndayiragije, Omer Preminger, Kristina Riedel, Ken Safir, Patricia Schneider-Zioga, Tarald Taraldsen, Jenneke van der

Wal, and Hedde Zeijlstra. I'm thankful as well to my colleagues and students in the Institute of Linguistics at the University of Minnesota for their support throughout the writing process. Special thanks go to Omer Preminger and Jessica Coon for their wisdom on the book-making process; to Richard Kayne for his careful and extremely useful suggestions in editing this book; and to three anonymous reviewers, whose feedback has made the book stronger in numerous ways.

Final words of thanks go to everyone who has supported me in all of the ways that go beyond the linguistic discussions in this book. I'm especially grateful to Aleysia and Ellen for their unwavering long-distance support and to Eva for the sanity-preserving coffee breaks! I am also deeply thankful for my entire family, whose encouragement goes back to the very beginning, and above all for Dan, who has kept me going through the ups and downs of the whole process.

The research in this book is based in part upon work supported by the National Science Foundation under Grant No. BCS-1122426. Any opinions, findings, and conclusions or recommendations expressed in this material are my own and do not necessarily reflect the views of the National Science Foundation. I have received additional support from an MIT Dean's Fund Grant and the University of KwaZulu-Natal, Howard College, Linguistics Department. I am very grateful for all of the financial support that has made this work possible.

LIST OF ABBREVIATIONS

ABS	absolutive
ACC	accusative
AOR	aorist
APPL	applicative
ASP	aspect
ASSOC	associative
AUG	augment
AUX	auxiliary
CAUS	causative
CONT	continuous
COP	copula
CS	case
DAT	dative
DEM	demonstrative
DET	determiner
DUR	durative
EXCL	exclusive
F	feminine
FOC	focus
FUT	future
FV	final vowel
GEN	genitive
IMP	imperfective
IMPER	imperative
INF	infinitive
LOC	locative
M	masculine
MOD	modal
NEG	negation
NOM	nominative
O	object agreement
OBJ	object case

OBL	oblique
PART	partitive
PASS	passive
PST	past
PF	perfect
PFV	perfective
PL	plural
POSS	possessive
PRES	present
PROG	progressive
PRT	participial
REFL	reflexive
REL	relative
REM	remote
SG	singular
S	subject agreements
SJC	subjunctive
AgrS	subject agreement head
C	complementizer head
DO	direct object
EPP	Extended Projection Principle
Ext. Arg.	External Argument
IO	indirect object
L	licenser head
NPI	Negative Polarity Item
Nr	number head
P	preposition
PIC	Phase Impenetrability Condition
Pn	person head
v^o	voice head
V	verb head
RtO	raising-to-object
RtS	raising-to-subject
TEC	transitive expletive construction

Argument Licensing and Agreement

CHAPTER 1
Introduction

1.1 BANTU EXCEPTIONALISM: WHAT VARIES, AND WHY?

Viewed from the perspective of, say, the Indo-European languages, the Bantu language family has a number of properties that are comfortingly familiar—such as a robust system of Spec–Head subject agreement—and many others that are bewilderingly unfamiliar—including the ability of a single nominal to control many instances of such agreement. Even at a glance, it is clear that certain of these properties that are broadly shared throughout the Bantu family require some parameterization of certain core syntactic properties and processes, as many researchers before me have proposed for various aspects of Bantu syntax (e.g., Harford Perez, 1985; Baker, 2003a, 2008; Carstens, 2005; Collins, 2005; Diercks, 2012).

This book investigates these questions of syntactic variation through an examination of some core grammatical phenomena—case licensing, agreement, the EPP—centered around the Bantu language Zulu. Zulu has a number of remarkable and puzzling properties, many of which are shared with other Bantu languages, whose analysis affords us new insight on the interaction between these components.

Many of these exceptional-looking syntactic issues are encapsulated in the alternations found with *subject raising* predicates in Zulu:

(1)   a. ku- bonakala [ukuthi **uZinhle**   u- zo- xova ujeqe   ]
       17s- seem   that   AUG.1Zinhle 1s- FUT- make AUG.1steamed.bread

    b. **uZinhle**$_i$ u- bonakala [ukuthi t$_i$ **u**- zo- xova ujeqe   ]
       AUG.1Zinhle 1s- seem   that   1s- FUT- make AUG.1steamed.bread

    c. **uZinhle**$_i$ **ku**- bonakala [ukuthi t$_i$ **u**- zo- xova ujeqe   ]
       AUG.1Zinhle 17s- seem   that   1s- FUT- make AUG.1steamed.bread
       'It seems that Zinhle will make steamed bread.'

The trio of sentences in (1) are judged to be semantically equivalent and are used interchangeably by speakers of Durban Zulu. In all of these sentences, a matrix raising predicate, *bonakala*, takes a finite CP complement, with three different options for placement and agreement of the embedded subject. The sentence in (1a) most closely resembles familiar patterns from languages like English: the embedded subject remains in the finite CP while the matrix predicate bears expletive agreement. In (1b), the embedded subject has moved to Spec,TP of the matrix clause and agrees with *both* the matrix and embedded verbs. Finally, the construction in (1c) also involves movement of the embedded subject to Spec,TP of the matrix clause, but in this case it only controls embedded—and not matrix—agreement. Again, in every case, the CP complement is *identical*, containing an overt complementizer and a finite predicate that agrees with the embedded subject.

The existence of this type of alternation in Zulu gives rise to several puzzles. First, we can ask why the raising in these constructions is *optional*. Raising is often assumed to be driven by the structural case needs of a nominal: required when the subject lacks case, but ruled out when the subject receives case in the embedded clause, as in a language like English:

(2) a. It seems that Zinhle will make steamed bread.

    b. * Zinhle$_i$ seems that t$_i$ will make steamed bread.

    c. * It seems Zinhle to make steamed bread.

    d. Zinhle$_i$ seems t$_i$ to make steamed bread.

In Zulu, by contrast, the raising is freely available and apparently independent of any particular properties of the embedded clause. This optionality fits into a larger pattern in Zulu—and the Bantu language family more generally—of a distribution of nominals that is relatively unrestricted.

In light of this type of evidence, a number of proposals suggest that much of the variation displayed by the Bantu family as a whole arises from the parameterization of case: in particular, they argue that we can make sense of the unrestricted distribution of nominals in many Bantu languages if syntactic case is simply not a part of the grammar of these languages (e.g., Harford Perez 1985; Diercks 2012 and others).

In this book, I argue in favor of a different conclusion. In particular, I propose that the main sources of the cross-linguistic variation that we find between Bantu languages like Zulu and those with more familiar case patterns are the *mechanisms* through which case is assigned and the *relationships* between case and agreement.

In chapters 3–5, I amass evidence that Zulu has a system of structural *and* morphological case. I argue that structural case effects of the type we have come to expect based on cross-linguistic patterns are obscured in Zulu for two main reasons. First, the positions of structural case-licensers differ from those found in more familiar case systems; notably, T in Zulu is not a case-assigner. Second, I argue that Zulu has available a type of freely-applying case morphology that can *intrinsically* license a nominal, independent of the syntax. I show that when we compare this Zulu morphological case system with more familiar systems, such as the well-studied case system of Icelandic, the existence of such morphology becomes less surprising.

Given these novel conclusions about case in Bantu, we can return to the raising puzzle to ask how raising and agreement work in a language without a nominative effect. As the constructions in (1) illustrate, any account of this raising pattern must answer the questions of what allows nominals in Zulu to raise out of a CP with a finite complement and why there are two options for agreement when the nominal has raised. More specifically, the raising in Zulu seems to be occurring out of the finite complement of an (overt) C^o, a type of movement that is generally ruled out by the *Phase Impenetrability Condition* (PIC, Chomsky, 2000, 2001). Furthermore, as I establish in chapter 2, elsewhere in Zulu, preverbal subjects obligatorily agree with the verb, so the fact that they do not need to agree in raising constructions like (1c) is surprising. I argue that these two puzzles are related. Following Rackowski and Richards (2005), I reduce the PIC to an instance of intervention, arguing that the embedded CP in Zulu functions as a potential goal for higher phi-agreement probes. Once that CP has been agreed with, however, it no longer intervenes and the embedded subject can therefore be probed by elements that are outside of the embedded CP. In the raising construction, I propose that the obviation of the PIC and the optional agreement both stem from the fact that the matrix predicate agrees *twice*—first with the embedded CP and then with the embedded subject. A final question raised by these constructions is the question of what *does* drive the raising, since it does not happen due to the needs of the raising subject. I argue in chapter 6 that this type of raising, and subject agreement in Zulu more generally, results from the EPP, requiring that Spec,TP be filled by a syntactic category, a connection proposed by Baker (2003a, 2008), Carstens (2005), and Collins (2005), among others. As I discuss throughout the book, the existence of separate systems of syntactic case and syntactic agreement that result from the lack of nominative assignment by T allow us to see unusual interactions between these two grammatical components.

1.2 FAMILIARITY IN THE UNFAMILIAR: INSIGHTS ON SYNTAX AND VARIATION

One of the most striking conclusions of this work is the discovery that Zulu has a system of case-licensing, realized both in terms of structural licensing and case morphology on nominals. As noted above, this conclusion goes against the prevailing view that case is not relevant in the grammar of Bantu languages (Harford Perez, 1985; Baker, 2003a, 2008; Carstens and Diercks, 2013; Diercks, 2012; and others). Though the type of case system that I propose for Zulu is at its core similar to our current understanding of case, there are a number of differences between the case system I argue for in Zulu and the more familiar systems of languages like Icelandic and English. These differences give us insight into how case functions in the grammar.

Chapter 2 sets the stage for our investigations into case and agreement. I establish in this chapter that while Zulu subjects display a fair amount of flexibility in terms of the syntactic position in which they may appear, agreement is always accompanied by A-movement of the subject to Spec,TP, yielding the observed correlation between Agree and the EPP. The choice of subject position, as I will show, correlates with information structure properties of the subject. I also return to the raising constructions illustrated in (1) at the beginning of this chapter, focusing on the alternation between non-raised subjects and agreeing raised subjects. I show that these constructions require a raising analysis and therefore raise the puzzles that I discussed above.

In chapters 3–5, I focus on the puzzle of Zulu's relatively unrestricted nominal distribution patterns that emerges from chapter 2. I demonstrate in chapters 3 and 4 that the positions in which structural licensing occur in Zulu are *not* the familiar positions of structural licensing found in languages like English or Icelandic. As we will see, neither T nor v^o appear to structurally license Zulu nominals. Instead, Zulu case-licensing seems to occur fully inside the vP domain. I argue that in chapter 3 that Zulu has a "higher" case associated with a Licensing head that licenses the highest element in vP and a "lower" case that is assigned by APPL or CAUS. The fact that licensing is associated with these unfamiliar positions in Zulu is one factor that has helped to obscure its effects. The other factor is that evidence for structural licensing comes from the behavior of *augmentless* nominals, which are restricted to the syntactic positions mentioned above, in contrast to nominals that are marked with an augment vowel. As I discuss in chapter 3, a number of other Bantu languages show similar syntactic restrictions correlated to the distribution of the augment, which suggests that evidence for case in these languages may have been similarly obscured by the prevalence of augment morphology.

In chapter 4, I examine additional evidence for this view of structural licensing in Zulu and argue that another syntactic phenomenon, the *conjoint/disjoint* alternation that marks verbal predicates, is in fact simply the head-marking morphological realization of the syntactic licensing process I propose in chapter 3. This conclusion is also an important one for our understanding of syntactic variation in Bantu; as I discuss in that chapter, work by Kavari et al. (2012) notes that the Bantu language Otjiherero shows a distribution of tonal patterns on nominals that they demonstrate coincides with exactly the instances where I posit that nominals are probed by the Licensing head in Zulu.

One striking similarity between the licensing of augmentless nominals and the conjoint/disjoint alternation is that both appear to be sensitive only to the *surface* position of arguments. I establish in chapters 3 and 4 that we can in fact distinguish these processes from truly surface-oriented ones. I argue on the basis of this evidence that both phenomena should therefore be considered part of the syntactic derivation. I propose that their apparent surface-oriented properties arise from the ability of the licensing relationship to be freely ordered with respect to A-movement. These ordering possibilities include one in which arguments move *before* they can be structurally licensed. I attribute the absence of the opposite order of operations—in which arguments would first be licensed by the L^o head and subsequently move—to the Activity Condition (Chomsky, 2001): once a nominal is licensed, it is inactive for all further A-processes. As I discuss in chapter 4, we find a number of remarkable similarities between these timing processes in Zulu and those that have been proposed to account for case and agreement interactions in Icelandic (Holmberg and Hróarsdóttir, 2004; Sigurðsson and Holmberg, 2008).

The structural licensing picture that emerges is thus both familiar and unfamiliar: the locations of licensing differ from a standard nominative–accusative picture, but the syntactic operations and ways in which they interact with each other are deeply familiar.

(3) **Sources of structural case in a NOM–ACC language**

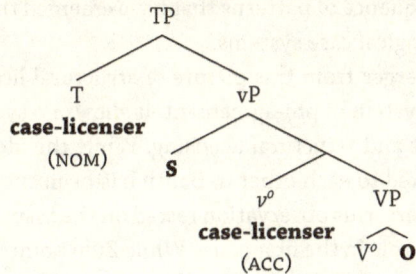

(4) **Sources of structural case in Zulu**

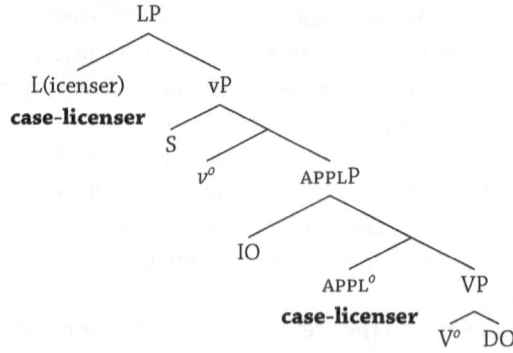

Zulu also displays some novel properties of morphological case, though again housed within a broadly familiar system. As I establish in chapters 3 and 4, the structural licensing effects that we find in Zulu appear to constrain only augmentless nominals; though there is ample proof that augmented nominals also interact with these licensing operations, they do not seem dependent on structural licensing in the same way. In chapter 5, I investigate the question of why augmented nominals in Zulu do not require structural licensing. I argue in this chapter that the *augment* vowel that marks most nominals functions as an intrinsic case licenser, allowing nominals that it marks to appear in unlicensed positions. I extend my investigation of nominal licensing beyond core arguments, to compare augmented nominals to nominals with oblique prefixes in Zulu. Through this comparison, I show that Zulu has a familiar system of case morphology, corresponding to the *structural, quirky,* and *inherent* cases found in languages like Icelandic (e.g., Schütze, 1997). At the same time, I argue that the augment itself is a novel type of case—one that inherently licenses nominals but is able to agree with the verb. I argue that these four types of case, as represented in table 1.1 on the following page, are predicted based on the two parameters that delineate the typology of case in languages like Icelandic. In this regard, the pattern we find in Zulu is in fact an expected one: a logical consequence of patterns that have emerged through investigation of other morphological case systems.

Another conclusion that emerges from this picture of structural licensing is that while Zulu has a robust system of phi-agreement, it shows no syntactic overlap between phi-agreement and structural licensing. While the idea that case and agreement are not linked to each other in Bantu has been suggested by Baker (2003a, 2008) and others, this observation rested on the assumption that case was playing little to no role in the first place. While Zulu points to the same higher-level conclusion, it does so by showing that case and agreement are both active in a language yet do not overlap or show any dependencies.

Table 1.1. LICENSING STRATEGIES AND
NOMINAL MORPHOLOGY IN ZULU

+ intrinsic + agreeable **augment**	– intrinsic + agreeable (*"structural"*) **augmentless**
+ intrinsic – agreeable (*"inherent"*) **aug-replacing**	– intrinsic – agreeable (*"quirky"*) **aug-permitting**

All of these conclusions lead us back to the original Zulu puzzle posed in (1) above. As we will see in chapter 6, I argue on the basis of agreement and raising facts that the EPP, and not case, functions as the driving engine for many of the A-processes, including phi-agreement and A-movement, that we find in the grammar of Zulu. On the surface, the fact that phi-agreement tends to correlate with movement to Spec,TP in Zulu is in line with theories of "reverse agree," which reduce the EPP to a by-product of the agreement process by arguing that goals must c-command their probes (e.g., Bošković, 2007; Wurmbrand, 2011; Zeijlstra, 2012). In chapter 6, however, I show that this generalization does not always hold in Zulu. In particular, I argue on the basis of constructions like (1c) above that Agree is crucially a downward-probing operation that is not simply a reflection of how the EPP is satisfied. Instead, I propose that phi-agreement with an embedded CP does *not* satisfy the EPP in Zulu, but rather serves to unlock the embedded CP phase for subsequent movement of the raised subject. This analysis extends an account of phase obviation proposed by Rackowski and Richards (2005) from A-bar processes to the A-movement found in Zulu raising constructions. In short, the typologically unusual raising patterns that we find in Zulu (and many other Bantu languages, see Harford Perez, 1985; Ura, 1994; Carstens, 2011; Carstens and Diercks, 2013; Diercks, 2012) are a natural outcome of the ways in which Zulu's case and agreement systems differ from the standard nominative–accusative system.

Chapter 7 discusses some of these higher-level conclusions that Zulu suggests concerning the organization of syntax. I review the insights we gain on case, agreement, and the EPP and compare the properties of Zulu in these domains with those of Icelandic. I close with some thoughts on how the discoveries presented here for Zulu may shape our understanding of the similarities and variations found in a broader cross-Bantu perspective.

Before I begin, I offer a brief note of orientation on Zulu, the language whose patterns will drive the investigation in this book. Zulu (also written isiZulu) is a Bantu language in the Nguni subgroup. The Bantu language family comprises over 500 languages[1] that are spoken indigenously in twenty-seven African countries, as well as by populations living in the United States, Europe, and elsewhere (Nurse and Philippson, 2003). The Bantu languages are divided into sixteen lettered subgroups ("Guthrie zones"), which are further broken down by number into more closely related subgroups. Zulu has the Guthrie classification of S42. Zone S contains languages spoken in the southern part of the continent, including Zimbabwe, Mozambique, Botswana, South Africa, Lesotho, and Swaziland. The Nguni subgroup (S40) contains Zulu's closest relatives: Xhosa, Swati, and Ndebele, which have a fair degree of mutual intelligibility with Zulu. Zulu is spoken by over 10 million speakers worldwide, primarily living in South Africa, with other Zulu-speaking communities in Botswana, Lesotho, Malawi, Mozambique, and Swaziland (Ethnologue). As of 2001, 10.7 million South Africans, 23.8% of the population, claimed Zulu as their first language, making it the most prevalent first language in the country (2001 Census).

The main Zulu-speaking areas in South Africa are the provinces of KwaZulu-Natal (81% native Zulu speakers) and Gauteng (21.5% native Zulu speakers). While Zulu is prevalent throughout the province of KwaZulu-Natal, including its major urban center of Durban, most Zulu speakers in Gauteng are located in and around Johannesburg, South Africa's largest city (2001 Census). The majority of Zulu speakers in Zulu-dominant regions receive Zulu-medium education in the early years of their schooling, and typically at least some Zulu-based instruction throughout their later academic career.

The data in this book come from my original fieldwork with native speakers of Durban Zulu, collected between September 2008 and December 2014. The majority of the data was collected on two research trips to South Africa in 2011 and 2012, with the rest of the data coming from in-person elicitation sessions with three speakers in the Boston area and phone consultations with three speakers from Durban. In Durban, I conducted interviews with 38 different speakers, mainly from Umlazi Township, though much of the data reported here comes from regular meetings with six of these speakers. In addition to direct elicitation, some examples are taken from naturally-occurring conversation and from the Internet. As I have noted throughout the book, the judgments of Durban Zulu speakers sometimes contrast with those reported in previous linguistic literature and grammar books. In addition, my

---

1. The exact number is in dispute. Recent estimates include 501 (Grimes, 2000) and 660 (Maho, 2003). See Nurse and Philippson (2003) for discussion.

fieldwork uncovered some systematic variation within the Durban population, which I have noted where relevant.

Finally, I would like to note that while Zulu is a tone language, its syntactic tonal properties are largely predictable (see Khumalo, 1981, 1982). Throughout the book, I do not mark tone unless specific tonal properties are directly relevant to the syntactic analysis.

CHAPTER 2

A-movement and Phi

Building Blocks of Zulu Syntax

A central concern of this book is the syntactic factors that govern the distribution of nominals in Zulu. In particular, which syntactic properties are responsible for the surface differences that we find between a Zulu-type language and one with a more familiar structural case-driven system? In chapters 3–6 I investigate a number of interactions between the distribution of Zulu nominals and their ability to agree with verbs that will allow us to identify the relevant factors that yield the variation we find between Zulu and other Bantu languages, and between Bantu and non-Bantu languages more generally. To analyze these constructions, we must first develop a solid understanding of the different syntactic positions available to nominals in Zulu and of the different agreement properties associated with these positions. This chapter provides a foundation for our investigation, establishing which syntactic positions are typically available to Zulu nominals and what the constraints on and consequences of appearing in such positions are. As we will see, the syntactic position of the subject correlates with both agreement patterns and information structure. This intersection between syntactic position and information structure will be crucial when we consider the restricted distribution of certain nominals in chapter 3 and when we examine the properties of non-agreeing preverbal subjects in chapter 6. In addition to addressing the basic syntactic constituencies associated with particular subject positions, I also address the nature of the morphological dependency between the verb and the subject. I argue in favor of treating the subject marker as the result of syntactic agreement between T and a nominal in Spec,TP—and not as a pronominal clitic. This distinction allows us to better understand the relationship between phi-agreement with subjects and structural case that we will see in subsequent chapters. In section 2.4, I extend the discussion of agreement and subject positions in Zulu to raising constructions. I show that Zulu allows optional raising out of finite agreeing clauses, a fact that will serve as background to my investigation of case in chapter 3. I return to raising predicates and their unique agreement properties in chapter 6, where I propose an analysis for why raising can occur out of finite clauses in the language. In section 2.5, I shift away from the agreement properties of subjects to examine argument structure within *v*P. I establish how different types of arguments, particularly those associated with applicative and causative constructions, are introduced in the language. In chapter 3, I build upon these observations to discuss the specific configurations in which arguments are case-licensed in Zulu.

2.1 ANATOMY OF A NOMINAL

Zulu nouns are divided into 14 different noun classes, a distinction that is realized both in terms of morphology on the nominal and in a variety of agreement and concord processes throughout the grammar.[1] Every Zulu noun stem is marked with prefixal morphology that corresponds to the noun class of the nominal. This prefixal morphology typically consists of two parts. The first part, which appears on every nominal, is the noun class prefix, a C/CV/CVC/Ø morpheme that attaches to the stem and indicates noun class. This noun class prefix is optionally preceded by an *augment* vowel (also referred to as the *initial vowel* or *pre-prefix*), that reflects the vowel in the noun class prefix (see Taraldsen, 2010). The full paradigm of noun class prefixes and augments is given in table 2.1 on the following page.[2]

In the remainder of this chapter, I focus on nominals that have augment morphology and do not discuss the internal morphological makeup of these nominals any further. I revisit the issue of the augment in chapter 3, where I argue that augmentless nominals require case-licensing, and in chapter 5, where I address the syntactic role of augment morphology and propose that it functions as a case morpheme that licenses nominals independently of the syntactic structure.

---

1. This type of noun class system is pervasive in the Bantu language family. The numbers associated with each noun class correspond to the reconstructed noun class system for Proto-Bantu, which includes approximately 24 noun classes (see Katamba, 2003, for an overview). Zulu, like other attested modern Bantu languages, does not retain the full set of noun class markers, which leads to some of the numbering gaps in table 2.1.

2. I do not distinguish between classes 1/1a and 2/2a in the glossing of examples. While classes 1a and 2a have distinct nominal prefix morphology from classes 1 and 2, they pattern with these classes for all other morphological processes. One exception to this pattern is that inanimate nouns in class 1a take a class 3 object agreement marker.

Table 2.1. NOUN CLASS PREFIXAL MORPHOLOGY

NOUN CLASS	AUGMENT	PREFIX	EXAMPLE	TRANSLATION
1	u-	m(u)-	umuntu	'person'
1a	u-	Ø	ugogo	'grandmother'
2	a-	ba-	abantu	'people'
2a	o-	Ø	ogogo	'grandmothers'
3	u-	m(u)-	umunwe	'finger'
4	i-	mi-	iminwe	'fingers'
5	i-	(li-)	iqanda	'egg'
6	a-	ma-	amaqanda	'eggs'
7	i-	si-	isipho	'gift'
8	i-	zi-	izipho	'gifts'
9	i-	N-	indawo	'place'
10	i-	ziN-	izindawo	'places'
11	u-	(lu-)	uthando	'love'
14	u-	(bu-)	ubuntu	'humanity'
15	u-	ku-	ukudla	'food'
17	u-	ku-	ukwindla	'autumn'

2.2 FLEXIBLE WORD ORDER

The canonical word order in Zulu transitive clauses is SVO:

(5) uZinhle   u- xova ujeqe
    AUG.1Zinhle 1s- make AUG.1steamed.bread
    'Zinhle is making steamed bread.'

In addition to SVO word order, however, Zulu also permits a number of non-canonical word orders. The use and acceptability of the different word order possibilities in Zulu depends on a number of independent factors, including agreement and information structure, as I will show in more detail later in this chapter. Setting aside these factors for a moment, we can see that all possible orderings of subject, verb, and object are permitted (Buell, 2005):

(6) a. uZinhle   u- ya- wu- xova ujeqe   SVO
       AUG.1Zinhle 1s- YA- 1o- make AUG.1steamed.bread

    b. ujeqe   u- ya- wu- xova uZinhle   OVS
       AUG.1steamed.bread 1s- YA- 1o- make AUG.1Zinhle

    c. uZinhle   ujeqe   u- ya- wu- xova   SOV
       AUG.1Zinhle AUG.1steamed.bread 1s- YA- 1o- make

d. ujeqe   uZinhle   u- ya- wu- xova   OSV
   AUG.1steamed.bread AUG.1Zinhle 1s- YA- 1O- make

e. u- ya- wu- xova ujeqe   uZinhle   VOS
   1s- YA- 1O- make AUG.1steamed.bread AUG.1Zinhle

f. u- ya- wu- xova uZinhle   ujeqe   VSO
   1s- YA- 1O- make AUG.1Zinhle AUG.1steamed.bread
   'Zinhle is making steamed bread.'

Furthermore, we find in Zulu that certain word orders can be associated with multiple syntactic structures. Because the verb in Zulu raises to a head that is above vP,[3] there are two possible locations for nominals that follow the verb: they may either be vP-internal or in a higher, right-dislocated position.

We can observe this contrast in postverbal subject positions if we look at the behavior of the low adverb *kahle* 'well', which Buell (2005) shows always appears within vP, at its right edge. Postverbal arguments may either appear to the left of *kahle*, and thus inside vP, or to its right:

(7)   a. ku- xova uZinhle   ujeqe   **kahle**
         17s- make AUG.1Zinhle AUG.1steamed.bread well

      b. u- wu- xova **kahle** uZinhle   ujeqe
         1s- 1O- make well   AUG.1Zinhle AUG.1steamed.bread
         'Zinhle makes steamed bread well.'

Using *kahle* as a marker of the right edge of the vP domain, we can conclude that the postverbal arguments in (7a) are between the verb and *kahle*, and thus presumably *inside* vP, while the arguments in (7b) follow *kahle* and thus are *outside* of vP. As we will see throughout this chapter and chapter 4, a number of other properties also reliably correlate with the right edge of vP, including *penultimate lengthing* of vowels at the vP edge (see Cheng and Downing, 2009) and the *conjoint/disjoint* alternation in verbal morphology that I discuss in detail in chapter 4. As we will see in chapter 4, the disjoint form (*-ya-*) appears when the vP is empty, as in (10a) below, and the conjoint (Ø) appears if not. In addition to the difference in word order that the subject displays with respect to *kahle* in (7), in the next section we will see that these two positions further correspond to obligatory differences in agreement patterns and interpretation. I will also show in the next section that preverbal arguments

3. See Julien (2002), Buell (2005), Cheng and Downing (2012), and Zeller (2013) for a discussion of the morphological evidence for head movement in Zulu, and in Bantu more generally. For Buell, the verb raises to a position called "Aux", which hosts the final vowel that appears at the end of verbal complexes; Cheng and Downing simply denote the position to which the verb raises as "X." For Julien (2002), who focuses specifically on Shona, head movement of the verb reaches "Mood", which is located above vP or CausP, which introduce the highest argument.

Table 2.2. SUBJECT AGREEMENT MORPHOLOGY

NOUN CLASS	INDIC.	SUBJUNCT.	PARTICIP.	REL.	OBJECT MARKER	PRONOUN
1SG	ngi-	ngi-	ngi-	engi-	-ngi-	mina
1PL	si-	si-	si-	esi-	-si-	thina
2SG	u-	u-	u-	owu-	-ku-	wena
2PL	ni-	ni-	ni-	eni-	-ni-	nina
1	u-	a-	e-	o-	-m(u)-	yena
2	ba-	ba-	be-	aba-	-ba-	bona
3	u-	u-	u-	o-	-wu-	wona
4	i-	i-	i-	-yi-	-yi-	yona
5	li-	li-	li-	eli-	-li-	lona
6	a-	a-	a-	a-	-wa-	wona
7	si-	si-	si-	esi-	-si-	sona
8	zi-	zi-	zi-	ezi-	-zi-	zona
9	i-	i-	i-	e-	-yi-	yona
10	zi-	zi-	zi-	ezi-	-zi-	zona
11	lu-	lu-	lu-	olu-	-lu-	lona
14	bu-	bu-	bu-	obu-	-bu-	bona
15	ku-	ku-	ku-	oku-	-ku-	kona
17	ku-	ku-	ku-	oku-	-ku-	kona

face similar ambiguities in structural position, which again correlate with particular agreement and information structure properties.

2.3 SUBJECTS AND AGREEMENT

Zulu finite predicates always contain a subject agreement morpheme. In addition to first and second person agreement, third person agreement tracks *noun class*, which I introduced in section 2.1. The subject agreement paradigm for these noun classes is given above in table 2.2.

When the subject appears outside of *v*P—or is pro-dropped—this subject morpheme matches the noun class of the subject:[4]

(8) **Pre-verbal agreed-with subjects**

    a. (**uZinhle**) **u-** xova ujeqe
       AUG.1Zinhle 1s- make AUG.1steamed.bread
       'Zinhle is making steamed bread.'

---

4. Though see chapter 6 for a discussion of some exceptions to this pattern.

b. **(omakhelwane) ba-** xova ujeqe
AUG.2neighbor   2s- make AUG.1steamed.bread
'The neighbors are making steamed bread.'

c. **(iqhawe) li-** xova ujeqe
AUG.5hero 5s- make AUG.1steamed.bread
'The hero is making steamed bread.'

(9) **Post-*v*P agreed-with subjects**

a. **u-** xova ujeqe   kahle $_{vP}$] **Zinhle**
1s- make AUG.1steamed.bread well   AUG.1Zinhle
'Zinhle makes steamed bread well.'

b. **ba-** xova ujeqe   kahle $_{vP}$] **omakhelwane**
2s- make AUG.1steamed.bread well   AUG.2neighbors
'The neighbors make steamed bread well.'

c. **li-** xova ujeqe   kahle $_{vP}$] **iqhawe**
5s- make AUG.1steamed.bread well   AUG.5hero
'The hero makes steamed bread well.'

When no external argument is present, as in the weather predicate in (10a)—which lacks arguments altogether—and the unaccusative in situ *wh*-question in (10b) below, the verb bears a default noun class 17 marker, *ku*- (Buell, 2005):

(10)   a. **ku-** ya- banda
17s- YA- be.cold
'It's cold.'

b. **kw-** ezneka- ni?
17s- happen- 9what
'What's happening?'

Similarly, when the external argument remains inside *v*P, the verb must also bear the default *ku*- marker instead of reflecting the noun class of the subject. In (11) below, the post-verbal subject appears between the verb and the low adverb *kahle*, and is thus inside *v*P. In these constructions, the default *ku*-marker is required:

(11)   ***v*P-internal subjects: agreement prohibited**

a. *****u-** pheka uZinhle kahle
1s- cook   1Zinhle well

b. **ku-** pheka uZinhle   kahle
17s- cook   AUG.1Zinhle well
'Zinhle cooks well.'

c. * **li**- pheka iqhawe   kahle
        5s- cook   AUG.5hero well

d.   **ku**- pheka iqhawe   kahle
        17s- cook   AUG.5hero well
        'The hero cooks well.'

What emerges from the data in (9)–(11) is that the appearance of the subject marker is sensitive to syntactic structure:

(12) **Subject agreement generalization:** *v*P-external subjects *must* agree; *v*P-internal subjects *cannot* agree.

Next I will look in more detail at the nature of this subject marker and the positions of nouns that trigger it.

2.3.1 Properties of *v*P-external Subjects

As I showed above, when the subject surfaces outside of *v*P in Zulu, the verb *must* bear a subject marker, regardless of whether that subject is pre- or post-*v*P. I will follow Buell (2005) in analyzing this subject marker as an agreement morpheme and will treat it as the result of agreement with a nominal in Spec,TP. In this section, I motivate these proposals in the face of the ongoing debate in the Bantu and Zulu literature over the syntactic status of both the subject marker and of the positions that agreeing subjects can occupy. There are two main points of contention. First is the question of whether the subject marker is itself a pronominal clitic that saturates the external argument of the verb (for example Givón, 1976; Van der Spuy, 2001; Schneider-Zioga, 2007; Zeller, 2008) or is in fact an agreement marker that reflects the noun class of a DP argument (for example Carstens, 2001; Baker, 2003b; Buell, 2005; Henderson, 2006a; Diercks, 2010). A distinct, but related, question is the issue of whether agreed-with subjects occupy Spec,TP or are always dislocated.

On the pronominal clitic view of the subject marker, the overt subject always appears in a dislocated, A-bar position because the subject marker itself occupies the argument position for the subject in the syntax, as Van der Spuy (2001) argues for Zulu. This analysis accounts for the fact that the subject can only be pro-dropped if a subject marker is present—in those cases the subject marker fulfills the actual role of the subject, which the full DP must do in the absence of the subject marker.

Corbett (2006) proposes that one way to distinguish between clitic doubling and agreement morphology is the appearance of multiple instances of the morpheme: multiple agreement markers are permitted, but only one clitic will occur per clause. If the subject marker is a pronominal clitic, then we expect only one agreement marker to be possible in a single clause. In fact, however, as Buell (2005) notes for Zulu, in line with work on several other Bantu languages (including Kinyalolo, 1991; Carstens, 2001; Baker, 2003b; Henderson, 2006a; Thwala, 2006a; Zeller, 2008), constructions that involve auxiliary verbs, such as so-called compound tenses, require multiple subject markers, one for each verbal element:

(13) **Multiple subject markers in compound tenses**

    a. **thina si**- zo- be **si**-   sa- dlala ibhola
       we   1PL- FUT- be 1PL.PRT- DUR- play AUG.5ball
       'We will still be playing soccer.'

    b. **abafana ba**- zo- be **be**-   nga- ka- dlal- i   ibhola
       AUG.2boy 2s- FUT- be 2s.PRT- NEG- EXCL- play- NEG AUG.5ball
       'The boys will not yet be playing soccer.'   (Nyembezi, 1991, pp. 168, 172)

We also find this pattern in Zulu with the numerous auxiliary verbs historically called 'deficient verbs' that tend to carry an adverbial meaning (see Slattery, 1981, for an exhaustive list):

(14) **Multiple subject markers with deficient verbs**

    a. uma zi-   sukuma, **izingane**   **zi**- phinde **zi**- w- e
       when 10PRT- stand.up AUG.10children 10s- again   10s- fall- SJC
       'Every time they stand up, the children fall down again.'

    b. **abazali**   **bami**   **ba**- yaye **ba**- vuk- e ngo-five
       AUG.2parents 2ASSOC.1SG 2s- usually 2s- awake- SJC NGA.AUG-1.five
       'My parents usually wake up at 5.'

By Corbett's diagnostic, the appearance of multiple subject markers in (13) and (14) is an argument in favor of an agreement analysis over a pronominal clitic analysis.

    Preminger (2009a) provides a different diagnostic for distinguishing agreement markers from clitic-doubling. He claims that only agreement morphology can surface in a 'default' form in the absence of anything to agree with; pronominal clitics, by contrast, simply do not appear at all when there is nothing to double. By this measure as well, the Zulu subject markers behave more like agreement than like pronominal clitics. We have already seen that default agreement marker *ku*- appears when the verb does not agree with a thematic subject, even in constructions such as weather predicates, which presumably have no thematic subject to begin with, as shown in this example repeated from (10a) above:[5]

5. Note that these facts contrast with the behavior of the object marker: in intransitive clauses, or when the object is *v*P-internal, no object marker morpheme appears on

(10a) **ku-** ya- banda
17s- YA- be.cold
'It's cold.'

In light of this type of evidence that favors an agreement analysis of the subject marker throughout Bantu, Baker (2003b) develops an alternative to the pronoun analysis: he argues that while the subject marker in Bantu languages is an agreement morpheme, rather than a pronominal clitic, it is always agreement with a null *pro* in Spec,TP. The optional overt DP, on this view, is in a dislocated position (Baker, 2003b). Both the pronominal clitic view and the agreement-with-*pro* view share the assumption that the agreeing subject is *always* in a dislocated, A-bar position. Both of these analyses therefore predict that agreeing subjects will always have A-bar properties.

Sabel and Zeller (2006) and Zeller (2008) show that some subjects with identificational, or exhaustive, focus (following Kiss, 1998), such as *wh*-words and DPs modified by *only*, cannot appear in agreeing subject position. These elements, they point out, must instead appear either inside *v*P or in a cleft:

(15) a. *** ubani   u- fik-   ile?
       AUG.1who 1s- arrive- PFV

     b. ku- fik-   e   **bani**?
         17s- arrive- PFV 1who

     c. ng- **ubani**   o-   fik-   ile?
         COP- AUG.1who 1REL- arrive- PFV
         'Who came?'   (Sabel and Zeller, 2006, ex. (5))

(16) ngi- mem- e   wonke umuntu,   kodwa...
     1SG- invite- PFV 1every AUG.1person but
     'I invited everyone, but...'
     a. *** uJohn   kuphela u- fik-   ile
        AUG.1John only   1s- arrive- PFV

     b. ku- fik-   e   **uJohn   kuphela**
         17s- arrive- PFV AUG.1John only
         'only John came.'   (Zeller, 2008, ex. (37))

the verb at all. Unlike the subject marker, the object marker does not appear to have a morphological default (Buell, 2005; Adams, 2010; Zeller, 2012). This asymmetry is reminiscent of the classic characterization of the EPP—that clauses uniformly require a subject, though there is no uniform requirement for there to be an object (Chomsky, 1981). I return to the connection between the subject agreement patterns in Zulu and the EPP in chapter 6, where I argue that the EPP is responsible for all subject agreement patterns in Zulu.

Sabel and Zeller (2006) and Zeller (2008) argue that this ban on these identificational focus elements in preverbal subject position is expected if agreeing DPs have the status of dislocated, clitic-doubled elements in Zulu, since such elements are cross-linguistically bad in dislocated positions. As van der Wal (2009) points out in reply, however, preverbal subjects in Bantu do not always display the behavior expected of dislocated elements. Van der Wal (2009) shows that in Makhuwa-Enahara, as in many other Bantu languages, universal quantifiers, which are often restricted in dislocated positions (see Rizzi, 1986; Baker, 1996), may appear in agreeing subject position, though they are prohibited in unambiguously dislocated positions. In addition, van der Wal (2009) shows that DPs with nonspecific indefinite interpretations are also permitted as agreeing preverbal subjects, again unexpected on a dislocation analysis.

Both of these patterns that van der Wal (2009) demonstrates for Makhuwa-Enahara hold in Zulu as well: universal quantifiers and nonspecific indefinites are both permitted as preverbal subjects, but not as right-dislocated postverbal subjects or as high left-dislocated subjects:

(17) **Universal quantifiers in agreeing subject position**

    a. **wonke umuntu**   **u-** ya- wa- thanda amaswidi
        1every AUG.1person 1s- YA- 6O- like   AUG.6candy
        'Everyone likes candy.'

    b. * **u-** ya- wa- thanda amaswidi **wonke umuntu**
        1s- YA- 6O- like   AUG.6candy 1every AUG.1person

    c. * **wonke umuntu**   amaswidi **u-** ya- wa- thanda
        1every AUG.1person AUG.6candy 1s- YA- 6O- like

(18) **Nonspecific indefinites in agreeing subject position**

    a. namhlanje **abantu**   **aba-thathu ba-** zo- li- wina iloto
        today   AUG.2people 2REL-three 2s- FUT- 5O- win AUG.5lottery
        'Today, three people will win the lottery.'

    b. # namhlanje **ba-** zo- li- wina iloto   **abantu**   **aba-thathu**
        today   2s- FUT- 5O- win AUG.5lottery AUG.2people 2REL-three

    c. # namhlanje **abantu**   **aba-thathu** iloto   **ba-** zo- li- wina
        today   AUG.2people 2REL-three AUG.5lottery 2s- FUT- 5O- win

In (17a) and (18a), the strong quantifier or nonspecific indefinite DP agrees with the verb in immediate preverbal position. In the ungrammatical (17b,c) and infelicitous (18b,c), the subject attaches to the left of the agreeing left-dislocated object (Buell, 2005; Cheng and Downing, 2009; Zeller, 2012) and is therefore presumably itself in an A-bar position. This contrast in grammaticality between the immediately preverbal agreeing subject and those in higher positions suggests that a true argument position in Spec,TP is available for agreeing subjects.

In addition to the ability of strong quantifiers and indefinites to agree with the verb, the preverbal agreed-with position is also grammatical for subjects with *information* focus—that is subjects that are non-presupposed new information (following Kiss, 1998).

(19)   **New information agreed-with subject**

    Q: kw- ezneka- ni?
       17s- happen- what
       'What's happening?'

    A: **uZinhle**   **u**- xova ujeqe
       AUG.1Zinhle 1s- make AUG.1steamed.bread
       'Zinhle is making steamed bread.'

Perhaps even more striking, the *answer* to a subject *wh*-question can appear in an agreeing preverbal position:

(20)   **Agreed-with subject as answer to *wh*-question**

    Q: ng- **ubani**   o-   fik-   ile?
       COP- AUG.1who 1REL- arrive- PFV
       'Who came?'

    A: **uMfundo**   **u**- fik-   ile
       AUG.1Mfundo 1s- arrive- PFV
       'Mfundo came.'

In (19), the response to the question merely has information focus, encompassing the whole sentence. Everything, including the subject, is new information but the subject is nevertheless able to agree with the verb. Moreover, even though *wh*-words themselves are unable to occupy agreeing subject positions, as (15) above illustrated, the *answer* to a subject *wh*-question, which Kiss (1998) classifies as an identificational focus because of its exhaustivity, as in (20), is able to agree. This pattern would be unexpected if agreeing subjects were always dislocated. Indeed, in (21), we can see that a truly dislocated subject that precedes the dislocated object is infelicitous as a response to a *wh*-question, in contrast to the subject that follows the dislocated object:

(21)   Q: ng- **ubani**   o-   theng- e amaqhoks   lawa?
          COP- AUG.1who 1REL- buy-   PFV AUG.6high.heels 6DEM
          'Who bought these high heels?'

     A1:   amanye   amaqhoks   **uZama**   u- wa- theng- ile
          6REL.some AUG.6high.heels AUG.1Zama 1s- 6o- buy-   PFV
          'Some of the high heels, Zama bought.'

A2: #**uZama**   amanye   amaqhoks   u- wa- theng- ile
AUG.1Zama 6REL.some AUG.6high.heels 1s- 6O- buy-   PFV
'(As for) Zama, she bought some of the high heels.'

In light of these contrasts, we can conclude that agreeing subjects are *not* necessarily dislocated and *can* appear in Spec,TP position, as van der Wal (2009) concludes for subjects in Makhuwa-Enahara.

While the examples in (17) through (20) indicate that Zulu has a position for agreeing subjects that does not exhibit properties of dislocation, agreeing subjects in Zulu also seem able to appear in *dislocated* positions at both the left- and right-peripheries. The strong quantifier and indefinite subjects in (17) and (18) above, which were grammatical in an agreeing preverbal position, were *ungrammatical* both in a postverbal, *v*P-external position and in a preverbal position to the left of the preverbal object. Cheng and Downing (2009) argue that these pre- and post-verbal dislocation positions in Zulu correlate with specific information structure properties: left-dislocated elements are discourse topics, while right-dislocated elements are merely old information. Since these positions are A-bar positions, the ungrammaticality of nonspecific indefinites and strong quantifiers that we observed above is expected. Cheng and Downing (2009) show the difference in interpretation of the two types of dislocation by demonstrating that discourse topics cannot appear in right-dislocated positions:[6]

(22) a.   ma-ní:ng') amátha:ng') e-nsím-íní   ká-Si:pho)
            COP.6-many AUG.6pumpkin LOC-9garden-LOC ASSOC-1Sipho
            'There are many pumpkins in Sipho's garden.'

      b.   **ámá-ny' ámátha:ng')** uSíph'   u- zo- wa- ník' ízihlóbo
            6-some   AUG.6pumpkin AUG.1Sipho 1s- FUT- 6O- give AUG.8relative
            z-á:khe)
            8ASSOC-his
            'Sipho will give his relatives some pumpkins.'

      c.   #úSípho   u- zo- wa- ník' ízihlóbo   z-á:khe)   **ámá-ny'**
            AUG.1Sipho 1s- FUT- 6O- give AUG.8relative 8ASSOC-his 6-some
            ámátha:ng')
            AUG.6pumpkin

                                            (Cheng and Downing, 2009, ex. (6))

In the discourse in (22) above, the sentence in (22a) establishes *amath-anga* 'pumpkins' as a discourse topic. The sentence in (22b) is a felicitous continuation, because the discourse topic *amathanga* is left-dislocated, while

6. The examples below are reproduced with markings as in the original: the apostrophes indicate vowel elision in rapid speech, while the closing parentheses indicate prosodic boundaries.

Table 2.3. PROPERTIES OF VP-EXTERNAL SUBJECTS

POSITION	AGREEMENT	INFORMATION STRUCTURE	
		Permitted	Prohibited
Spec,TP	required	indefinites new information answers to *wh*-Q	*wh*-words *only*-DPs
Left-dislocated	required	discourse topic	focus new information
Right-dislocated	required	old information	focus discourse topic

(22c) is infelicitous because right-dislocation is incompatible with a topic reading.

We can conclude from the evidence in this section that agreeing subjects in Zulu do not have a uniform syntactic status. While they may appear in an A-position, as specifier of Spec,TP, they may also occur in dislocated positions to the left and right of the verb. In other words, even when an agreeing subject is preverbal in Zulu, it may appear either in Spec,TP or in a dislocated preverbal position. Bresnan and Mchombo (1987) come to the same conclusion about preverbal subjects in Chichewa, and Schneider-Zioga (2007) makes a similar point about Kinande, for which she argues that only under special circumstances can an agreeing subject actually surface in Spec,TP.

To summarize what we have seen in this section, the Zulu verb is marked with an obligatory subject agreement morpheme, which is realized as a default class 17 *ku-* when the verb does not agree with a subject. Agreeing subjects either appear outside of *v*P, or are pro-dropped. Agreeing subjects may either surface in Spec,TP, or in a right- or left-dislocated position. In Spec,TP, subjects cannot involve certain types of identificational focus, but they can be new information, strong quantifiers, or answers to *wh*-questions. Left-dislocated elements must be discourse topics, while right-dislocated elements are merely old information—and cannot be discourse topics. These patterns are outlined in table 2.3.

2.3.2 Properties of *v*P-internal Subjects

As we saw earlier in the chapter, while *v*P-external subjects must agree, subjects that remain inside *v*P cannot agree with the verb, illustrated in (11), repeated below:

(11) **vP-internal subjects: agreement prohibited**
    a.   * **u-** pheka uZinhle kahle
           1s- cook   1Zinhle well

b. **ku**- pheka uZinhle   kahle
   17s- cook   AUG.1Zinhle well
   'Zinhle cooks well.'

c. * **li**- pheka iqhawe   kahle
   5s- cook   AUG.5hero well

d. **ku**- pheka iqhawe   kahle
   17s- cook   AUG.5hero well
   'The hero cooks well.'

The examples in (11) show that vP-internal subjects are permitted with unergative verbs; example (23) below shows that they are also grammatical, with the same agreement pattern, with unaccusatives:

(23) a. * **i**- w- e   inkomishi $_{vP}$]
         9s- fall- PFV AUG.9cup

      b. **ku**- w- e   inkomishi $_{vP}$]
         17s- fall- PFV AUG.9cup
         'The/a cup fell.'

In contrast to vP-external subjects, which can appear in multiple positions, these non-agreeing subjects that appear inside vP have a more rigid word order with respect to the other elements inside vP. A low subject always appears before any other vP-internal arguments.[7]

So far, we have only examined vP-internal subjects in intransitive constructions. The example below in (24) shows that Zulu similarly allows a vP-internal subject with expletive agreement with a *transitive* predicate—a *transitive expletive construction* (TEC):

(24) a. ku- fund- isa **uSipho**   isiZulu
         17s- learn- CAUS AUG.1Sipho AUG.7Zulu
         'Sipho teaches Zulu.'

      b. * ku- fund- isa isiZulu   **uSipho**
         17s- learn- CAUS AUG.7Zulu AUG.1Sipho

In TECs in Zulu, as illustrated above, the subject must precede the object, as in (24a), and cannot follow it, as the ungrammatical sentence in (24b) shows. Note that if the predicate in (24b) agreed with the subject, the subject

---

7. As Buell (2005), Adams (2010), and Zeller (2012) discuss, non-agreeing objects are also typically inside vP—with a few exceptions—while agreeing objects are always dislocated. The presence or absence of object agreement is a useful way to determine whether a postverbal object is inside vP: agreeing postverbal objects are always vP-external, while non-agreeing objects are nearly always vP-internal.

would be located in a *v*P-external position after the object and would thus be grammatical:

(25) u- fund- isa   isiZulu   *v*P] **uSipho**
     1s- learn- CAUS AUG.7Zulu   AUG.1Sipho
     'Sipho teaches Zulu.'

Zulu further allows *ditransitive* expletive constructions, where the subject remains inside *v*P with a ditransitive predicate. The word order in these constructions is again rigid:

(26) a. ku- fund- isa **uSipho**   abantwana   isiZulu
         17s- learn- CAUS AUG.1Sipho AUG.2children AUG.7Zulu
         'Sipho teaches the children Zulu.'

     b. * ku- fund- isa abantwana   isiZulu   **uSipho**
         17s- learn- CAUS AUG.2children AUG.7Zulu AUG.1Sipho

     c. ku- fund- isa abantwana   **uSipho**   isiZulu
         17s- learn- CAUS AUG.2children AUG.1Sipho AUG.7Zulu
         'The children teach Sipho Zulu.'
         * 'Sipho teaches the children Zulu.'

     d. * ku- fund- isa **uSipho**   isiZulu   abantwana
         17s- learn- CAUS AUG.1Sipho AUG.7Zulu AUG.2children

As with the TECs, in the ditransitive expletive constructions, the subject must precede the internal arguments, as (26a) shows. The examples in (26b–c) show that the subject cannot follow the internal arguments. The example in (26d) shows that the rigidity in word order extends beyond the relative position of the subject: reordering of the internal arguments with respect to each other also yields ungrammaticality. To summarize, *v*P-internal subjects seem to require a rigid word order of *subject > (indirect object) > direct object* within *v*P. I return to the specific structure of these *v*P-internal arguments in TECs and ditransitive expletive constructions in section 2.5.

This rigidity in word order of *v*P-internal arguments contrasts with the more flexible ordering of adjuncts with respect to the *v*P-internal subject that Buell (2009) reports. Buell claims that the interpretation of the subject is linked to its ordering possibilities with respect to adjuncts. He shows that a focused *v*P-internal subject necessarily precedes adjuncts, as in (27) below:

(27) a. yin'   indaba ku-   hlala **uSipho**   khona?
         COP.what AUG.9news 17PRT- stay AUG.1Sipho there
         'Why does SIPHO live there?'

     b. * yin'   indaba ku-   hlala khona **uSipho**?
         COP.what AUG.9news 17PRT- stay there AUG.1Sipho

(Buell, 2009, ex. (6))

In contrast, when the subject is *not* an identificational focus, such adjuncts may precede it, as in (28) – (30):

(28)   indawo   lapho ku-   hlala khona **uSipho**
        AUG.9place where 17PRT- stay there AUG.1Sipho
        'the place where Sipho lives'   (Buell, 2009, ex. (14))

(29)   a. ng- a-   ya lapho ku-   hlala **uSipho**   khona
          1SG- PST- go where 17PRT- stay AUG.1Sipho there

        b. ng- a-   ya lapho ku-   hlala (khona) **uSipho**
          1SG- PST- go where 17PRT- stay (there) AUG.1Sipho
          'I went to where Sipho lives.'   (Buell, 2005, ex. (282))

(30)   a-   ng- azi   isikhathi o- ku- cula nga- so   **uSipho**
        NEG- 1SG- know AUG.7time REL- 17s- sing NGA- 7DEM AUG.1Sipho
        'I don't know (the time) when Sipho sang.'   (Buell, 2005, ex. (284))

In (28) and (29), the resumptive locative adjunct *khona* may precede the subject in relative clauses with *v*P-internal subjects. In (30), Buell shows the same pattern with a temporal adjunct.[8]

It is perhaps unsurprising that the interpretation of the subject is tied to its relative position inside *v*P. We saw in the previous section that the interpretive possibilities of the subject correlate with its position outside of the *v*P: dislocated subjects required a topic interpretation while non-dislocated preverbal subjects resisted certain types of focus elements. Here we will see that while there is some overlap between preverbal and *v*P-internal subjects, as Buell (2005) demonstrates, the only restriction on *v*P-internal subjects is that they cannot be topics.

We saw in the previous section that while *wh-* subjects and subjects modified by *only* cannot appear outside of *v*P, they are grammatical within *v*P, repeated below:

(15)   a. * **ubani**   **u-** fik-   ile?
           AUG.1who 1s- arrive- PFV

        b. ku- fik-   e   **bani?**
          17s- arrive- PFV 1who
          'Who came?'   (Sabel and Zeller, 2006, ex. (5))

---

8. Note that in all of these constructions, the verb does *not* agree with the subject *Sipho*; rather, class 17 *ku-* agreement appears instead. This lack of agreement is evidence that the subject is necessarily inside *v*P in all of these constructions, and not in a right-dislocated position.

(16) ngi- mem- e   wonke umuntu,   kodwa...
1SG- invite- PFV 1every AUG.1person but
'I invited everyone, but...'

   a. *uJohn   kuphela u- fik-   ile
      AUG.1John only   1s- arrive- PFV

   b. ku- fik-   e uJohn   kuphela
      17s- arrive- PFV AUG.1John only
      'only John came.'   (Zeller, 2008, ex. (37))

These subjects fit into the class of identificational focus subjects that Buell (2009) describes as having rigid word order with respect to adjuncts. Identificational focus is not *required* for *v*P-internal subjects, however; Buell (2005) identifies circumstances in which a subject can appear inside *v*P when it is not focused. In the following inversion constructions, for example, the low subject does not necessarily receive a focus interpretation. The example in (31) illustrates *quotative inversion*, where a quotation is fronted with expletive agreement on the verb and the subject remains inside *v*P. As Buell (2005) notes, this construction has a counterpart in English (Branigan, 1992; Collins and Branigan, 1997):

(31) "U- zo- pheka- ni?" Kw- a-   buza uSipho.
2SG- FUT- cook- what 17s- PST- ask AUG.1Sipho
'"What will you cook?" asked Sipho.'   (Buell, 2005, ex. (269))

Nkabinde (1985), Buell (2007), and Zeller (2010) document additional inversion constructions in Zulu, where locative and instrument arguments appear in the canonical subject position, while the subject remains inside *v*P:

(32) **Locative inversion**

   a. lezi   zindlu   zi- hlala **abantu abadala**
      10these 10houses 10s- stay 2people 2REL.old

   b. abantu abadala ba-hlala ku- lezi   zindlu
      2people 2REL.old 2s-stay KU- 10these 10houses
      'Old people live in these houses.'   (Buell, 2007, ex. (7))

(33) a. lesi   silonda si- phuma **ubovu**
      7this 7sore   7s- exit   AUG.11pus
      'Pus is coming out of this sore.'   (Nkabinde, 1985, p. 47)

   b. indlela   i- mila **utshani**
      AUG.9path 9s- grow AUG.14grass
      'Grass grows on the path.'   (Nkabinde, 1985, p. 47)

(34) **Instrument inversion**

   a. i-   sipuni si- dla **uJohn**.
      AUG- 7spoon 7s- eat AUG.1John

b. u- John u- dla nge- sipuni
   AUG- 1John 1s- eat NGA.AUG- 7spoon
   'John is eating with a spoon.'   (Zeller, 2010, ex. (50))

While the verb in the quotative inversion constructions bears class 17 agreement morphology,[9] the verb in these locative and instrument inversions agrees with the fronted locative or instrument.[10] I return to the locative and instrument inversion constructions in greater detail in chapter 5, where they will be crucial to our understanding of the relationship between case and agreement in Zulu.

Again, in all of these inversion constructions, the subject does not require a identificational focus interpretation; in fact, as Buell (2005) notes, the most natural interpretation of such sentences is with information focus on the entire predicate. In general, the other instances of non-focused vP-internal subjects that Buell identifies all involve broad, or information, focus on the predicate as well. The subject itself can be definite or indefinite, specific or nonspecific, as long as it is not a topic:

(35) ku- fund- e **umfana nga-munye**$_i$ incwadi   yakhe$_i$
      17s- read- PFV AUG.1boy NGA-1.each   AUG.9book 9ASSOC.his
      'Each boy$_i$ read his$_i$ book.'   (Buell, 2005, ex. (277))

(36) njalo nje ku- thol- wa **impendulo entsha**
      always just 17s- find- PASS AUG.9answer 9.new
      'Every time, a new solution is found.'   (Buell, 2005, ex. (278))

The sentence in (35) shows that strong quantifiers are permitted with vP-internal subjects. The sentence in (36) shows a context in which the sentence asserts the existence of the indefinite subject. As with the inversion constructions, these constructions show that a range of interpretations are available for vP-internal subjects in Zulu.

In contrast, in a context that forces a topic reading for the subject, the vP-internal position is ungrammatical:

(37) Q: uMlu   w- enza- ni   manje?
          AUG.1Mlu 1s- do-   9what now
          'What is Mlu doing now?'

9. See chapter 6 for a discussion of *ku*- agreement in non-default contexts.

10. Unlike in some other Bantu languages such as Chichewa (see Bresnan and Kanerva, 1989), the inverted noun does not keep its "locative morphology." Instead, the locative/instrumental morphology does not appear when the noun is in subject position and the verb agrees with its underlying noun class. I address this ability of the locative/instrumental morphology to disappear in section 5.5.2.

Table 2.4. PROPERTIES OF VP-INTERNAL AND EXTERNAL SUBJECTS

POSITION	AGREEMENT	INFORMATION STRUCTURE	
		Permitted	Prohibited
Spec,TP	required	indefinites new information answers to *wh*-Q	*wh*-words *only*-DPs
Left-dislocated	required	discourse topic	focus new information
Right-dislocated	required	old information	focus discourse topic
*v*P-internal	prohibited	focus new information	topic

A1: # ku- bhukuda uMlu   manje
     17s- swim   AUG.1Mlu now

A2:   uMlu   u- ya- bhukuda manje
      AUG.1Mlu u- YA- swim   now
      'Mlu is swimming now.'

To summarize, *v*P-internal subjects never agree with the verb. While they can support a wider variety of identificational focus readings than *v*P-external subjects, the only interpretive requirement for subjects inside *v*P is that *they not be topics*. The full set of subject properties in different positions is given in table 2.4.[11]

2.3.3 Optionality for Subjects

In this section, we have seen that there are a number of positions that subjects in Zulu may occupy. I have focused on the basic difference between *v*P-external and *v*P-internal subjects, which correlates with subject agreement patterns: *v*P-external subjects must agree with the verb, while *v*P-internal subjects cannot agree with the verb. While this difference is robust throughout the language, in chapter 6 I will introduce novel data that involve two *exceptions* to the generalization that *v*P-external subjects must agree with the verb: constructions in which the preverbal subject optionally does not control agreement morphology on the verb.

11. In table 2.4, note that only for Spec,TP do I separate out particular types of focus. As we have seen in this section, it is only in this position that there is a split in the behavior of focused elements. In the other positions I have discussed, all focused elements seem to pattern together and thus I do not retain the distinction.

In addition to the difference regarding agreement patterns, we saw some differences in the available interpretations for subjects in these different positions. Most basically, certain elements that unambiguously always receive a identificational focus interpretation, such as *wh*-words and *only* DPs cannot appear in *v*P-external positions, though other elements can occupy these positions. Topics, by contrast, cannot appear in *v*P-internal positions, though other elements can.

At the same time, there is a certain amount of overlap in the possible interpretations for *v*P-internal and (non-dislocated) *v*P-external subjects. Both can be new information, including answers to subject-oriented *wh*-questions and strong quantifiers:

(38) **Optionality: new information**

Q: kw- eznek- e- ni izolo?
  17s- happen- PFV- 9what yesterday
  'What happened yesterday?'

A1: **uMfundo** **u-** fik- ile
   AUG.1Mfundo 1s- arrive- PFV
   'Mfundo came.'

A2: ku- fik- e **uMfundo**
   17s- arrive- PFV AUG.1Mfundo
   'Mfundo came.'

(39) **Optionality: answers to *wh*-questions**

Q: ku- fik- e bani?
  17s- arrive- PFV 1who
  'Who came?'

A1: **uMfundo** **u-** fik- ile
   AUG.1Mfundo 1s- arrive- PFV
   'Mfundo came.'

A2: ku- fik- e **uMfundo**
   17s- arrive- PFV AUG.1Mfundo
   'Mfundo came.'

(40) **Optionality: strong quantifiers**

a. **wonke umuntu** u- fik- ile namhlanje
   1.all AUG.1person 1s- arrive- PFV today

b. ku- fik- e **wonke umuntu** namhlanje
   17s- arrive- PFV 1.all AUG.1person today
   'Everyone came today.'

In (38)–(40), speakers judge both the *v*P-external and *v*P-internal subject to be felicitous in the same contexts. While the choice of subject position may sometimes be dictated by the interpretation of the subject, these examples show that in other cases, Zulu appears to permit true optionality.

2.4 RAISING CONSTRUCTIONS IN ZULU

In the previous section, we saw that there are a number of positions available for subjects in monoclausal Zulu sentences and that different positions have different consequences for agreement morphology. In particular, I showed that there are two non-dislocated positions for the subject: one vP-internal— the in situ position of the subject—and one vP-external, in Spec,TP. In this section, I examine another type of construction in which we find optionality with respect to the position of the subject and in which subject position has consequences for agreement: bi-clausal *raising* constructions, which we first saw at the beginning of chapter 1. In these constructions, the thematic subject of an embedded clause can optionally appear in an A-position in the matrix clause—either as a vP-external matrix subject in *raising-to-subject* (RtS) constructions, or as a vP-internal matrix object in *raising-to-object* (RtO) constructions.

In this section I will show that these constructions involve A-movement out of finite, agreeing embedded clauses and will show that we can distinguish these constructions from surface-similar *control* configurations in the language.

2.4.1 Raising-to-subject

In this subsection, I will focus on the properties of RtS out of finite embedded clauses in Zulu. I will compare the properties of these constructions with those of two surface-similar constructions: the compound tense/deficient verb constructions discussed in section 2.3.1 and subject control constructions. I will show that RtS in Zulu has the following properties:

(41) **Properties of raising-to-subject in Zulu**

    a. RtS involves a full embedded CP that may have an overt complementizer.

    b. RtS is optional—subjects may appear in one of three (non-dislocated) positions:[12]

12. Subjects in these constructions may also appear in dislocated positions where independently permitted, as discussed in section 2.2. In chapter 6 I return to this issue of optionality and develop an analysis of subject-to-subject raising in Zulu that accounts for why the fourth position—vP-internal in the matrix clause—does not occur.

    i. *v*P-internal position in the embedded clause

    ii. Spec,TP position in the embedded clause

    iii. Spec,TP position in the matrix clause

c. Raised subjects agree with both the matrix and embedded verb.

d. Raised subjects are thematically related only to the embedded verb.

e. Raised subjects create a new antecedent for binding.

Multi-verb constructions

In section 2.3.1 I showed that Zulu "complex tense" and "deficient verb" constructions involve a single thematic subject that agrees with multiple verbal elements:

(13) **Multiple subject markers in compound tenses**

   a. **thina si**- zo- be **si**-　　sa- dlala ibhola
      we　1PL- FUT- be 1PL.PRT- DUR- play AUG.5ball
      'We will still be playing soccer.'

   b. **abafana ba**- zo- be **be**-　　nga- ka- dlal- i　ibhola
      AUG.2boy 2S- FUT- be 2S.PRT- NEG- EXCL- play- NEG AUG.5ball
      'The boys will not yet be playing soccer.'　　(Nyembezi, 1991, p. 168, 172)

(14) **Multiple subject markers with deficient verbs**

   a. uma zi-　　sukuma, **izingane**　　**zi**- phinde **zi**-　　w-　e
      when 10PRT- stand.up AUG.10children 10S- again　10S.SJC- fall- SJC
      'Every time they stand up, the children fall down again.'

   b. **abazali**　　**bami**　　**ba**- yaye **ba**-　　vuk- e　ngo-five
      AUG.2parents 2ASSOC.1SG 2S- usually 2S.SJC- awake- SJC NGA.AUG-five
      'My parents usually wake up at 5.'

    Carstens and Kinyalolo (1989) argue that such auxiliary verbs in Bantu have the properties of raising verbs in that the two verbal elements in these constructions share a single subject that is thematically related only to the lower verb. We can observe this property through the behavior of idioms, which show that the subject in these constructions is selected by the lower verb.

    Zulu has several idioms that include an idiomatic subject (see Nyembezi, 1963):[13]

---

13. The younger speakers of Durban Zulu who I have encountered through my fieldwork are unfamiliar with the majority of the documented idioms in Zulu, and particularly with the subject idioms discussed here. All subject idiom judgments and data were collected from older residents of Umlazi Township, Durban. While some

(42) **Zulu subject idioms**

    a. iqhina   li- phum- e   embizeni
       AUG.5steinbok 5s- exit-   PFV LOC.9pot
       'The secret came out.'

       lit. 'The steinbok exited the cooking pot.'[14]

    b. insimba   y- esul- ela   nge-gqumusha
       AUG.9genet 9s- wipe- APPL NGA.AUG-5bushshrike
       'Blame was shifted to an underling.' / 'Abuse of power occurred.'

       lit. 'The genet wiped itself on the bushshrike.'[15]

With the multi-verb constructions above, the idiomatic subject is able to retain its idiomatic meaning even when it appears before—and agrees with—the higher auxiliary verb:

(43) **Idiomatic subjects with auxiliary verbs**

    a. iqhina   li- zo- be li-   nga- ka-   phum- i   embizeni
       AUG.5steinbok 5s- FUT- be 5PRT- NEG- EXCL- exit-   NEG LOC.9pot
       'The secret will not yet be out.'

    b. insimba   i- phinde y-   esul- ela   nge-gqumusha
       AUG.9genet 9s- again   9SJC- wipe- APPL NGA.AUG-5bushshrike
       'Blame was shifted again.'

Despite the presence of two verbal elements (and two agreement markers), there is no clear evidence that these constructions are truly biclausal, rather than involving a single inflectional domain. In all of these constructions, the subject may either appear inside the vP of the lower verb, with *ku*-agreement on both verbal elements, as in (44a), *or* it may appear in a vP-external position preceding the higher verb, in which case it agrees with both verbal elements, as in (44b). The subject may not appear between the two elements, regardless of agreement pattern, as shown in (45):

(44)   a.   emini   ku- zo- be ku-   sa-   dla **abafana**
               LOC.noon 17s- FUT- be 17PRT- DUR- eat AUG.2boy

       b.   emini   **abafana** ba- zo- be be-   sa-   dla
               LOC.noon AUG.2boy 2s- FUT- be 2PRT- DUR- eat
               'At noon, the boys will still be eating.'

of these older speakers moved to the Durban area as adults, their production and judgments of other aspects of the relevant grammatical phenomena matches that of younger Durban speakers.

14. A steinbok is a small antelope that typically reaches a height of 1½–2 feet tall.

15. A genet is a small predator related to civets and mongooses. A bushshrike is a small species of bird.

(45) a. *emini   ku- zo- be **abafana** be- sa- dla
         LOC.noon 17s- FUT- be AUG.2boy 2PRT- DUR- eat

    b. *emini   ba- zo- be **abafana** be- sa- dla
         LOC.noon 2s- FUT- be AUG.2boy 2PRT- DUR- eat

    c. *emini   ku- zo- be **abafana** ku- sa- dla
         LOC.noon 17s- FUT- be AUG.2boy 17PRT- DUR- eat

    d. *emini   ba- zo- be **abafana** ku- sa- dla
         LOC.noon 2s- FUT- be AUG.2boy 17PRT- DUR- eat

As we will see, this behavior contrasts with the behavior of truly biclausal constructions, which always allow a vP-external subject to immediately precede the lower verb.

In addition, the temporal relationships between the verbal elements in these constructions appears to be more tightly linked than in truly biclausal constructions. For the compound tenses, the auxiliary verb is always a light verb and the temporal morphology on each verbal component combines to apply to the single event, as in the "overflow" patterns described by Bjorkman (2011). In the deficient verb constructions, while the higher verb does have some semantic content, it serves to modify the lower verb. Temporal morphology on the lower verb is highly restricted and dependent on the higher verb; the morphology that determines the tense of the entire event is realized on the higher verb, as in (44a). We will see below that this behavior contrasts with that of biclausal constructions, which support independent temporal morphology and interpretations in the two clauses.[16]

Finally, nonverbal elements that can typically appear at clause boundaries or edges in Zulu are unable to intervene between the verbal elements in these constructions. First, while overt complementizers in Zulu are typically permitted (if not required) to introduce embedded clauses, as in (47), no complementizer may appear between the verbal elements in these constructions, as in (46):

(46) uma zi-   sukuma, **izingane**   **zi**- phinde (*ukuthi) **zi**-   w- e
      when 10PRT- stand.up AUG.10children 10s- again *that   10SJC- fall- SJC
      'Every time they stand up, the children fall down again.'

---

16. These are reminiscent of restructuring predicates, where clauses that contain multiple inflected verbal elements appear to behave as a single unit with respect to phenomena such as tense, aspect, or passivization (e.g. Cinque, 2004, 2006; Wurmbrand, 2001, 2007). In recent work on Mayrinax Atayal, Chen (2012) has argued for a restructuring analysis of multiverb constructions that strongly resemble the "deficient verb" constructions in Zulu in terms of the range meanings of the higher element.

(47) si- funa **(ukuthi)** izingane   zi-   w- e
      1PL- want (that)   AUG.10child 10sJC- fall- SJC
      'We want the children to fall.'

Similarly, adverbial phrases, which can appear at the left edge of an embedded clause, as in (49), cannot appear between the verbal elements, as in (48):

(48) a. **namhlanje** izingane   zi-   phinde za-   wa
          today   AUG.10child 10s- again   10.SJC.PST- fall
          'Today, the children fell again.'

      b. * izingane   zi-   phinde **namhlanje** za-   wa
            AUG.10child 10s- again   today   10.SJC.PST- fall

(49) a. **namhlanje** si-   funa (ukuthi) izingane   zi- w- e
          today   1PL- want (that)   AUG.10child 10s- fall- SJC
          'Today we want the children to fall.'

      b. si-funa (ukuthi) **namhlanje** izingane   zi-   w- e
          1PL-want (that)   today   AUG.10child 10.SJC- fall- SJC
          'We want the children to fall today.'

To summarize, while these multi-verb constructions involve more than one verbal element that appear to share a single thematic subject, there is no clear evidence in favor of a biclausal analysis of these constructions. Rather, it appears that the two verbal elements are part of a single articulated temporal domain. As we will see next, this class of constructions contrasts in various ways with clearly biclausal raising constructions that share a single thematic subject.

Raising predicates

In this subsection, I focus on two Zulu predicates that allow raising-to-subject: the deontic modal *fanele* 'be necessary'[17] and *bonakala* 'seem'. In contrast to the constructions in the previous subsection, these predicates clearly take a full CP complement and allow the complementizer to appear in the embedded clause. *Fanele* takes an embedded CP with an optional complementizer and a *subjunctive* predicate (Zeller, 2006). *Bonakala* takes an embedded CP with an obligatory complementizer and an *indicative* predicate. While the multi-verb constructions in the previous subsection only allowed the subject to appear inside *v*P, following the second verb, or to precede the first verb,

17. A second deontic necessity modal *mele* is also found in the language and to my knowledge is interchangeable with *fanele*. For simplicity, I focus on *fanele* here.

these constructions allow the subject to appear in a *v*P-external position immediately preceding *either* verb: In both constructions, the embedded subject may either remain in a preverbal position in the embedded clause, controlling agreement on the embedded verb while default *ku*-agreement appears on the raising verb (50a, 51a), or it may raise to subject position in the matrix clause, controlling agreement on both verbs (50b, 51b):

(50) **Raising-to-subject:** *fanele* **(subjunctive complement)**

    a. ku- fanele   (ukuthi) **uZinhle**   a-   xov- e
         17s- be.necessary that   AUG.1Zinhle 1sJC- make- sJC
         ujeqe   manje
         AUG.3steamed.bread now

    b. **uZinhle**   u- fanele   (ukuthi) **a-**   xov- e
         AUG.1Zinhle 1s- be.necessary that   1sJC- make- sJC
         ujeqe   manje
         AUG.3steamed.bread now

    c. ku- fanele   (ukuthi) ku-   xov- e   uZinhle
         17s- be.necessary that   17sJC- make- sJC AUG.1Zinhle
         ujeqe   manje
         AUG.3steamed.bread now
         'Zinhle must make steamed bread now.'

(51) **Raising-to-subject:** *bonakala* **(indicative complement)**

    a. ku- bonakala [ukuthi **uZinhle**   u- zo- xova ujeqe   ]
         17s- seem   that   AUG.1Zinhle 1s- FUT- make AUG.1steamed.bread

    b. **uZinhle**   u- bonakala [ukuthi **u-** zo- xova ujeqe   ]
         AUG.1Zinhle 1s- seem   that   1s- FUT- make AUG.1steamed.bread
         'It seems that Zinhle will make steamed bread.'

    c. ku- bonakala [ukuthi ku- zo- xova **uZinhle**   ujeqe   ]
         17s- seem   that   17s- FUT- make AUG.1Zinhle AUG.1steamed.bread
         'It seems that Zinhle will make steamed bread.'

Speakers judge the (a) and (b) constructions in (50) and (51) to be equivalent; whether the subject appears in the matrix or the embedded clause does not impact grammaticality. This free variation is similar to the optionality between certain *v*P-internal and *v*P-external subjects that I showed in the previous section. For non-quantified subjects, there are no observable interpretive differences between the two constructions, which is expected for raising, but not for similar constructions, such as copy-raising or control, whose contrasting behavior we will see shortly.[18]

18. I have not yet been able to demonstrate interpretive differences between raised and non-raised quantifier expressions, though more work on such constructions is needed.

As with the multi-verb constructions above, the subject in these raising predicates is thematically related only to the embedded verb. Again, the behavior of subject idioms reveals this connection, since the subject can maintain its idiomatic reading even when it appears in the higher clause:

(52) **Subjunctive raising preserves idiom**

    a. **ku**- fanele   [(ukuthi) iqhina   li-   phum- e   embizeni]
       17s- necessary that   AUG.5steinbok 5sJC- exit-   SJC LOC.9pot
       The secret must come out.

    b. **iqhina**   **li**- fanele   [(ukuthi) **li**-   phum- e   embizeni]
       AUG.5steinbok 5s- necessary that   5sJC- exit-   SJC LOC.9pot
       The secret must come out.

(53) **Indicative raising preserves idiom**

    a. **ku**- bonakala [ukuthi iqhina   li-   phum- ile   embizeni]
       17s- seem   that   AUG.5steinbok 5s- exit-   PFV LOC.9pot
       'It seems that the secret came out.'

    b. **iqhina**   **li**-bonakala [ukuthi **li**-phum- ile   embizeni]
       AUG.5steinbok 5s-seems   that   5s-exit-   PFV LOC.9pot
       'The secret seems to have come out.'

While the idiom data in (52) and (53) above show that the subject originates as an argument of the lower verb, we saw in the previous section that preverbal subjects can appear in dislocated positions, which allows for the possibility that the subject is "raising" into the matrix clause without undergoing A-movement. In (54), I show that this type of movement does in fact create an A-chain. The raised subjects of *fanele* and *bonakala* create a new antecedent for binding:

(54) **Raising-to-subject creates new antecedent for binding**

    a.   ku- fanele   [ukuthi [ngo-buhlakana   bukaSipho$_i$]   *pro$_i$* **a**-
       17s- necessary that   NGA-AUG.14wisdom 14ASSOC.1Sipho *pro* 1sJC-
       m- siz- e   uThemba]
       1o- help- SJC AUG.1Themba
       'It's necessary that out of Sipho$_i$'s wisdom, he$_i$ helps Themba.'

    b. **pro$_i$* **u**- fanele   [ukuthi [ngo-buhlakana   bukaSipho$_i$]   t$_i$ **a**-
       pro 1s- necessary that   NGA-AUG.14wisdom 14ASSOC.1Sipho   1sJC-
       m- siz- e   uThemba]
       1o- help- SJC AUG.1Themba

In (54a), the R-expression inside the adverbial phrase in the embedded clause is grammatical because the *pro* subject of the embedded clause has not undergone raising. If the *pro* subject does raise, as in (54b), the R-expression that it has raised over becomes ungrammatical.

To summarize, raising predicates in Zulu optionally allow the subject to raise out of a tensed, agreeing CP with an overt complementizer. When the subject raises into the matrix clause, it agrees with both the matrix and embedded verbs. These subjects behave as though they are thematically related to the embedded verb, since idiomatic subjects retain their idiomatic reading through raising, but they also seem to involve A-movement in that they create new antecedents for binding.

Raising look-alikes

The raising properties of *fanele* and *bonakala* become even clearer if we compare them to other biclausal constructions where the two verbs 'share' a single subject. Since, as we saw in section 2.3, Zulu allows *pro*-drop with agreeing subjects, we could in principle have two possible syntactic configurations for a biclausal sentence with a single shared subject:

(55) **Possible configurations for shared subject constructions**

    a. SUBJ_i AGR_i-V $[_{CP}$ C^o t_i AGR_i-V $]$

    b. SUBJ_i AGR_i-V $[_{CP}$ C^o pro_i AGR_i-V $]$

I have argued that *fanele* and *bonakala* have the syntactic configuration in (55a), where the subject is only thematically related to the lower predicate. In the construction in (55b), by contrast, the subject is selected by both predicates; this thematic relationship should be detectable in its interpretation. I will briefly show a few contrasts between the properties of the raising verbs discussed above and the behavior of control and copy-raising verbs in Zulu.

Like constructions with raised subjects, control and copy-raising constructions involve an overt subject in the matrix clause and agreement with that subject in the embedded clause. Unlike the raising construction, I will assume that control verbs involve a null PRO in the embedded clause while copy-raising involves a *pro* (see Asudeh, 2002; Asudeh and Toivonen, 2012; Carstens and Diercks, 2013; Landau, 2011; Polinsky and Potsdam, 2006; Postal, 1974; Potsdam and Runner, 2001, and others for discussion of copy-raising structures):

(56) **(Optional) control**

    a. uMandla   u- thanda ukuthi a-   cul- e
       AUG.1Mandla 1s- like   that   1SJC- sing- SJC
       'Mandla likes to sing.' (also: 'Mandla likes him to sing.')

b. uSipho   u- funa ukuthi a-   phek- e   iqanda
   AUG.1Sipho 1s- want that   1sJC- cook- SJC AUG.5egg
   'Sipho wants to cook an egg.' (also: 'Sipho wants him to cook an egg.')

(57) **Copy-raising**

a. uMandla   u- zw-   akala sengathi u-smugglisha amadrugs
   AUG.1Mandla 1s- perceive- able as.if   1s-smuggle AUG.6drugs
   'Mandla sounds like he smuggles drugs.'

b. uSipho   u- buk- eka sengathi u- bhema iwunga
   AUG.1Sipho 1s- look- able as.if   1s- smoke AUG.5wunga
   'Sipho looks like he smokes *wunga*.'[19]

One major difference between these structures and raising-to-subject is that while raising predicates permit an idiomatic reading for the raised nominal, these constructions do not. The raising data is repeated in (52b), while the contrasting control and copy-raising constructions are in (58) and (59):

(52b)   **iqhina   li**- fanele   [(ukuthi) **li**-   phum- e   embizeni]
         5steinbok 5s- necessary that   5sJC- exit-   SJC LOC.9pot
         'The secret must come out. '

(58)   #**iqhina   li**- thanda [(ukuthi) **li**-   phum- e   embizeni]
         5steinbok 5s- like   that   5sJC- exit-   SJC LOC.9pot
         'The steinbok likes to come out of the cooking pot.'

         *'The secret likes to come out.'

(59)   #**iqhina   li**- zwa-   akala [(ukuthi) **li**- phum- e   embizeni]
         5steinbok 5s- perceive- able that   5s- exit-   PFV LOC.9pot
         'The steinbok sounds like it came out of the cooking pot.'

         *'The secret sounds like it came out.'

In addition, the full CP embedded clause in the control constructions in Zulu alternates with an infinitival complement, as shown below in (60):

(60) **Control with infinitival complement**

a. uMandla   u- thanda uku-cula
   AUG.1Mandla 1s- like   INF-sing
   'Mandla likes to sing.'

b. uSipho   u- funa uku-pheka iqanda
   AUG.1Sipho 1s- want INF-cook AUG.5egg
   'Sipho wants to cook an egg.'

19. Hearsay suggests that *wunga* is the latest local street drug in Durban, a mix of antiretrovirals, cleaning powder, and rat poison (though opinions on the ingredients vary). Typically in powder form, it is mixed into marijuana and smoked.

This type of alternation is impossible in raising—and copy-raising—constructions that otherwise take an indicative complement for nearly all speakers I worked with, as shown in (61) and (62) below:[20]

(61) * uMandla   u- bonakala uku-cula
      AUG.1Mandla 1s- seem   INF-sing
      intended: 'Mandla seems to sing.'

(62) * uMandla   u- bukeka   uku-bhema iwunga
      AUG.1Mandla 1- look.able INF-smoke AUG.5wunga
      intended: 'Mandla looks/seems to smoke wunga.'

Speakers consistently report an interpretive contrast between raising and copy-raising: while the raised subject of *bonakala* 'seem' is judged to be felicitous in contexts based on indirect evidence, the copy-raising construction requires direct evidence:

(63) Context: We go to Sipho's apartment and find *wunga*-making paraphernalia and supplies.

      a. √ uSipho   u- bonakala ukuthi u- bhema iwunga
         AUG.1Sipho 1s- seem   that   1s- smoke AUG.5wunga
         'Sipho seems to smoke *wunga*.'

      b. # uSipho   u- bukeka/ zwakala   sengathi u- bhema iwunga
         AUG.1Sipho 1s- look.able/ perceive.able as.if   1s- smoke AUG.5wunga
         #'Sipho looks like/sounds like he smokes *wunga*.'

By contrast, when we do have direct evidence, both constructions are appropriate:

(64) Context: We see Sipho accept a *wunga* joint or hear him talking about smoking *wunga*.

      a. √ uSipho   u- bonakala ukuthi u- bhema iwunga
         AUG.1Sipho 1s- seem   that   1s- smoke AUG.5wunga
         'Sipho seems to smoke *wunga*.'

20. By contrast, some speakers who do not allow an infinitival complement for *bonakala* do allow an infinitival complement with the predicate *fanele* 'be necessary', which normally takes a subjunctive complement:

(i)   wena   u- fanele   uku- bong-wa, ngi- ya- ku- bonga nami
      2SG.DEM 2SG- be.necessary INF- praise-PASS 1SG- YA- 2SG- praise 1SG.DEM
      'You are worthy of praise, and I praise you.'

Interestingly, speakers consistently translate *fanele* in this type of construction as meaning 'worthy of', suggesting that these are most likely control constructions and not raising.

b. ✓ uSipho   u- bukeka/   zwakala   sengathi u- bhema iwunga
   AUG.1Sipho 1s- look.able/ perceive.able as.if   1s- smoke AUG.5wunga
   'Sipho looks like/ sounds like he smokes *wunga*.'

We therefore have multiple ways to distinguish raising from the surface-similar control and copy-raising constructions. Though these constructions raise many questions of their own, I set them aside for the remainder of this discussion and simply conclude that these differences help solidify the analysis of constructions like (50b) and (51b) as raising-to-subject.

Theoretical implications

The optional raising constructions in Zulu that I discuss in this section pose problems for our understanding of raising constructions cross-linguistically. In particular, abstract case, in the sense of Vergnaud (2006 [1976]) and Chomsky (1980, 1981), is often invoked to explain the patterns found in raising constructions. When the embedded clause of a raising predicate is finite, the embedded subject can receive nominative case. This case assignment not only satisfies the case needs of the subject, but in fact renders it *inactive* for further A-movement to a cased position. The cased subject's inability to move is what accounts for the requirement that an expletive subject appear in the matrix clause in languages like English. By contrast, when the embedded predicate is nonfinite, the embedded subject cannot receive case and must raise to the matrix clause to get nominative case. This type of analysis accounts for the fact that in languages like English, raising is never optional, and is always dependent on the finiteness of the embedded clause:

(65) a.   It seems [that **Sipho** will cook an egg.]

      b.   * **Sipho**$_i$ seems [that t$_i$ will cook an egg.]

      c.   **Sipho**$_i$ seems [t$_i$ to cook an egg.]

      d.   * It seems [**Sipho** to cook an egg.]

In a language like Zulu, such an account cannot be adapted straightfor-wardly. Any account of Zulu raising constructions must capture the optionality of subject raising and the fact that the raising can take place out of finite, agreeing clauses in which subjects are typically grammatical – both subjunctive and indicative.[21]

---

21. The case-driven analysis of the Zulu raising predicate *fanele* by Zeller (2006), who follows Alexiadou and Anagnostopoulou (1998), runs into this problem. Zeller ties the raising to the presence of a defective subjunctive CP, which lacks nominative case, but does not have an independent criterion for distinguishing defective subjunctives from

The fact that the embedded predicates are identical in both the raised and non-raised variants of constructions involving the raising verbs *fanele* and *bonakala* thus presents difficulties for a case-driven theory of raising in Zulu. The optionality suggests that the embedded subject is equally well licensed in either position.

On the basis of similar facts in other Bantu languages, Harford Perez (1985), Diercks (2012), and others simply argue that Bantu languages display no case effects whatsoever. By removing case as a potential factor, the fact that non-raised subjects are grammatical does not mean that they will be rendered inactive, and thus they should be able to raise. I return to this influential stance on the lack of case in Bantu in chapter 3 and argue that despite these appearances, Bantu *does* have a system of structural case. In addition, while a theory of Zulu that completely lacks case may account for the lack of Activity effects governing the nominals in these raising constructions, it still leaves open the question of what drives the raising—and of why these nominals are permitted to leave an agreeing finite clause. I return to these questions in chapter 6, where I argue that some novel agreement facts provide the answer to both of these questions.

2.4.2 Raising-to-object

Zulu also allows raising-to-object out of embedded subjunctives with certain verbs.[22] In the relevant constructions, an overt DP can appear either before or after the complementizer *ukuthi*:[23]

(66) **Raising-to-object (subjunctive complement)**
    a. ngi- funa [ukuthi **uSipho**   a-pheke iqanda]
       1SG- want that   AUG.1Sipho 1SJC-cook AUG.5egg

    b. ngi- funa **uSipho**   [ukuthi a-pheke iqanda]
       1SG- want AUG.1Sipho that   1SJC-cook AUG.5egg
       'I want Sipho to cook an egg.'

(67) a. ngi-funa [ukuthi **impi**   i- gcin- e]
       1SG-want that   AUG.9war 9SJC- finish- SJC

---

non-defective subjunctives. In addition, this analysis does not have a logical extension to the *indicative* raising facts introduced in this chapter. In chapter 6, I return to this question of what permits the raising and of what Zulu has in common with other unusual cases of raising, such as the one in Greek.

22. So far, all raising-to-object verbs I have encountered require a subjunctive complement. I am unsure whether this pattern reflects a categorical restriction on raising-to-object or merely a gap in the data.

23. The complementizer is optional throughout these examples.

b. ngi-funa **impi**   [ukuthi i-   gcin- e]
   1SG-want AUG.9war that   9SJC- finish- SJC
   'I want war to end.'

In pre-complementizer position, the DP behaves as though it is inside the matrix *v*P. The nominal in this position can undergo object agreement in the matrix clause as in (68). In the non-agreeing position in the higher clause, it must receive a *v*P-internal information structure interpretation, i.e. new information or focus; it cannot receive a topic interpretation—which we saw in section 2.3 is associated with the left periphery—as illustrated in (69) below.

(68) **Raising-to-object feeds object agreement in the higher clause**

    a.   ngi- ya- **m**- funa uSipho   (ukuthi) a-   pheke iqanda
        1SG- YA- 1O- want AUG.1Sipho (that)   1SJC- cook AUG.5egg
        'I want Sipho to cook an egg.'

    b. *ngi- (ya)- **m**- funa ukuthi uSipho   a-   pheke iqanda
        1SG- YA- 1O- want that   AUG.1Sipho 1SJC- cook AUG.5egg
        'I want Sipho to cook an egg.'

(69) **Raising-to-object has *v*P-internal information structure**

    A: yini indaba   u- ngi- cela uku- thola uSipho?
        what AUG.9matter 2SG- 1SG.O- ask INF- get   AUG.1Sipho
        'Why did you ask me to get Sipho?'

    B: #ngi- funa uSipho   ukuthi a-   pheke iqanda
        1SG- want AUG.1Sipho that   1SJC- cook AUG.5egg
        Either (66a) or (68a) would work in this context.

However, while the pre-complementizer DP participates in matrix phenomena, it behaves thematically like a part of the lower clause. We can see this effect most clearly in the behavior of idioms. If we place an idiom like (42) in the complement of a verb like *lindela* 'expect', the idiomatic reading in the lower clause is retained even when the idiomatic subject appears in pre-complementizer position, as illustrated by (70) below. The behavior of idioms in (70) contrasts with (optional) object control constructions like (71): with a verb like *khuthaza* 'encourage', the idiomatic reading is lost if the embedded subject appears in pre-complementizer position. The optionality of raising-to-object in (70) again suggests that the DPs involved in the constructions are licensed in either position.

(70) **Raising-to-object: idiomatic reading retained**

    a. Ngi- lindela [(ukuthi) **iqhina**   **li**-phume embizeni]
       1SG- expect that   AUG.5steinbok 5SJC-exit LOC.9pot
       'I expect the secret to come out.'

b. Ngi-lindela **iqhina**   [(ukuthi) **li**-phume embizeni]
1SG-expect AUG.5steinbok that   5SJC-exit LOC.9pot
'I expect the secret to come out.'

(71) **(Optional) object control: idiomatic reading lost**

a. A- ngi- khuthaz- anga   [(ukuthi) iqhina   li-   phum-
    NEG- 1SG- encourage- NEG.PST that   AUG.5steinbok 5SJC- exit-
    e   embizeni]
    SJC LOC.9pot
    'I didn't encourage that the secret get out.'

b. # A- ngi- khuthaz- anga   iqhina   [ukuthi li-   phum- e
    NEG- 1SG- encourage- NEG.PST AUG.5steinbok that   5SJC- exit- SJC
    embizeni]
    LOC.9pot
    'I didn't encourage the steinbok to leave the pot.' (literal meaning only)

The behavior of idioms in the raising constructions discussed above suggests that the element that can appear in either the higher or lower clause is always thematically linked to the lower clause. We saw in section 2.3.1 that raising-to-subject creates a new antecedent for binding. This same pattern holds in the raising-to-object construction, as illustrated in (72):

(72) **Raising-to-object creates new antecedent for binding**

a. ngi-lindele [ukuthi [*ngo-kutatazela*   *kukaSipho*   ] **(yena)** a-
    1SG-expect that   NGA.AUG-17haste 17ASSOC.1Sipho (1PRO) 1SJC-
    khohlw- e   ukupheka idina   ]
    forget- SJC INF.cook AUG.5dinner
    'I expect that in Sipho's haste he forgets to cook dinner.'

b. ngi- lindele **yena**$_i$ [ukuthi [*ngo-kutatazela*   *kwakhe*$_i$] t$_i$ a-
    1SG- expect 1PRO that   NGA.AUG-17haste 17ASSOC.1his   1SJC-
    khohlw- e   ukupheka idina   ]
    forget- SJC INF.cook AUG.5dinner
    'I expect him to forget to cook dinner in his haste.'

c. * ngi- lindele **yena**$_i$ [ukuthi [*ngo-kutatazela*   *kukaSipho*$_i$] t$_i$ a-
    1SG- expect 1PRO that   NGA.AUG-17haste 17ASSOC.1Sipho 1SJC-
    khohlw- e   ukupheka idina   ]
    forget- SJC INF.cook AUG.5dinner
    intended: *'I expect him$_i$ to forget to cook dinner in Sipho$_i$'s haste.'

In the sentences in (72) above, when the adverbial phrase in the embedded clause contains an R-expression, the embedded subject cannot raise to object if it co-refers with the R-expression. It must either remain in the embedded clause, below the R-expression, or the adverbial must contain a pronoun instead. In addition, agreement patterns furnish an additional argument that these instances of raising-to-object involve A-movement: raising-to-object can feed object agreement in the higher clause, as (73) shows:

(73) ngi- ya- m- lindela ukuthi a-   khohlw- e   ukupheka idina
      1SG- YA- 1O- expect that   1SJC- forget- SJC INF.cook AUG.5dinner
      'I expect him to forget to cook dinner.'

If the target for this movement operation is an A-position, then, we expect the *origin* site for the moved element—in other words, the embedded agreeing subject position—to also be an A-position as well, given the apparent ban on improper movement (Chomsky, 1973, 1981; May, 1979).

2.5 BEYOND SUBJECT DISTRIBUTION: ADDING ARGUMENTS

In this chapter, I have focused on the distribution of subject nominals, and in particular, on their behavior in agreeing, *v*P-external positions. In this final section, I turn to the behavior of nominals in situ and the ways in which they are introduced into the structure. I will show that Zulu has both applicative and causative verbal morphology capable of introducing an applied or causer argument into the structure and that these morphemes are able to combine on a single predicate to produce four-argument structures. Based on the behavior of these constructions, I will argue that the syntax for the causative and applicative supports the structures proposed in (74) and (75). These conclusions concerning the internal organization of *v*P will be essential to understanding the relationship of *v*P-internal nominals to higher probing heads in the syntax, as we will see in chapter 3.

(74) **Zulu three-argument structures**

      a. **Applicative**

b. **Causative**

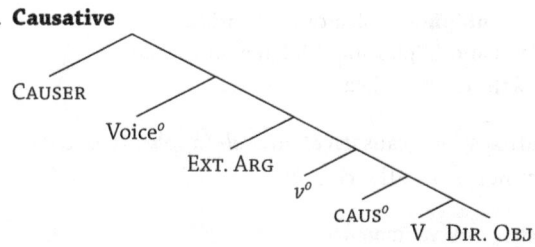

(75) **Zulu four-argument structure**

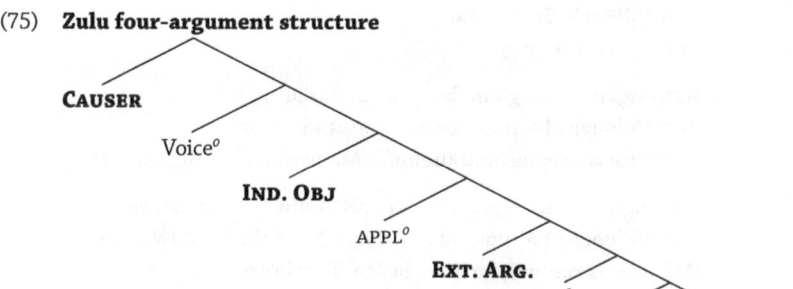

So far, I have mainly focused on constructions that involve subjects generated in Spec,*v*P, and objects generated as complements to the verb. As we saw in previous sections, we can observe these arguments in their base positions in a Transitive Expletive Construction (TEC):[24]

(76) ku- xova uZinhle   ujeqe
17s- make AUG.1Zinhle AUG.1steamed.bread
'Zinhle makes steamed bread.'

(77)

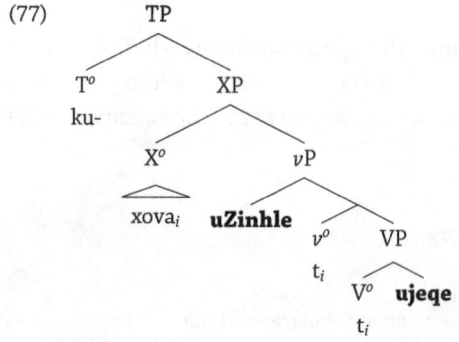

In section 2.3.2, we also saw that Zulu allows more arguments to appear inside *v*P as in the *ditransitive* expletive construction repeated as (78) below:

24. For now, I follow the convention of Cheng and Downing (2012) of marking the position to which the verb raises simply as "X." For simplicity, though I will assume verb raising of this type throughout this book, I will not indicate it in subsequent trees.

(78) ku- fund- isa **uSipho** abantwana isiZulu
17s- learn- CAUS AUG.1Sipho AUG.2children AUG.7Zulu
'Sipho teaches the children Zulu.'

Zulu has two suffixes, -is- (causative) and -el- (applicative) that are capable of introducing arguments into the clause:

(79) a. uMlungisi u- ya- gijima
AUG.1Mlungisi 1s- YA- run
'Mlungisi is running.'

b. **uMlungisi** u- gijim- **is-** a uSimaku
AUG.1Mlungisi 1s- run- CAUS- FV AUG.1Simaku
'Mlungisi is making Simaku run.' / 'Mlungisi is chasing Simaku.'

c. uMlungisi u- gijim- **el-** a **uNtombi** / **kwaNtombi**
AUG.1Mlungisi 1s- run- APPL- FV AUG.1Ntombi / LOC.1Ntombi
'Mlungisi is running for Ntombi / to Ntombi's house.'

In (79b), the inclusion of -is- morphology coincides with the addition of a causer argument. In (79c), the -el- morphology introduces a benefactive or locative argument. These two morphemes can apply in combination to a single verb, with each introducing a separate argument. As we saw with the *v*P-internal arguments in TECs, the order of arguments is rigid here: the benefactive must precede the direct object.

(80) uMlungisi u- gijim- **is-** **el-** a **uNtombi** **uSimaku**
AUG.1Mlungisi 1s- run- CAUS- APPL- FV AUG.1Ntombi AUG.1Simaku
'Mlungisi is chasing Simaku for Ntombi.'
*Mlungisi is chasing Ntombi for Simaku.'

The examples above involve an underlyingly intransitive verb. The causative and applicative can also combine with a transitive verb, yielding four arguments associated with a single predicate, as we can see in the examples in (81) below:

(81) a. uSipho u- funda isiZulu
AUG.1Sipho 1s- learn AUG.7Zulu
'Sipho is studying Zulu.'

b. **uSipho** u- fund- **is-** a amantombazane isiZulu
AUG.1Sipho 1s- learn- CAUS- FV AUG.6girls AUG.7Zulu
'Sipho is teaching the girls Zulu.'

c. uSipho u- fund- is- **el-** a **uthisha** **omkhulu**
AUG.1Sipho 1s- learn- CAUS- APPL- FV AUG.1teacher 1REL.big
amantombazane isiZulu
AUG.6girls AUG.7Zulu
'Sipho is teaching the girls Zulu for the principal.'

While we saw earlier that Zulu allows ditransitive expletives, with the subject and two lower arguments all appearing inside *v*P, speakers uniformly reject expletive constructions with four *v*P-internal arguments:

(82) *ku- fund- is- **el**- a uSipho   uthisha   omkhulu
17s- learn- CAUS- APPL- FV AUG.1Sipho AUG.1teacher 1REL.big
amantombazane isiZulu
AUG.6girls   AUG.7Zulu
'Sipho is teaching the girls Zulu for the principal.'

Unlike the restrictions on (augmentless) nominals that I discuss in chapter 3, this ban on four *v*P-internal arguments is not sensitive to nominal morphology or any other factor that I have identified. In the absence of evidence that would distinguish between whether the restriction is due to syntactic factors or extra-syntactic concerns (such as processing or pragmatics), I set aside this issue for the purposes of this investigation.

In constructions like (81c), where the the APPL and CAUS morphemes appear together on a single predicate, they always appear in the same order, *-is-* causative followed by *-el-* applicative. This order is common throughout Bantu and, as Hyman (2003) discusses, in at least some languages the morpheme ordering appears to be somewhat independent of syntactic structures. We can see that in examples like (81c), the causer argument is syntactically higher than the applied argument. I will return to this issue at the end of this section; first, however, I'll examine the syntactic structures that result when either the APPL or the CAUS morphemes appear separately.

First, turning to the applicative construction, I will show that applicative morphology in Zulu introduces an applied argument *above* the verb: a *high applicative* (McGinnis, 2001; Pylkkänen, 2002, 2008). This type of applicative relates the applied argument to the event described by the VP, as in (83). Low applicatives, by contrast, introduce the applied argument below the verb and thus only relate it to the direct object. The structures for these two types of applicatives are given below:

(83) **High Applicative (Zulu type)**

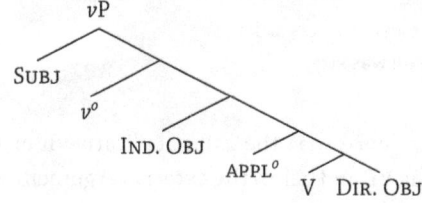

(84) **Low Applicative**

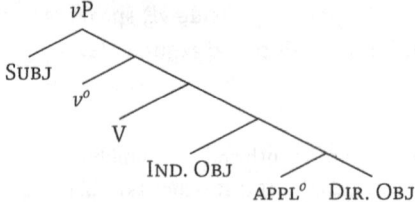

We can see that the applicative head in Zulu is above VP by its ability to combine with any predicate type, including unergatives, as in (79c) above, repeated below:

(79c) uMlungisi u- gijim- **el-** a **uNtombi** / **kwaNtombi**
AUG.1Mlungisi 1s- run- APPL- FV AUG.1Ntombi / LOC.1Ntombi
'Mlungisi is running for Ntombi / to Ntombi's house.'

The independence of the Zulu applicative head from the argument structure of the predicate rules out a low applicative analysis; since low applicative heads must combine with a direct object, they are only available in constructions that have an underlying internal argument.

Furthermore, low applicatives show a semantic restriction not faced by high applicatives: because they directly relate the indirect object to the direct object, they imply a transfer of possession and are thus incompatible with static predicates such as *hold*. As example (85) below shows, Zulu allows the applicative to combine with a static predicate:

(85) uMfundo u- phath- el- a umama ingane
AUG.1Mfundo 1s- hold- APPL- FV AUG.1mother AUG.9child
'Mfundo is holding the baby for mother.'

Pylkkänen (2008) also shows that high applicatives allow for the applied argument to be modified by a depictive, while low applicatives do not. Again, we find that Zulu patterns with the high applicative languages, allowing the applied argument to control a depictive, as in (86) below.

(86) ngi- phek- el- e umama e- gula
1SG- cook- APPL- PFV AUG.1mother 1PRT- sick
'I cooked for mother while she was sick.'

We thus have a variety of evidence that the Zulu applicative morpheme introduces an argument above the VP and below the external argument, which remains the structurally highest argument in all of the examples we have seen.[25]

The causative morpheme in Zulu, -is-, can attach to all types of predicates, including unaccusatives, unergatives, and transitives, as the examples in (87)–(89) below show.

(87) a. indlu   yami   i- ya- sha!
          AUG.9building 9ASSOC.1SG 9S- YA- burn
          'My house is on fire!'

      b. *izigebengu   zi- sha indlu   yami
          AUG.8criminals 8S- burn AUG.9building 9ASSOC.1SG

      c. izigebengu   zi- sh- is- a indlu   yami!
          AUG.8criminals 8S- burn- CAUS- FV AUG.9house 9ASSOC.1SG
          'Criminals are burning down my house!'

(88) uMlungisi   u- gijim- is-   a uSimaku
      AUG.1Mlungisi 1S- run-   CAUS- FV AUG.1Simaku
      'Mlungisi is making Simaku run.' / 'Mlungisi is chasing Simaku.'

(89) uSipho   u- fund- is-   a amantombazane isiZulu
      AUG.1Sipho 1S- learn- CAUS- FV AUG.6girls   AUG.7Zulu
      'Sipho is teaching the girls Zulu.'

From these patterns, we can see that the causative construction introduces a causer argument above the agent of an unergative or transitive predicate. At the same time, we find that certain unaccusative verbs in Zulu allow causative morphology without seeming to add a causer agent, such as (90) below:

(90) indlu   yami   i- ya- sh- is- a
      AUG.9house 9ASSOC.1SG 9S- YA- burn- CAUS- FV
      'My house gets warm.' / 'My house is well-insulated.'

Pylkkänen (2002, 2008) concludes on the basis of this type of pattern in a number of other languages that a causative construction does not necessarily

25. Note that Zulu also has morphologically simple telic verbs of transfer such as *pha/nika* 'give', which seem to involve low applicatives, given the inability of the applied argument to control a depictive:

(i) ngi- nik- e umama   amaphilisi (*e- gula)
     1SG- give- PFV AUG.1mother AUG.6pills 1PRT- sick
     'I gave mother pills (*when she was sick).'

These particular verbs do not require transparent APPL morphology in order to function ditransitively, though Adams (2010) argues that they do involve silent applicative structure. I am not aware of verbs in which the APPL -el- morpheme is used to form a low applicative.

introduce a causer *argument*. In this type of language, which she dubs "non-voice-bundling," causative morphology introduces a causative event, while a separate Voice head introduces the causer argument. The existence of these unaccusative causatives is in line with Pylkkänen's non-voice-bundling construction, where the actual causer argument is introduced in the specifier of a higher Voice head that is separate from the CAUS head.

We can pinpoint the attachment site of the CAUS head as *below* the causee argument using Pylkkänen's observation that causatives that attach to VP permit manner adverbs, but not agent-oriented adverbs to modify a causee argument. As (91) below shows, a manner adverb may scope below the causative, modifying the external argument of *gijima*:

(91) uMlungisi u- gijim- **is-** a **uSimaku** *ngokushesha*
     AUG.1Mlungisi 1s- run- CAUS- FV AUG.1Simaku quickly
     'Mlungisi is making Simaku run quickly.'

By contrast, an agent-oriented adverb like *ngamabomu* 'on purpose' can only modify the causer argument, and not the causee, as the examples in (92) and (93) below show:

(92) a. uSipho$_i$ u- khal- is- a izingane$_k$ *ngamabomu$_{i/*k}$*
      AUG.1Sipho 1s- cry- CAUS- FV AUG.10children deliberately
      'Sipho$_i$ made the children$_k$ cry *on purpose$_{i/*k}$*

       i. **Felicitous context:** Sipho pulls the children's hair to get them to cry.

       ii. **Infelicitous context:** Sipho tells the children that MaMkhize always gives sweets to crying children, so they go over to her and begin to cry deliberately.

(93) a. uThemba$_i$ u- fail- is- a uSipho$_k$ itesti *ngamabomu$_{i/*k}$*
      AUG.1Themba 1s- fail- CAUS- FV AUG.1Sipho AUG.5test deliberately
      'Themba$_i$ made Sipho$_k$ fail the test *on purpose$_{i/*k}$*

       i. **Felicitous context:** Themba is Sipho's lifeline on a gameshow. Sipho calls Themba to ask the answer to a question. Themba knows the correct answer but tells him an incorrect one anyways.

       ii. **Infelicitous context:** Right before Sipho takes the military academy entrance exam, Themba convinces him that he doesn't want to attend so Sipho deliberately messes up the test.

Outside of causatives, the agent-oriented adverb *ngamabomu* is available to modify the external argument of the predicates above, as shown in (94) below. In these constructions, the infelicitous contexts from (92) and (93) become felicitous.

(94) a. izingane zi- khala *ngamabomu*
      AUG.10children 10s- cry deliberately
      'The children are crying on purpose.'

b. uSipho   u- fail- e itesti   *ngamabomu*
AUG.1Sipho 1s- fail- PFV AUG.5test deliberately
'Sipho failed the test on purpose.'

To summarize, Zulu has a high applicative that appears to attach to VP, adding an applied argument that is structurally below the external argument but above the verb and internal arguments. The causative morpheme also appears to attach at the VP level, but instead adds a causer argument *above* the external argument, via a separate Voice head (following Pylkkänen, 2002, 2008):

(95) **Zulu causative**

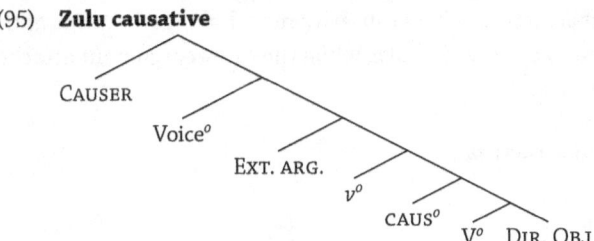

When the causative and applicative combine on a single predicate, the resulting structure suggests that these two processes are interleaved. As noted above, causative morphology must be structurally lower (closer to the verb) than applicative morphology in Zulu, while the causer argument is structurally *higher* than the applied argument. The applied argument is in turn is structurally higher than the external argument of the predicate, yielding rigid *Causer > Applied argument > External Argument > Direct Object* order. As we saw in section 2.3, non-agreeing arguments must appear in their base-generated positions, which suggests that this linear order reflects syntactic height of arguments. We can see this pattern in (96) below. The causer is the argument that raises to *v*P-external subject position, and the word order of the remaining DPs inside *v*P always places the benefactive argument above the external argument and the direct object:

(96) a. uSipho   u- fund- is- el- a **uthisha   omkhulu**
AUG.1Sipho 1s- learn- CAUS- APPL- FV AUG.1teacher 1REL.big
amantombazane isiZulu
AUG.6girls   AUG.7Zulu
'Sipho is teaching the girls Zulu for the principal.'
*'Sipho is teaching the principal Zulu for the girls.'

b. ubaba   u- cul- is- el- a inkosi   abantwana   i-
AUG.1father 1s- sing- CAUS- APPL- FV AUG.9chief AUG.2children AUG5-
Nkosi Sikelel' iAfrika
9lord bless AUG.5Africa
'Father made the children sing the chief the national anthem.'
*'Father made the chief sing the national anthem for the children.'

At the same time, the *meaning* of the predicate reinforces the morphological evidence that APPL is structurally higher than CAUS. This contrast is clearest in (96a): speakers find the sentence to be felicitous in contexts where the *teaching* is done on behalf of the principal, but not when the *learning* is.

Harley (2013) discusses a similar interaction between causative and applicative in Hiaki, which also shows evidence for causative morphology that is structurally lower than the applicative, while the causer argument is structurally higher than the applied argument. Harley concludes that the Hiaki pattern involves low causative morphology, with a high Voice head introducing the causer *above* the applied argument. Given what we have seen for Zulu, we can imagine a similar structure, where causative morphology can attach at the VP-level, for the reasons discussed above, while the causer argument attaches outside of the applicative:[26]

(97)   **Zulu argument structure**

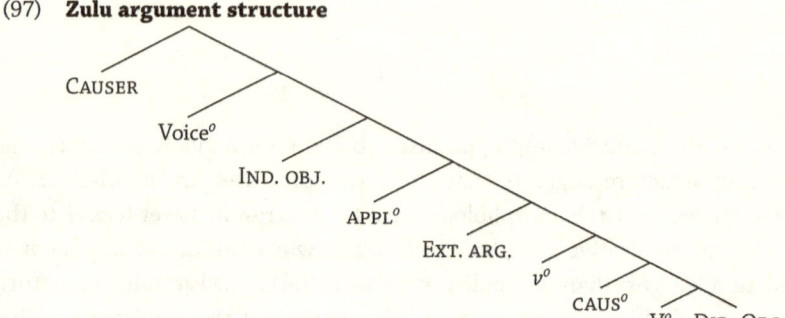

If, as Harley does, we assume that applicative morphology, unlike the causative, directly introduces the applied argument, then in constructions with both CAUS and APPL, the applicative must attach outside of *v*P, as illustrated in (97) above. One consequence of this conclusion is that the position of the applicative head does not appear to be absolute. Rather, it seems to be relative to the highest argument-introducing head: as we saw in examples like (85), the applied argument attaches *below* the external argument in predicates that are not causative.

The main generalization that emerges is that both CAUS and APPL attach at the VP level when acting alone, though the causer argument attaches higher. When both appear on the predicate, CAUS still shows evidence of VP-level attachment, whereas APPL appears to introduce an applied argument above *v*P. This understanding of the articulated argument structure in the extended *v*P domain will be crucial as we investigate structural licensing of in situ

---

26. Harley (2013) argues that the external argument of the predicate is also introduced by a separate Voice head, rather than by *v°* directly. For simplicity here, and throughout the rest of the book, I maintain Spec,*v*P as the position for the external argument, though nothing crucial in the discussion hinges on this choice.

arguments in chapter 3. As I will show, both applicative and causative heads interact with the process of argument licensing that we find in Zulu.

2.6 SUMMARY

In this chapter, I have introduced a number of constructions that are central to the questions investigated in this book. In particular, I have focused on the positions available for subjects in Zulu, and the ways in which subject agreement interacts with movement and subject position in the language. While Zulu prohibits agreement with vP-internal subjects, agreement is required when subjects appear outside of vP. These agreeing subjects can surface in multiple vP-external positions, including a preverbal position that I have identified as a Spec,TP argument position, a preverbal A-bar position, and a postverbal A-bar position.

I also showed that Zulu has a selection of predicates that optionally allow an embedded subject to raise to matrix subject or object position out of a finite, agreeing clause with an overt complementizer. In the raising-to-subject constructions, the raised subject agrees both in the embedded and matrix clause. With raising-to-object, the raised subject behaves like a vP-internal argument in the matrix clause.

Finally, I outlined the positions in which arguments are introduced in Zulu, showing that Zulu has a high applicative phrase and a verb-selecting causative. These structures can combine to yield a total of four arguments associated with single verbal predicate, three of which can appear inside vP.

So far in this discussion, I have shown that there is a link between phi-agreement and syntactic position and a link between syntactic position and interpretation. With only these two factors at play, we've seen that nominals in Zulu exhibit a certain amount of optionality in which syntactic positions they appear in, particularly when it comes to leaving a large number of arguments inside vP. Given this picture, we can ask what role—if any—structural case plays in the distribution of nominals in Zulu. In the next chapter, I turn to this question and investigate a new set of contexts in which nominal distribution becomes more limited in Zulu.

CHAPTER 3
Uncovering Argument Licensing

We saw in chapter 2 that Zulu allows a certain degree of optionality in the position of subjects, both in monoclausal sentences and in biclausal raising constructions. In particular, the grammaticality of subject nominals was not linked to syntactic position in Zulu—though certain information structure considerations do influence subject position. In monoclausal sentences subjects may appear in either vP-internal or vP-external A-positions; in raising constructions, the subject is equally grammatical in the matrix vP-external subject position and in the embedded clause. We also saw that agreement with subjects is not necessary for grammaticality, but instead correlates with syntactic position. This type of optionality is notable because it contrasts with common cross-linguistic distributional restrictions on the syntactic position of nominals. In particular, Zulu allows full optionality in raising constructions: subjects may remain inside the embedded complement of a raising predicate *or* raise out of the finite, agreeing full CP. Many other languages, by contrast, seem to disallow raising out of finite, tensed clauses, but require it out of nonfinite clauses.

Based on this type of difference between languages in the Bantu family and languages with well-studied cases systems like English, researchers on Bantu languages have debated whether *case* is globally relevant in the language family. In this chapter, I argue that despite the distributional freedom we have observed for nouns in Zulu so far, a certain class of nominals in the language does exhibit distributional restrictions that are determined by syntactic configuration. I introduce several novel constructions to show that nouns that appear without their initial *augment* vowel are restricted to specific structural positions within vP. These augmentless nominals are structurally licensed either by a licensing head above vP that I call L, which licenses the highest element in vP, or by lower causative or applicative heads, which can license a direct object.

As we will see, augmentless nominals in Zulu also correspond to particular interpretations in certain syntactic environments; I will show in section 3.3 that we can separate these interpretive properties of augmentless nominals from syntactic restrictions that seem purely tied to structural position, as outlined in the preceding paragraph. At the same time, the combination of interpretive properties and structural restrictions shares certain properties with bare nominal phenomena in other languages (e.g., Longobardi, 1994, 2000, for Romance), a connection I will explore in section 3.4.

3.1 NOMINAL DISTRIBUTION AND CASE THEORY IN BANTU

For several decades, researchers have been investigating how nominals are licensed in various Bantu constructions and whether standard Case Theory is at all relevant to the distribution of nominals in these languages. Research on this question has tended to address whether case is *globally* relevant in Bantu languages. Crucially, most of this work has focused on the presence or absence of case-type effects associated with preverbal subjects.

Before we turn to the specifics of the Zulu patterns, it is useful to consider the debate on the status of case in the Bantu language family and to examine the arguments that case effects are absent in the language. Zulu shares many properties with Bantu languages that have been argued to lack case effects, including the optionality of movement of the embedded subject in the raising constructions discussed in chapter 2. Nonetheless, I argue in this book that nominals in Zulu *are* subject to case licensing, just like their counterparts in more familiar case-licensing languages.

In this chapter, I show that Zulu nominals do face syntactic distributional restrictions and argue that these can be understood in terms of case licensing that takes place within vP. These syntactic restrictions are visible primarily for nominals that lack an *augment* vowel, as discussed in the next section. As I will argue in chapter 5, the augment vowel itself signals local licensing for nominals, and thus eliminates any dependency on the type of syntactic licensing discussed in this chapter. Crucially, I show that all of the structural case-licensing effects that we find in Zulu occur at the vP-level. The preverbal subject position (Spec,TP) is not a licensing position for these nominals.

The patterns of nominal distribution in Zulu that I present in this chapter provide counter-evidence to the claim that case is inoperative in Bantu. At the same time, my finding that structural case is associated with particular syntactic positions within vP, but not with Spec,TP (or Spec,vP) is in fact in line with the findings of researchers arguing against a standard application of case theory in Bantu (for example Harford Perez, 1985; Ndayiragije, 1999; Alsina,

2001; Baker, 2003a; Carstens and Diercks, 2013; Diercks, 2012), who focus only on showing that Bantu lacks case effects associated with these expected positions. Thus Zulu not only gives us new insight on the issue of case in Bantu, but it expands the typology of structural case cross-linguistically.

3.1.1 The Profile of Abstract Case

By this point, we have seen ample evidence that Zulu does not display typical morphological case patterns that reflect the position in which a nominal is licensed: the morphological form of an argument nominal is independent of where it is merged in the structure—or, as the expletive and raising constructions show, of where it moves. This morphological identity of nominals in different positions is illustrated below in (98).

(98) **Apparent lack of structural case morphology in Zulu**

    a. **u-mntwana** u- cul- e   i-ngoma
       AUG-1child   1s- sing- PFV AUG-9song
       'The child sang a song.'

    b. u-Mfundo   u- nik- e **u-mntwana** u-jeqe
       AUG-1Mfundo 1s- give- PFV AUG-1child   AUG-1steamed.bread
       'Mfundo gave the child steamed bread.'

    c. u-Mfundo   u- nik- e u-gogo   **u-mntwana**
       AUG-1Mfundo 1s- give- PFV AUG-1granny AUG-1child
       'Mfundo gave granny the child.'

This pattern of morphological identity contrasts with the pattern found in languages like Icelandic, where the morphological form of a nominal reflects aspects of its syntactic position (and sometimes of its thematic role):

(99) **Icelandic NOM–ACC pattern**

    a.   Við   kusum   **stelpuna**
       We.NOM elected.1PL the.girl.ACC
       'We elected the girl.'

    b.   **Stelpan**   var   kosin
       the.girl.NOM was.3SG elected
       'The girl was elected.'   (Sigurdsson, 1992 ex. (1))

Though Zulu, and Bantu more broadly, lacks this familiar type of morphological case pattern, the question of whether it displays familiar patterns of *abstract* case (e.g., Vergnaud, 2006 [1976]; Chomsky, 1981) requires more investigation.

Rules of case assignment, in combination with some form of *Case Filter*, as in (100) below, reflect the claim that the distribution of nominals is determined by whether they are "licensed" in the grammar:

(100) **Case Filter:** *DP without case

That is, there are certain structural configurations in which nominals are grammatical and others in which they are not. While in some languages these positions tend to correlate with particular case morphology on the nominal, it is clear from languages like Icelandic that this system of abstract case operates independently of morphological case (see Zaenen et al., 1985, and others), as I will discuss in chapter 5.

In a language like English, which is argued to have structural, but not morphological, case, we see evidence that nominal arguments are case-licensed by finite T (nominative) or (some structure associated with) transitive v^o (accusative). In the absence of appropriate licensing elements, a nominal must move to a position where it can receive structural case or it will yield ungrammaticality.

(101) **Finite T as a licenser**
    a.   It is likely [that *Sipho* **will** win the race].

    b.   * It is likely [*Sipho* **to** win the race].

    c.   *Sipho$_i$* is likely [t$_i$ **to** win the race.]

(102) **v^o as a licenser**
    a.   Sipho sang *a song*.

    b.   *A song* was sung.

    c.   * It/there was sung *a song*.

At the same time, the *inability* of nominals to undergo A-movement of this type when they originate in a case-licensed position has led researchers to assume an *Activity Condition* that prevents a nominal from being the target of further agreement relationships after its case needs have been satisfied (Chomsky, 2000, 2001). As we saw in chapter 2, this view of licensing and raising does not capture the raising patterns found in Zulu: raising is optional out of *finite* embedded clauses, as in (103) and these raising predicates typically do not take nonfinite complements at all, at least for speakers of Durban Zulu (104):

(103) **Optional raising-to-subject**

    a. ku- bonakala [ukuthi **uZinhle**   u- zo- xova ujeqe   ]
       17s- seem   that   AUG.1Zinhle 1s- FUT- make AUG.3steamed.bread

    b. **uZinhle**   u- bonakala [ukuthi u- zo- xova ujeqe   ]
       AUG.1Zinhle 1s- seem   that   1s- FUT- make AUG.3steamed.bread
       'It seems that Zinhle will make steamed bread.'

    c. ku- bonakala [ukuthi ku- zo- xova **uZinhle**   ujeqe   ]
       17s- seem   that   17s- FUT- make AUG.1Zinhle AUG.3steamed.bread
       'It seems that Zinhle will make steamed bread.'

(104)   a. *uMandla   u- bonakala uku-cula
          AUG.1Mandla 1s- seem   INF-sing
          intended: 'Mandla seems to sing.'

       b. *ku- bonakala uMandla   uku-cula
          17s- seem   AUG.1Mandla INF-sing
          intended: 'Mandla seems to sing.'

Similarly, we find that in Zulu, while passivization predictably removes the external argument, it does not require the object to move or to agree with the verb:

(105)   a.   intombazane i- bona uMandla
          AUG.9girl   9s- see   AUG.1Mandla
          'The girl sees Mandla.'

       b.   uMandla   u- bon- wa (y-   intombazane)
          AUG.1Mandla 1s- see- PASS (COP- AUG.9girl)

       c.   ku- bon- wa uMandla   (y-   intombazane)
          17s- see- PASS AUG.1Mandla (COP- AUG.9girl)
          'Mandla is seen (by the girl).'

In languages like English, the distributional patterns of nominals contrast with those of CP arguments: for CP complements to V, passive movement and raising-to-subject are optional:

(106)   a.   It is likely [that Mandla sang.]

       b.   [That Mandla sang] is likely.

(107)   a.   It was explained [that Mandla sang.]

       b.   [That Mandla sang] was explained.

The nominals that we've seen so far in Zulu seem to behave more like English CPs than English DPs, with optional movement and agreement. In Zulu, speakers rule out CPs in preverbal subject position, an issue that I will return to in chapter 6, so we cannot directly compare CPs to DPs in this configuration in Zulu:

(108)   a.   ku- bonakala [ukuthi uMandla   u- cul- ile].
             17s- seem   that   AUG.1Mandla 1s- sing- PFV
             'It seems that Mandla sang.'

        b.   * [ukuthi uMandla   u- cul- ile] ku- bonakala
            that   AUG.1Mandla 1s- sing- PFV 17s- seem

(109)   a.   ku- chaz-   wa [ukuthi uMandla   u- cul- ile].
             17s- describe- PASS that   AUG.1Mandla 1s- sing- PFV
             'It was explained that Mandla sang.'

        b.   * [ukuthi uMandla   u- cul- ile] ku- chaz-   wa
            that   AUG.1Mandla 1s- sing- PFV 17s- describe- PASS

The behavior of CP arguments compared to DP arguments is also central to discussions of case on arguments of certain non-verbal predicates. In particular, DP arguments of adjectives and nouns must be licensed by a preposition or an oblique case marker in languages like English, while CP arguments do not require this licensing:

(110)   a.   I am proud **of** Mandla.

        b.   * I am proud Mandla.

        c.   I am proud (*of) [that Mandla sang].

(111)   a.   the news **of** my family

        b.   * the news my family

        c.   the news (*of) [that my family is well]

In Zulu, oblique morphology also appears on arguments of these types of predicates. Unlike in English, however, Zulu requires this type of morphology on *both* DP and CP arguments. In (112), the predicate *qhenya* requires an instrumental marker *nga-*[1] on both nominal complements and clausal complements:

(112)   a.   ngi- ya- zi-   qhenya **ngo**-Mandla
             1SG- YA- REFL- proud   NGA.AUG-1Mandla
             'I'm proud of Mandla.'

        b.   * ngi- ya- zi-   qhenya uMandla
            1SG- YA- REFL- proud   AUG-1Mandla
            'I'm proud of Mandla.'

1. See chapter 5 for more on this marker.

c. ngi- ya- zi- qhenya **ngo**-kuthi uMandla u- cul- ile
1SG- YA- REFL- proud NGA-that AUG.1Mandla 1s- sing- PFV
'I'm proud that Mandla sang.'

d. *ngi- ya- zi- qhenya ukuthi uMandla u- cul- ile
1SG- YA- REFL- proud that AUG.1Mandla 1s- sing- PFV
'I'm proud that Mandla sang.'

As (113) shows, we find the same type of pattern for complements of a noun, where the associative marker[2] is required, regardless of whether the complement is a DP or a CP:

(113) a. indaba **yo**-mndeni wa- mi
AUG.9news 9ASSOC.AUG-3family 3ASSOC- 1SG
'the news of my family'

b. *indaba umndeni wa- mi
AUG.9news AUG.3family 3ASSOC- 1SG
'the news of my family'

c. indaba **yo**-kuthi umndeni wa-mi u- ya- phila
AUG.9news 9ASSOC-that AUG.3family 3ASSOC-1SG 3s- YA- live
'the news that my family is well'

d. *indaba ukuthi umndeni wa-mi u- ya- phila
AUG.9news that AUG.3family 3ASSOC-1SG 3s- YA- live
'the news that my family is well'

I return to the role of these morphemes in chapters 5 and 6. For now, we can see that the initial picture of case in Zulu looks rather different than what we would expect based on familiar case patterns: A-movement of DP arguments appears to be optional, regardless of whether the DP originates in a position that we would expect to be associated with case or in one that we would expect to be caseless. In addition, while CPs appear to be restricted from appearing in pre-verbal subject position, Zulu treats DP and CP arguments the same with respect to licensing in non-verbal predicates. Given this divergence from expected patterns, we might wonder whether the standard case theory has any relevance to Zulu syntax.

3.1.2 Against Standard Case Theory in Bantu

The types of issues noted above for Zulu have been a point of concern for a number of syntacticians working on Bantu languages. Since Harford Perez

---

2. This marker will be discussed in more detail in chapter 5 and chapter 6.

(1985), there has been work on Bantu suggesting that case does not play a role in the grammar of Bantu languages (Ndayiragije, 1999; Alsina, 2001; Baker, 2003a; Carstens and Diercks, 2013; Diercks, 2012). Many of these claims stem from the absence in Bantu of effects that we associate with case-licensing in Spec,TP. As we saw with Zulu above, one notable divergence from standard case patterns is the ability of subjects to raise out of finite clauses, which has been documented in a number of Bantu languages. (114) repeats the pattern that we have observed for Zulu; Harford Perez (1985) shows similar patterns for Shona in (115) and Kirundi in (116a).

(114) a. ku- bonakala [ukuthi **uSipho**   u- pheka iqanda]
          17s- seem   that   AUG.1Sipho 1s- cook AUG.5egg
          'It seems that Sipho is cooking an egg.'

       b. **uSipho**   u- bonakala [ukuthi u- pheka iqanda]
          AUG.1Sipho 1s- seem   that   1s- cook AUG.5egg
          'Sipho seems to be cooking an egg.'   *Zulu*

(115) a. mbavhá í- no- fungir- w- a kuti y- áka-   vánd- á mú- bako
          9thief   9s- PRES- suspect- PASS- FV that 9s- REM.PST- hide- FV 18- cave
          'The thief is suspected to be hidden in the cave.'

       b. zvi- no- fungir- w- a kuti mbavhá y- akak-   vánd- á mú- bako
          8s- PRES- suspect- PASS- FV that 9thief 9s- REM.PAST- hide- FV 18- cave
          'It is suspected that the thief is hidden in the cave.'
                                                      (Harford Perez, 1985) *Shona*

(116) a. inzovu   z- aa- menyeekan- ye kó z- iish- e báa-   ba- antu
          10elephants 10s- PST- be.known   PF that 10s- kill- PF 2those- 2- people
          'Elephants are renowned for having killed those people.'

       b. vy- aa- menyeekan- ye kó inzovu   z- iish- e báa-   ba- antu
          8s- PST- be.known-   PF that 10elephants 10s- kill- PF 2those- 2- people
          'Elephants are renowned for having killed those people.'
                                                      (Harford Perez, 1985) *Kirundi*

In addition to this type of raising pattern, we also find licit subjects of nonfinite clauses in some Bantu languages, as in (117), (e.g., Harford Perez, 1985; Diercks, 2012). The boldface nominals in (117) below are all understood as the subject of a following infinitive-marked (non-agreeing) verb. Comparable constructions in languages like English would require a case-licensing complementizer to immediately precede the nominal (as the translations of the a and b examples reflect).

(117) **Licit subjects of nonfinite clauses**
       a. i- na- wezakana (*kwa) **Maiko** ku- m- pig- i-   a Tegani simu
          9s- PRES- possible (*for) Michael INF- 1o- beat- APPL- FV Tegan phone
          'It's possible for Michael to call Tegan.'   (Diercks, 2012) *Swahili*

b. **Sammy** khu- khila ku-mw-inyawe o- kwo khu- la- sanga- sya
1Sammy INF- win 3-3-game DEM- 3 15- FUT- please- CAUS
mawe
mother
'For Sammy to win the game will please his mother.' (Diercks, 2012) *Lubukusu*

c. **a-rutwo** gŭ- thooma ŭŭrú kŭ- ráákáragi- a mŭ- rutani
2-students INF- read badly 15s- anger.CONT- FV 1- teacher
'Students reading badly angers the teacher.' (Harford Perez, 1985) *Kikuyu*

d. **va-nhu** ku- rwa daka u- ku-ha= kú- ná- kú- naka
2-people INF- fight 5grudge this- 15 NEG- 15s- be INF- be.good
'This fighting grudges on the part of people is no good.'

(Fortune, 1977) *Shona*

The prevalence of inversion constructions, as in (118), where a preverbal object or locative phrase controls 'subject' agreement while the subject remains after the verb (e.g., Harford Perez, 1985; Ndayiragije, 1999), has also been taken as evidence against a standard application of case in Bantu. In particular, as these examples show, subjects in inversion constructions neither move to Spec,TP nor do they agree with T. Instead, an internal argument or oblique may both move *and* control agreement, suggesting that in these constructions subjects do not establish the type of syntactic relationship with T that standard theories of case would expect.

(118) **Inversion constructions**

a. **olukwi** si- **lu-** li- seny- a (*a-)bakali
11wood NEG- 11s- PRES- chop- FV (AUG-)2women
'WOMEN do not chop wood.' (Baker, 2003, ex. (24a)) *Kinande,*

b. **omo-mulongo mw-** a- hik- a (?o-)mukali
18LOC-3village 18s- T- arrive- FV (AUG-)1woman
'At the village arrived a woman.' (Baker, 2003, ex. (25)) *Kinande*

Finally, as discussed above for Zulu, expletive constructions, as in (119), where the subject again remains low and expletive agreement appears on the verb (e.g., Harford Perez, 1985; Van der Wal, 2012), essentially raise the same question about how case is assigned to subjects. In particular, on any theory of case assignment for which subjects receive case through the establishment of a relationship with T (signaled by movement and/or Agree), expletive constructions that show neither movement or agreement of the subject become problematic.

(119) **Expletive constructions**[3]

    a. **kw**- á-   uray- iw-   a   mu-rúmé né- shumba ku- ru- kova
        17s- PST- kill- PASS- FV 1-man   by- 9lion 7- 11- river
        'There was a man killed by a lion at the river.' (Harford Perez, 1985) *Shona*

    b. **ku**- fund- is-   a uSipho   izingane   isiZulu
        17s- learn- CAUS- FV AUG.1Sipho AUG.10children AUG.7Zulu
        'Sipho teaches the children Zulu.'   *Zulu*

As the constructions above illustrate, the focus of discussions of case in Bantu tends to be on the behavior of subject DPs and on the position that is typically associated with nominative case, finite T. As the examples make clear, movement to Spec,TP is not required to license DPs—and DPs in a finite Spec,TP are not rendered "inactive" for further A-movement—in a variety of Bantu languages. Given this pattern, some researchers have concluded that the presence of case in a grammar is parametrized; in Bantu, case is simply "switched off" (Harford Perez, 1985; Carstens and Diercks, 2013; Diercks, 2012). A related line of argumentation proposes that all movement to Spec,TP in Bantu languages is driven purely by phi-agreement with T—but not case— which again fits with the Zulu patterns we observed in the previous chapter (Collins, 2004; Carstens, 2005; Baker, 2003a, 2008; Henderson, 2006b).

Building on Baker (2003a), Baker (2008) breaks the patterns down into two parameters to capture the range of possible relationships between EPP effects, phi-agreement with T, and nominative case assignment. His first parameter, the *Directionality of Agreement Parameter*, specifies whether Agree operations trigger EPP effects that require movement of the goal to the probe's specifier. The second, the *Case-Dependency of Agreement Parameter*, divides languages into those that achieve case-valuation and Agree via the same operation and those that do not. For most Bantu languages, he argues, Agree requires EPP, but is not dependent on case. The result, then, is that movement in these Bantu languages is triggered by phi-agreement, which is not linked to case. These parameters therefore combine to give the absence of a nominative effect: movement of subjects (and movement to and from Spec,TP more generally) under this system will not show evidence of a direct link to finiteness of T, the need of a nominal to receive case, or any other hallmarks of the English-type pattern.

Note that this type of approach does not in fact rule out the presence of case requirements in languages that do display these properties; in fact, many of these proposals assume that nominative case is being assigned to the subject in Bantu languages—even when another element appears in Spec,TP.

---

3. The noun class used for expletive/default subject agreement differs across Bantu languages, but is typically a class that is also associated with gerunds or locatives. In Zulu, as we saw in chapter 2, class 17 is the default agreement class.

For example, Carstens (2005) spells out a case assignment mechanism for inversion constructions. She proposes that nominative case can be assigned to an in situ subject in Kilega inversion constructions because an inverted object (which has, on her view, already received case from v^o) can agree only for phi-features with T, moving to Spec,TP as a result. A separate nominative probe on T can then probe the subject, assigning it case. Carstens (2005, 2011) also develops an explanation for why nominals in many Bantu languages seem to move from case position to case position (including inverted objects and raised subjects): she argues that nominals in Bantu are "hyperactive" because they enter the derivation with a valued, but uninterpretable, gender feature that remains unchecked throughout the derivation.

While these types of approaches can capture the basic Bantu patterns without needing to sacrifice a standard view of case assignment, Diercks (2012) observes that despite the ability to incorporate a standard case assignment mechanism, we don't really see any direct evidence for the nominative effect; he concludes that a more efficient theory would simply eliminate case from the grammar of Bantu, with a macro-parameter determining whether case is present in a language or not. In recent work, Van der Wal (2012) returns to the issue of the correct granularity of parameters surrounding case in Bantu. She argues that there is more variation across Bantu languages in whether they show case effects. In particular, she demonstrates that Bantu languages like Matengo allow true in situ agreeing subjects, which are ruled out in many other Bantu languages (in favor of the non-agreeing in situ subjects shown above). On this basis, she argues that Bantu languages like Matengo, which do not link agreement with the EPP, are languages where agreement with T may be driven by case assignment, in contrast with the rest of the Bantu family, whose patterns have been described above.

The consensus of this literature, then, is that Bantu languages like Zulu lack any direct evidence for nominative case assignment, with the further conclusion by some researchers that abstract case plays no role in the grammar of these languages. If we expand the empirical picture in Zulu beyond the patterns associated with subject positions and subject agreement, a different set of patterns and conclusions emerges. In particular, examining nominal distribution patterns in the syntactic domain below T reveals a set of behaviors that bear familiar hallmarks of structural case, which I will argue should be represented in terms of structural case-licensing inside vP. Because this licensing takes place only at the vP level, this proposal does not contradict the narrower conclusion of previous research that there is no nominative case associated with finite T in most Bantu languages—though it does present a challenge to the broader conclusion that has often been drawn in this research, that Bantu lacks the effects of case-licensing altogether.

I begin our exploration of syntactic case in Zulu by focusing on the structural restrictions that govern the distribution of a subclass of nominals:

those without the *augment* vowel. While these augmentless nominals are subject to particular distributional restrictions related to their interpretation, I will show that in addition to these semantic restrictions, there are further purely syntactic restrictions on their distribution that should be analyzed as abstract case effects just like those we saw earlier in this chapter. While the discussion in this chapter is limited to augmentless nominals and the ways in which they contrast with augmented nominals, I will argue in the following chapters that these case effects are merely one aspect of a larger case system in Zulu, which encompasses all nominals.

3.2 AUGMENTLESS NOMINALS

The remainder of this chapter focuses on a distinction between two categories of nominal in Zulu: those that bear an *augment* vowel and those that lack the vowel. While there are a variety of contexts that require a nominal to appear without the augment vowel in Zulu, we will see that when augmentless nominals appear as arguments of a predicate, they are limited to a subset of the environments in which augmented nominals may appear as arguments. Specifically, I will show that augmentless nominal arguments are restricted to *v*P-internal positions:

(120) **Augmentless nominal generalization** (preliminary): An augmentless nominal argument must appear in a *v*P-internal position.

We first saw in chapter 2 that every Zulu noun stem is marked with prefixal morphology that indicates the noun class of the nominal. This prefixal morphology includes both the noun class prefix itself—a C/CV/CVC/Ø morpheme that attaches to the stem—and the preceding *augment* vowel.

I repeat the full paradigm of noun class prefixes and augments from the previous chapter in table 3.1 on the following page.

While nearly every Zulu nominal that we have seen so far in this book has been marked with an obligatory augment vowel, examples like (121) below show that there are circumstances in which the augment may be omitted:

(121) ni- bona (**u**)- **bani**?
      2PL- see (AUG)- 1who
      'Who do you see?'

In the example in (121), the *wh*-word *(u)bani* 'who' may appear either with or without its initial augment vowel *u-*. As we investigate the particular circumstances under which an augmentless nominal like the one in (121) is grammatical, we begin to see evidence that nominals in Zulu are subject to structural licensing conditions after all.

Table 3.1. NOUN CLASS PREFIXAL MORPHOLOGY

NOUN CLASS	AUGMENT	PREFIX	EXAMPLE	TRANSLATION
1	u-	m(u)-	umuntu	'person'
1a	u-	Ø	ugogo	'grandmother'
2	a-	ba-	abantu	'people'
2a	o-	Ø	ogogo	'grandmothers'
3	u-	m(u)-	umunwe	'finger'
4	i-	mi-	iminwe	'fingers'
5	i-	(li-)	iqanda	'egg'
6	a-	ma-	amaqanda	'eggs'
7	i-	si-	isipho	'gift'
8	i-	zi-	izipho	'gifts'
9	i-	N-	indawo	'place'
10	i-	ziN-	izindawo	'places'
11	u-	(lu-)	uthando	'love'
14	u-	(bu-)	ubuntu	'humanity'
15	u-	ku-	ukudla	'food'
17	u-	ku-	ukwindla	'autumn'

3.2.1 The Distribution of Augmentless Nominals

Nouns appear without an augment vowel in several different environments (Mzolo, 1968; von Staden, 1973; de Dreu, 2008; Taraldsen, 2010; Buell, 2011). The full range of such environments reported in these earlier works does not completely match the judgments of the speakers of Durban Zulu with whom I worked, however. In general, my consultants were less willing to omit the augment vowel than what has traditionally been reported. Consequently, Durban Zulu speakers judged a number of contexts reported as prohibiting the augment, particularly by von Staden (1973), as allowing—or even requiring—an augment. In addition, many younger speakers describe the use of augmentless nominals in argument positions as marked and "rude", a register distinction that, to my knowledge, has not been noted in earlier descriptions of augmentless nominals. Table 3.2 compares the environments that have been described in earlier research as permitting augmentless nominals, as collected in Buell (2011), with the recent judgments I have collected from speakers of Durban Zulu.

The focus of this chapter, and of subsequent discussion in the following chapters, is the distribution and behavior of augmentless nominals that function as arguments. Specifically, in order to approach the issue of structural case, we will be concerned with the clause-level configurations that license augmentless nominals. I turn my attention, therefore, to the final two

Table 3.2. COMPARATIVE DISTRIBUTION OF AUGMENTLESS NOMINALS

	ENVIRONMENT	AUGMENT STATUS	
		Reported in Buell (2011)	Durban Zulu
NP-level:	2nd member of compound	omitted	omitted
	noun class transposition	omitted	omitted
	denominal adjectives	omitted	omitted
	denominal adverbs	omitted	omitted
DP-level:	following a demonstrative pronoun	omitted	omitted
	following an 'absolute' pronoun	optional	optional/preferred
	proper names after titles	strongly dispreferred	strongly dispreferred
	before -ni 'what kind/amount'	omitted	dispreferred
	before -phi 'which'	omitted	preferred (construction dispreferred)
	before numeral quantifiers and 'all'	optional	required
Vocatives:		omitted	omitted
Clause-level:	wh-words	no discussion	optional
	Negative Polarity Items	omitted	omitted (within vP)/optional

categories in table 3.2: *negative polarity items* (NPIs) and *wh*-words, which I will show are licensed only in particular syntactic configurations. I return to the NP-level and DP-level occurrences of augmentless nominals in chapter 5, discussing in section 5.6 how we might understand these patterns in terms of case licensing.

Nominal arguments that can appear without an augment in Zulu tend to have a limited set of interpretations: these nominals are typically either *wh*-words or NPIs. We can see an example of both of these uses of augmentless arguments in (122) below:

(122)   a. u-   bona **bani**?
          2SG- see   1who
          'Who do you see?'

    b. a-   ngi- bon- i   **muntu**
          NEG- 1SG- see- NEG 1person
          'I don't see anyone.'

In (122a), the *wh*-object *bani* 'who' appears without its augment vowel, just as we saw was possible in example (121). As *v*P-internal elements, *wh*-words in Zulu optionally bear an augment, both as subjects and as objects:

(123)   **Optional augments on *v*P-internal** *wh*-
    a. ku- fik-   e   **bani**?
       17s- arrive- PFV 1who

    b. ku- fik-   e   **u-   bani**?
       17s- arrive- PFV AUG- 1who
       'Who came?'

    c. u-   funa- **ni**?
       2SG- want- 9what

    d. u-   funa **i-   ni**?
       2SG- want AUG- 9what
       'What do you want?'

The examples in (123a,b) show that a *v*P-internal subject *wh*-word may optionally bear an augment, while (123c,d) show the same for an object *wh*-word. The object *wh*-word *(i)ni* 'what' cliticizes to the verb when it appears without the augment vowel.

Crucially, this optionality of the augment with *wh*-words is only observable inside *v*P. We saw in chapter 2 with (15), repeated with slight modifications below, that *wh*-words cannot appear in a *v*P-external subject position (regardless of augment status). When *wh*-words appear in a cleft, as in (15c'), the augment is required:

(15') a. *(**u)bani** **u**- fik- ile?
        AUG.1who 1s- arrive- PFV

b. ku- fik- e **(u) bani**?
   17s- arrive- PFV AUG.1who

c. ng- ***(u)bani** o- fik- ile?
   COP- AUG.1who 1REL- arrive- PFV
   'Who came?'   (Sabel and Zeller, 2006, ex. (5), adapted)

As we have already seen, *wh*-words in Zulu, including those with an aug-ment vowel, have a more limited distribution than other types of nominals. As Buell (2009) and Adams (2010) point out, *wh*-words also display restrictions within *v*P that appear to be related to their focal properties. While these authors imply that the distribution of *wh*-words—including those with an augment—matches the distribution of the augmentless NPIs that I discuss below, I will show that while both (augmented) *wh*-words and augmentless nominals have a more restricted distribution than augmented nominals, they do not in fact have the same profile. There are some systematic differences between the distribution of (augmented) *wh*-words in general and that of augmentless nominals, including the difference illustrated in (15') above and differences in the distribution of multiple *v*P-internal arguments that I will discuss in section 3.3.2 (see footnote 6 for comparison)

The other main use of augmentless arguments, as illustrated by (122b) above, is as NPIs. It has been claimed in the literature, as summarized recently, for example, by de Dreu (2008), that under negation, augmented nominals are interpreted as definite or specific, while augmentless nominals are interpreted as indefinite/NPIs:

(124) **Reported meaning contrast with augment**

a. a- ka- limaz-i **a- bantwana**
   NEG- 1s- hurt-NEG AUG- 2children
   'He doesn't hurt (some particular) children.'

b. a- ka- limaza-i **bantwana**
   NEG- 1s- hurt-NEG 2children
   'He doesn't hurt any children.'   (de Dreu, 2008, ex. (2b), (3b), adapted)

Before I turn to the distributional details of these augmentless NPIs, I will again note that though the existing literature on Zulu describes the omission of an augment vowel as a general, unmarked NPI strategy in the language, for the majority of speakers of Durban Zulu with whom I have worked, most augmentless NPIs are possible only in a marked register. These speakers describe augmentless NPIs as being informal to the point of rudeness, and thus can be reluctant to use or consider this construction in more formal settings.[4] Two generic NPIs, *muntu* 'anyone' and *lutho* 'anything', are exceptions to this register distinction. Speakers tend to accept these forms in all registers, even where another augmentless NPI would be judged inappropriate. The judgments that I report that do not involve the generic augmentless NPIs come from speakers who are accessing an informal register or from those who seem to have less of a register distinction for augmentless NPIs.

While most discussions of augmentless NPI nominals focus on sentential negation as the relevant licensing environment, as illustrated in (125), it is clear that these elements are licensed by a variety of other nonveridical environments as well.

(125) a. **A**- ngi- bon- **i**   muntu
          NEG- 1SG- see- NEG 1person
          'I don't see anybody.'/ *'I don't see the person.'

    b. * ngi- bona muntu
         1SG- see 1person

The example in (125a) illustrates that the augment may be omitted under sentential negation, forcing an NPI interpretation. It may not be omitted in an affirmative sentence, as (125b) shows. In (126), we can see that a negative adverb, *ngeke* 'never' will also license an augmentless NPI:

(126) **Ngeke** ngi-   sho lutho
      never 1SG.SJC- say 11thing
      'I'll never say anything.'

The example in (127) shows that a minimizing preposition, *ngaphambi* 'before' licenses an augmentless NPI as well:

(127) ... **ngaphambi** ko-ku-ba   ba- sho lutho...
        before   LOC-INF-be 2s- say 1thing
      '...before they said anything...'[5]

Finally, the example in (128) shows that polar questions also license augmentless NPIs:

(128) **u- ke**   w- a-   funda ncwadi ku-le-mpelasonto?
      2SG-occasionally.do 2SG- PST- read   9book LOC-DEM-9weekend
      'Did you read any book on the weekend?

4. This register distinction seems to be particularly pronounced for younger speakers.
5. <http://vcmstatic.sabc.co.za>, accessed May 19, 2009.

As is often the case for NPIs cross-linguistically (see Giannakidou, 2011), not all nonveridical environments license augmentless nominals in Zulu, as the ungrammatical example with *few* in (129) below shows. Nevertheless, the examples above indicate that a range of nonveridical contexts do serve to license augmentless nominals.

(129) *abantu   abambalwa ba- bon- e   muntu
        AUG.2people 2REL.few   2S- see- PFV 1person
        intended: 'Few people saw anyone.'

While the examples in (126)–(128) show augmentless NPI licensing in monoclausal sentences, the constructions in (130) show that there is no clausemate restriction on the licenser: negation in the higher clause can license an NPI in the embedded clause (as discussed in Giannakidou 2000, for example). This ability of higher negation to license an augmentless nominal in the embedded clause will be crucial in our understanding of the syntactic restrictions on nominals, as we will see in section 3.3.[6]

(130) **Cross-clausal licensing of augmentless nominals**

   a. **A-** ngi- fun- **i** [ukuthi uSipho   a-   phek- e **qanda**]
      NEG- 1SG- want- NEG that   AUG.1Sipho 1SJC. cook- SJC 5egg
      'I don't want Sipho to cook any egg.'

   b. **A-** ngi- cabang- **i** [ukuthi uSipho   u- bon- e   **muntu/lutho**]
      NEG- 1SG- think- NEG that   AUG.1Sipho 1S- see- PFV 1person/11thing
      'I don't think Sipho saw anyone/anything.'

The restriction of augmentless nominals to nonveridical environments limits their distribution considerably. Previous discussions of their distribution have assumed that this restriction, and the accompanying NPI interpretation, fully accounts for the distribution of augmentless nominals (e.g., Adams, 2008; Cheng and Downing, 2009). I argue in this chapter that this conclusion is incorrect, and that the distribution of augmentless nominals is also restricted by additional syntactic licensing principles—in particular by principles that mirror the effects of the Case Filter in languages like English and Icelandic. To show that this new characterization of the pattern is correct, I first outline the system of structural licensing and then demonstrate how it accounts for the full picture of augmentless nominal distribution in Zulu.

6. In chapter 6, I show that not all speakers accept constructions like those in (130b), where an NPI in an indicative clause is licensed by matrix negation. As I will show in that chapter, a certain group of speakers has a set of related restrictions involving indicative complement clauses. For now, I follow the judgments of speakers who display no contrast between embedded subjunctives and embedded indicatives.

While the restriction to nonveridical environments already limits the syntactic positions available to augmentless nominals, there is evidence that there are additional syntactic restrictions on the placement of augmentless nominals that cannot be explained by the requirements for NPI licensing. We will first see that augmentless nominals must appear inside vP, as stated above in (120), repeated below:

(120) **Augmentless nominal generalization** (preliminary): An augmentless nominal must appear in a vP-internal position.[7]

Beyond this restriction to vP-internal positions, I will show that there are further distributional limitations on augmentless nominals and that these additional restrictions point to case licensing as a factor in Zulu grammar. While we will not see case licensing associated with the familiar finite T and transitive v^o in Zulu, we will find that nominals are licensed through particular structural relationships within vP. Inside vP, only one nominal may appear without the augment in an intransitive or transitive construction— constructions with zero or one external argument. When a construction involves causative or applicative arguments, an additional augmentless nominal may appear. To capture these generalizations, I propose that licensing of augmentless nominals takes place within vP via two structural relationships. First, a L(icensing) head immediately above vP can license the most local nominal in its c-command domain. Second, when an *additional* head beyond v^o, such as APPL or CAUS, is introduced into the structure, the direct object is also licensed. I will suggest in section 3.3.2 that this pattern may be a special case of the broader pattern that includes Burzio's Generalization (Burzio, 1986).

(131) **Augmentless nominal generalization** (revised): An augmentless nominal argument must be local to a nominal-licensing head (L or APPL/CAUS).

These licensing processes are schematized in (132) and (133) on the following page.

---

7. Given the discussion of causative constructions in the previous chapter, the relevant domain for licensing in situ arguments is more precisely the entire extended domain of vP, including the Voice head that we saw introduces the causer in section 2.5. This more articulated structure will become relevant to the discussion of licensing additional arguments in section 3.3.2; outside of that discussion, I will continue to use vP to refer to this domain.

(132) **Licensing via L**

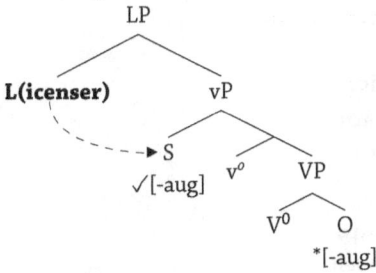

(133) **Licensing via extra 'external' arguments**

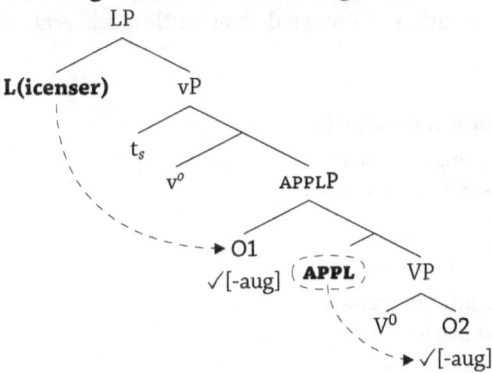

The schema in (132) and (133) capture the fact that at most one augmentless nominal can be licensed in transitive and intransitive constructions, while two augmentless nominals can be licensed in the presence of CAUS or APPL—"external argument" introducing heads. As we have seen so far throughout this chapter, nominals that bear an augment vowel are not subject to any of these restrictions. At the same time, as we shall see, they act as intervenors for the licensing heads, and can therefore block lower augmentless nominals from being licensed (along the lines of Chomsky, 2000). As I will show in the following sections, this licensing mechanism accounts for the aspects of the distribution of augmentless nominals that cannot be attributed to the more general licensing conditions discussed above, and that are not faced by their augmented counterparts.

3.3.1 The *v*P-internal Restriction on Augmentless Nominals

In this section, I examine the restriction of augmentless nominals to *v*P-internal positions. In addition to seeing evidence of this restriction, we will also see evidence that the licensing head L is located above *v*P in (132). To investigate these issues, we will need to look beyond the grammatical instances of augmentless nominals in preceding sections, which all involved non-agreeing, in situ objects, as in (134) below:

(134) **Augmentless *v*P-internal objects**

    a. a-   ngi- bon- anga   **muntu**
        NEG- 1SG- see- NEG.PST 1person
        'I didn't see anybody.'

    b. ngeke ngi-   bon- e   **muntu**
        never 1SG.SJC- see- SJC 1person
        'I'll never see anyone.'

Zulu also permits postverbal *v*P-internal augmentless *subjects*, as (135) below shows.

(135) **Augmentless *v*P-internal subjects**

    a. a-   ku- fundis- anga   **muntu**
        NEG- 17s- teach- NEG.PAST 1person
        'Nobody taught.'

    b. ngeke ku-   fundise **muntu**
        never 17s.SJC- teach.SJC 1person
        'Nobody will ever teach.'

The grammaticality of augmentless *external* arguments in *v*P-internal position means that Spec,*v*P is part of the domain of licensing for augmentless nominals. With the downward-looking licensing mechanism introduced in (132), this fact motivates the placement of the Licensing head *above* *v*P, where it can access both internal and external arguments. Further evidence in support of this type of licensing mechanism comes in section 3.3.2, where I show that the subject can behave as an intervenor for object licensing.

Once we move from non-agreeing *v*P-internal positions to *v*P-external positions, the behavior of augmentless nominals ceases to be a predictable by-product of their NPI/*wh*- properties. Contrary to what is assumed by Adams (2008), Cheng and Downing (2009), and others, I show here that the interpretive factors governing augmentless nominals are insufficient to account for their restriction to *v*P-internal positions.

First I will show that we cannot understand the prohibition on augmentless nominals in agreeing object positions as a result of their NPI interpretation (contra Adams, 2008). The examples in (136) show that augmentless nominals cannot appear in agreeing object position.[8]

8. Though I do not focus on the properties of agreeing and non-agreeing objects, I will follow Buell (2005) in treating agreed-with objects—like agreed-with subjects—as *v*P-external. Buell shows that on a variety of measures, the agreed-with object behaves

(136) **Augmentless nominals ungrammatical as agreeing objects**

    a. * A-   ngi- **m**- bon- i   *v*P] **muntu**
         NEG- 1SG- 1O- see- NEG   1person
         intended: 'I don't see anybody.'

    b. * A-   ngi- **yi**- fun- i   *v*P] **mali**
         NEG- 1SG- 9O- want- NEG   9money
         intended: 'I don't want any money.'

Even though these nominals are located in a right-peripheral position, outside of *v*P, the examples in (137) below show that elements in this position still scope under negation—and thus that the constructions in (136) meet the requirement for a nonveridical licensing environment. As Buell (2008) demonstrates, right-dislocated material in Zulu appears within the scope of sentential negation realized on the verb:

(137) **Negation scopes over right-dislocated elements**

    a. Izingane   a-   zi- thand- i   amaswidi   ]*vP* zonke.
       AUG.10child NEG- 10S- like-   NEG AUG.6sweets   10all
       'Not all children like sweets.' $\neg > \forall, *\forall > \neg$

    b. A-   ngi- yi- bon- anga   ]*vP* le   ndoda **nakanye**.
       NEG- 1SG- 9O- see- NEG.PST   DEM9. 9man even-once(NPI)
       'I didn't see this man even once.'   (Buell, 2008, ex. (12), (17))

In (137a), a right dislocated quantifier *zonke* 'all' must be interpreted as taking low scope with respect to negation. In (137b), the adverbial NPI *nakanye* 'even once' is grammatical in a right-dislocated, *v*P-external position. This NPI attaches to the right of an agreeing, dislocated object *le ndoda* 'this man,' which suggests that the agreeing object is also in the scope of negation.

    Adams (2008) suggests that the inability of augmentless objects to appear in these dislocated agreeing positions is due to the fact that an NPI interpretation is incompatible with the interpretive properties of a right-dislocated object position. Speakers of Durban Zulu, however, have no problem interpreting an *augmented* agreeing object in a right-dislocated position as a low scope indefinite NPI, as illustrated in (138) below:

(138) **Right-dislocated augmented objects: NPI interpretation possible**

    Q: U- bon- e   izindlovu   ezingaki   eBoston?
       2SG- see- PFV AUG.10elephant REL.10.how.many LOC.5Boston
       'How many elephants did you see in Boston?'

like a dislocated element. In chapter 4, we will see evidence of this type with respect to the *conjoint/disjoint* morphological alternation.

A: A- ngi- zi- bon- anga $_{vP}$] **izindlovu**.   A- zi- kho
NEG- 1SG- 10O- see- NEG.PST   AUG.10elephant. NEG- 10S- exist
laphaya.
over.there
'I didn't see any elephants. There aren't any over there.'

We can observe a similarly unexplained restriction for augmentless nominals in preverbal subject position. As we saw in the previous section, matrix negation can license an augmentless nominal in the embedded clause. In (139), we see that *muntu* in (139a) is in the same domain as the licit augmentless objects in (130), an embedded clause under negation, yet is ungrammatical. Grammatical counterparts to (139a) involve either adding an augment to the agreeing subject, as in (139b), or placing the augmentless subject in non-agreeing, postverbal position, as in (139c).

(139) **Augmentless preverbal subjects ungrammatical**

    a. * A- ngi- sho- ngo   [ukuthi **muntu u**- fik-ile]
        NEG- 1SG- say- NEG.PAST that   1person 1S- arrive-PFV
        'I didn't say that anyone came.'

    b. A- ngi- sho- ngo   [ukuthi **u**muntu **u**- fik-ile]
        NEG- 1SG- say- NEG.PAST that   1person 1S- arrive-PFV
        'I didn't say that a/the person/anyone came.'

    c. A- ngi- sho- ngo   [ukuthi **ku**- fik-e   **muntu**]
        NEG- 1SG- say- NEG.PAST that   17S- arrive-PFV 1person
        'I didn't say that anyone came.'

Note that the ungrammaticality of (139a) is not predicted by the NPI-licensing requirement on augmentless nominals, since the embedded subject is in the scope of the matrix negation. Rather, it appears that the ungrammaticality must stem from the fact that the subject is in an agreeing, preverbal position. We can further narrow down the diagnosis of the problem to the *position* of the subject in (139a), rather than the subject agreement. As I will show below, it is not the case that agreement with an NPI is always ruled out. Augmentless nominals may control subject agreement just in case they further raise to a *v*P-internal, non-agreeing position:

(140) **Augmentless nominal surface generalization**: An augmentless nominal must appear in one of the *v*P-internal positions specified in (132) and (133).

So far, we have only examined cases in which augmentless nominals are grammatical in situ inside *v*P. In (141) below, we see an augmentless nominal undergoing raising-to-object through an agreeing position in the lower clause:

(141) A- ngi- lindel- i **muntu a-** phek- e iqanda
      NEG- 1SG- expect- NEG 1person 1SJC- cook- SJC AUG.5egg
      'I don't expect anyone to cook an egg.'

Recall from section 2.4.2 that raising-to-object for augmented nominals is an optional process, as in (66), repeated below:

(66) a. ngi- funa [ukuthi uSipho a- phek- e iqanda]
       1SG- want that AUG.1Sipho 1SJC- cook- SJC AUG.5egg
       'I want Sipho to cook an egg.'

     b. ngi- funa uSipho [ukuthi a- phek- e iqanda]
       1SG- want AUG.1Sipho that 1SJC- cook- SJC AUG.5egg
       'I want Sipho to cook an egg.'

In contrast, the raised variant is *required* with an augmentless nominal. When we add an overt complementizer to the construction, it must follow, and cannot precede, the augmentless noun, indicating that the nominal is outside of the embedded clause, as (142) shows:

(142) a. a- ngi- fun- i **muntu** [ukuthi a- phek- e (i)qanda]
        NEG- 1SG- want- NEG 1person that 1SJC- cook- SJC (AUG).5egg
        'I don't want anyone to cook an egg.'

     b. *a- ngi- fun- i [ukuthi **muntu a-** phek- e (i)qanda]
        NEG- 1SG- want- NEG that 1person 1SJC- cook- SJC (AUG).5egg

These facts yield the surprising conclusion that augmentless nominals face purely structural restrictions on their distribution beyond basic NPI requirements. The distribution of augmentless nominals is schematized in (143) below. In a raising-to-object structure with an augmentless embedded subject, the augmentless nominal can either remain in situ (inside embedded *v*P) or can raise to the matrix *v*P *through* the position of lower subject agreement, but it cannot surface in the agreeing subject position. In essence, augmentless nominals in Zulu behave the way *every* nominal behaves in English in raising-to-object environments: they cannot remain in the embedded subject position and must raise to matrix object position. However, unlike subjects in English raising constructions, Zulu augmentless nominals have a second licit structural position, inside the embedded *v*P.

(143)   angifuni √**muntu** [*CP* ukuthi [*TP* ***muntu** apheke [*vP* √**muntu** iqanda

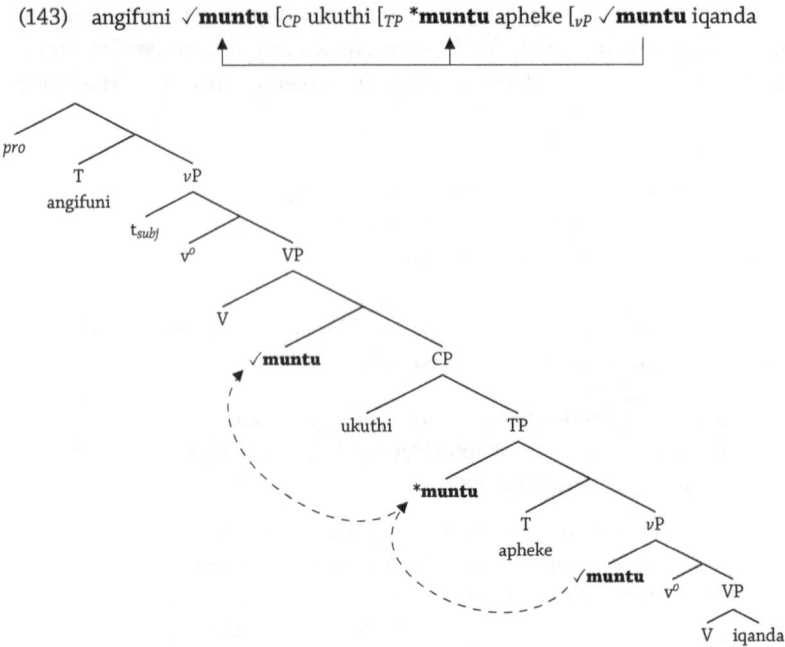

From the pattern schematized in (143), it appears that augmentless nominals are grammatical only inside *v*P, with no intervening CP boundary. We learn from raising-to-object configurations that an augmentless nominal can satisfy this requirement either by remaining in situ or by undergoing movement to a higher *v*P, even though it bears no thematic relation to the higher verb. Now that I have established that augmentless nominals must appear inside a *v*P, we can start to investigate the specifics of this restriction.

3.3.2 Augmentless Nominals within *v*P

In addition to the restriction that augmentless nominals surface in *v*P-internal position, augmentless nominals face further restrictions *within v*P. These *v*P-internal restrictions on augmentless nominals provide evidence that the distribution of augmentless nominals is governed by syntactic locality relationships, rather than linearity or mere restriction to a specific domain. In particular, we will see both that higher nominals serve as intervenors to licensing of lower elements and that the licensing of more than one augmentless nominal correlates with the introduction of applicative or causative heads in the syntactic structure.

Restrictions on the distribution of augmentless nominals inside *v*P emerge when the nominals in *v*P outnumber the licensers, on the assumption that L is a licensing head that is always present in the structure and that APPL and CAUS act as an additional source of licensing. When nominals outnumber licensers in these configurations, only those that are most locally c-commanded by a licenser can appear without an augment. Nominals that are not closest to a licenser must bear an augment.

In chapter 2, we saw several constructions that can in principle yield more nominals within *v*P than licensing heads. First, we saw that Zulu allows transitive expletive constructions (TECs), as in (144) below:

(144) ku- phek- e uSiphokazi amaqanda
     17s- cook- PFV AUG.1Siphokazi AUG.6eggs
     'Siphokazi cooked eggs.'

In these constructions, there are two *v*P-internal nominals, the subject and the object, but only a single licensing head, L, on the theory proposed here.

In ditransitive constructions, APPL/CAUS adds a second licensing head. As we saw in chapter 2, repeated below, Zulu also allows ditransitive expletives, with three *v*P-internal elements:[9]

(26) a. ku- fund- isa **uSipho** abantwana isiZulu
      17s- learn- CAUS AUG.1Sipho AUG.2children AUG.7Zulu
      'Sipho teaches the children Zulu.'

In the acceptable examples in (144) and (26) above, all of the nominals bear augments, as expected for non-NPI contexts. As I will show in this section, augmentless nominals are restricted in just such situations—even when the rest of their licensing requirements are met. These restrictions are explained if augmentless nominals must be licensed under the conditions described above, via proximity to L or as the direct object of an applied or causative construction.

L as a licensing head

We have seen that both postverbal *v*P-internal subjects and *v*P-internal objects can be augmentless, as in (145a–b) below. The fact that augmentless subjects in Spec,*v*P can be licensed suggested that the structural licenser L can access nominals anywhere in *v*P. When the subject is postverbal in a TEC, however, there are two *v*P-internal arguments and only one licenser, as discussed above.

---

9. Recall from the discussion in chapter 2 that causer arguments are introduced above the external argument, as specifier of a VoiceP projection (following Harley, 2013). I continue to use the term "*v*P-inernal" to refer to the syntactic domain including the initial positions of all arguments, though we can perhaps better think of this domain as the extended *v*P, including VoiceP in constructions with a causer argument.

If augmentless nominals were licensed simply by appearing inside *v*P, then the presence of multiple arguments would not cause ungrammaticality in this type of sentence. By contrast, the one-to-one relationship between licensers and augmentless nominals that I proposed above would ensure that only one nominal in a TEC may appear without its augment. In particular, since L is located above *v*P, we expect it to be most local to, and thus to license, the subject in such a construction. In (145), we see that this expectation is borne out. As mentioned earlier, the examples in (145a–b) confirm that either an external or an internal argument of the predicate *pheka* 'cook' may be augmentless when they are alone in *v*P. By contrast, when these two arguments both remain in *v*P, the only grammatical position for an augmentless nominal is as the external argument, as (145d) shows.[10]

(145)   **Mono-/intransitives: one augmentless argument licensed**

    a. ✓ **VS with augmentless subject**
       a-   ku- phek- anga   muntu
       NEG- 17S- cook- NEG.PAST 1person
       'Nobody cooked.'

    b. ✓ **SVO with augmentless object**
       umuntu   a-   ka- phek- anga   qanda
       AUG.1person NEG- 1S- cook- NEG.PST 5egg
       'A/the person didn't cook any egg.'

    c. * **VSO augmentless–augmentless**
       *a-   ku- phek- anga   muntu qanda
       NEG- 17S- cook- NEG.PST 1person 5egg

    d. ✓ **VSO augmentless–augmented**
       a-   ku- phek- anga   muntu i**q**anda
       NEG- 17S- cook- NEG.PST 1person AUG.5egg
       'Nobody cooked the/an/any egg.'

    e. * **VSO augmented–augmentless**
       *a-   ku- phek- anga   umuntu   qanda
       NEG- 17S- cook NEG.PST AUG.1person 5egg

10. Note that *wh*-words, if they retain the augment, are subject to looser restrictions than augmentless nominals. In (i), for example, an augmented *wh*-in-situ object can be separated from the verb by an intervening subject, in contrast to the augmentless nominal object in (145e) above.

(i)   ku- phek- e   bani ini?
     17S- cook- PFV 1who AUG.9what
     'Who cooked what?'

In both of the ungrammatical sentences above, (145c) and (145e), the object is augmentless and ungrammaticality results regardless of whether the subject bears an augment. The pattern that emerges is that the *highest* nominal inside *v*P is licensed, as schematized in the tree in (146) below:

(146)

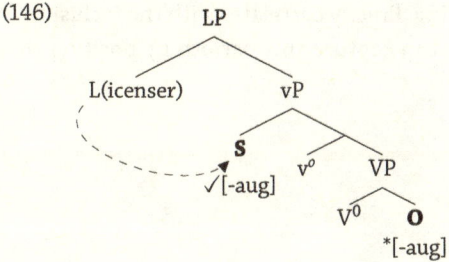

As (146) illustrates, the L head can license a single argument inside *v*P. A *v*P-internal subject will always be closest to L and will thus block L from licensing an augmentless object.

Additional Licensing: Echoes of Burzio's Generalization

In a double object structure, a more complicated pattern emerges. In TECs in the previous subsection, we observed that only the highest nominal in *v*P is licensed as an augmentless nominal. In constructions that contain causative or applicative morphology, we are no longer limited to a single augmentless nominal inside *v*P. As the constructions in (147) below illustrate, in double object constructions with an APPL head, *any* combination of augmented and augmentless nominals is permitted within *v*P, including two augmentless objects as in (147a):

(147) **Applicative double object: two augmentless arguments licensed**

    a. **DOC: Augmentless–Augmentless**

        uThemba   a- ka- phek- el-   i   muntu nyama

        AUG.1Themba NEG- 1s- cook- APPL- NEG 1person 9meat

        'Themba doesn't cook anyone any meat.'

    b. **DOC: Augmented–Augmentless**

        uThemba   a- ka- phek- el-   i   uSipho   nyama

        AUG.1Themba NEG- 1s- cook- APPL- NEG AUG.1Sipho 9meat

        'Themba doesn't cook Sipho any meat.'

c. **DOC: Augmentless–Augmented**

uThemba   a-   ka- phek- el-   i   muntu **inyama**
AUG.1Themba NEG- 1S- cook- APPL- NEG 1person AUG.9meat
'Themba doesn't cook anyone meat/the meat.'

As (147a) suggests, the extra licensing directly correlates with the inclusion of an APPL head in the structure. We can capture this pattern by positing that APPL itself is a licensing head:

(148)

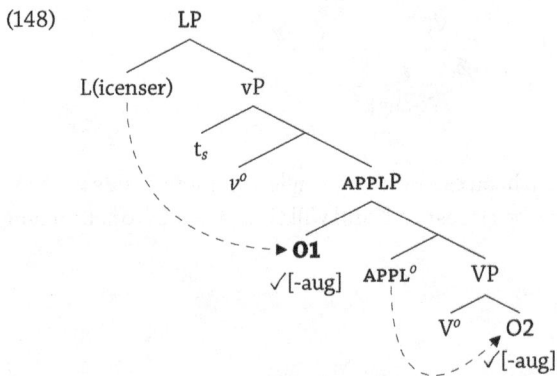

The examples in (149) show that causative structures behave in the same way. Just as with applicatives, predicates with a CAUS head also display an unrestricted distribution of augmentless nominals inside the extended vP:

(149) **Causative double object: two augmentless nominals licensed**

a. uSipho   a-   ka- fund- is-   anga   muntu   lutho
AUG.1Sipho NEG- 1S- learn- CAUS- NEG.PST 1person 11thing
'Sipho didn't teach anyone anything.'

b. uSipho   a-   ka- fund- is-   anga   abafana   lutho
AUG.1Sipho NEG- 1S- learn- CAUS- NEG.PST AUG.1boys 11thing
'Sipho didn't teach the boys anything.'

c. uSipho   a-   ka- fund- is-   anga   muntu   isiZulu
AUG.1Sipho NEG- 1S- learn- CAUS- NEG.PST 1person AUG.7Zulu
'Sipho didn't teach anyone Zulu.'

Recall from chapter 2 that causative morphology attaches at the VP level, while the causer argument itself is introduced by a higher Voice head above vP. In this structure, just as in the applicative structure in (148) above, we can think of the additional licensing as coming from the added CAUS head:

(150)

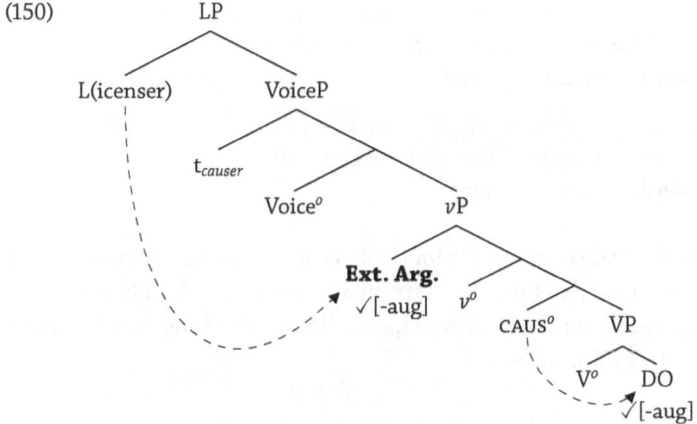

The trees in (148) and (150) above represent the licensing associated with APPL and CAUS in the same way as licensing from L, via assignment to the most local element in the c-command domain of a head. In principle, though, the data in (147a) and (149) are also compatible with saying that APPL and CAUS simply license an extra argument regardless of syntactic position. If we look more closely at constructions involving APPL and CAUS, however, we find evidence that this licensing is sensitive to syntactic configuration in precisely the way licensing by L is.

One striking piece of supporting evidence comes from TECs. Although in the previous subsection we saw that TECs without APPL/CAUS morphology only permit a single augmentless nominal (the subject), the picture is different for TECs that do involve APPL/CAUS. For example, if we consider a causative verb like *fundisa* 'teach' in (151), we find that it can optionally drop either the external argument (causee) or the direct object:

(151) a. uSipho   u- fund- isa   amantombazane isiZulu
          AUG.1Sipho 1s- learn- CAUS AUG.6girl   AUG.7Zulu
          'Sipho teaches girls Zulu.'

     b. uSipho   u- fund- isa   amantombazane
          AUG.1Sipho 1s- learn- CAUS AUG.6girl
          'Sipho teaches girls.'

     c. uSipho   u- fund- isa   isiZulu
          AUG.1Sipho 1s- learn- CAUS AUG.7Zulu
          'Sipho teaches Zulu.'

As we would expect, these monotransitive versions of *fundisa* permit either object to appear without an augment under negation:

(152) a. uSipho   a-   ka- fund- is-   anga   mantombazane
          AUG.1Sipho NEG- 1S- learn- CAUS- NEG.PST 6girl
          'Sipho didn't teach any girls.'

     b. uSipho   a-   ka- fund- is-   anga   lutho
          AUG.1Sipho NEG- 1S- learn- CAUS- NEG.PST 11thing
          'Sipho didn't teach anything.'

If we consider the TEC counterparts for (152), however, we find that they show different licensing patterns for each type of argument: specifically, augmentless *causee* arguments cannot be licensed, as in (153a), while augmentless *direct objects* can, as in (153b).

(153) a. * a-   ku- fund- is-   anga   muntu mantombazane
          NEG- 17S- learn- CAUS- NEG.PST 1person 6girl
          intended: 'Nobody taught any girls.'

     b.   a-   ku- fund- is-   anga   muntu lutho
          NEG- 17S- learn- CAUS- NEG.PST 1person 11thing
          'Nobody taught anything.'

On any account where the impossibility of augmentless objects in TECs like (145) was due to a general ban on augmentless objects in VSO configurations, the grammaticality of (153b) would be unexpected. On the other hand, if CAUS always allowed an additional augmentless nominal into the structure, the ungrammaticality of (153a) would be unexpected: the external argument (causee) would be licensed by CAUS even though CAUS is lower in the structure. It seems that instead, CAUS can only license a nominal in its c-command domain. In the ungrammatical example in (153a), then, it is not the case that the number of nominals exceeds the number of licensers; rather, the *position* of the second licenser is too low to license the augmentless causee argument:

(154)

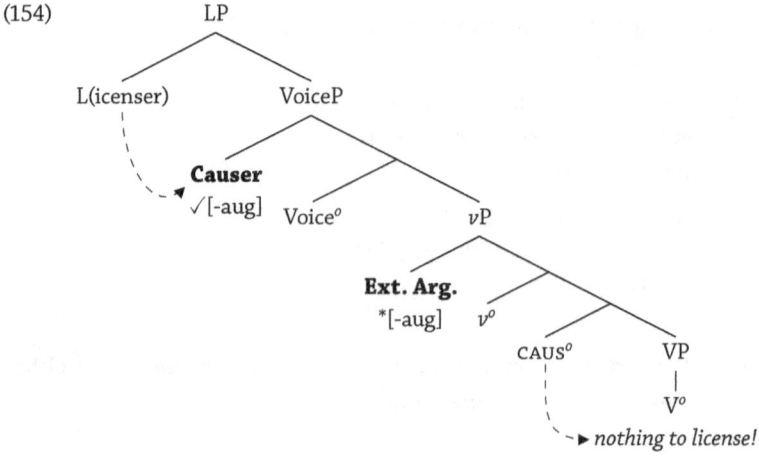

In other words, since CAUS attaches at the VP level, it can license a VP-internal argument, the direct object, but not a VP-external argument. Since APPL also attaches at the VP level, we expect the same generalization if licensing is parallel to licensing by L. By keeping all three arguments inside vP, we can see this generalization made explicit. In these ditransitive expletive constructions, two arguments can be licensed: the subject and the direct object. Crucially, the middle argument must bear an augment. In the proposal developed here, we can understand this pattern as a result of the fact that the middle argument is too high to be licensed by APPL or CAUS, but too low to receive licensing from L, which picks out the subject.

(155) **Ditransitive expletive applicative: two augmentless arguments licensed**

    a. ✓ **Augmentless–Augmented–Augmentless**

        A- ku- thum- el-   anga   muntu **i**zingane   mali

        NEG- 17s- send- APPL- NEG.PST 1person AUG.10child 9money

        'Nobody sent the/any children any money.'

    b. * **Augmentless–Augmentless–Augmentless**

        *A- ku- thum- el-   anga   muntu zingane mali

        NEG- 17s- send- APPL- NEG.PST 1person 10child 9money

    c. * **Augmented–Augmentless–Augmentless**

        *A- ku- thum- el-   anga   **u**muntu   zingane mali

        NEG- 17s- send- APPL- NEG.PST AUG.1person 10child 9money

    d. * **Augmentless–Augmentless–Augmented**

        *A- ku- thum- el-   anga   muntu zingane **i**mali

        NEG- 17s- send- APPL- NEG.PST 1person 10child AUG.9money

This construction is schematized illustrated in (156):

(156)

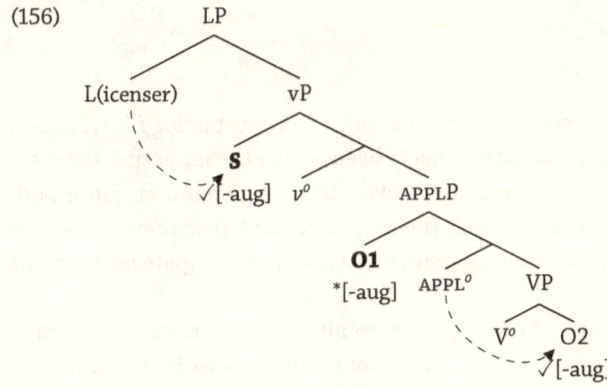

Again, we find the same pattern with causatives: in a ditransitive expletive, only the causer and direct object may be augmentless, just as with the TEC versions of causative predicates in (153) above:

(157) a. ✓ **Augmentless–Augmented–Augmentless**
         a-   ku- fund- is-   anga   muntu amantombazane lutho
         NEG- 17s- learn- CAUS- NEG.PST 1person AUG.6girl   11thing
         'Nobody taught (any) girls anything.'

       b. * **Augmentless–Augmentless–Augmentless**
          *a-   ku- fund- is-   anga   muntu mantombazane lutho
           NEG- 17s- learn- CAUS- NEG.PST 1person 6girl   11thing

       c. * **Augmented–Augmentless–Augmentless**
          *a-   ku- fund- is-   anga   umuntu   mantombazane lutho
           NEG- 17s- learn- CAUS- NEG.PST AUG.1person 6girl   11thing

       d. * **Augmentless–Augmentless–Augmented**
          *a-   ku- fund- is-   anga   muntu mantombazane isiZulu
           NEG- 17s- learn- CAUS- NEG.PST 1person 6girl   AUG.7Zulu

The tree in (158) illustrates this pattern:

(158)

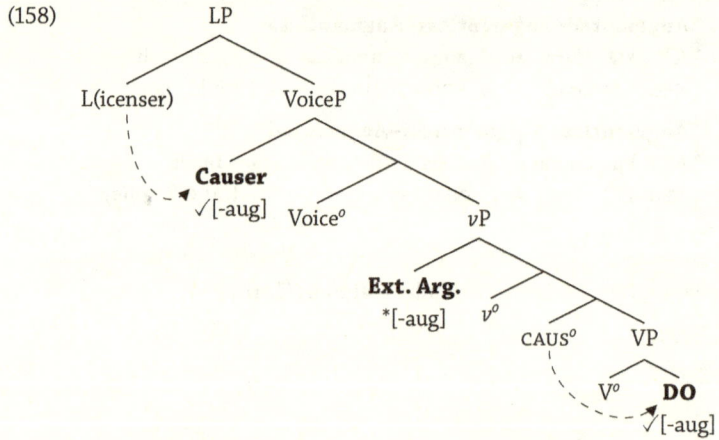

In general, then, it seems that CAUS and APPL morphology introduce a licensing process that is exactly parallel to licensing by L: they permit the most local argument in their c-command domain to be augmentless. Since both morphemes attach at the VP level, the only argument that they can license is the direct object. All arguments above CAUS and APPL compete for licensing from L.

Curiously, when APPL and CAUS are combined on the same predicate, yielding a four-argument structure, we do not see an increase in the number of possible augmentless nominals. Recall from chapter 2 that Zulu permits constructions with CAUS+APPL, though still with a maximum of three arguments expressed inside vP:

(159)   uSipho   u- fund- is- **el-** a **uthisha**   **omkhulu**
        AUG.1Sipho 1s- learn- CAUS- APPL- FV AUG.1teacher 1REL.big
        amantombazane isiZulu
        AUG.6girls   AUG.7Zulu
        'Sipho is teaching the girls Zulu for the principal.'

As we saw in section 2.5, the applied argument appears to be introduced *above* the causee in these constructions, which we took as evidence that the APPL head attaches at the vP level instead of at VP. If each CAUS and APPL head is a licenser, we might expect that all three in situ arguments could appear without their augment in (160), but this is contrary to fact:

(160)   * uSipho   a- ka- fundis- el- i   muntu mantombazane zilimi
          AUG.1Sipho NEG- 1s- teach- APPL- NEG 1person 6girls   8language
          intended: 'Sipho doesn't teach any girls any languages for anyone.'

Instead, the pattern in these triple object constructions mirrors that of the ditransitive expletives in (155): only the highest out of the first two arguments may be augmentless, as (161a) and (161b) show. The direct object may appear either with or without its augment, with no impact on grammaticality (161c).

(161)   **Triple-object: two augmentless arguments licensed**
      a. √**Augmentless–Augmented–Augmentless**
           uSipho   a- ka- fundis- el- i   muntu **a**bantwana   lutho
           AUG.1Sipho NEG- 1s- teach- APPL- NEG 1person AUG.2children 11thing
           Sipho doesn't teach (any) kids anything for anyone.

      b. *****Augmented–Augmentless–Augmentless**[11]
          * uSipho   a-ka- fundis- el- i   **u**Themba   bantwana lutho
          AUG.1Sipho NEG-1s- teach- APPL- NEG AUG.1Themba 2children 11thing

      c. *****Augmentless–Augmentless–Augmented**
          * uSipho   a- ka- fundis- el- i   muntu bantwana
          AUG.1Sipho NEG- 1s- teach- APPL- NEG 1person 2children
          izilimi
          AUG.8language

---

11. For some speakers, this construction was judged to be marginally acceptable. The majority of speakers, however, found it to be ungrammatical. Here I focus only on the ungrammatical judgment.

It is important to note that for sentences like (161a), speakers will accept an NPI translation for the augmented nominal—despite the presence of the augment. By contrast, the presence of the augment under negation typically forces a specific/definite reading for the nominal, as we saw earlier in this chapter. The same speakers who report that the NPI reading is available for augmented *abantwana* in (161a) require NPI readings to correspond to *augmentless* nominals only in contexts where the nominal is local to a licenser. The ambiguity of the augmented nominal in (161a) shows that the interpretive correlation with the augment—augmented nominals are non-NPIs—is severed just under these specific structural conditions. In other words, the augment must be absent *when structurally possible* to yield an NPI reading, but when the structure requires the augment, the NPI reading is not ruled out. I return to this issue in section 3.4.3, and again in chapter 5.

The ungrammaticality of an augmentless middle argument in (160) and (161) above introduces a wrinkle into our understanding of APPL and CAUS as licensers. In particular, it appears that while CAUS continues to license the direct object in these constructions, APPL does not introduce additional licensing for the specifier of *v*P.

(162)

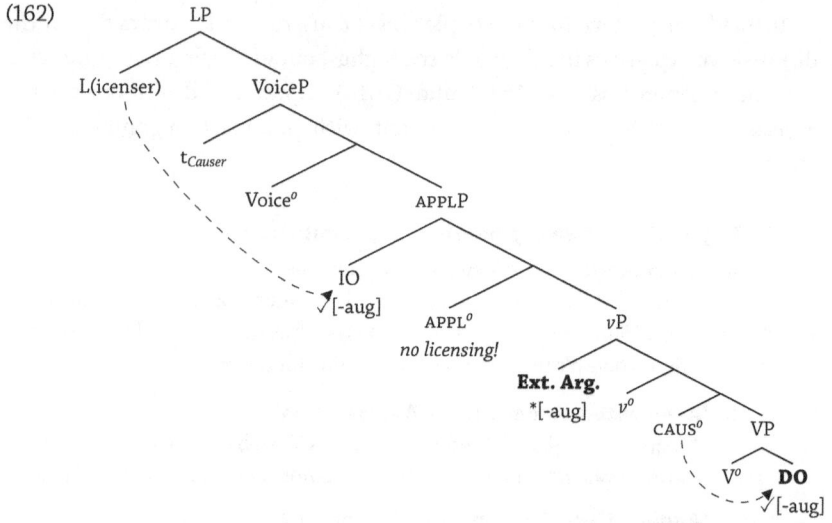

As (162) shows, we can capture the pattern in (160) and (161) by stating that only the lowest CAUS or APPL head in the structure is a licenser. Alternatively, we could capture this generalization in other ways, by saying that the CAUS or APPL head must be inside *v*P to be a licenser, or that it must work in conjunction with VP in order to license the direct object (perhaps along the lines of *feature inheritance*, as discussed by Chomsky, 2008). Another possibility is that like CAUS, APPL in Zulu does not directly introduce an applied argument, but instead always attaches *below* v^o even in cases where the applied argument is introduced above vP. In the absence of distinguishing evidence, I will not offer a precise formulation for this generalization.

Despite the complication introduced by the combination of causative and applicative, we have seen clear evidence in this section that CAUS and APPL heads in Zulu can license augmentless nominals. While we might typically think of causative and applicative morphemes as licensing the arguments that they introduce, we have seen that this is *not* the case in Zulu; instead, these heads appear to license an element in their c-command domain, namely the direct object. While this type of licensing may seem novel, it is reminiscent of Burzio's Generalization, which states that only constructions that contain an external argument can structurally license the direct object (Burzio, 1986). That is, transitive predicates in languages like English license accusative case, but unaccusatives and passives do not—the licensing of *internal arguments* is thus directly linked to the introduction of *external arguments* in the structure. Just as in English, Zulu seems to have a form of structural licensing that is entirely dependent on the appearance of certain argument-introducing heads—APPL and CAUS. Unlike the familiar instantiation of Burzio's Generalization in languages like English, however, in Zulu it appears that v^o itself is not involved in licensing. Instead, only the introduction of an *additional* "external argument"—APPL or CAUS appearing below v^o—yields the familiar licensing pattern. Thus while the particulars of Zulu are perhaps novel, the signature of this type of structural licensing is familiar. Moreover, as I will discuss in chapter 7, this licensing is in line with the fact that while Zulu exhibits familiar types of licensing, none of the expected heads seem to be licensers in Zulu. More specifically, the licensers that we have seen in this chapter, L and APPL/CAUS, are both lower in the structure than the typical case licensers, T and v^o.

3.3.3 Summary

We have now seen various structural restrictions on augmentless nominals in Zulu that don't apply to augmented nominals. Augmentless nominals are only licit inside vP, though they may pass through vP-external agreeing positions if they further move to a vP-internal position, as in raising-to-object constructions. Within vP there are further restrictions on augmentless nominals: when no applicative morphology is present, only the highest vP-internal argument may be augmentless. With applicative morphology, both the highest and lowest arguments may be augmentless, but any intermediate arguments cannot. I argued that we can capture this distribution by positing two sources of licensing for agumentless nominals: 1) a structural licenser, L, located above *v*P and 2) additional licensing from a CAUS or APPL head inside *v*P. As I showed in this section, L is capable of licensing only the argument closest to it; while augmented nominals do not require structural licensing, they function as intervenors, blocking the licensing of lower augmentless nominals. The licensing mechanisms that play a role in Zulu, while being novel in their specifics, display all of the elements of familiar licensing systems from other languages. Licensing by L is dependent only on local structural relationships, just as licensing by finite T is. Licensing via APPL/CAUS is akin to accusative licensing, in that it is dependent of the argument structure of non-local heads. While it is notable that the heads responsible are not the usual suspects, we can nevertheless recognize the nature of these heads and the processes involved as being in line with other attested systems of licensing.

The patterns of augmentless nominal distribution that we have seen so far, and my analysis of them, raise a number of questions. In chapter 4, I'll return to the specifics of the licensing processes proposed in this chapter; for the remainder of the chapter, I will explore how the Zulu patterns fit in the broader picture of nominal distribution, both within Bantu and outside.

3.4 AUGMENTLESS NOMINALS AND THE CASE FOR CASE: A CROSS-LINGUISTIC COMPARISON

At this point, it is clear that Zulu augmentless nominals have a restricted distribution, beyond nonveridicality requirements, in places where augmented argument nominals do not face distributional restrictions. I have advocated for a case-based analysis of these patterns, arguing that augmentless nominals require abstract case licensing via specific structural configurations within *v*P. This characterization of the pattern departs from previous approaches to structural case in the Bantu language family, which, as we saw earlier in the chapter, tend to assume either that case is completely absent from the grammar of Bantu languages or that its effects are obscured by the lack of direct links between case and agreement/movement. Given this context, we can ask whether distributional restrictions on augmentless nominals require a structural case-based analysis in Zulu. Alternatively, one might maintain the assumptions of a non-case-based approach to nominal distribution patterns in Bantu (e.g., Ndayiragije, 1999; Alsina, 2001; Baker, 2003a; Carstens and Diercks, 2013; Diercks, 2012) and instead seek a separate explanation for the restricted distribution of augmentless nominals.

Beyond simply considering how a non-case-based approach would fare for the Zulu facts that I introduce in this chapter, we must also consider whether the approach I develop for Zulu can generalize to other Bantu languages, which, as we saw, share similar profiles for augmented nominal distribution. As we will see in the remainder of this chapter, gaps in our current knowledge make it difficult to directly compare the behavior of augmentless nominals in other Bantu languages to the Zulu patterns; in a recent study of Xhosa (Carstens and Mletshe, 2013a,b), based directly off the patterns discussed in this chapter (as first discussed in Halpert, 2012a), the broad patterns of augmentless nominal distribution appear similar, including their basic restriction to *wh-* and NPI contexts, though the languages differ in the details. In other languages, such as Kinande and Luganda, where only basic patterns are known, we see certain syntactic properties remaining constant, while the interpretive properties of augmentless expressions differ from Zulu, suggesting that reducing the distribution of these expressions to conditions on their interpretive properties may miss more fundamental syntactic generalizations. In addition, as we will see in the next chapter, recent work on Otjiherero (Kavari et al., 2012) shows a clear parallel to the Zulu patterns *outside* the domain of the augment: in this Bantu language, the basic distribution of tonal melodies on nominals mirrors the augmented/augmentless distinction in Zulu.

Finally, we can consider parallels to the distribution of augmentless nominals from outside of the Bantu family and investigate whether any such parallels may shed light on the correct interpretation of the Zulu facts. Two phenomena in particular seem to share basic properties with augmentless nominals in Zulu: the distribution of bare negative indefinite NPs in Romance languages (e.g., Kayne, 1981) and the behavior of accusative case drop on objects in languages like Turkish (e.g., Enç, 1991; Kornfilt, 1997). Both types of phenomena involve the same basic ingredients as the Zulu pattern: a "missing" piece of nominal morphology, predictable interpretive effects, and syntactic restrictions on distribution. As we will see in section 3.5, Romance bare NPs also share the NPI interpretation that most augmentless nominals in Zulu have. I will suggest, however, that the types of analyses proposed for bare NPs in Romance cannot be extended to the Zulu patterns; instead, comparisons to caseless nominals may be more on the right track, an issue I return to in more detail in chapter 5.

3.4.1 Revisiting the Question of Case in Bantu

As we saw earlier in this chapter, Bantu languages display a number of properties that appear to not conform to the familiar patterns of structural case licensing in any straightforward way. The consensus that emerged from earlier literature on this subject was that Bantu languages lack evidence for nominative case assignment, with some researchers concluding that case plays no role whatsoever in the grammar of Bantu languages (e.g., Harford Perez, 1985; Diercks, 2012; Carstens and Diercks, 2013) and others maintaining a place for case in Bantu syntax, while accounting for the apparent lack of case effects in other ways (e.g., Baker, 2003b; Carstens, 2005, 2011).

Zulu exhibits many of the same constructions that led to the conclusion that Bantu languages lack (standard) syntactic case. I argued earlier in this chapter that these constructions, including the availability of optional hyperraising and non-agreeing subject inversion, really provide evidence only for a lack of *nominative* case in Spec,TP. While the detailed investigation of augmentless nominals in this chapter has not challenged this generalization, I argued that Zulu augmentless nominals provide evidence in favor of a system of case-licensing more generally. From this perspective, we can return to previous implementations of case-licensing in Bantu languages to see whether there are aspects that can be reconciled with the new Zulu facts.

One family of proposals attempts to provide explanations for the absence of classic case effects without eliminating the notion of a case- or licensing-type mechanism. In particular, they tend to suggest that the mismatch between case positions and Bantu nominals stems from a one-sided relationship between the case-assigning head and the nominal. In this way, they depart from the logic behind approaches to case that assume both the probe *and* the goal require feature-checking of some type (e.g., Chomsky, 2000, 2001).

Ndayiragije (1999) proposes that case is active in the grammar of Bantu languages, but that in these languages only the features of functional heads, and not of lexical items (which includes nominals on this theory), need to be checked for the derivation to converge. Specifically, uninterpretable features like case on nouns do not have to be checked, which leads to a relatively free distribution of nominals in non-case positions in Bantu. He claims that case does not appear to drive the distribution of nominals in Bantu languages since case assignment depends purely on the requirements of functional heads. Ndayiragije applies this approach to OVS inversion constructions in Kirundi. In these constructions, as in the Kinande constructions we saw at the beginning of the chapter in (118), an internal argument may appear in Spec,TP, controlling "subject" agreement, while the external argument appears in a non-agreeing postverbal position. Kirundi also allows TECs, where expletive agreement appears on the verb and both arguments are in post-verbal positions. These possibilities are illustrated in (163a) below:

(163)   a. Amatá y- á- nyôye   abâna
           6milk 6s- PST- drink.PERF 2child
           [Lit.: 'Milk drank children.']
           'Children (and not parents) drank milk.'

        b. pro$_{EXP}$ ha- á- nyôye   amatá abâna
               16s- PST- drink.PERF 6milk 2child
           [Lit.: 'There drank milk children.']
           'Children (and not parents) drank milk.'   (Ndayiragije, 1999, ex. (1b,c))

Ndayiragije argues that in Kirundi, subject and object agreement markers are straightforward indicators of nominative and accusative case assignment, respectively. Following this assumption, he claims that the inverted object in (163a) receives nominative case from T, while in the TEC in (163b) nominative is assigned to the expletive *pro*. In both of these constructions, he argues that the subject *abâna* A-bar moves to a rightward focus specifier, causing it to follow the object in a TEC and leaving the possibility that the object can be a goal for T in the inversion construction. Crucially, Ndayiragije concludes from the Kirundi patterns that case-checking is not a requirement for nominals, but rather only for functional heads: as long as T can assign nominative (to the object or an expletive), it doesn't matter if the focused subject receives no case.

Carstens (2005, 2011) and Carstens and Diercks (2013) argue for a different type of probe-goal mismatch, as we saw earlier in the chapter. For them, case is not only active in Bantu, but is in fact "hyperactive." Carstens (2005) claims that only feature *valuation*, and not feature checking, renders goal inactive and further that Bantu nominals enter the derivation with an already-valued gender feature. Following these assumptions, she concludes that Bantu nominals will always be active since they contain at least one uninterpretable feature—gender—that will never be valued during the derivation. Consequently, Bantu nominals can enter case-checking relationships multiple times over the course of the derivation, which is why they appear to be equally well licensed in a number of positions. While I set aside the implications of this view of Activity for the moment, I will return to the question in chapters 4 and 5, where I will argue that case assignment of the type I propose here *does* in fact render a nominal inactive in Zulu, leading to some unusual timing patterns in the order of case and Agree operations sketched in this chapter.

Finally, as we saw at the beginning of the chapter, Baker (2003a, 2008), Henderson (2006b), and others argue that case in Bantu may exist independently of A-movement and agreement, unlike in language families like Indo-European for which nominative case appears to be a reflex of subject agreement. As I noted earlier, severing case assignment from EPP and phi-agreement effects can help to explain why many Bantu languages lack the standard nominative case effects (movement to and from Spec,TP and agreement with T are not directly tied to finiteness), without necessarily sacrificing the notion of a Case Filter in Bantu. Baker (2003a) in particular assumes that the Case Filter does apply to nondislocated nominals in Kinande; like Ndayiragije (1999), he assumes that nominals in A-bar positions do not require case and suggests that all agreeing nominals are in fact A-bar dislocated. In section 3.4.3 we will see how Baker applies these assumptions to the properties of augmentless nominal in Kinande.

These proposals typically strive to account for the unrestricted distribution of *augmented* nominals in Bantu languages, though some do not consider the differences in distribution between augmented and augmentless nominals at all. As we have seen in this chapter, any approach to Zulu requires that the distinction be made: we need an account that will capture both the relatively unrestricted distribution of augmented nominals and the relatively restricted distribution of augmentless ones. We have seen that the augment morpheme is the sole difference between grammaticality and ungrammaticality of nominals in certain structural positions, suggesting that its presence is directly linked to the grammaticality of nominals in these positions. I proposed in this chapter that the restrictions on augmentless nominals reflect structural case requirements. Augmented nominals, by contrast, are intrinsically cased and therefore are not subject to these case-licensing requirements, an issue I return to in chapter 5. At the same time, they act as defective intervenors for case-licensing heads, suggesting that they are not incompatible with structural case, along the lines of Legate's account of inherent ergatives in Warlpiri (Legate, 2005). In this sense, my view on augmented nominals is similar to Ndayiragije's (1999): while these nominals can occupy case-licensed positions, they are essentially indifferent to any case-licensing processes. In chapter 4, I provide independent morphological evidence that augmented nominals inside *v*P can be targets of the licensing head.

3.4.2 Restricting Augmentless Nominals without Case?

I showed in section 3.3 that Zulu augmentless nominals must *surface* in a *v*P-internal position; when augmentless nominals originate in licit positions but undergo movement to non-licensed positions over the course of the derivation, they are ungrammatical. The fact that the pattern seems to necessitate a surface-oriented generalization is at odds with the general cross-linguistic pattern of case assignment: evidence from languages like English suggests that case-licensing can be followed by subsequent movement out of the position in which licensing occurs. By contrast, the empirical generalization that emerges from the Zulu data is that augmentless nominals are licensed only in their final position. In chapter 4, I return to this issue and argue that this apparent surface-oriented pattern is in fact a predictable outcome of the syntactic derivation. An alternative approach, however, might avoid the complications inherent in a syntactic case analysis and instead construe this pattern in terms of a more surface-oriented process, such as incorporation, clitic attachment, or mere linear adjacency to a verb. These mechanisms, unlike our standard assumptions about structural case, require transparent adjacency between two elements. While such approaches would have a natural account for the surface-true structural generalizations, I will show here that adjacency-based analyses fail to account for all of the Zulu data.

We can take as a starting point for this investigation a set of related proposals concerning word order restrictions on double object constructions in Bantu. A number of these proposals claim that word order restrictions in double object constructions arise not due to case licensing, but rather from the need for a nominal to surface adjacent to the element that assigns it a grammatical function or theta role (Alsina, 2001; Alsina and Mchombo, 1993; Bresnan and Moshi, 1990, among others). In other words, these proposals suggest that (non-agreeing) Bantu nominals must remain local to their selecting verb. While these accounts focus on augmented nominals in the Bantu languages they discuss, we could imagine extending this logic to the distribution of *augmentless* nominals in Zulu.

In particular, if non-agreeing nominals must remain local to their theta licenser and augmentless nominals typically don't control agreement, then the restriction of these nominals to vP-internal positions is expected: maintaining the local relationship between the argument and its introducer would essentially force arguments to remain in situ. Such an approach fails to capture the Zulu patterns in two major respects, however. First, though the augmentless nominals in a monoclausal construction always maintain proximity to the theta-assigner, we saw that this locality is lost in a raising construction. As the evidence from raising-to-object constructions shows, augmentless nominals are grammatical if they raise out of the clause where they receive their theta role and into a *higher* vP, where they do not receive a theta role. On an account where theta assignment determines licensing, this type of grammatical movement is unexplained.[12] The availability of raising-to-object with augmentless nominals also shows that agreement with augmentless nominals cannot simply be ruled out, as we saw earlier, which weakens the premises of this type of approach (and, as we saw, approaches like Adams, 2008; Cheng and Downing, 2009). Second, this type of analysis cannot account for the restrictions on augmentless nominals *within* vP. While we saw that a single augmentless nominal—in any argument position—is grammatical in vP, and that certain combinations of augmentless nominals are grammatical, other combinations are ruled out but can be "rescued" by adding augment vowels. Since the same theta role relationships are at play in all of these constructions, theta role assignment alone cannot account for these contrasts.

Another semantically-driven adjacency approach to the restrictions on augmentless nominals would be to analyze Zulu augmentless nominals as incorporated nouns. Under this type of approach, the restriction of augmentless nominals to vP-internal position would be a result of incorporation: these nominals are vP-internal because incorporation of a N head to the verb results in strict adjacency to the verb (Baker, 1988; Farkas and de Swart, 2003;

12. It is perhaps possible, however, to rework this type of account in terms of the relationship "argument of," rather than as a direct link to theta assignment.

van Geenhoven, 1998; Mithun, 1984, among others). We can rule out head-incorporation in Zulu by adding additional structure to augmentless nominals. Augmentless nominals in Zulu need not be simple N head, but are instead capable of the same levels of complexity as their augmented counterparts, including modification by adjectives and relative clauses, as illustrated below:

(164) a. a- ngi- bon- i [**muntu** o- gqoka isigqoko]
       NEG- 1SG- see- NEG 1person 1REL- wear AUG.7hat
       'I don't see anyone wearing a hat.'

       b. a- ngi- bon- i [**muntu** o- mu- bi]
       NEG- 1SG- see- NEG 1person 1REL- 1- ugly
       'I don't see anyone ugly.'

The availability of this type of construction suggests that it would be more appropriate to consider augmentless nominals as a potential instance of pseudo-incorporation, which can involve complex nominals, as Massam (2001) demonstrated for Niuean:

(165) ne inu [kofe kono] a Mele
       PST drink [coffee bitter] ABS Mele
       'Mary drank bitter coffee.'   (Massam, 2001, ex. (6a)) *Niuean*

One attractive outcome of a pseudo-incorporation analysis for Zulu would be the predicted interpretation of augmentless nominals under negation. Incorporated nominals of all types generally behave as though they are scopally inert (e.g., Farkas and de Swart, 2003; Geenhoven, 2002; Mithun, 1984); in particular, incorporated nominals obligatorily scope below negation, yielding NPI readings (e.g., Bittner, 1994; van Geenhoven, 1998, see Dayal, 2011, for discussion with respect to pseud-incorporation). While this type of account would not explain why these elements must appear in nonveridical environments in Zulu, it would correctly predict the NPI interpretation that they receive in these environments.

Another potentially desirable outcome, as mentioned above, would be the ability to capture surface position restrictions. However, as we have seen, augmentless nominals are not simply restricted to being adjacent to the verb. First, in constructions with applied or causative arguments, multiple augmentless nominals may appear inside *v*P, and augmentless nominals may be separated from the verb by multiple other arguments, including augmented nominals, as *mali* 'money' is in (166).

(166) A- ku- thum- el- anga mama izingane **mali**
       NEG- 17s- send- APPL- NEG.PST 1motherAUG. 10child 9money
       'Mother didn't send the children any money.'

Second, as with the thematic-role locality approach, raising-to-object constructions present another complication, since an augmentless nominal that would be ungrammatical in Spec,TP is grammatical inside the *higher* vP:

(167) a.　a-　ngi- fun- i　**muntu** [ukuthi **a**-　phek- e　(i)qanda]
　　　　NEG- 1SG- want- NEG 1person that　1SJC- cook- SJC (AUG).5egg
　　　　'I don't want anyone to cook an egg.'

　　 b.　*a-　ngi- fun- i　[ukuthi **muntu a**-　phek- e　(i)qanda]
　　　　NEG- 1SG- want- NEG that　1person 1SJC- cook- SJC (AUG).5egg

It is not entirely clear what the predictions of a pseudo-incorporation account would be for these structures. While certain instances of pseudo-incorporation require strict adjacency between the incorporated NP and the verb (e.g., Niuean, Massam, 2001), other cases, such as Hindi, appear to allow the incorporated NP to be separated from the verb in certain circumstances (see Dayal, 1999; Day, 2003; Dayal, 2011). For the Hindi case, Dayal (2011) concludes that "[o]ther things being equal, an incorporated nominal enjoys the same freedom that all arguments do in the language." An approach to Zulu along these lines would lack a clear way to account for these facts, since the patterns in (166) and (167) do *not* follow from any principles that govern the freedom of all arguments in Zulu. It seems, then, that any incorporation analysis would solve the surface effects that we find in Zulu, but would still need an additional (perhaps completely independent) component to explain the precise distribution of augmentless nominals.

Perhaps more problematic to an incorporation account are the ways in which the Zulu pattern diverges from the shared semantic characteristics of incorporation cross-linguistically. First, while incorporated elements are typically scopally inert, we have already seen that *wh*-words in Zulu may be augmentless (in exactly the same syntactic positions as augmentless NPIs):

(168)　uMfundo　　u- cabanga ukuthi ni- bon- e　**bani**?
　　　　AUG.1Mfundo 1s- think　that　2PL- see- PFV 1who
　　　　'Who does Mfundo think that you saw?'

In addition, while (pseudo-)incorporation typically involves internal arguments, we have seen in Zulu that all arguments, including the agent, are potential candidates for augmentless nominals, provided they meet the syntactic restrictions.[13] More strikingly, incorporation of all types tends to

---

13. Öztürk (2003) discusses apparent pseudo-incorporation of agents in Turkish, but argues that that these incorporated arguments are not in fact true subjects, since they cannot, for example, undergo passivization. More generally, Baker (2014) argues that a predicate cannot involve more than one instance of pseudo-incorporation, a generalization that is incompatible with the Zulu facts.

result in what Mithun (1984) describes as a "unitary concept" conveyed by the incorporated predicate. As Dayal (2011) points out, pseudo-incorporation typologically seems to display limited productivity, yielding both opaque (idiomatic) readings in certain cases and restrictions to institutionalized or canonically recognized activities in others. Zulu, by contrast, seems to share none of these properties: as long as the syntactic conditions are met, any argument seems able to lose its augment—including a *wh*-word—in combination with any verb. The meanings of structures with augmentless nominals are predictably transparent as well. In short, any gains that we might make with an incorporation account of these nominals are balanced (or perhaps outweighed) by additional complications that arise in applying this type of approach to the Zulu pattern. In particular, given that strict adjacency is clearly not required in Zulu, no clear predictions that would impose the necessary surface restrictions on augmentless nominals emerge from this type of account.

To avoid the semantic issues involved in an incorporation approach to the *v*P-internal restriction on augmentless nominals, we could instead pursue a clitic analysis of these elements. That is, rather than linking these elements to a particular surface position for syntactic or semantic reasons, we might instead propose that as clitics, they must appear adjacent to verbs for morpho-phonological reasons. This type of account faces some of the same empirical issues discussed above. First, the same non-adjacency pattern seen in (166) remains a problem for a clitic account of augmentless nominals. What this type of account *can* capture, however, is the pattern in (167), where adjacency to the *higher* verb yields grammaticality.

At the same time, if phonological adjacency to a verb (or a [verb + clitic] unit) were the only relevant factor in licensing, we might expect to find other constructions in which an augmentless embedded subject would be adjacent to a matrix verb and thus licensed by the matrix verb. In fact, Zulu rules out such constructions:

(169) a. ngi- fisa (ukuthi) uSipho a-   phek- e   iqanda
           1SG- wish (that)   1Sipho 1SJC- cook- SJC AUG.5egg
           'I wish that Sipho would could an egg.'

    b. *ngi- fisa uSipho ukuthi a-   phek- e   iqanda
           1SG- wish 1Sipho that   1SJC- cook- SJC AUG.5egg

    c. *a-   ngi- fis- i   **muntu** a-   phek- e iqanda
           NEG- 1SG- wish- NEG 1person 1SJC- cook- SJC AUG.5egg

While the verb *fisa* 'wish' takes a subjunctive complement with an optional complementizer, the ungrammaticality of (169b) shows that it does not have the option for object control or raising-to-object,[14] which means that nominals that appear between the matrix and embedded verbs must be in subject position in the lower clause. In (169c), we see that the augmentless nominal, in subject position in the lower clause, is ungrammatical, despite being adjacent to the higher verb.

A final possible approach that could potentially capture the surface-oriented properties of augmentless nominal distribution without resorting to syntactic licensing is one based on information structure. We saw in section 3.2 that the ban on augmentless nominals in post-vP (agreeing) positions cannot be attributed to the information structure properties of NPIs, since augmented NPIs may appear in these positions. At the same time, we might consider whether the distribution of augmentless nominals *within* vP is restricted by information structure requirements. In particular, Buell (2009) and Cheng and Downing (2009) have shown that there is a strong preference for focused elements in vP to be adjacent to the verb in Zulu. Cheng and Downing (2009) link this fact directly to the prosodic structure of Zulu, proposing that focused elements need to both be *highest* in vP and at the *edge* of vP in order to align with a natural prosodic boundary. This need to interface with prosodic boundaries, they claim, can drive the syntax to create structures in which a focused element is verb-adjacent and at vP's edge, which captures the surface-oriented pattern. If augmentless nominals are subject to the same conditions on focus, we might expect similar surface restrictions on their distribution.

While focused elements are typically adjacent to the verb, certain circumstances allow a focused element to appear elsewhere in vP (Buell, 2009; Adams, 2011; Halpert, 2011).[15] Despite the potential to have a focused element in multiple vP-internal positions, there are few problems with a focus-based approach. First, as we've already seen in section 3.2, an NPI interpretation does not necessitate a focus reading. This fact is perhaps clearest in cases where an agreeing element in a right-dislocated (old information) position is understood as an NPI:

(138) **Right-dislocated augmented objects: NPI interpretation possible**

Q: U- bon- e izindlovu ezingaki eBoston?
2SG- see- PST AUG.10elephant REL.10.how.many LOC.5Boston
'How many elephants did you see in Boston?'

---

14. While *fisa* 'wish' does not behave as a raising verb for the majority of Zulu speakers with whom I have worked, for a few speakers, it does allow raising-to-object under certain circumstances. Here I report the judgements of non-raising speakers. In chapter 4, I examine some constructions in which raising-to-object in a *fisa* clause is permitted.

15. These circumstances tend to involve a configuration where the syntax independently prevents a focused element from being adjacent to the verb, as I argue in Halpert (2011) for constructions with focused objects and postverbal subjects. Many of these constructions simply involve multiple focused elements inside of vP, not all of which can be adjacent to the verb.

A: A-   ngi- zi- bon- anga   _vP_] **izindlovu**.   A-   zi- kho
   NEG- 1SG- 1OO- see- NEG.PST   AUG.10elephant. NEG- 10s- exist
   laphaya.
   over.there
   'I didn't see any elephants. There aren't any over there.'

Second, even if we were to assume that all _v_P-internal augmentless NPIs are necessarily focused, they do not in fact have the same distribution as other focused elements. Buell (2009) shows that in a double object construction with two _wh_-elements, the second _wh_-, which receives a focus interpretation, is grammatical in a _v_P-internal position following the focused _wh_-indirect object:

(170)   u-   zo- nika bani ini?
        2SG- FUT- give 1who AUG.9what
        'Who will you give what?   (Buell, 2009, ex. (18))

While the account I presented in this chapter distinguishes between a construction like (170), which involves a double object structure and is thus predicted to be grammatical, and a VSO construction, a focus account of augmentless nominal distribution would not straightforwardly make such a distinction; since multiple foci are in fact grammatical in Zulu, we would expect multiple augmentless nominals to be grammatical in the same positions. Strikingly, though, if we look at the result of a multiple _wh_-question with VSO structure, we find that not only is such a construction is grammatical, it requires an augment to appear on the second argument:

(171)   ku- phek- e   bani ini?
        17s- cook- PFV 1who AUG.9what
        'Who cooked what?'

Compare (171) to a VSO construction with augmentless nominals, in which an augmentless object is ungrammatical, though speakers report that an emphatic, NPI-type reading for the augmented object is available:

(172)   a-   ku- phek- anga   muntu *(i)- qanda
        NEG- 17s- cook- NEG.PST 1person AUG- 5egg
        'Nobody cooked an/any egg.'

As the contrast between (171) and (172) shows, focus alignment cannot be the reason why VSO constructions rule out an augmentless nominal, since Zulu allows two foci to follow the verb in VSO constructions more generally. Based on this type of difference, I set aside the possibility that a prosody-driven account can give us the distribution of augmentless nominals.

It seems, then, that deriving the apparent surface-oriented nature of the licensing requirement on augmentless nominals is non-trivial; a number of approaches that typically yield surface-order effects fail to capture the Zulu patterns, including theta-based and incorporation accounts that would treat augmentless nominals as bound to particular positions due to some semantic effect, as well as clitic and prosody accounts, which would derive the surface effects via phonological interface conditions. Given the difficulties that these accounts face, I conclude that identifying specific syntactic positions as the locus of augmentless nominal licensing remains the best characterization of the distribution. The question of why the *final* position of an augmentless nominal seems to be the relevant position for syntactic licensing remains, however. While I set aside the issue for the moment, I will argue in the next chapter that this apparent surface property is in fact a predictable consequence of the syntactic derivation.

3.4.3 Clues from the Broader Bantu Landscape

While it is clear at this point that the structural restrictions on Zulu nominals explored in this chapter are limited to those without the augment vowel, any deeper understanding of these distributional patterns requires insight on the precise differences between nominals with an augment vowel and those without. As we've already seen in this chapter, it is difficult to map the structural differences between augmented and augmentless nominals directly onto their semantic properties (for example, as NPIs or *wh*-words) or interpretive properties (such as any possible tendency to map to focus, as discussed above). In chapter 5, I will argue that this indirect relationship between interpretation and the distribution of the augment is a cross-linguistically common property of morphological case marking. Looking closer to home, we find that other Bantu languages also display complicated interactions between augment morphology and syntactic distribution of nominals. Although there are few syntactically detailed accounts of augment distribution across Bantu, by comparing these patterns to Zulu we can begin to identify similarities and differences that will shed light on the fundamental properties of the phenomenon.

Recall that many previous discussions on structural case in Bantu have advocated for a unified treatment across the Bantu languages (e.g., Harford Perez, 1985; Baker, 2003a; Diercks, 2012, though see van der Wal, 2012, for evidence that a more fine-grained approach is necessary). Since I have argued that augment distribution patterns in Zulu constitute evidence for a structural case system in the language, we can ask whether augment patterns across the rest of the language family show similar evidence. At a very basic level, we find what appears to be a wide range of variation with respect to the augment. Some languages lack an augment morpheme—or a contrast between augmented and augmentless forms—altogether; some appear to have an augment whose distribution can be defined along semantic lines; while others seem to display the type of interaction between syntax and interpretation that characterizes the Zulu contrast. As I will show, while languages that display this type of contrast vary in the precise semantic conditions required for augmentless nouns, they seem to target roughly the same syntactic domains that Zulu augmentless nouns are licensed in. In addition to languages in which augment distribution seems to have a syntactic dimension, we also find languages in which tonal morphology seems to follow a similar syntactic distribution.

The first major point of variation across the Bantu languages is whether segmental augment morphology is present in a given language at all. A number of Bantu languages show no evidence of an augment morpheme, including Swahili, Makhuwa, and Lingala (see Katamba, 2003, for an overview). In the Swahili example below, nominals have retained their noun class prefixes, but pre-prefixal augment morphology is completely absent:

(173) a. M-toto m-dogo   a-mefika
          1-child 1REL-little 1s-arrived
          'The little child arrived.'

       b. Ki-kapu ki-dogo   ki-mefika
          7-basket 7REL-little 7s-arrived
          'The little basket arrived.'   (Katamba, 2003, ex. (7))

Note, however, that the lack of an augment on Swahili nominals does not trigger behavior akin to that of augmentless nominals in Zulu. Swahili is among those languages whose relatively unrestricted nominal distribution caused researchers to propose that Bantu lacked case in the first place, as the ability for nominals to appear as the subjects of nonfinite clauses illustrated:

(174) i- na- wezakana (*kwa) **Maiko** ku- m- pig- i-   a Tegani simu
       9s- PRES- possible (*for) Michael INF- 1O- beat- APPL- FV Tegan phone
       'It's possible for Michael to call Tegan.'   (Diercks, 2012, ex. (7b))

Unlike in Zulu, then, we cannot say for a language like Swahili that the presence of an augment is what permits certain nouns to appear outside of syntactically licensed positions. Whether Swahili and other languages without an augment contrast employ some other licensing mechanism or perhaps in fact lack case altogether remains to be seen; as the discussion of Otjiherero below will demonstrate, some Bantu languages seem to signal licensing contrasts between nominals by other means, including tonal distinctions.

The class of Bantu languages that lack augment morphology includes languages like Matengo, as well as languages like Swahili. It is worth considering these languages separately from the Swahili-type languages in the context of van der Wal (2012), who argues that these particular languages show evidence of a nominative effect in T. In particular, Matengo allows subject agreement with a vP-internal subject:

(175) Ju- a-   teleka María wâ:le $_{vP}$]
       1s- PST- cook/SF 1Maria 9rice
       'Maria cooked rice.' (subject focus)   (Yoneda, 2011, ex. (32a))

Van der Wal (2012) observes that in languages of this type—in contrast to Swahili, Zulu, and many other Bantu languages—subject agreement is not linked to the EPP; instead, it seems to always track the subject, even when it remains low, which she suggests may indicate that languages with this property show the effects of structural case. Interestingly, the languages that van der Wal (2012) discusses as having low agreeing subjects (Matengo, Makwe, Makhuwa, Matuumbi) all appear to be languages without an augment morpheme. If van der Wal's observation is on the right track, then it is worth investigating whether there is a unidirectional implication between evidence for a more extensive structural case system (such as in situ agreement and a nominative effect) and lack of an augment contrast.

The question of whether a language contains augment morphology is further complicated by the apparent existence in a number of Bantu languages of a tonal, rather than segmental, augment (see, for example, Hombert, 1980; Puech, 1988; Hyman, 2005; Barlew and Clem, 2014; Clem, 2014). Barlew and Clem (2014) argue that Bulu has two different types of augment, a segmental augment and a tonal one, which have different distributions. As Clem (2014) shows for Bulu, the tonal augment is a high tone that is realized on the initial syllable of nouns that are followed by post-nominal modifiers, such as the relative clause in (176c) below:

(176) a. bìtétám
          8okra
          'okra' (pl)

       b. mə̆kùs   **bì**tétám
          1sg.bought 8okra
          'I bought okra.'

       c. mə̆kùs   **bí**tétám   màkə̀jì
          1sg.bought AUG.8okra 1sg.wanted
          'I bought the okra that I wanted.'   (Clem, 2014, ex. (16i), (22i))

Note that in the example above, Bulu nominals lack segmental augment morphology. Barlew and Clem (2014) point out that in Bulu, the (segmentally) augmentless form of a nominal seems to be the default, unlike in Zulu and other languages that we will see shortly. They demonstrate that the segmental augment in Bulu appears only on nominals that have both a discourse referent and a set of relevant alternatives in the discourse context:

(177) a. mà-kɔ́   mbò   lúk   **ə̀-mìngá** á-bìlí bə̀-ɲàk
           1SG-want to.marry AUG-1woman 1s-own   2cow
           'I want to marry a woman who has cows.' (existence commitment, relevant
           set of women)   (Barlew and Clem, 2014, ex. (6))

       b. mà-kɔ́   mbò   lúk   **mìngá** á-bìlí bə̀-ɲàk
           1SG-want to.marry 1woman 1s-own 2cow
           'I want to marry a woman who has cows.' (no existence commitment,
           nonspecific)   (Barlew and Clem, 2014, ex. (7/8))

Barlew and Clem (2014) conclude from this type of pattern that the segmental augment in Bulu does not depend on syntactic structure, but rather entirely on the discourse context. This type of straightforward correlation between the presence of an augment and a particular interpretation suggests that in some Bantu languages, a purely semantic account of the augment may be possible.

Otjiherero is also a language with limited augment contrast, though unlike in Bulu, Otjiherero nominals nearly always require an augment (Elderkin, 2003). Unlike in Zulu, the Otjiherero augment is typically an invariable o-[16] that does not depend on the vowel of the noun class prefix. Elderkin cites vocatives and negative copular constructions as the only two syntactic environments where the augment is consistently dropped in Otjiherero.[17] While Otjiherero is an augment language, then, it is unlikely that the augment is participating in the same type of syntactic processes that I have argued for Zulu. At the same time, Otjiherero does show evidence of syntactically-determined alternations in nominal marking in terms of *tone*. As Kavari et al. (2012) demonstrate, prefixal morphology (the augment and noun class marker) can surface in four different tone patterns, depending on syntactic environment:

16. Except with class 5 nominals, which have an *e*- augment.
17. Elderkin (2003) also notes that the augment is not preserved when a noun stem undergoes category change to a verb or is the second member of a noun–noun compound.

(178) **Otjiherero nominal tone patterns** (Kavari et al., 2012, (2)–(5))[18]

    a. **òtjì**- hávérò tj-á   ù
       7D- chair 7S-PST fall.down
       'The chair fell down.'   *Default:* LL

    b. vé   múná **òtjí**- hávérò
       2S.HAB see   7C- chair
       'They usually see the chair.'   *Complement:* LH

    c. **ótjì**- hávérò
       7P- chair
       'It's a chair.'   *Copulative/predicative:* HL

    d. **tjì**- hávérò
       7V- chair
       'O chair!'   *Vocative:* ØL

As we will see in the next chapter, aspects of this tonal process suggest that tonal alternations—and not augment distribution—in Otjiherero are equivalent to the Zulu case-licensing process. For now, we can simply note that both Bulu and Otjiherero show evidence of both tonal and segmental nominal marking and that these different markers have different distributions.

Beyond languages like Bulu or Otjiherero, we find a number of Bantu languages in which, as in Zulu, segmental augment contrasts seem to have a more complicated distribution. Research on the function of the augment in Bantu languages has noted that multiple factors seem to govern its distribution, in varying combinations from language to language. In many languages, semantic and pragmatic factors such as definiteness, specificity, and focus seem to interact with syntactic factors, including position within the clause and presence of c-commanding negation (Hyman and Katamba, 1991, 1993; Katamba, 2003; Buell, 2011; de Dreu, 2008). These disparate factors have made it difficult for researchers who have attempted to pinpoint a precise meaning for the augment morpheme. I have advocated an approach to Zulu in this chapter in which we isolate the syntactic factors governing augmentless nominals and treat them as a form of structural case-licensing. In chapter 5, I argue that the augment itself functions as an intrinsic case marker in Zulu. My proposal takes the syntactic restrictions on the distribution of the augment to be primary: the absence of an augment is only permitted in constructions where structural case is assigned. In these constructions, the presence or absence of the augment can have interpretive consequences (as in

18. Kavari et al. (2012) use D for default tone pattern, C for complement, P for predicative, and V for vocative. Their glossing convention does not indicate augments, which are present in all forms except the vocative.

determining whether the nominal receives an NPI interpretation), but outside of case-assigning environments, such distinctions are neutralized and only the augmented version is permitted. I show in chapter 5 that this type of pattern is not uncommon cross-linguistically. Here we can look at the limited evidence available on augment distribution patterns in other Bantu languages that have the contrast to see that this characterization seems to capture the basic properties of the alternation: augmentless nominals (which are interpretively marked) are available only in certain syntactic positions, which tend to be low in the clause.

In Kinande, augmentless nominals can be NPIs, *wh*-words, and nonspecific indefinites (e.g., Progovac, 1993a; Schneider-Zioga, 2007; Mujomba, p.c.); Progovac (1993a), focusing on the NPI use of augmentless nominals in Kinande, argues that they are licensed by a downward-entailment operator, which fits with the broad semantic pattern that we saw in Zulu. For at least some speakers of Kinande, the semantic licensing conditions are a bit broader: low-scoping indefinites may be augmentless even without a nonveridical environment. Regardless of the semantic licensing, Kinande augmentless nominals are restricted to specific syntactic positions. Strikingly, we find a clear contrast between *v*P-internal positions and preverbal subjects. In a low position, absence of the augment yields a nonspecific indefinite; in the higher position, the augment is required even when a nonspecific indefinite interpretation is conveyed:

(179)   a.   **o**mundu   a- ma- gonga
             AUG.1person 1S- PRES- knock
             'Someone's knocking.' (specific or nonspecific)
             or 'The person is knocking.'

        b.   * mundu a- ma- gonga
             1person 1S- PRES- knock
             indended: 'Someone's knocking.'

        c.   ha- ma- gonga mundu
             16S- PRES- knock 1person
             'Someone's knocking.' (nonspecific)

        d.   ha- ma- gonga **o**mundu
             16S- PRES- knock AUG.1person
             'A/the person is knocking.' (specific)   (Pierre Mujomba, p.c.)

This contrast in the availability of augmentless nominals between *v*P-internal and *v*P-external positions mirrors what we saw in Zulu. In both languages as well, the augmented version is required, despite semantic interpretation, outside of certain syntactic positions. At the same time, it's clear even from preliminary data that just as the interpretive consequences of the alternation vary between the languages, there are perhaps syntactic differences as well. For example, as Schneider-Zioga (2007) demonstrates for *wh*-elements in Kinande, while preverbal *wh*-words must generally bear an augment—as we saw for non-*wh*-words in (179) above—they can be augmentless just in case they follow another (focus clefted) *wh*-word:

(180) **Kinande preverbal augmentless nominal**

    a. *ekitabu,   **ndi** a-a-ki-soma
         AUG.7book, 1who 1S-PST-7O-read

    b. ekihi   kyo   **ndi** a-alangira
         AUG.7what that-FOC 1who 1s-saw
         'Who saw what?'   (Schneider-Zioga, 2007, ex. (35), gloss adapted)

Schneider-Zioga (2007) argues that the correct interpretation of these facts is that the augmentless nominal in (180b) is grammatical only when it appears in a lower position (for her, Spec,TP) than the normal position for preverbal subjects and that nominals only surface in this lower position when the higher one is occupied (here by the other *wh*-word).

Returning to the distinction between the availability of augmentless nominals in low positions and their exclusion from higher positions in Kinande, Baker (2003a) turns to the issue of case. As we saw earlier in this chapter, his focus is the apparent lack of nominative case effects in Kinande, which he analyzes as de-linking of case and agreement in the Bantu family. He argues that agreed-with augmented nominals always occupy dislocated, A-bar positions and thus do not require case at all. While Baker does not directly address whether accusative case is affected by his analysis, his discussion of augmentless nominals assumes that it is lacking. He claims that augmentless nominals in Kinande are inherently cased as a way to explain why these nominals can appear in *v*P-internal non-agreeing A-positions. However, while Baker notes that *v*P-internal nominals in Kinande are often augmentless, his explanation does not provide an account for the appearance of augmented nominals in these same positions, as in (181b) below:

(181) a. mo- nga- langira simba
        PST- 1SG- see   9lion
        'I saw a lion.' (nonspecific)

     b. mo- nga- langira **e**simba
        PST- 1SG- see   AUG.9lion
        'I saw a/the lion.' (specific)   (Pierre Mujomba, p.c.)

Indeed, exactly as in Zulu, the distribution of augmentless nominals in Kinande is a subset of the syntactic environments in which augmented nominals may appear. In these particular environments, the presence or absence of an augment is meaningful: it conveys something about the interpretation of the nominal (such as specificity). Outside of these environments, the augment is required but the full range of meanings is possible. Regardless of the status of agreeing nominals in the language, the ability of both types of nominals to appear in vP-internal A-positions is beyond the scope of Baker's (2003a) account, but in line with the type of analysis proposed here for Zulu.

Luganda is another language that, like Zulu and Kinande, displays an interaction between syntactic and interpretive properties of augment distribution (e.g., Dewees, 1971; Hyman and Katamba, 1991, 1993). At the clause level, negation and focus both play a central role in augmentless nominal licensing in Luganda.[19] Nominals in the c-command domain of negation must be augmentless in Luganda, even if they receive a definite interpretation:

(182) tè-bááwà   báànà   bìtábó
NEG-2s.gave 2children 8books
'They didn't give the children books.'
(*a-baaana e-bitabo, *a-baana bitabo, *baana e-bitabo)
(Hyman and Katamba, 1993, ex. (18a))[20]

This pattern extends to elements inside relative clauses, as in (183a), but not across all clausal boundaries. As (183b) shows, matrix negation does not license an augmentless nominal inside the complement CP of a complex DP:

(183)   a. tè-báálàbà bìtábó byé twááwá báàná
NEG-2s.saw 8books REL 1PL.gave 2children
'They didn't see (the) books we gave to (the) children.'

    b. t-ákkírìzà   lùgámbó ntì báágulà è-bítábó
NEG-1s.believe rumor   that 2s.bought AUG-8books
'He doesn't believe the rumor that they bought books.' (Hyman and Katamba, 1993, ex. (19b), (20b))

While negation seems to be a common trigger for augmentless nominals in Zulu, Kinande, and Luganda, only in Luganda does augment drop under negation lack interpretive consequences for the nominal itself.

Focus is also a trigger for augment drop in Luganda: post-verbal focused elements are uniformly augmentless:

---

19. In addition to clause-level licensing, Luganda displays several DP- and PP-level licensing environments that appear to be parallel to Zulu, including augmentless nominals in certain locative constructions and in *which/how many* constructions. See Hyman and Katamba (1993) for an overview of these environments.

20. Glosses modified from original to reflect noun class and augments.

(184)   a. yàgúlà   è-bítábó   (bìnó)
        1s.bought AUG-8books (8these)
        'He bought (these) books.' [even focus]

     b. yàgúlà   bìtábó (bìno)
        1s.bought 8books (8these)
        'He bought (THESE) BOOKS. [postverbal focus] (Hyman and Katamba, 1993, ex. (24))

When multiple elements appear after the verb, if both are arguments, either the first or both may drop the augment to receive a focus interpretation—but not the second by itself, as the ungrammaticality of (185d) shows:

(185)   a.   yàgílìrà   à-báànà   è-bítábó
             1s.brought AUG-2children AUG-8books
             'He brought the children books.'

        b.   yàgílìrà   báànà   bítábó
             1s.brought 2children 8books
             'He brought THE CHILDREN BOOKS.'

        c.   yàgílìrà   báànà   èbítábó
             1s.brought 2children AUG-8books
             'He brought THE CHILDREN books.'

        d. * yàgílìrà   à-báànà   bítábó
             1s.brought AUG-2children 8books
             intended: 'He brought the children BOOKS.' (Hyman and Katamba, 1993, ex. (25))

When an argument and an adverb are both present in the postverbal field, only the highest element may drop the augment for a focus interpretation, though either order of elements is permitted, as (186) illustrates:

(186)   a. yàgúlà   **bìtábó** á-mángú
           he.bought books AUG-quickly
           'He bought (the) books quickly.'

           (*amangu ebitabo, ?*mangu bitabo, *amangu bitabo)

        b. yàgúlà   **màngú** é-bítábó
           he.bought quickly AUG-books
           'He bought (the) BOOKS quickly.'

           (*ebitabo amangu, *bitabo mangu, *ebitabo mangu) (Hyman and Katamba, 1993, ex. (27))

This dependence of augment-drop for focused elements on specific details of the syntactic structure is the same type of pattern that we have observed for Zulu. Indeed, while we lack information about the precise cause of the differences between the pattern in (185) and (186), it is interesting to note that the grammatical instances of multiple augmentless focused nominals given by Hyman and Katamba (1993) all involve an applicative construction, while the examples in which only the highest element may be augmentless in (186) involve a plain transitive verb. The dependence of these phenomena on specific syntactic positions becomes even more evident when Hyman and Katamba (1993) consider the phenomenon of "exbraciation," which they argue involves a post-verbal nominal that is not "internal to a clause" but not as high as agreeing right-dislocated nominal. In other words, they seem to be talking about *v*P-external elements that still have a fairly low attachment site. Remarkably, these exbraciated nominals require an augment, even under negation:

(187) a. tè-bááwà   báànà   bànó bìlábò
          NEG-2s.gave 2children 2these 8gifts
          'They didn't give these children gifts.'

       b. tè-bááwà   bànò] **àbáànà**   **èbìlábò**
          NEG-2s.gave 2these] AUG.2children AUG.8gifts
          'They didn't give these children gifts.' (Hyman and Katamba, 1993, foot-note 17)

To summarize this initial picture from Luganda, it seems that although the class of licensers is perhaps heterogeneous—with negation forcing augment drop in its c-command domain while focus has a slightly different effect—they both target the same syntactic domain, low in the postverbal field, a region that is plausibly the same *v*P-internal domain we found in Zulu. We've also seen initial evidence for further restrictions within this low domain, though we lack information that would determine what principles are at play in these distinctions. Hyman and Katamba (1993) conclude that the structural configuration is a necessary component for "licensing" of augmentless ([−A]) nominals: "Specifically, we have argued that a constituent marked [−A] must be licensed by one of two syntactic operators, NEG and FOC, vs. the [+A] specification which is self-licensing" (p. 254), the same rough conclusion that I reached for the Zulu pattern.

While these cross-Bantu snapshots leave open a number of questions regarding the details of augment patterns, it is also clear that for those languages that appear to have a structural component to their distribution, a number of common factors emerge. The meaning of these augmentless nominals seems to be centered around (negative) indefiniteness or focus and beyond interpretive restrictions, there seems to be a common restriction to a domain that is roughly equivalent to *v*P, as the contrast between preverbal and postverbal augmentless nominals in Kinande and Luganda show, as well as the contrast between in situ and "exbraciated" augmentless nominals in Luganda. In the following section, I will consider one additional case study of augmentless nominals in Xhosa (Carstens and Mletshe, 2013b), a close relative of Zulu, and the parallel to other bare negative NP and negative indefinite phenomena that Carstens and Mletshe raise.

3.5 AUGMENTLESS NOMINALS AS BARE NEGATIVE NPS?

A final case of augmentless nominal distribution that we can consider comes from recent work by Carstens and Mletshe (2013b) on Xhosa, a language closely related to Zulu, investigating the patterns and claims developed in a previous version of the proposals in this book Halpert (2012a,b). Carstens and Mletshe (2013b) are able to replicate the Zulu patterns discussed in this chapter for Xhosa, with some minor differences. One point of difference they observe is that in a transitive expletive construction in Xhosa, unlike in Zulu, both post-verbal arguments may be augmentless, a pattern that matches the one we saw for focused arguments in Luganda:

(188)   A-ku-phek-anga   m-ntu   qanda
        NEG-17S-cook-NEG.PST 1person 5egg
        'Nobody cooked any egg,   (Carstens and Mletshe, 2013b, ex. (25b)) *Xhosa*

(189)   * A-ku-phek-anga   muntu   qanda
        NEG-17S-cook-NEG.PST 1person 5egg
        'Nobody cooked any egg.   *Zulu*

Focusing only on augmentless nominals with a negative indefinite interpretation, Carstens and Mletshe (2013b) characterize their distribution as follows:

Table 3.3. XHOSA AUGMENTLESS NPI DISTRIBUTION (CARSTENS AND MLETSHE, 2013B, EX. (8))

Licit sites for [–A] NPIs	Illicit sites for [–A] NPIs
a. Phasal Spec,*v*P of SVO clauses	d. Sister to V
b. Spec of a middle-field FocP	e. Preverbal subject position
c. Phasal Spec, Appl, or Caus of symmetrical double object constructions	f. Externally merged Spec, Appl, or Caus

Carstens and Mletshe claim that augmentless nominals in Xhosa are *n*-words, negative indefinite elements with an uninterpretable negative feature [uNeg] that requires syntactic licensing via an Agree relationship with a higher negative operator (e.g., Zeijlstra, 2004, 2008). Furthermore, they argue that this type of licensing is an A-bar relationship that requires licensed elements to move to an A-bar position. They analyze the licit positions in table 3.3 as A-bar landing sites for movement; crucially, for them, augmentless nominals are never licensed in situ. In this way, their account is similar to proposals by Progovac (1993a) for Kinande and Hyman and Katamba (1993) for Luganda, in requiring syntactic licensing via an operator, with the added requirement that licensed elements must additionally appear in an A-bar position:

(190) **Carstens-Mletshe augmentless nominal licensing hypothesis:** Xhosa and Zulu [−A] NPIs are n-words which must:
    i. be licensed through Agree with a local, c-commanding negation operator, AND
    ii. move leftwards to enter this relation.

(Carstens and Mletshe, 2013b, ex. (39))

Following a recent body of research on augment vowels in Nguni (Buell, 2011; Taraldsen, 2010; Visser, 2008), they further claim that the augment vowel is a D^o head, heading a DP that requires syntactic case. Augmentless nominals, by contrast, are bare NPs that do not need case. As Carstens and Mletshe (2013b) point out, such an analysis of augment vowels in languages like Zulu and Xhosa yields an interaction between augment distribution and NPI licensing that resembles a familiar pattern of article drop in Romance languages like French and Italian (Kayne, 1981; Longobardi, 1994, 2000). A main claim of their research is that all of the structural properties of augmentless nominal distribution can in this way reduce to conditions on n-word licensing. They argue that this treatment allows a simpler account than the one proposed here for Zulu, in which NPI licensing and augmentless nominal licensing are separate mechanisms. In order to fully account for the distribution on augmentless nominals in these terms, Carstens and Mletshe synthesize a number of observed properties of negative indefinites (NPIs and n-words) cross-linguistically.

3.5.1 Syntactic Licensing of Negative Indefinites

As Carstens and Mletshe note, a number of languages exhibit restrictions on bare negative indefinites that go beyond simple licensing by a negative operator. In French, for example, Kayne (1981) observed that a bare indefinite like *personne* can be licensed by matrix negation in embedded object position, but not in embedded subject position:

(191) a. ? Je n' ai exigé qu' ils arrêtent **personne**
        I NEG have required that they arrest nobody
        'I didn't require that they arrest anyone.'

b. * Je n'   ai   exigé   que **personne** soit arrêté
I   NEG have required that nobody   be   arrested
intended: 'I didn't require that anyone be arrested.'

(Kayne, 1981, ex. (3)–(4))

This subject/object asymmetry in French looks strikingly like the pattern in Zulu (which also holds in Xhosa), repeated in (139) below, where an embedded augmentless nominal is grammatical *except* in preverbal subject position:

(139) **Augmentless preverbal subjects ungrammatical**

a. * A- ngi- sho- ngo   [ukuthi **muntu u**- fik-ile]
NEG- 1SG- say- NEG.PAST that   1person 1S- arrive-PFV
'I didn't say that anyone came.'

b. A- ngi- sho- ngo   [ukuthi **u**muntu **u**- fik-ile]
NEG- 1SG- say- NEG.PAST that   1person 1S- arrive-PFV
'I didn't say that a/the person/anyone came.'

c. A-   ngi- sho- ngo   [ukuthi **ku**- fik-e   **muntu**]
NEG- 1SG- say- NEG.PAST that   17S- arrive-PFV 1person
'I didn't say that anyone came.'

In both languages, a negative indefinite in an embedded clause is ungrammatical in Spec,TP but grammatical in a postverbal position. As Kayne (1981) discusses, the restriction in French is not simply on the bare indefinite in preverbal position, since it is grammatical in that position as long as it occurs with clausemate negation:

(192)   J' ai   exigé   que **personne** ne   soit arrêté
I have required that nobody   NEG be   arrested
'I have required that nobody be arrested.'   (Kayne, 1981, ex. (5))

Kayne concludes that the ungrammaticality of the preverbal negative indefinite in (191b), and the subject/object asymmetry that we see in (191) more generally, results from the need for the negative indefinite to take scope in the same clause as the negative element *ne*. This requirement causes quantifier raising of *personne* from object position in (191a); QR from preverbal subject position is ruled out as part of a more general set of restrictions on syntactic movement out of preverbal subject position, such as the ECP.

As we've seen in this chapter, the licensing conditions for augmentless nominals in Zulu cannot be precisely the same as those that govern the French patterns in (191) and (192); Zulu clearly rules out preverbal augmentless nominals in Spec,TP, even when clausemate negation is present:

(193) a. a- ku- fundis- anga   **muntu**
           NEG- 17S- teach- NEG.PAST 1person

       b. * **muntu** a- ka- fundis- anga
           1person NEG- 1S- teach- NEG.PAST
           'Nobody taught.'

We can further rule out the possibility that the ungrammaticality of (193b) is simply due to a c-command requirement on negation by comparing to constructions that involve a high negative adverb. As with sentential negation, the adverb can license a vP-internal subject, but not one in Spec,TP:

(194) a. ngeke ku-   fundise **muntu**
           never 17S.SJC- teach.SJC 1person

       b. * ngeke **muntu** a-   fundise
           1person never   1S.SJC- teach.SJC
           'Nobody will ever teach.'

So while French plausibly involves a movement-based subject/object asymmetry for embedded negative indefinites under matrix negation, Zulu has a more general prohibition on augmentless nominals in Spec,TP. Beyond these surface differences, extending the story for French to cover the Zulu cases faces additional difficulties. Kayne suggests that the embedded subject in (191b) cannot undergo QR from Spec,TP following an overt complementizer for the same reason that overt movement from that position is ruled out: a *that*-trace effect (e.g., Chomsky and Lasnik, 1977). In Zulu, overt movement of the preverbal subject around a complementizer is grammatical, as we saw in chapter 2: a nominal may raise from embedded subject position to a matrix object position.

(195) a. ngi-funa [ukuthi **impi**   i-   gcin- e]
          1SG-want that   AUG.9war 9SJC- finish- SJC

       b. ngi-funa **impi**   [ukuthi i-   gcin- e]
          1SG-want AUG.9war that   9SJC- finish- SJC
          'I want war to end.'

Given that overt movement of this type does not induce *that*-trace effects in Zulu, an account along these lines would require an independent reason why covert movement would. These crucial differences in the subject/object asymmetries in French and Zulu suggest that a unified account would face a number of challenges. Indeed, while Carstens and Mletshe (2013b) emphasize the parallel between the languages, they do not directly address these differences between the two constructions. Notably, they do not consider the raising-to-object pattern at all and instead seem to conclude that the movement possibilities for augmentless nominals are even more restricted in Zulu than they are in French. They also do not address the availability of the preverbal bare indefinite that we saw in French monoclausal constructions in (192) above, the existence of which seems at odds with their conclusion that all of these syntactic negative indefinites must appear in an A-bar position and therefore are barred from preverbal subject position.

In motivating their A-bar requirement, Carstens and Mletshe (2013b) find parallels in other negative indefinite phenomena. In particular, they point out that negative concord phenomena in languages like West Flemish require that *n*-words undergo overt leftward movement, following Haegeman (1995, 1997):

(196) a. da   Valère **van niemand** ketent   en- was
           that Valère of   no.one   contented *en-* was

       b. * da Valère ketent   **van niemand** en- was
             that Valère contented of   no.one   *en-* was
             'that Valère was not pleased with anyone.'

                    (Carstens and Mletshe, 2013b, ex. (35), citing Haegeman 1997)

Multiple lines of research have proposed explanations for the required shift illustrated in (196), though a common thread that unites them is locality with a higher negative head/operator (e.g., Haegeman, 1995; Haegeman and Lohndal, 2010; Zeijlstra, 2004, 2008). Carstens and Mletshe (2013b) go one step further, claiming that negative concord requires locality *and* an A-bar position for the *n*-word. Crucially, the A-bar positions that they claim are licit in Zulu and Xhosa are all ones that involve string-vacuous movement. This type of restriction is perhaps particularly surprising given that other types of negative indefinites are grammatical in post-*v*P A-bar positions in Zulu, as I showed earlier in this chapter.

In addition to the significant differences between the patterns of negative indefinites in Zulu and those in languages like French or West Flemish, the type of account that Carstens and Mletshe (2013b) proposes falls short in another respect: as we saw at the beginning of the chapter, augmentless nominals are not always negative elements. The fact that augmentless NPIs and augmentless *wh*-elements exhibit the same syntactic restrictions suggests that any licensing mechanism that relies on negative features is too narrow to capture the full picture. As the snapshots of augmentless nominal behavior in other Bantu languages made clear in the previous section, any unified licensing account across the Bantu languages will need to be robust enough to capture a wider variety of interpretive effects. As we'll see in chapter 5, we find precisely these sorts of interactions between interpretive effects, structural position, and morphological marking in a number of case alternations found cross-linguistically. By framing these facts as a case pattern, we are better equipped to deal with the variety of interpretive effects that are difficult to capture with a negative feature-driven account.

3.6 SUMMARIZING THE CASE FOR CASE

As we've now seen in detail, augmentless nominals in Zulu, and in Bantu languages more generally, not only come with syntactic restrictions, but also with particular interpretive consequences, compared to their augmented counterparts. Perhaps most salient of these consequences in Zulu is the negative indefinite interpretation licensed in the presence of sentential negation (or certain other nonveridical environments). The structural restrictions on augmentless nominals exceed those expected by simple NPI or negative concord licensing, however; as the previous section shows, parallels to other complex negative indefinite patterns break down, and it is impossible to build a unified account for augmentless nominals based on syntactic negative indefinite licensing. Approaching augmentless nominal distribution as pseudo-incorporation, which builds on another aspect of augmentless nominal interpretation—indefiniteness—also runs into problems with empirical coverage. Given these difficulties, I have instead advocated for an analysis of augmentless nominals based on other structural properties of the clause. I showed that augmentless nominals are restricted to certain positions within vP and argued that we can understand this distribution in terms of case licensing via local licensing heads L, APPL, and CAUS.

In proposing such a system, I depart from previous treatments of (the lack of) case effects in the language family (Ndayiragije, 1999; Alsina, 2001; Baker, 2003; Carstens and Diercks, 2013; Diercks, 2012). While my analysis illustrates a familiar mechanism at work in Zulu, Zulu conspires to camouflage the presence of the Case Filter throughout most of the grammar. As I have shown, structural case licensing effects only emerge for the class of augmentless nominals, whose distribution is also subject to independent grammatical restrictions. The class of augmented nominals, which I argue to bear inherent case, does not exhibit structural restrictions. In the case of augmentless nominals, it is only when the independent grammatical requirements are met that we can see the role that structural licensing plays. Once we consider the right environments, we see that these nominals are only licensed in specific syntactic configurations, and will undergo A movement from a nonlicensed position to a licensed position, just as in more familiar languages like English. I presented evidence from raising-to-object constructions and from the behavior of vP-internal arguments to show that all structural licensing in Zulu occurs within vP, mediated by a licensing head (L) directly above vP and by APPL/CAUS heads.

In the following two chapters, I address two major outstanding issues raised by these data and my analysis of them. The first concerns the licensing process itself. I have proposed that a syntactic head, L, is located above vP and licenses the highest nominal within vP, but I have not addressed the question of L's role in the structure and the timing of its licensing process in the derivation. Chapter 4 examines licensing by L more closely. I show that when we consider the syntactic domain in which L appears to operate, we find a (seemingly) independent morphological process that shares the syntactic distribution of augmentless nominals: the *conjoint/disjoint* alternation. I argue that this process is also mediated by L and specifically propose that the *disjoint* morpheme is an overt instance of L. With this new information about the licensing head, I return to the issue of timing and propose that the unusual timing effects of the licensing process proposed in this chapter are a result of the Activity Condition.

In chapter 5, I return to the question of what makes augmentless nominals special, compared to their augmented counterparts, in terms of structural restrictions and interpretive properties. By casting a wider net, including other nominal prefixes in our investigation, we see that certain parallels emerge between the augment and oblique prefixes in the language. I argue on the basis of these parallels that the augment is simply one element in a larger system of morphological case in Zulu. Augmented nominals appear to be exempt from structural licensing in Zulu because they receive case in a more local relationship, signaled by the augment itself. Once we consider the augment to be overt morphological case, we gain a new tool for investigating the interpretive properties of augmentless nominals discussed in this chapter: instead of treating the interpretive properties as primary, they can instead be understood as yet another instance of the interpretative consequences that are associated with morphological case in a variety of languages (e.g., de Hoop, 1996).

CHAPTER 4

Licensing and *v*P

Evidence from the Conjoint/Disjoint Alternation

4.1 INTRODUCTION

In chapter 3, we saw that augmentless nominals in Zulu are subject to syntactic licensing conditions. Specifically, augmentless nominals are licensed either as the highest element within *v*P or as the direct object under CAUS or APPL. To account for this distribution, I argued that the higher licensing occurred by means of a licensing head that is outside of *v*P and can therefore license even an in situ external argument.

(197)

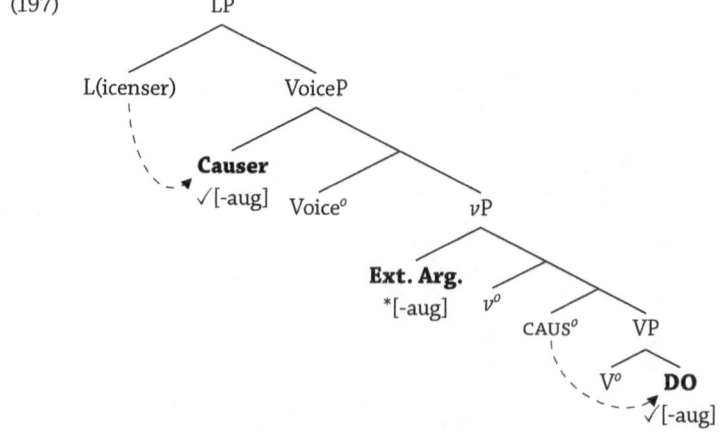

In this chapter, I focus on this higher licensing process. I argue that there is independent motivation to posit a syntactic category above the extended *v*P (including Voice in a causative structure) that probes the entire *v*P. This evidence comes from the so-called conjoint/disjoint (or "long/short") alternation on verbal predicates (Doke, 1997 [1927]; Van der Spuy, 1993; Buell, 2005, among others). As we will see, not only is the conjoint/disjoint alternation sensitive to the contents of *v*P, which is the basic licensing domain for augmentless nominals, but this process is also sensitive to movement, just like the licensing of augmentless nominals. I propose that the common syntactic signature of these two phenomena can be understood in terms of the licensing head L that I introduced in chapter 3, as illustrated above. L probes the derivation in every construction in search of *v*P-internal material and can structurally license its goal—the highest element inside *v*P.

(198) **Conjoint/disjoint: basic proposal**

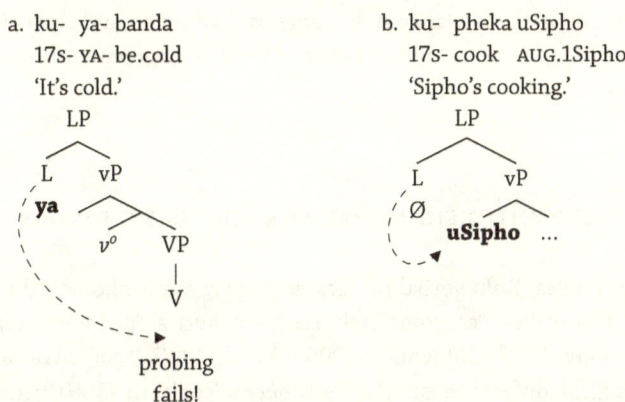

a. ku- ya- banda
   17s- YA- be.cold
   'It's cold.'

b. ku- pheka uSipho
   17s- cook AUG.1Sipho
   'Sipho's cooking.'

Section 4.2 lays out the distribution of the conjoint/disjoint alternation. As we will see, evidence that the conjoint/disjoint alternation is sensitive to syntactic configuration comes from the behavior of a variety of elements, including the argument nominals, locatives, and adverbs discussed in Van der Spuy (1993) and Buell (2005). I review the diagnostics for these authors develop for constituency, which all indicate that the conjoint form occurs in the presence of *v*P-internal material, while the disjoint occurs when the *v*P is empty.

This distribution shares with the distribution of augmentless nominals a sensitivity to movement: material that moves out of *v*P during the derivation does not count as *v*P-internal for the conjoint/disjoint alternation. As I discussed for the distribution of augmentless nominals in the previous chapter, this sensitivity to movement has been taken as evidence that the conjoint/disjoint alternation is a reflection of surface configuration (Buell, 2005, 2006). I present new evidence, however, that the conjoint/disjoint alternation is *not* merely sensitive to the surface syntax and argue that it should instead be treated as the result of a syntactic agreement process. On the basis of the parallels in distribution between the conjoint/disjoint alternation and the licensing of augmentless nominals, I argue in section 4.3 that the licensing head L accounts for the distribution of both phenomena.

The remainder of the chapter is devoted to addressing outstanding issues related to the conjoint/disjoint alternation and to the nature of the agreement process that the head L undergoes. Section 4.4 discusses the nature of the L probe. I show that the participation of non-nominal categories in the conjoint/disjoint alternation follows from independent evidence that these categories all contain accessible nominal elements. In section 4.5, I return to the question of sensitivity to movement that we saw with augmentless nominals in the previous chapter, and propose that we can understand this sensitivity in terms of the Activity Condition. I present new evidence about the distribution of the conjoint/disjoint alternation in environments with clausal complements and adjuncts and discuss how this data helps us understand how to characterize the agreement process that L undergoes.

4.2 THE CONJOINT/DISJOINT ALTERNATION: BASIC DISTRIBUTION

In certain tenses, Zulu verbal predicates display a morphological alternation between a so-called "conjoint" (short) form and a "disjoint" (long) form[1] (Van der Spuy, 1993; Güldemann, 2003; Buell, 2005, 2006). We can see this morphological difference on the verb *pheka* 'cook' in (199) below. In the present tense, the verb is marked with the morpheme *ya* in the present tense intransitive construction in (199b), but with Ø in the present tense transitive construction in (199a):

(199)   **Conjoint/disjoint: present tense alternation**

a. uMlungisi   u- pheka iqanda
   AUG.1Mlungisi 1s- cook AUG.5egg
   'Mlungisi is cooking an egg.'

b. uMlungisi   u- **ya**- pheka
   AUG.1Mlungisi 1s- YA- cook
   'Mlungisi is cooking.'

1. The use of the terms *conjoint* and *disjoint* date to Meeussen (1959). The terms *short* and *long* first appear in Doke's 1927 grammar of Zulu and are also frequently used to describe this alternation in the literature on Nguni.

In the so-called near or recent past (perfective) construction, we also find a morphological realization of the conjoint disjoint: a high-toned suffix -é appears in conjoint environments and -ile in disjoint environments, as illustrated in (200) below.

(200) **Conjoint/disjoint: recent past tense alternation**

 a. uMlungisi   u- phek- **é** iqanda
    AUG.1Mlungisi 1s- cook- PFV AUG.5egg
    'Mlungisi cooked an egg.'

 b. uMlungisi   u- phek-**ile**
    AUG.1Mlungisi 1s- cook- PFV
    'Mlungisi cooked.'

We find a similar contrast in relativized predicates, where a disjoint environment triggers a -yo suffix:

(201) **Conjoint/disjoint: relativized predicate**

 a. umuntu   o-   pheka iqanda
    AUG.1person 1REL- cook AUG.5egg
    'a person who cooked an egg'

 b. umuntu   o-   pheka-**yo**
    AUG.1person 1REL- cook- YO
    'a person who cooked'

As Buell (2005) discusses, these alternations are sensitive to the same morphosyntactic environments as the present tense. For simplicity, I restrict my discussion to present tense forms for the remainder of the chapter. Zulu also has tense forms that lack a morphological distinction between conjoint and disjoint. As (202) shows, the future and remote past both take the same morphological form, whether or not a non-agreeing object is present:

(202) **No conjoint/disjoint: future and remote past**

 a. uMlungisi   u- **zo**- pheka (iqanda)
    AUG.1Mlungisi 1s- FUT- cook (AUG.5egg)
    'Mlungisi will cook (an egg).'

 b. uMlungisi   w- **a**-   pheka (iqanda)
    AUG.1Mlungisi 1s- REMPST- cook- (AUG.5egg)
    'Mlungisi cooked (an egg).'

Although we see no morphological distinction for these forms, postverbal material is sensitive to the same morphosyntactic environments as in the other tenses, so I will assume that the clausal structure of LP proposed above, which I motivate below in the present tense, holds.[2] In this section I show, following Buell (2005) and Van der Spuy (1993), that in the present tense, the disjoint *ya* morpheme appears when the *v*P is empty *after* any A-movement has taken place, while the null conjoint occurs if *v*P contains material after A-movement. I will argue that this alternation is a reflection of probing by L: the disjoint appears when L fails to find a goal inside *v*P, while the conjoint appears when L does find a goal.

(203)   **Conjoint–disjoint generalization:**

   Conjoint (Ø): appears when *v*P contains material (after A movement)

   Disjoint (*ya*): appears when *v*P does not contain material (after A movement)

While this morphological alternation has been analyzed as a means of encoding focus, both in Zulu and in related Bantu languages (Creissels, 1996; Güldemann, 2003; Ndayiragije, 1999; Voeltz, 2004; van der Wal, 2011), Van der Spuy (1993) and Buell (2005, 2006) show that the choice between conjoint and disjoint forms is predictable from the syntactic configuration and is independent of focus. Specifically, Buell (2005, 2006) argues that the alternation encodes the surface contents of a particular syntactic domain: the conjoint (null in present tense) appears when the verb is *not* final in the relevant syntactic domain (for van der Spuy, IP; for Buell, AgrSP), while the disjoint (*ya* in present tense) appears when the verb *is* final in this domain.

This section discusses the evidence that the conjoint/disjoint alternation is sensitive to syntactic constituency, along the lines proposed by van der Spuy (1993) and Buell (2005, 2006). While Buell characterizes this constituent as one containing the verb itself and argues that the alternation depends on whether the verb is final in this constituent, I will argue that we can capture the facts in terms of whether *v*P is "empty" or not, as stated in (203).

In addition, previous accounts of the conjoint/disjoint alternation identify it as being sensitive only to the surface structure. I present novel evidence that shows that while the alternation does seem to be sensitive to most instances of movement, it is not the case that it merely reflects surface structure. While Buell (2005, 2006) suggests that there is a perfect correspondence between disjoint verb forms and phrase-final prosody on the verb, the evidence in this

2. See Zeller et al. (in preparation) for a more detailed discussion of the morphosyntax of the conjoint/disjoint alternation in these tenses. In particular, they provide initial evidence that Durban Zulu speakers may use grammatical tone to mark the conjoint/disjoint distinction in remote past constructions, suggesting that there may be morphological correlates in that domain as well. Notably, they show that in the remote past, the *conjoint* is marked by a final high tone, while the disjoint receives no special marking. Given this pattern, we see all possibilities for morphological realization of the distinction: marked disjoint in the present tense, both marked in the near past, and marked conjoint in the remote past.

section suggests that the disjoint does not reflect verb finality and is in fact deeply syntactic in nature. In particular, I show that in certain coordination constructions with a shared object the verb in the first conjunct receives phrase-final prosody and is not followed by any overt element in the relevant syntactic domain, yet requires the conjoint form.

To return to the example in (199), we saw that the null conjoint form is used when an object follows the transitive verb in (199a), while the disjoint morpheme appears when nothing follows the intransitive verb in (199b). Van der Spuy (1993) and Buell (2005, 2006) show that the conjoint/disjoint alternation does not simply reflect on whether the verb is sentence final. Instead, as they discuss, the alternation is sensitive to the syntactic position of elements following the verb. Specifically, we find the conjoint form in the presence of in situ post-verbal arguments and low adjuncts. We find the disjoint form in the absence of such elements, even when the verb is sentence-medial and followed by high adjuncts or dislocated arguments.

4.2.1 The Conjoint/Disjoint Alternation and Argument Position

In constructions where the verb presumably takes no thematic arguments, such as the weather predicate in (204) below, the disjoint form is required. In this construction, the verb bears class 17 expletive agreement.

(204)   **Weather predicate: disjoint required**

    a.   ku- ya- banda
          17s- YA- be.cold
          'It's cold.'

    b. *ku- banda
          17s- be.cold

When the verb does take thematic arguments, the conjoint/disjoint alternation correlates with the syntactic position of those arguments. Recall from chapter 2 that non-agreeing arguments are always inside vP, while agreed-with arguments occupy vP-external positions, either to the left or the right of the verb. The generalization in (203) suggests that the choice between conjoint and disjoint forms should reflect this difference between vP-internal and vP-external postverbal arguments. Given the correlation between agreement and syntactic position, we therefore expect the conjoint/disjoint alternation to be sensitive to whether arguments are agreed with. As we see in examples (205) and (206) below, this expectation is met. In intransitive and mono-transitive constructions, the conjoint form is required whenever there are non-agreeing arguments:

(205) **Non-agreeing subject: conjoint required**

    a.   ku- pheka uSipho
            17s- cook AUG.1Sipho
            'Sipho's cooking.'

    b. * ku- **ya**- pheka uSipho
            17s- YA- cook AUG.1Sipho

(206) **Non-agreeing object: conjoint required**

    a.   uSipho   u- pheka iqanda
            AUG.1Sipho 1s- cook AUG.5egg
            'Sipho is cooking an egg.'

    b. * uSipho   u- **ya**- pheka iqanda
            AUG.1Sipho 1s- YA- cook AUG.5egg

By contrast, when the verb agrees with *both* arguments, the disjoint form is always required, regardless of whether the overt DPs are preverbal, postverbal, or pro-dropped:

(207) **Intransitive agreeing subject: disjoint required**

    a.   (uSipho) u- **ya**- pheka
            AUG.1Sipho 1s- YA- cook
            'Sipho is cooking.'

    b. * uSipho   u- pheka
            AUG.1Sipho 1s- cook

    c.   u- **ya**- pheka uSipho
            1s- YA- cook AUG.uSipho
            'Sipho is cooking.'

    d. * u- pheka uSipho
            1s- cook AUG.1Sipho

(208) **Monotransitive agreeing object: disjoint required**

    a.   (iqanda) (uSipho) u- **ya**- li- pheka
            AUG.5egg AUG.1Sipho 1s- YA- 5o- cook
            '(As for) the egg, Sipho is cooking it.'

    b. * iqanda   uSipho   u- li- pheka
            AUG.5egg AUG.1Sipho 1s- 5o- cook

    c.   uSipho   u- **ya**- li- pheka iqanda
            AUG.1Sipho 1s- YA- 5o- cook AUG.5egg
            'Sipho is cooking the egg.'

    d. * uSipho   u- li- pheka iqanda
            AUG.1Sipho 1s- 5o- cook AUG.5egg

In double object constructions, since only one object may agree with the verb, the non-agreeing object typically remains in situ. As (203) would predict for these cases, the conjoint form must appear.

(209) **Double object construction: conjoint required**

    a.   uSipho   u- phek- ela uMfundo   iqanda
        AUG.1Sipho 1s- cook- APPL AUG.1Mfundo AUG.5egg
        'Sipho is cooking Mfundo an egg.'

    b.   **uMfundo**   uSipho   u- **m**- phek- ela iqanda
        AUG.1Mfundo AUG.1Sipho 1s- 1O- cook- APPL AUG.5egg
        '(As for) Mfundo, Sipho is cooking an egg for him.'

    c.   *uMfundo   uSipho   u- **ya**- m phek- ela iqanda
        AUG.1Mfundo AUG.1Sipho 1s- YA- 1O- cook- APPL AUG.5egg

    d.   **iqanda**   uSipho   u- **li**- phek- ela uMfundo
        AUG.5egg AUG.1Sipho 1s- 5O- cook- APPL AUG.1Mfundo
        'As for the egg, Sipho is cooking it for Mfundo.'

    e.   *iqanda   uSipho   u- **ya**- li phek- ela uMfundo
        AUG.5egg AUG.1Sipho 1s- YA- 5O- cook- APPL AUG.1Mfundo

These double object constructions in (209) rule out a theory in which the disjoint form simply correlates with movement out of vP. As long as even one object is left inside vP, the conjoint form is still required, even though movement and agreement of the other arguments has occurred.

This pattern crucially contrasts with the double dislocation pattern described by Voeltz (2004), Adams (2010), and Zeller (2015). While maximally one object may agree with the verb, these researchers have shown that if the verb agrees with the indirect object and the underlying IO > DO word order is maintained, the disjoint form may be used. Both objects in these double dislocation constructions otherwise behave like right-dislocated elements in single dislocations, requiring an old information interpretation and appearing outside of vP, as Zeller (2015) demonstrates:

(210) uSipho   u- **ya**-**m**- phek- ela] uMfundo   iqanda
       AUG.1Sipho 1s- YA- 1O- cook- APPL] AUG.1Mfundo AUG.5egg
       'Sipho (did) cook Mfundo an egg.'

This contrast again shows that the conjoint/disjoint alternation does not track the occurrence of movement. Rather, in all of the cases above, the disjoint morphology appears precisely when *all* of the arguments of the verb have moved out of vP, leaving it empty after A-movement has occurred. As (204) showed, we also find disjoint morphology when no movement has occurred—but where there are no arguments to begin with. When any argument stays inside the vP, conjoint morphology is required. The examples in this section thus illustrate that the alternation is dependent on the syntactic position of the arguments: the conjoint is used in the presence of *v*P-internal arguments while the disjoint is used in the absence of *v*P-internal arguments. These examples also illustrate that the relevant syntactic position for arguments is the one that they occupy *after* movement. Throughout the section, we will see how the data and my analysis of them compare to the previous approaches to the conjoint/disjoint alternation (e.g., Van der Spuy, 1993; Güldemann, 2003; Buell, 2005, 2006). While my observations on and characterization of the phenomenon largely follow Buell (2005, 2006), some crucial data that I introduce in section 4.2.4 lead me to favor an account based on syntactic agreement, rather than surface configuration.

4.2.2 The Conjoint/Disjoint Alternation with Locatives and Adverbs

In addition to its sensitivity to nominal argument position, as discussed in section 4.2.1, the conjoint/disjoint alternation is also sensitive to the position of elements that one might assume are non-nominals, including adverbs and locatives. Just as with the nominals, we can see that when these elements attach inside *v*P, they trigger the conjoint form, even in the absence of *v*P-internal arguments. When these elements have a higher attachment site, by contrast, they trigger the disjoint form.

First, we can see that VP-modifying adverbs with a uniformly low attachment site, such as the adverb *kahle* 'well' that we saw in chapter 2, typically require the conjoint form of the verb:

(211) **Low adverb: conjoint required**

    a.   uSipho   u- gijima **kahle**
           AUG.1Sipho 1s- run   well
           'Sipho runs well.'

    b. * uSipho   u- **ya**- gijima **kahle**
           AUG.1Sipho 1s- YA- run   well

Despite the strong tendency for such low adverbs to trigger the conjoint, speakers will accept the disjoint form under the right discourse conditions. In particular, if the adverb itself is old information and the predicate receives verum focus, the disjoint morpheme is permitted:

(212) **Old information low adverb: disjoint permitted**

    Q: uMfundo   a-   ka- bhukud- i   kahle, a-   ngi- thi?
        AUG.1Mfundo NEG- 1s- swim-   NEG well   NEG- 1SG- say
        'Mfundo doesn't swim well, does he?

A: cha, u- ya- bhukuda kahle, kodwa uMthuli   u- ya- m- hlula
   no 1s- YA- swim   well   but   AUG.1Mthuli 1s- YA- 1O- surpass
   'No, he does swim well, but Mthuli is better.'

Other adverbs, such as *kakhulu* 'a lot' can appear with either form of the verb:

(213) **Conjoint/disjoint optionality with adverb**

    a. uSipho   u- gijima **kakhulu**
       AUG.1Sipho 1s- run   a.lot.'
       'Sipho runs a lot.'

    b. uSipho   u- **ya**- gijima **kakhulu**
       AUG.1Sipho 1s- YA- run   a.lot
       'Sipho runs a lot.'

With this set of adverbs, speakers report that the conjoint and disjoint forms are equally good in many contexts, though there is a tendency to prefer the conjoint when the adverb is in focus, as in the question in (214) below, and the disjoint for verum focus (with an old information adverb), as illustrated by the possible responses:

(214) Q: UNokukhanya   u- bhukuda kakhulu yini?
       AUG.1Nokukhanya 1s- swim   a.lot   what
       'Does Nokukhanya swim a lot?'

    A1: U- (ya)- bhukuda kakhulu uma e-   seThekwini.
       1s- (YA)- swim   a.lot   when 1PRT- be.at.AUG5Durban
       'She swims a lot when she's in Durban.'

    A2: U- ya- bhukuda kakhulu uma e-   seThekwini,   kodwa hhayi
       1s- YA- swim   a.lot   when 1PRT- be.at.AUG5Durban but   not
       uma e-   seMelika.
       when 1PRT- be.at.AUG5America
       'She does swim a lot when she's in Durban, but not when she's in America.'

With locative phrases, there is a strong contrast between goal readings and location readings. Goal readings require a conjoint form (and typically co-occur with an applicative marker on the verb), as in (215):

(215) **Goal reading: conjoint required**

    a.   uMfundo   u- gijim- ela   **esitolo**
        AUG.1Mfudno 1s- run-   APPL LOC.7store
        'Mfundo is running to the store.'

    b. *uMfundo   u- **ya**- gijim- ela   **esitolo**
        AUG.1Mfundo 1s- YA- run-   APPL LOC.7store

Location readings can co-occur with either the conjoint or the disjoint form of the verb—and show the same context-sensitivity to old information and focus as the adverbs above. In (216), the locative is new information and triggers a conjoint verb; in (217), the old information locative in the response triggers disjoint morphology:

(216) **Location reading: conjoint**

    Q: UMfundo   w- enza- ni?
       AUG.1Mfundo 1s- do-   9what?
       'What is Mfundo doing?'

    A: UMfundo   u- gijima esitolo.
       AUG.1Mfundo 1s- run   LOC.AUG.7store
       'Mfundo is running in the store.'

(217) **Location reading: disjoint**

    Q: UMfundo   u- gijima esitolo   yini?
       AUG.1Mfundo 1s- run   LOC.7store what
       'Is Mfundo running in the store?

    A: Yebo, u- ya- gijima esitolo!
       yes   1s- YA- run   LOC.7store
       'Yes, he is running in the store!'

In these examples, we can see that while a goal reading requires a conjoint form, location readings for locative phrases are context sensitive: focus on the locative phrase correlates with a conjoint form, as in (216), while an old information locative phrase yields a disjoint form, as in (217). If the generalization in (203) is correct, these patterns suggest that goals and new or focused locations appear inside *v*P, while old information locations appear outside *v*P. As we saw in chapter 2, this type of positional distinction based on information structure seems to hold independently in Zulu (e.g., Cheng and Downing, 2009), and in section 4.2.3, we will see some additional ways to confirm these predicted structures.

4.2.3 Diagnostics for *v*P Edge

The pattern that emerges from the data in the previous subsections is that, as described by van der Spuy (1993) and Buell (2005, 2006), the conjoint/disjoint alternation tracks the contents of *v*P:

(203) **Conjoint-disjoint generalization:**

    Conjoint (Ø): appears when *v*P contains material (after A-movement)

    Disjoint (*ya*): appears when *v*P does not contain material (after A-movement)

An empty *v*P triggers disjoint marking (*-ya-*) while material inside *v*P, including both arguments and adjuncts, triggers the null conjoint. As we saw from the subject and object data, this generalization appears to hold *on the surface*: elements that start out inside *v*P but move during the course of the derivation, such as the subjects and objects in (207) and (208) trigger disjoint, rather than conjoint, marking.

It is crucial that the relevant domain for the conjoint/disjoint alternation is not defined linearly—for example, as the entirety of the postverbal field including everything that follows the verb until the end of the sentence. Rather, as we have seen, the alternation is sensitive to different *syntactic* positions following the verb. We can observe the relevance of the *v*P domain to the conjoint/disjoint alternation by examining how the alternation lines up with independent diagnostics for the right edge of *v*P.

Van der Spuy (1993) and Buell (2006) develop syntactic and prosodic diagnostics for the syntactic boundary that the conjoint/disjoint alternation is sensitive to. The syntactic evidence comes from the possibility of inserting elements such as vocative phrases or question particles in sentence medial position, as well as from the behavior of agreed-with, dislocated DPs. The prosodic evidence involves processes such as penultimate lengthening and high tone shift that target particular syntactic constituents.

(218) **Syntactic evidence for *v*P boundary**

    a. Vocative insertion: must occur to the right of a *v*P boundary.

    b. Question particle insertion: must occur to the right of a *v*P boundary.

(219) **Prosodic evidence for *v*P boundary**

    a. Penultimate lengthening: occurs on the penultimate syllable of *v*P.

    b. High tone shift: shifts to antepenult at a *v*P boundary, penult otherwise.

Syntactic evidence

Van der Spuy (1993) notes that a vocative phrase, in addition to appearing sentence initially or finally, may also appear sentence medially. When it follows a sentence medial verb, however, the disjoint form is required:

(220) **Zulu vocative: sentence-initial and sentence-final**

    a. **Mama**   uSipho   u- gijima phandle
        1mother AUG.1Sipho 1s- run   outside
        'Mom, Sipho is running outside.'

b. uSipho   u- gijima phandle **Mama**
    AUG.1Sipho 1s- run   outside 1mother
    'Sipho is running outside, Mom.'

(221) **Sentence-medial vocative: must follow disjoint form**

  a.   uSipho   u- **ya**- gijima **Mama**   phandle
       AUG.1Sipho 1s- YA- run   1mother outside
       'Sipho is running, Mom, outside.'

  b. *uSipho   u- gijima **Mama**   phandle
       AUG.1Sipho 1s- run   1mother outside

With a direct object, the vocative can either follow the non-agreeing direct object (which follows a conjoint form of the verb) or precede the agreeing object, in which case it follows a disjoint verb form.[3] The vocative cannot appear between a conjoint form of the verb and the object:

(222) **Sentence-medial vocative with object**

  a.   uSipho   u- (*ya-) dlala ibhola   **Mama**   (phandle)
       AUG.1Sipho 1s- (*YA-) play AUG.5soccer 1mother (outside)
       'Sipho is playing soccer, Mom, outside.'

  b.   uSipho   u- **ya**- li- dlala **Mama**   ibhola
       AUG.1Sipho 1s- YA- 5o- play 1mother 5soccer
       'Sipho is playing, Mom, soccer.'

  c. *uSipho   u- (li-) dlala **Mama**   ibhola
       AUG.1Sipho 1s- (5o-) play 1mother 5soccer

Buell (2005) shows a similar pattern with the question particles *na/yini*, which typically appear sentence finally to mark a yes/no question:[4]

(223) **Zulu question particle** *na*

  a. uSipho   u- ya- wu- thanda lo-   mculo
    AUG.1Sipho 1s- YA- 3o- love   DEM3- 3song
    'Sipho likes this song.'

---

3. The vocative can also follow an agreeing, dislocated object, in which case the verb must appear in the disjoint form, as expected for dislocated objects. I do not discuss this construction here because it does not add to our understanding of the conjoint/disjoint alternation.

4. While Buell (2005) only addresses the use of *na*, the speakers of Durban Zulu with whom I have worked prefer *yini* 'what' over *na* to mark yes/no questions. To my knowledge, the distribution of *yini* in this use mirrors the distribution of *na* described by Buell (2005), though see Thwala (2006b) for an argument they they occupy slightly different positions in the closely related language SiSwati. Since both positions that Thwala indentifies are outside of vP, the existence of a similar distinction in Zulu would not affect the diagnostics here.

b. uSipho   u- ya- wu- thanda lo-   mculo **na**?
AUG.1Sipho 1s- YA- 3o- love   DEM3- 3song Q
'Does Sipho like this song?'   (Buell, 2005, ex. (123), adapted)

(224)   **Zulu question particle** *yini*

     a. uSipho   u- pheka iqanda
        AUG.1Sipho 1s- cook   AUG.5egg
        'Sipho is cooking an egg.'

     b. uSipho   u- pheka iqanda   **yini**?
        AUG.1Sipho 1s- cook   AUG.5egg what
        'Is Sipho cooking an egg?'

Like the vocative, the question particle can never be inserted directly after the conjoint form of the verb. Instead, it must appear either after the disjoint form of the verb, or after the conjoint verb and a following object or low adjunct. In (225a–b), we can see that in an intransitive construction with no other elements, *yini* must follow the disjoint form of the verb. The sentences in (225c–e) show that when the adjunct *phandle* appears to the left of *yini*, the conjoint form is grammatical, but when it appears to the right, only the disjoint is allowed.

(225)   **Question particle (with adjunct): cannot immediately follow conjoint verb**

     a.   uSipho   u- **ya**- gijima **yini**?
          AUG.1Sipho 1s- YA- run   what
          'Is Sipho running?'

     b.   * uSipho   u- gijima **yini**?
          AUG.1Sipho 1s- run   what

     c.   uSipho   u- **ya**- gijima **yini** phandle?
          AUG.1Sipho 1s- YA- run   what outside
          'Is Sipho running outside?'

     d.   uSipho   u- gijima phandle **yini**?
          AUG.1Sipho 1s- run   outside what
          'Is Sipho running outside?'

     e.   * uSipho   u- gijima **yini** phandle?
          AUG.1Sipho 1s- run   what outside

In (226), we see a similar pattern with objects. When the (non-agreeing) object appears to the left of *yini*, the verb takes the conjoint form. When the object agrees and appears to the right of *yini*, the disjoint is required.

(226) **Question particle (with object): cannot immediately follow conjoint verb**

    a.   uSipho   u- pheka iqanda **yini**?
           AUG.1Sipho 1s- cook   AUG.5egg what
           'Is Sipho cooking an egg?'

    b. *uSipho   u- pheka **yini** iqanda?
           AUG.1Sipho 1s- cook   what AUG.5egg

    c.   uSipho   u- **ya**- li- pheka **yini** iqanda?
           AUG.1Sipho 1s- YA- 5o- cook   what AUG.5egg
           'Is Sipho cooking the egg?'

Van der Spuy (1993) and Buell (2005, 2006) argue that the vocative and the question particle attach outside of *v*P. When these elements immediately follow the verb, therefore, nothing else that follows the verb can be *inside v*P. On a view of the conjoint/disjoint alternation that tracks constituency (or *v*P contents), the obligatoriness of the disjoint form in this configuration is expected, since the *v*P is empty.

Prosodic evidence

In addition to the syntactic markers of phrase edges discussed above, Van der Spuy (1993) and Buell (2005, 2006) also discuss some prosodic diagnostics for determining syntactic boundaries. One such diagnostic is *penultimate lengthening,* or *prepausal lengthening,* a process that lengthens the penultimate syllable of a word (and inserts a subsequent pause) at the right edge of a syntactic phrase boundary. I will discuss this process and subsequent research on it in more detail in section 4.2.4, but for now I will simply note the observations that bear on the conjoint/disjoint alternation. Since penultimate lengthening applies at the right edge of a syntactic phrase, Van der Spuy (1993) uses it to demonstrate that conjoint forms in Zulu have a different syntactic constituency than disjoint forms.

In a sentence where the verb appears in the conjoint, Van der Spuy (1993) shows that the verb itself cannot bear penultimate lengthening, suggesting that there is no right edge of any relevant syntactic phrase intervening between the verb and what follows:

(227) **Conjoint verb: no penultimate lengthening**

    a.   uSipho   u- gijima **pha:ndle**)
           AUG.1Sipho 1s- run   outside
           'Sipho is running outside.'

    b. *uSipho   u- **giji:ma**) phandle
           AUG.1Sipho 1s- run   outside

By contrast, when the verb appears in the disjoint form, penultimate lengthening *must* apply to the verb:

(228) **Disjoint verb: penultimate lengthening required**

    a.   uSipho   u- ya- **giji:ma**) phandle
           AUG.1Sipho 1s- YA- run   outside
           'Sipho is running outside.'

    b.   * uSipho   u- ya- gijima **pha:ndle**)
           AUG.1Sipho 1s- YA- run   outside

Van der Spuy (1993) takes this pattern as additional evidence that the disjoint verb does not form a syntactic constituent with following material.

Buell (2005) highlights a second prosodic process, *high tone shift*, that also targets the right edge of syntactic phrases. In a construction with an underlyingly toneless verb, when a preverbal morpheme introduces a high tone, the high tone shifts to the right, surfacing either on the penult or the antepenult of the verb. When the verb is phrase-final, the high tone shifts to the antepenult, but when the verb is phrase-medial, the high tone shifts all the way to the penult. This shift correlates with the conjoint/disjoint alternation: conjoint forms allow high tone shift to the penult, while disjoint forms require the high tone to surface on the antepenult. In the following examples, the noun class 2 subject agreement morpheme *bá-* has an underlying high tone, in contrast to the first person singular *ngi-*. With the low-tone verb *gijima* 'run', the high tone of *bá-* shifts to the antepenult of a disjoint verb, as in (229b), but all the way to the penult of a conjoint verb, as in (230):

(229) **High tone shift with disjoint verb**

    a. /ngi- ya- gijima/ → ngì- yà- gìjì:mà
        1SG- YA- run
        'I run.'

    b. /**bá**- ya- gijima/ → bà- yà- gíji:ma
        2s- YA- run
        'They run.'   (Buell, 2005, ex. (117))

(230) **High tone shift with conjoint verb**

    /bá- gijima nge-   jubane/ → bà- gìjímà ngejuba:ne
    2s- run   with.AUG 5speed
    'They run fast.'   (Buell, 2005, ex. (119))

As with the penultimate lengthening evidence, this tonal evidence indicates that Zulu has a systematic means of marking the right edge of certain prosodic constituents.[5] When these prosodic boundaries fall on the verb itself, the disjoint morpheme typically appears; the conjoint form is used when the verb is not at the edge of a prosodic constituent. In the next subsection, I examine the strength of this prosodic correlation.

4.2.4 Against a Prosodic Account of the Conjoint/Disjoint Alternation

The evidence in section 4.2.3 shows a strong correlation between the conjoint/disjoint alternation and prosodic markers of the *v*P edge. The disjoint appears when the verb is the final element in a prosodic phrase, while the conjoint appears when the verb is not at the edge of a prosodic phrase. Given this correlation, it is tempting to consider the conjoint/disjoint alternation as merely another marker of the prosodic phrase. In this subsection, I present novel data to show that we can in fact distinguish the conjoint/disjoint alternation from purely prosodic processes.

Cheng and Downing (2009) argue specifically that prosodic phrase boundaries in Zulu occur at the right edges of *v*Ps and CPs. They identify the prosodic boundary that the conjoint/disjoint alternation seems to align with as the right edge of *v*P. They tie this observed correlation between prosodic and syntactic phrases in Zulu into the cross-linguistic tendency for prosodic phrases to align with syntactic phase boundaries (An, 2007; Ishihara, 2007; Kahnemuyipour, 2004; Kratzer and Selkirk, 2007, among others). If the conjoint/disjoint alternation is merely another expression of the prosodic boundary of *v*P, we would expect it to consistently pattern with prosodic processes. Here I discuss two processes that allow us to separate the conjoint/disjoint alternation from the processes outlined in section 4.2.3: the behavior of clitics and the behavior of shared objects in coordination.

First, as Buell (2005) points out, certain *wh-* enclitics in Zulu form a single prosodic word with the verb. As Buell (2005) and Cheng and Downing (2009) describe, the prosodic phrase markers discussed above typically fall on the final prosodic word in a particular prosodic phrase. If the disjoint morpheme is merely a prosodic phrase marker that appears on the verb when it is final in the prosodic phrase, we would expect it to appear in constructions where the verb and its *wh-* clitic are not followed by other material. Buell (2005) shows that contrary to this expectation, the *conjoint* is required in these cases:

(231)   *wh-* **clitics: final prosody, conjoint verb**

    a.   ba- dlala:-phi?
           2s- play-   where
           'Where are they playing?'

---

5. As Zeller et al. (in preparation) note, this type of prosodic process is robust across all tenses in Durban Zulu, not just those that have a morphologically marked conjoint/disjoint alternation.

b. * ba- ya- dlala- phi?
   2s- YA- play- where

c. u- fundisa:- ni?
   2SG- teach- what
   'What do you teach?'

d. * u- ya- fundisa- ni?
   2SG- YA- teach- what

(Buell, 2005, adapted from ex. (255))

In (231), the *wh*-clitics form part of the same prosodic word as the verb, as indicated by penultimate lengthening, but the conjoint form is required. The data in (231) show that the disjoint does not uniformly appear on the verb when it is the final *prosodic* word in the phrase, but they do not rule out an account in which the disjoint morpheme appears on the verb when it is the final *lexical* word in the phrase. If we look beyond the *wh*-clitics that Buell considers, however, we find more striking evidence against a simple prosodic or lexical finality account. The relevant contrast emerges if we compare the behavior of the *wh*- clitics to the behavior of another clitic, *-ke* 'so, then'. While *-ke* also forms a prosodic word with the verb, again illustrated by the penultimate lengthening in (232), and acts as a unit for the purpose of phrase-final prosodic markers, in these constructions, it is the *disjoint*—and not the conjoint—that is required:

(232) **Non-*wh* clitics: final prosody, disjoint required**

a. ngi- ya- hamba:- ke
   1SG- YA- go- KE
   'So I'm going.'

b. * ngi- hamba- ke
   1SG- go- KE

We can conclude from these differences between *wh*-clitics and *-ke* with respect to the conjoint/disjoint alternation that we cannot predict the choice of conjoint or disjoint form simply from whether the verb is the final prosodic (or lexical) word or not. By contrast, markers of prosodic boundaries such as penultimate lengthening or high tone shift *do* simply track the final prosodic word boundary and are insensitive to the appearance—and type—of clitics on the prosodic word that contains the verb stem.

I return to the differing behavior of the two clitic types later in section 4.4.3, but for now I simply highlight the fact that both clitic types trigger identical prosodic behavior but different behavior with respect to the conjoint/disjoint alternation.

A second way in which the behavior of the disjoint morpheme differs from the behavior of markers of prosodic phrase finality emerges from the behavior of certain coordination constructions in Zulu. Typically, the first member of a pair of coordinated verb phrases in Zulu has a prosodic boundary at its right edge:

(233) **Coordination: first member has prosodic boundary at right edge**

a. ngi- ya- cu:la) futhi ngi- ya- da:nsa)
    1SG- YA- sing   and 1SG- YA- dance
    'I sing and I dance.'

b. * ngi- cula futhi ngi- ya- dansa
    1SG- sing and 1SG- YA- dance

(234) bà- yà- gíjì:mà) futhi ba- dlala ibhola
       2S- YA- run   and 2S- play AUG.5ball
       'They run and they play soccer.'

The first verb in the coordination constructions in (233) and (234) behaves as though it were final in a prosodic constituent: it receives penultimate lengthening, which is consistent with the right edge of a prosodic boundary, and in (234), the underlying high tone of the subject marker shifts to the antepenult, as expected for a prosodic phrase-final verb. The verb is also required to appear with disjoint morphology, which, as we have seen, correlates with a verb that is final in *v*P.

With a transitive verb in the first conjunct, we still see a prosodic phrase boundary at the end of the first conjunct—on the *object*, which is the final prosodic word in the phrase. As expected, the conjoint form of the verb is required here:

(235) a. ba- dlala ibho:la   ) futhi ba- ya- gijima
          2S- play AUG.5ball   and 2S- YA- run
          'They play soccer and they run.'

b. * ba- ya- dlala ibhola   futhi ba- ya- gijima
    2S- YA- play AUG.5soccer and 2S- YA- run

To summarize, so far we have seen that the first conjunct in coordinated structures in Zulu behaves as though there is a prosodic boundary at its right edge: the final prosodic word in the conjunct receives a prosodic phrase boundary and the verb requires the conjoint form if it is not final in the first conjunct, but disjoint form if it is.

Zulu also allows coordinated verb phrases to share a single object, which is realized inside the second conjunct.[6] In these constructions, the verb in

---

6. I do not assume any particular analysis of these shared object constructions. For the purposes of this discussion, we can compare the prosodic and morphological properties to other conjoined verb phrases without any deeper understanding.

the first conjunct still receives a prosodic phrase boundary, but appears in the *conjoint* form, despite being the final prosodic word in the phrase:

(236) **Shared object: prosodic boundary in first conjunct, conjoint required**

ngi-buk-**e**:la   ) futhi (ngi-phinde) ngi-dlal-e   ibho:la   )
1SG-watch-APPL) and 1SG-again   1SG-play-SJC AUG.5soccer
'I watch and I (also) play soccer.'

In (236), the shared object *ibhola* 'soccer' appears in the second conjunct, where it receives a prosodic phrase boundary. In the first conjunct, the verb is marked with an object-introducing applicative marker, indicating that it shares *ibhola* with the second conjunct. The first verb must appear in the *conjoint* form, even though it still behaves as though it is at the edge of a prosodic phrase, which as we've seen, typically induces a disjoint morpheme. I return this construction and its implications in section 4.5 to argue that in contrast to agreeing *v*P-external objects, the shared object in the coordination construction is available as a goal throughout the entire syntactic derivation.

To summarize the evidence in this subsection, we have now seen two ways in which the distribution of the conjoint/disjoint alternation differs from that of prosodic phrase markers such as penultimate lengthening or high tone shift. Both the clitic data and the coordination data show that even when the verb behaves prosodically as though it is the final prosodic word in the phrase, there are cases where the conjoint form, rather than the disjoint form, is required.

4.2.5 The Conjoint/Disjoint Alternation as a Marker of Syntactic Constituency

Given the evidence that despite the close correlation between disjoint morphology and prosodic markers that correlate with the *v*P edge, the disjoint morpheme does not have the same distribution as prosodic phrase boundaries, we can conclude (following Buell, 2005, 2006) that the conjoint/disjoint alternation is purely a reflection of *syntactic* structure. Buell (2005, 2006) characterizes the conjoint/disjoint alternation as a reflection of the syntactic constituent that contains the verb. The conjoint form appears when the verb is phrase-medial in its constituent, while the disjoint appears when the verb is final in its constituent, as we will see shortly. In this chapter, I instead model this distribution in terms of a syntactic agreement relationship—exactly like the licensing mechanism that I proposed in chapter 3. The head responsible for the conjoint/disjoint alternation, again L, has *v*P as its syntactic search domain. When it finds phrasal material to agree with in *v*P, it spells out as Ø (the conjoint). When it fails to find phrasal material, the derivation converges

(Preminger, 2010, 2011), but the head L spells out as -*ya*-, marking the failure.[7]

(198)   **Conjoint/disjoint: basic proposal**

a. ku- ya- banda
   17s- YA- be.cold
   'It's cold.'

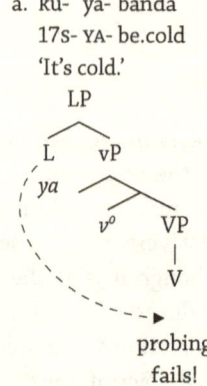

probing
fails!

b. ku- pheka uSipho
   17s- cook AUG.1Sipho
   'Sipho's cooking.'

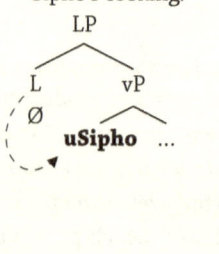

We can contrast this approach with Buell's own approach. As I will show below, when we take into account some new prosodic evidence, we are forced to conclude that the conjoint/disjoint alternation cannot simply be modeled in terms of surface constituency.

The syntactic analysis that Buell (2005, 2006) adopts is based on the claim that a certain syntactic constituent in Zulu, which he calls AuxP (and identifies as the syntactic phrase headed by the final vowel),[8] is required to contain "heavy (phrasal) overt material." This AuxP is dominated by the phrase that houses the conjoint/disjoint morphology, which Buell calls *ya*P. Buell claims that the macrostem of the verb always raises to Spec,*ya*P *unless* such movement would leave the lower AuxP empty. When the VP raises into Spec,*ya*P, the head of *ya*P remains null, due to the Doubly Filled Spec Filter (Koopman, 1996), which yields the conjoint form. When the VP remains inside AuxP, the head of *ya*P is able to be overtly realized, yielding the disjoint form. Buell's proposed structure is illustrated in the trees below:

---

7. As we saw earlier in the chapter, perfective verb forms are marked in both the conjoint (-*é*) and the disjoint (-*ile*), suggesting that L marks the distinction between successful and unsuccessful probing in different ways across the different tense/aspect paradigms.

8. Recall the discussion of verb position from chapter 2. Because the verb always precedes all *v*P-internal elements and shows evidence of head movement under other diagnostics, it has clearly itself evacuated *v*P to a higher position. For Buell, that position is (minimally) a phrase above *v*P he identifies as AuxP. As I established in chapter 2, I continue to abstract away from this verb movement, so trees in this chapter will not indicate a moved position for the verb.

(237) a. uSipho   u- ya- cul- a
           AUG.1Sipho 1S- YA- sing- FV
           'Sipho is singing.'

     b. uSipho   u- cul- a ingoma
           AUG.1Sipho 1S- sing- FV AUG.9song
           'Sipho is singing a song.'

(238) **Conjoint/disjoint analysis: Buell (2005)**

    a. Disjoint construction (Buell, 2005, ex. (310a))

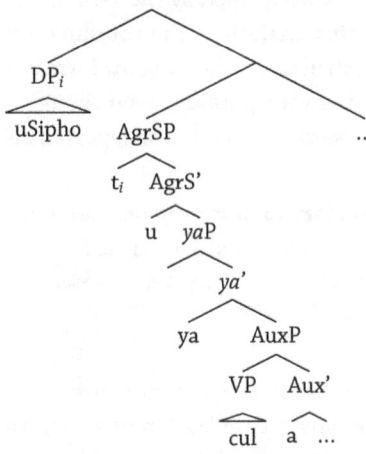

    b. Conjoint construction (Buell, 2005, ex. (311))

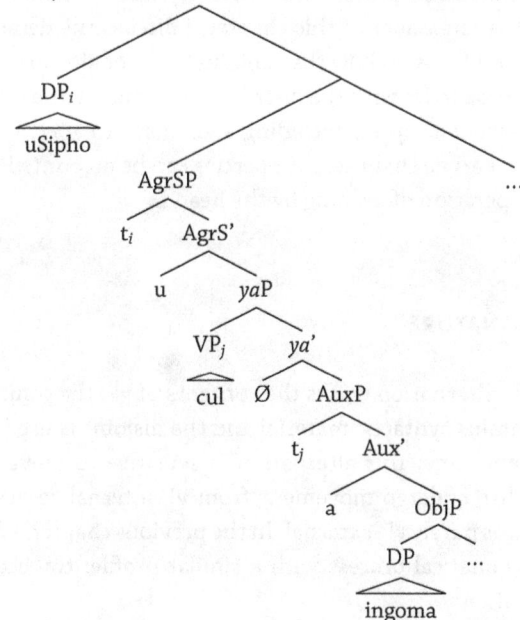

Though Buell (2005) explicitly argues against a prosodic account of the conjoint/disjoint alternation, his analysis is in fact phonological in nature. The contrast between conjoint and disjoint boils down to a requirement that the AuxP in the structures above be realized with overt (phrasal) phonological content. It is not immediately clear how this requirement should treat the *wh*-clitic data that Buell himself introduces, illustrated above in (231). In these examples, despite the fact that the clitic is part of the same phonological word as the stem, the verb nevertheless takes the conjoint form, which on Buell's analysis is consistent with it raising into *ya*P. On his analysis, then the *wh*-clitic must therefore both "count" as heavy phonological content inside AuxP but also be part of the phonological word formed by the verb.

Perhaps more problematic for this analysis is the coordination data discussed above in (236). In these constructions, the conjoint form is used in the first conjunct of the two coordinated verb phrases, even though the shared object is *overtly* realized only in the second conjunct, as repeated below:

(236) **Shared object: prosodic boundary in first conjunct, conjoint required**

ngi-buk-**e:**la   ) futhi (ngi-phinde) ngi-dlal-e   ibho:la   )
1SG-watch-APPL) and 1SG-again   1SG-play-SJC AUG.5soccer
'I watch and I (also) play soccer.'

Based on these facts, I conclude that the conjoint/disjoint alternation cannot be directly tied to the phonological realization of a construction—in particular, to whether an element is phonologically overt—and argue instead that it should be understood purely in terms of syntactic relationships, as outlined above. In the remainder of this chapter, I discuss the details of this analysis. In particular, I focus on how the conjoint/disjoint alternation shares numerous syntactic properties with the distribution of augmentless nominals discussed in the previous chapter, including sensitivity to specific types of syntactic movement. I argue that these properties can be accounted for using the same syntactic operation of probing by the head L.

4.3 A FAMILIAR SIGNATURE

The conjoint/disjoint alternation tracks the contents of vP: the conjoint form is used when vP contains syntactic material and the disjoint is used when vP is empty. At the same time, this alternation is sensitive to movement. As we saw, elements that undergo movement from vP-internal to vP-external positions are treated as purely vP-external. In the previous chapter, I discussed an independent grammatical process with a similar profile: the licensing of augmentless nominals.

Recall that augmentless nominals are restricted to syntactic positions within *v*P. In (239), we see that the augmentless subject *muntu* is licensed when it appears in a postverbal, *v*P-internal position, but not when it moves to a preverbal *v*P-external position. However, as (240) illustrates, when an ungrammatical preverbal augmentless subject further raises to *v*P-internal object position in the higher clause, the sentence is grammatical.

(239)   **Augmentless nominals licensed within *v*P**

    a.   a- ngi- sho- ngo   [ukuthi ku- fik-e   **muntu**]
         NEG- 1SG- say- NEG.PAST that   17s- arrive-PFV 1person
         'I didn't say that anyone came.'

    b. *a- ngi- sho- ngo   [ukuthi **muntu** u- fik-ile]
         NEG- 1SG- say- NEG.PAST that   1person 1s- arrive-PFV

(240)   **Raising-to-object licenses augmentless nominals**

    a. *a- ngi- fun- i   [ukuthi **muntu** a-   pheke iqanda]
         NEG- 1SG- want- NEG that   1person 1sJC- cook AUG.5egg

    b. a- ngi- fun- i   **muntu**$_i$ [ukuthi t$_i$ a-   pheke iqanda]
         NEG- 1SG- want- NEG 1person that   1sJC- cook AUG.5egg
         'I don't want anyone to cook an egg.'

Furthermore, in simple intransitives and monotransitives, an augmentless nominal must be the highest nominal within *v*P: when both the subject and object are postverbal, only the subject may be augmentless, as in (241a).

(241)   a. ✓ **VSO   –augment   +augment**
         a- ku- phek- anga   muntu **i**qanda
         NEG- 17s- cook- NEG.PST 1person AUG.5egg
         'Nobody cooked an egg.'

    b. * **VSO   –augment   –augment**
         *a- ku- phek- anga   muntu qanda
         NEG- 17s- cook- NEG.PST 1person 5egg

    c. * **VSO   +augment   –augment**
         a- ku- phek- anga   **u**muntu   qanda
         NEG- 17s- cook- NEG.PST AUG.1person 5egg

Crucially, just as with the conjoint/disjoint alternation, it is not enough for an augmentless nominal to *start out* inside *v*P. As (242) also illustrates, movement to a preverbal position, without subsequent raising-to-object, causes ungrammaticality:

(242) **Movement to *v*P-external position ungrammatical**

    a.   ngeke ku- fundise **muntu**
          never 17s- teach.SJC 1person
          'Nobody will ever teach.'

    b. *ngeke **muntu** a- fundise
          never 1person 1s- teach.SJC

The conjoint/disjoint alternation and the distribution of augmentless nominals thus have a similar profile: both involve elements that are within *v*P, and in both cases the grammatical operation is sensitive to elements that are inside *v*P at a point *after* movement of subjects and objects occurs. In other words, at a glance, in both cases the *surface* configuration seems to be relevant, as Buell (2005) tried to capture. However, as we saw in the previous section, we can identify constructions, where the conjoint/disjoint alternation does not merely track surface configuration. I return to the issue of movement in section 4.5 to examine how we can account for these surface-oriented tendencies for both phenomena.

In this section, I will show that we can understand both of these puzzles if we assume that a single head is responsible for both. As discussed in chapter 3, the participation of *v*P-internal subjects in both of these processes suggests that the probing head, L, must be immediately *above* *v*P (or VoiceP in the causative construction). I have proposed that the conjoint/disjoint alternation is a record of the probing operation. If the probe finds a target, it spells out as the conjoint, while if it *fails* to find a target, it spells out as the disjoint. This same probe, L, licenses augmentless nominals. The need for licensing by L causes augmentless nominals to surface only in the most local position to the probe, making them the highest nominals within *v*P. Augmented nominals, on the other hand, are inherently licensed and thus do not require licensing by L. This basic pattern is schematized in (243) and (244) below:

(243)

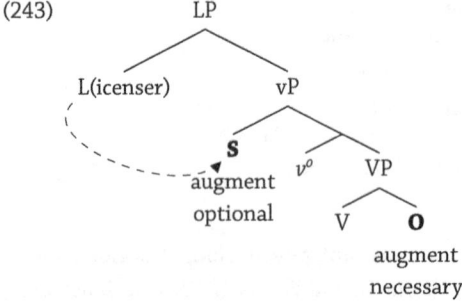

(244)

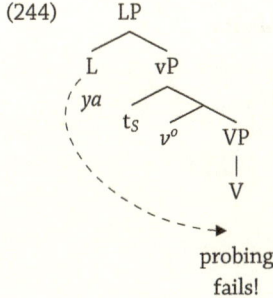

probing
fails!

The mechanics of this analysis depends on a particular understanding of the relationships between probes and goals. First, as I have mentioned above, to capture the conjoint/disjoint alternation in terms of probing, Agreement operations must be able to fail without causing a crash (Preminger, 2009b, 2010, 2011, 2014). Second, the relationship between the probe, L, and both augmented and augmentless nominals suggests that case relationships must have the potential to be one-sided (Ndayiragije, 1999; Legate, 2005). In the following subsection, I address these issues in more detail.

4.3.1 Asymmetric Probe–Goal Relationships

As we have seen, it is crucial to the analysis I propose here that the failure to find a goal by L does not yield a crash. Preminger (2009b, 2010, 2011, 2014) argues that it is in fact *not* obligatory for a probing head to successfully undergo Agreement in order for a derivation to be grammatical. However, Agree itself is not optional: a head obligatorily probes and thus will always Agree if a goal is present. As long as probing is attempted, the derivation can yield a grammatical output even if a probe fails to find a goal.

We can understand the Zulu conjoint/disjoint pattern in terms of this proposal. The head responsible for the conjoint/disjoint alternation probes the *v*P for an XP to agree with. When the *v*P is empty, and L thus lacks a goal, the derivation still converges, as predicted by Preminger. In Zulu present tense constructions, we see a morphological marker of this failure: where Agree does not occur, the probing head spells out as *-ya-*, rather than Ø. While I attach no particular import to the fact that it is the *failure* of Agree that is morphologically marked in this case, Preminger (p.c.) notes that this pattern is attested elsewhere, as in English verbal agreement morphology, where the default (which Preminger argues can arise as the *absence* of agreement) is overt *-s*, while true agreement with first and second person arguments is null.

(245) **Failure to Agree by L: no *v*P-internal arguments**

ku- ya- banda
17s- YA- be.cold
'It's cold.'

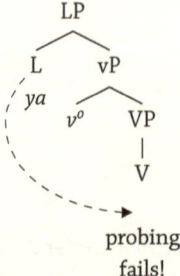

probing
fails!

On the other side of asymmetric probing relationships is the issue of how potential goals respond to probing. Ndayiragije (1999) argues that some *goals* can be probed in Bantu even when they do not need to undergo Agree, as I discussed in chapter 3. For Ndayiragije, nominals that don't require case in Bantu can still be goals, and not merely interveners, of case probing without causing a crash. Similarly, Legate (2005) argues that nominals that are inherently cased in Warlpiri can occur in positions where structural case is assigned. This type of configuration is exactly what arises on my account of these two puzzles in Zulu. Though augmentless nominals do require probing by L, *augmented* nominals apparently do not. However, it appears that though augmented nominals do not *require* licensing by the L head, they are licit targets for L, since their presence triggers the conjoint form of the predicate.[9]

(246) **Probing by L succeeds: postverbal subject**

ku- fundise **uMthuli**
17s- teach.PFV 1person
'Mthuli taught.'

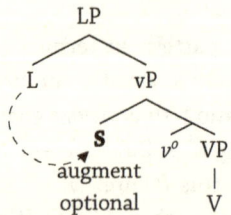

augment
optional

9. In section 4.5.1, and again in chapter 5, I return to the question of why augmented nominals can act as goals for L. I suggest that though the augment, which indepenently provides licensing, can coincide with structural licensing from L, it in fact enters the derivation *after* L has probed, so at the point when L probes, all nominals are in fact augmentless.

The fact that augmentless nominals, on the other hand, *do* require structural licensing by L allows us to understand the fact that they are only licensed as the highest nominal inside *v*P. If L, the head responsible for the conjoint/disjoint alternation, is also responsible for structural case, an augmentless nominal must be its most local potential target in order to be licensed. The presence of a higher nominal will thus always prevent a lower augmentless nominal from being licensed.

(247) **Augmentless nominal must be most local to L**

    a. √**VSO**   **–augment**   **+augment**
       a-   ku- phek- i   muntu iqanda
       NEG- 17s- cook- NEG 1person AUG.5egg
       'Nobody is cooking an egg.'

    b. *****VSO**   **+augment**   **–augment**
       a-   ku- phek- i   **u**muntu qanda
       NEG- 17s- cook- NEG 1person 5egg

    c. *****VSO**   **–augment**   **–augment**
      * a-   ku- phek- i   muntu qanda
       NEG- 17s- cook- NEG 1person 5egg

(248)

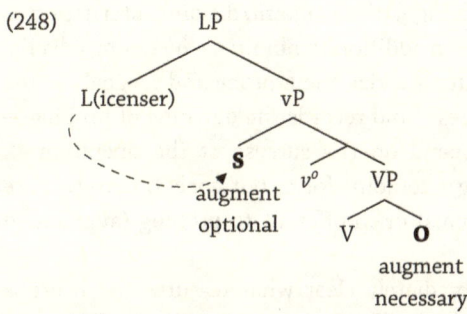

This type of asymmetry, where a *goal* requires a specific Agree relationship to hold, while the *probe* does not, is also discussed by Preminger (2011). Preminger shows that a probe that checks [participant] features in Kichean Mayan languages need not undergo Agree. Nominals that bear [participant] features, on the other hand, must be licensed via Agree with the [participant] probe (Person Licensing Condition, Béjar and Rezác, 2003).

The evidence in Zulu of asymmetrical relationships between the head L and its potential goals seems to be another case of the asymmetrical probe–goal patterns discussed above. While L is responsible for case-licensing augmentless nominals, it does not specifically probe for an augmentless nominal, instead interacting with any XP it finds within vP, yielding the conjoint/disjoint patterns that we have observed. In addition, L will not cause a crash whether or not it finds a goal. The conjoint/disjoint alternation reflects whether L has successfully Agreed but allows the derivation to converge either way. On the other hand, augmentless nominals that are not checked by L *do* cause a crash and thus must be local to L.

4.4 THE NATURE OF L AS A PROBE

On the analysis that I have developed in this chapter, conjoint/disjoint morphology spells out the head L, which probes the vP in every derivation. I have proposed that conjoint morphology is the result of a successful Agreement/licensing operation for L, while disjoint morphology results when L fails to find a goal to Agree with. I have not addressed the question of what L probes for in any detail, though the picture that emerges from the discussion of the conjoint/disjoint alternation is somewhat different from the simplest conclusions one could draw from the augmentless nominal licensing discussion in the previous chapter. I argued in chapter 3 that augmentless nominals arguments *must* be licensed by L; augmented nominals do not require L-licensing, but can intervene as goals when L probes. As we saw in section 4.2 of this chapter, though, the conjoint/disjoint alternation is sensitive to other types of phrases in addition to nominals, including adverbs and locatives. We can therefore characterize the L probe and its goals in the following way: L obligatorily probes—and records the outcome of probing—but grammaticality does not depend on the success of the operation. L treats all goals the same, yielding a conjoint form, but goals themselves are either needy (augmentless nominals) or indifferent to probing (augmented nominals, locatives, adverbs).

In other words, it is not immediately clear what features the L probe is relativized to. As we've seen, Zulu is a language that has rich person, number, and noun class agreement in the subject and object agreement paradigms. By contrast, neither the conjoint/disjoint alternation nor the syntactic restrictions on augmentless nominals overtly reflect any of these phi-features via agreement morphology. It also appears that the L probe is not sensitive to an argument/non-argument distinction. In (216), repeated below, the presence of a non-argumental locative inside vP triggers conjoint morphology and in (249) an adverb can also trigger the conjoint:

(216) **Location reading: conjoint**
      Q: uMfundo   w- enza:- ni?
        AUG.1Mfundo 1s- do-   what?
        'What is Mfundo doing?

A: uMfundo u- gijima **esito:lo**
AUG.1Mfundo 1s- run LOC.AUG.7store
'Mfundo is running in the store.'

(249) uSipho u- gijima **kakhu:lu**
AUG.1Sipho 1s- run a.lot
'Sipho runs a lot.'

Again, this behavior of these non-nominal elements suggests that the conjoint/disjoint alternation is not distinguishing nominals from non-nominals.[10] While this result is unproblematic in for an analysis such as that of Buell (2005), which depends purely on phonological weight inside a particular domain, it requires extra explanation in a theory based on syntactic Agree, such as the one I propose here.

In this section, I look more closely at the behavior of these non-nominal elements that participate in the conjoint/disjoint alternation, focusing first on CPs and then on locatives and adverbs. I will argue that while these categories may seem to have little in common with nominals at first glance, there are two different ways in which they behave as though they contribute an accessible nominal goal for L to the structure.

4.4.1 The Conjoint/Disjoint Alternation and Clausal Complements

In this subsection, I argue that the behavior of CPs parallels the behavior of nominals in a way that suggests that they can interact with the L probe in exactly as nominals do. From this stance, it is unremarkable that CPs participate in the conjoint/disjoint alternation. CPs inside vP trigger conjoint morphology, while those that appear outside vP trigger disjoint forms. Once this observation is established, I will show that not only do CPs show the same basic sensitivity to the conjoint/disjoint alternation as nominals, but certain CPs, such as those headed by *ukuthi*, can also trigger agreement on the verb in the same fashion as nominals. This agreement has the predicted result that agreeing CPs must dislocate. I will return to this property of CPs in chapter 6, where I discuss raising-to-subject constructions.

10. One measure in which it is difficult to directly compare the behavior of nominals and non-nominals is in terms of their status as intervenors. In the constructions that I have examined, speakers generally reject adverbs and locatives that are positioned between the verb and a subject or object nominal—regardless of whether the nominal bears an augment—so the question of whether an adverb of locative blocks augmentless nominal licensing remains open. In the next section, and again in chapter 5, we'll see some constructions where certain CPs and oblique adjuncts require the same type of licensing as augmentless nominals. As we will see, in these circumstances, augmented nominals do act as intervenors for licensing and the constructions are only grammatical when these CPs and adjuncts are highest in vP.

Next I will show that the complementizer *sengathi* has a different distribution from *ukuthi*. I show that CPs headed by *sengathi* must remain inside *v*P, and must furthermore be the *highest* element within *v*P—exactly like the augmentless nominals we saw in the previous chapter. Given this distribution, it appears that CPs interact with the L head in exactly the same manner as nominals: all CPs are licit targets for L probing, but only a subset of CPs, those headed by *sengathi*, require probing by L in order to be licensed.[11] These parallels between CPs and nominals are illustrated in table 4.1 on the following page. In light of these similarities, both in terms of the conjoint/disjoint alternation and in terms of other properties—such as agreement and structural licensing—I will conclude that CPs share the relevant properties of nominals that allow them to act as goals for L.

For the nominal arguments discussed earlier in this chapter, subject or object agreement with the argument correlates with displacement of the associated argument to a *v*P-external position, as we saw in chapter 2. Agreed-with nominals appear outside of *v*P, which can in turn yield disjoint morphology if the *v*P becomes empty as a result of such movement. Similarly, certain clausal complements in Zulu are able to control object agreement on the main predicate. When a CP complement agrees with the verb, it must appear outside the *v*P, triggering disjoint morphology:

(250) a. ngi- ya- **ku**- cabanga [ukuthi uMlungisi   u- ya- bhukuda manje]
           1SG- YA- 17O- think   that   AUG.1Mlungisi 1s- YA- swim   now
           'I think that Mlungisi is swimming now.'

       b. *ngi- **ku**- cabanga [ukuthi uMlungisi   u- ya- bhukuda manje]
           1SG- 17O- think   that   AUG.1Mlungisi 1s- YA- swim   now
           'I think that Mlungisi is swimming now.'

While nominal arguments require agreement with *v*P-external clausal complements, however, clausal complements in Zulu also allow for the main verb to appear in either the conjoint or the disjoint form *without* agreement, as we see for full CP complements in (251) and for infinitival complements in (252).

11. This difference is perhaps due to the different morphological makeups of the complementizers. While they are both based built from the same verbal stem *-thi* 'say', *ukuthi* is inflected like an inifinitival clause—or augmented class 15/17 nominal. By contrast, *sengathi* is inflected with aspect and mood morphology and does not bear anything like an augment vowel. While we cannot say that *sengathi* is merely an unaugmented form of *ukuthi*, the fact that it requires licensing is perhaps linked to its lack of an initial vowel.

Table 4.1. DISTRIBUTION OF NOMINALS AND CPS WITH RESPECT TO CONJOINT/DISJOINT

	NOMINALS		CPs	
	Augmented	Augmentless	*ukuthi*-headed	*sengathi*-headed
	*v*P-internal OK triggers conjoint no agreement	*v*P-internal required triggers conjoint no agreement	*v*P-internal OK triggers conjoint no agreement	*v*P-internal required triggers conjoint no agreement
	*v*P-external OK triggers disjoint agreement required	**v*P-external (must be local to licenser)	*v*P-external OK triggers disjoint agreement optional	**v*P-external (must be local to licenser)

(251) a. ngi- cabanga [ukuthi uMlungisi   u- ya- bhukuda manje]
       1SG- think   that   AUG.1Mlungisi 1S- YA- swim   now
       'I think that Mlungisi is swimming now.'

       b. ngi- **ya**- cabanga [ukuthi uMlungisi   u- ya- bhukuda manje]
       1SG- YA- think   that   AUG.1Mlungisi 1S- YA- swim   now
       'I think that Mlungisi is swimming now.'

(252) a. ngi- funa uku- bhukuda
       1SG- want INF- swim
       'I want to swim.'

       b. ngi- **ya**- funa uku- bhukuda
       1SG- YA- want INF- swim
       'I want to swim.'

With subjunctive CPs, the complementizer *ukuthi* can optionally be omitted. Both forms of the CP—with and without the complementizer—are compatible with either the conjoint or the disjoint:

(253) a. ngi- funa [ukuthi uXolani   a-   win- e   umjaho]
       1SG- want that   AUG.1Xolani 1SJC- win- SJC AUG.3race
       'I want Xolani to win the race.'

       b. ngi- ya- funa [ukuthi uXolani   a-   win- e   umjaho]
       1SG- YA- want that   AUG.1Xolani 1SJC- win- SJC AUG.1race
       'I want Xolani to win the race.'

(254) a. ngi- funa [uXolani   a-   win- e   umjaho]
       1SG- want AUG.1Xolani 1SJC- win- SJC AUG.3race
       'I want Xolani to win the race.'

       b. ngi- ya- funa [uXolani   a-   win- e   umjaho]
       1SG- YA- want AUG.1Xolani 1SJC- win- SJC AUG.1race
       'I want Xolani to win the race.'

Just as we saw with subjects in chapter 2, the position of a CP in Zulu is tied to information structure. In out-of-the-blue contexts, speakers often do not show systematic preferences between the conjoint and disjoint forms given above. When part of the contents of the complement clause is in focus, however, speakers show a preference for the conjoint form:

(255) Q: u-   cabanga ukuthi uMlungisi   w- enza- ni   manje?
       2SG- think   that   AUG.1Mlungisi 1s- do-   what now?
       'What do you think Mlungisi is doing now?

       A: ngi- cabanga ukuthi u- ya- bhukuda manje
       1SG- think   that   1s- YA- swim   now
       'I think that he is swimming now.'

Speakers also prefer the conjoint form when the clausal complement is followed by a clausal adjunct:

(256) uMandla   u- bona [ukuthi ngi- ya- m- thanda] [uma ngi- mu- pha
    AUG.1Mandla 1s- see   that   1SG- YA- 1O- like   when 1SG- 1O- give
    izipho]
    AUG.8presents
    'Mandla sees that I like him when I give him presents.'

By contrast, speakers use the disjoint form in contexts where the matrix verb is in focus, as in (257) below, or where there is verum focus on the predicate, as in (258):

(257) Q: W- enza- ni   uMlungisi   manje?
        1s- do- what AUG.1Mlungisi now
        'What's Mlungisi doing now?'

     A: Ngi- **ya**- cabanga [ukuthi uMlungisi   u- ya- bhukuda manje] ... kodwa
        1SG- YA- think   that   AUG.1Mlungisi 1s- YA- swim   now   ... but
        a-   ng- azi   kahle.
        NEG- 1SG- know well
        'I THINK that Mlungisi is swimming now... but I don't really know.'

(258) Q: UMandla   a-   ka- bon- i   ukuthi ngi- ya- m- thanda, a-   ngi- thi?
        AUG.1Mandla NEG- 1s- see- NEG that   1SG- YA- 1O- like   NEG- 1SG- say
        'Mandla doesn't see that I like him, does he?

     A: Cha, uMandla   u- **ya**- bona ukuthi u-   ya- m- thanda.
        no AUG.1Mandla 1s- YA- see   that   2SG- YA- 1O- like
        'No, he DOES see that you like him.'

Because the disjoint appears both in cases of verb focus and in cases of verum focus, it is sometimes used when the speaker wants to express doubt about the complement and sometimes when the speaker wants to express emphasis.

As we saw at the beginning of this section, both the full *ukuthi* CP complement and the infinitival complement are able to control object marking on the matrix verb, realized as *ku*. When *ku*- object marking occurs, only the disjoint form of the matrix verb is grammatical:

(259) a.   ngi- **ya**- **ku**- cabanga [ukuthi uMlungisi   u- ya- bhukuda manje]
        1SG- YA- 1?O- think   that   AUG.1Mlungisi 1s- YA- swim   now
        'I (do) think that Mlungisi is swimming now.'

      b.   * ngi- **ku**- cabanga [ukuthi uMlungisi   u- ya- bhukuda manje]
        1SG- 1?O- think   that   AUG.1Mlungisi 1s- YA- swim   now

(260) a. ngi- **ya- ku-** funa uku- bhukuda
1SG- YA- 17O- want INF- swim
'I (do) want to swim.'

b. *ngi- **ku-** funa uku- bhukuda
1SG- 17O- want INF- swim

With subjunctive CPs, the *ku-* object agreement construction is only possible with the overt complementizer *ukuthi*. When the complementizer is dropped, object agreement becomes ungrammatical:

(261) a. ngi- ya- ku- funa ukuthi uXolani a- win- e umjaho
1SG- YA- 17O- want that AUG.1Xolani 1SJC- win- SJC AUG.1race
'I (do) want Xolani to win the race.'

b. *ngi- ya- ku- funa uXolani a- win- e umjaho
1SG- YA- 17O- want AUG.1Xolani 1SJC- win- SJC AUG.1race

The dependence of object agreement on the presence of the overt complementizer suggests that the object marker reflects a direct agreement relationship with the complementizer (or the infinitival morphology) and is not merely a "default" morpheme, an issue I return to in chapter 6.

Just as we saw for indicative and infinitival complements, the *ku-* object agreement for subjunctive CPs requires the disjoint form of the verb:

(262) *ngi- ku- funa ukuthi uXolani a- win- e umjaho
1SG- 17O- want that AUG.1Xolani 1SJC- win- SJC AUG.1race

With these indicative, infinitival, and subjunctive clausal complements, then, it appears that agreement forces dislocation, yielding the disjoint form, just as in constructions with nominal arguments. Without agreement, these clausal complements may either remain in situ *or* dislocate, yielding the optionality that we saw above.

Not all clausal complements show such optionality, however. In contrast to these infinitival complements and CP complements introduced by *ukuthi*, CP complements introduced by *sengathi* require the conjoint form.

In CP complements of verbs like *bonakala* 'seem', *bona* 'see', or *fisa* 'wish', the complementizer *sengathi* 'as if' alternates with *ukuthi*, yielding meaning differences along the lines of those represented in (263) and (264) below. While *ukuthi* permits the disjoint with these verbs, *sengathi* does not:

(263) ***ukuthi: disjoint permitted***

a. uMandla u- bona [ukuthi ngi- ya- m- thanda]
AUG.1Mandla 1s- see that 1SG- YA- 1O- like
'Mandla sees that I like him.'

b. uMandla   u- ya- bona [ukuthi ngi- ya- m- thanda]
   AUG.1Mandla 1s- YA- see   that   1SG- YA- 1O- like
   'Mandla sees that I like him.'

(264) *sengathi*: conjoint required

a. uMandla   u- bona [sengathi ngi- ya- m- thanda]
    AUG.1Mandla 1s- see   as.if   1SG- YA- 1O- like
    'Mandla is of the opinion that I like him.' (implies that I don't)

b. * uMandla   u- ya- bona [sengathi ngi- ya- m- thanda]
    AUG.1Mandla 1s- YA- see   as.if   1SG- YA- 1O- like

In section 4.2.3 we saw independent evidence for determining whether elements are inside *v*P or not. By applying these diagnostics, we can see that the non-agreeing clausal complements that trigger the disjoint are attached outside *v*P, while those that trigger the conjoint are attached inside *v*P. We can conclude from these diagnostics that CPs introduced by *sengathi* must remain inside *v*P, in contrast to CPs introduced by *ukuthi* or without an overt complementizer.

(265) **Vocative insertion with *ukuthi* CP**

a. * uMandla   u- bona, Monwa, [ukuthi ngi- ya- m- thanda]
    AUG.1Mandla 1s- see   1Monwa that   1SG- YA- 1O- like

b. uMandla   u- ya- bona, Monwa, [ukuthi ngi- ya- m- thanda]
    AUG.1Mandla 1s- YA- see   1Monwa that   1SG- YA- 1O- like
    'Mandla sees, Monwa, that I like him.'

(266) *sengathi* CP: vocative insertion prohibited

a. * uMandla   u- (ya)- bona, Monwa, [sengathi ngi- ya- m- thanda]
    AUG.1Mandla 1s- (YA-) see   1Monwa as.if   1SG- YA- 1O- like
    intended: 'Mandla is of the opinion, Monwa, that I like him.'

b. uMandla   u- bona [sengathi ngi- ya- m- thanda], Monwa
    AUG.1Mandla 1s- see   as.if   1SG- YA- 1O- like   1Monwa
    'Mandla is of the opinion that I like him, Monwa.'

(267) **Q insertion with *ukuthi* CP**

a. * uMandla   u- (ya-) bona **yini** [ukuthi ngi- ya- m- thanda]
    AUG.1Mandla 1s- (YA-) see   what that   1SG- YA- 1O- like

b. uMandla   u- ya- bona **yini** [ukuthi ngi- ya- m- thanda]
    AUG.1Mandla 1s- YA- see   what that   1SG- YA- 1O- like
    'Does Mandla see that I like him?'

(268) *sengathi* CP: Q insertion prohibited

a. * uMandla   u- (ya) bona **yini** [sengathi ngi- ya- m- thanda]?
    AUG.1Mandla 1s- (YA-) see   what as.if   1SG- YA- 1O- like
    intended: 'Is Mandla of the opinion that I like him?'

b. uMandla   u- bona [sengathi ngi- ya- m- thanda] **yini**?
   AUG.1Mandla 1s- see as.if   1SG- YA- 1O- like   what
   'Is Mandla of the opinion that I like him?'

In the examples above, the CP complements headed by *sengathi* are required to remain within *v*P, which we can see from their inability to co-occur with the disjoint form of the matrix verb. The restriction on *sengathi* CPs goes beyond the requirement that they remain inside *v*P, however. If we attempt to combine CP complements with a *v*P-internal subject, we find that only *ukuthi* permits a low subject. A comparable construction with a *sengathi* clause is ungrammatical, as the contrast in (269) below illustrates:

(269) a. ku- bona uMandla   [ukuthi ngi- ya- m- thanda].
          17s- see AUG.1Mandla that   1SG- YA- 1O- like
          'MANDLA sees that I like him.'

       b. *ku- bona uMandla   [sengathi ngi- ya- m- thanda].
          17s- see AUG.1Mandla as.if   1SG- YA- 1O- like

The *sengathi* CPs show a similar restriction with raising-to-object verbs, again in contrast to *ukuthi* CPs. The optional raising-to-object verb *fisa*[12] 'wish' can either combine with an *ukuthi* (or null-complementizer) complement or with a *sengathi* complement:[13]

(270) a. ngi- fisa [**ukuthi** ubaba   a-   fik- e kusasa]
          1SG- wish that   AUG.1father 1SJC- arrive- SJC tomorrow
          'I wish that dad would arrive tomorrow.'

       b. ngi- fisa [**sengathi** ubaba   a-   nga- fika kusasa]
          1SG- with as.if   AUG.1father 1SJC- can- arrive tomorrow
          'I wish that dad would arrive tomorrow.'

While either complementizer is allowed when raising-to-object does not occur, only the *ukuthi* construction permits raising-to-object:

(271) a. ngi- fisa ubaba   [**ukuthi** a-   fik- e kusasa]
          1SG- wish AUG.1father that   1SJC- arrive- SJC tomorrow
          'I wish that dad would arrive tomorrow.'

12. In chapter 3, I reported on the behavior of *fisa* for speakers who do not allow it to function as a raising predicate. Here I report the judgments of those who do.

13. When *fisa* takes a *sengathi* complement, the embedded verb bears the possibility modal -*nga*- and receives a strongly counterfactual interpretation, in contrast to the *ukuthi* complement which takes a plain subjunctive complement and is not strongly counterfactual. I set aside these additional differences here.

b. *ngi- fisa ubaba   **[sengathi** a-   nga- fika   kusasa]
   1SG- wish AUG.1father as.if   1SJC- CAN- arrive tomorrow

We also find restrictions on *sengathi* clauses in adjunct position, which again contrast with the behavior of other clausal elements.

Small clause modifiers follow the familiar pattern of clausal complements – and of non-clausal adjuncts. As (272a) illustrates, this type of small clause typically triggers conjoint morphology on the main verb. In the new information context of (272), the disjoint form of the main verb is perceived as odd, as in (272b).

(272)   **Small clause new information: conjoint form**

a.   zo-nke izinsuku izingane   e-   zi- ningi zi- lala [zi-
      10-all 10days AUG.10children REL- 10s- many 10s- sleep 10PRT-
      lambile] lapha eThekwini
      hungry here LOC.5Durban
      'Every day, many children go to sleep hungry here in Durban.'

b.   # zo-nke izinsuku izingane   e-   zi- ningi zi- **ya**- lala [zi-
      10-all 10days AUG.10children REL- 10s- many 10s- YA- sleep 10PRT-
      lambile] lapha eThekwini
      hungry here LOC.5Durban

When we change the context to one where the small clause is old information and the main predicate receives verum focus, speakers to prefer the disjoint form on the main verb, as the exchange in (273) illustrates:

(273)   **Small clause old information: disjoint form**

A: Ngenxa   yomsebenzi   wa-   mi a-   yi- kho ingane
   because.of 9ASSOC.-AUG.1work 1ASSOC.- 1SG NEG- 9s- exist AUG.9child
   eThekwini   e-   lala [i-   lambile.]
   LOC.5Durban REL.9s- sleep 9PRT- hungry
   'Because of my work, there's no child in Durban who goes to sleep hungry.'

B: Hhayi-bo, zonke izinsuku izingane   e-   zi- ningi zi- **ya**- lala
   no   10-all 10days AUG.10children REL- 10s- many 10s- YA- sleep
   [zi-   lambile.]
   10PRT- hungry
   'No, every day, many children DO sleep hungry.'

While the small clause modifiers above typically trigger a conjoint main verb form, CP modifiers, such as the purpose clause in (274) and reason clause in (275), require a disjoint verb:

(274) a. uMfundo u- ya- shesha [ukuze a- fik- e nge-
     AUG.1Mfundo 1s- YA- hurry so.that 1SJC- arrive- SJC NGA.AUG-
     sikhathi e- kilasini]
     7time LOC- 5class.LOC
     'Mfundo is rushing to get to class on time.'

   b. *uMfundo u- shesha [ukuze a- fik- e nge- sikhathi
     AUG.1Mfundo 1s- hurry so.that 1SJC- arrive- SJC NGA.AUG- 7time
     e- kilasini]
     LOC- 5class.LOC

(275) a. ngi- ya- gijima [ngoba ngi- funa uku- fika nge- sikhathi]
     1SG- YA- run because 1SG- want INF- arrive NGA.AUG- 7time
     'I'm running because I want to arrive on time.'

   b. *ngi- gijima [ngoba ngi- funa uku- fika nge- sikhathi]
     1SG- run because 1SG- want INF- arrive NGA.AUG- 7time

The use of the disjoint form in these adjunct clause constructions is expected for elements that have a high attachment site. By contrast, *sengathi* CPs that function as modifiers must remain inside *v*P, just as *sengathi* complements did:

(276) a. u- (*ya-) khuluma sengathi u- phuz- ile
     1s- (*YA-) speak as.if 1s- drink- PFV
     'He's speaking like he's drunk.'

   b. u- (*ya-) hleka sengathi u- ya- qala uku- hleka
     1s- (*YA-) laugh as.if 1s- YA- start INF- laugh
     'He's laughing as if it's his first laugh ever.' (i.e., a lot)

Just as with *sengathi* complements, we see additional restrictions on these *sengathi* modifiers. While these modifiers are grammatical after an intransitive verb, they cannot follow a transitive predicate with a *v*P-internal object:

(277) a. *uMthuli u- dla **inyama** [sengathi u- ya- yi- qabuka]
     AUG.1Mthuli 1s- eat AUG.9meat as.if 1s- YA- 9O- discover
     intended: 'He's eating meat as if he's just discovered it.'

   b. inyama u- yi- dla [sengathi u- ya- yi- qabuka]
     AUG.9meat 1s- 9O- eat as.if 1s- YA- 9O- discover
     'He's eating meat as if he's just discovered it.'

   c. u- dla sengathi [inyama u- ya- yi- qabuka]
     1s- eat as.if AUG9meat 1s- YA- 9O- discover
     'He's eating as if he's just discovered meat.'

In (277a), we can see that the direct object cannot intervene between the verb and the *sengathi* CP. However, if the direct object *inyama* 'meat' moves out of the *v*P and controls object agreement, as in (277b), the sentence is grammatical. If *inyama* is instead realized inside the *sengathi* clause, as in (277c), the sentence is also grammatical. What both of these alternatives share is that the *sengathi* clause is able to appear immediately after the matrix verb, inside *v*P.

To summarize, I have shown in this section that *sengathi* CPs are required to appear inside *v*P, which in turn yields the conjoint form of the verb in all clauses in which they appear. This requirement holds whether the CP is introduced as a complement of the verb or as an adjunct. Furthermore, we saw that *sengathi* CPs cannot follow a nominal inside *v*P. In constructions that contain both an object and a *sengathi* CP, such as in raising-to-object and in modified clauses, the object *must* vacate the *v*P to leave the *sengathi* CP as the highest element.

This subsection illustrates that clausal elements behave in a parallel fashion to nominal elements with respect to the conjoint/disjoint alternation. When they appear inside *v*P, they trigger conjoint morphology, but movement out of *v*P—either co-occurring with object agreement *or* without the agreement—triggers disjoint morphology. While many CPs are grammatical in a variety of structural positions inside and outside of *v*P, those headed by the complementizer *sengathi* display structural restrictions akin to those that govern the distribution of augmentless nominals: *sengathi* CPs must appear inside *v*P and cannot follow a direct object within *v*P. These similarities are given in table 4.2 on the following page, repeated from above.

What we learn from this comparison of different CP behaviors is that CPs in Zulu (or perhaps more precisely their complementizer heads) show evidence of nominal-type behaviors. In particular, CPs appear to interact with phi-agreement and licensing processes a manner similar to Zulu nominals. While we don't see a single complementizer that shows both an ability to control phi-agreement *and* structural licensing sensitivity (i.e., one with an active augment contrast), the fact that we find both of these behaviors in the family of Zulu CPs makes their participation in the conjoint/disjoint alternation unsurprising: as we learned from the behavior of nominals, not all goals are "needy."

4.4.2 The Nature of Locative and Adverb Categories

In the previous subsection, we saw evidence that CPs behave in a manner that is akin to nominals. They are capable of controlling agreement in certain circumstances and a subset of these CPs, headed by the complementizer *sengathi*, are subject to the same licensing conditions that augmentless nouns face. In this section, I turn briefly to the nature of locatives and adverbs to illustrate a different way in which we find accessible nominal elements in these constructions.

Table 4.2. DISTRIBUTION OF NOMINALS AND CPS WITH RESPECT TO CONJOINT/DISJOINT

NOMINALS		CPs	
Augmented	Augmentless	*ukuthi*-headed	*sengathi*-headed
*v*P-internal OK triggers conjoint no agreement	*v*P-internal required triggers conjoint no agreement	*v*P-internal OK triggers conjoint no agreement	*v*P-internal required triggers conjoint no agreement
*v*P-external OK triggers disjoint agreement required	**v*P-external (must be local to licenser)	*v*P-external OK triggers disjoint agreement optional	**v*P-external (must be local to licenser)

Unlike the CPs discussed in the previous section, we do not find constructions in which adverbs control agreement in Zulu. This difference perhaps stems from the fact that adverbs are never *selected* by the predicate the way certain CPs are. Despite the absence of such evidence, the idea that adverbs and locatives are closely related to nouns is an old one in the literature on Bantu, and on Zulu in particular. For example, Nkabinde (1985) refers to them as "secondary" nouns. His argument is based on the fact that most adverbs in Zulu are formed from nouns that take locative or instrumental morphology:

(278) a. ngo-   kushesha
          NGA.AUG- 15speed
          'quickly'

       b. ngo-   buhlungu
          NGA.AUG- 14pain
          'painfully'

As I discuss in detail in chapter 5, the nominal components of such elements do seem to be visible to L in the syntactic derivation. Specifically, we see that the nominals *inside* these constructions subject to the same syntactic licensing conditions as argument nominals—and crucially are able to be licensed by L even though they are inside this prefixal morphology. As (279) shows, these prefixed oblique nominals must either be licensed by L as the highest element in *v*P or they must bear an augment:

(279) **Instrumental marked oblique: can be augmentless if highest in *v*P**

       a. ngi- bhala **nge-**   peni   (= nga+ipeni)
          1SG- write NGA.AUG- 5pen
          'I write with a pen.'

       b. a-   ngi- bhal- i   **nga-** peni
          NEG- 1SG- write- NEG NGA- 5pen
          'I don't write with any pen.'

(280) **Instrumental –AUG: must be highest in *v*P**

       a. u-Mfundo   u- bhala i-zincwadi **nge-**   peni   (nga+ipeni)
          AUG-1Mfundo 1s- write AUG-10letter NGA.AUG- 5pen
          'Mfundo writes letters with a pen.'

       b. *u-Mfundo   a-   ka-bhal- i   i-zincwadi **nga-** peni
          AUG-1Mfundo NEG- 1s- write- NEG AUG-10letter NGA- 5pen

       c. u-Mfundo   a-   ka-bhal- i   **nga-** peni i-zincwadi
          AUG-1Mfundo NEG- 1s- write- NEG NGA- 5pen AUG-10letter
          'Mfundo doesn't write letters with any pen.'

In short, the nominal components of these elements behave as though they are visible to the syntax, and show the same sensitivities to licensing that argument nominals face.

In addition to adverbs that are formed in the way described above, certain adverbs are formed from non-nominal stems, including adjective stems. These adverbs are prefixed by morphemes such as *ka-*, which Nkabinde (1985) analyzes as a (no longer productive) noun class prefix. In a discussion of adverbs formed from non-nominal stems in Zulu, Buell (2009) shows that such adverbs behave as though they have noun class 17 membership and that, like nominals, they are able to control possessive (associative) concord morphology, which tracks noun class:

(281) phakathi kw-   abantu
       inside   17ASSOC- AUG.2people
       'among the people'   (Buell, 2009, p. 23)

Given this type of construction, it is reasonable to conclude that adverbs in Zulu also have phi-features, or other accessible nominal properties. While their behavior is different from nominals and CPs, we do see multiple pieces of evidence that suggest that they share categorial or featural properties with nominals—or that such properties of the nominals that they contain are visible to outside syntactic processes. In particular, not only do we see that the nominals in such expressions are subject to familiar licensing restrictions that I argue are attributed to L, but we find that the adverbs themselves are capable of controlling class 17 associative morphology on nominals that they combine with. In short, as we discovered with Zulu CPs, a closer look at the adverb/locative class yields a similar conclusion: that all of these elements share some common features that may make them accessible to the L probe.

4.4.3 The Selectiveness of L

In the previous subsections, I argued that ostensibly non-nominal elements, such as CPs, adverbs, and locatives, all involve a nominal-(like) goal that is accessible to L head. At the same time, given the range of things that L is sensitive to, it is reasonable to ask whether there is any sort of selectiveness to different types of elements in its syntactic search domain. Here, I return to the issue of how different types of clitics behave with respect to the conjoint/disjoint alternation to explore the hypothesis that perhaps their differences can be attributed to whether they are potential goals for L in the first place. Despite the differing behavior of the two types of clitics—*wh*-clitics and *-ke*—I nevertheless conclude that there is insufficient evidence that any unambiguously vP-internal element is excluded from the class of possible goals for L.

As we saw in example (231), repeated below, *wh-* enclitics form a prosodic word with the verb but trigger a conjoint form:

(231)   *wh-* **clitics: final prosody, conjoint verb**

    a.   ba- dlala:- phi?
          2s- play- where
          'Where are they playing?'

    b.   * ba- ya- dlala- phi?
          2s- YA- play- where

    c.   u-   fundisa:- ni?
          2sG- teach-   what
          'What do you teach?'

    d.   * u-   ya- fundisa- ni?
          2sG- YA- teach- what

Buell (2005, adapted from ex. (255))

While this pattern is difficult to capture if we assume a prosodic account of the conjoint/disjoint alternation, it follows naturally from a syntactic account: the *wh-* clitic is syntactically present inside vP when L probes, which yields the predicted conjoint form.

By contrast, we saw in (232), repeated below, that the clitic *-ke*, which also forms a prosodic word with the verb, requires the disjoint form when the verb+clitic is phrase final:

(232)   *-ke* **clitic: final prosody, disjoint required**

    a.   ngi- ya- hamba:- ke
          1sG- YA- go-   KE
          'So I'm going.'

    b.   * ngi- hamba- ke
          1sG- go-   KE

The theory that I have developed in this chapter predicts that this difference is due to the fact that L finds a goal in the case of the *wh*-clitics but not in the case of *-ke*. As discussed above, the fact that L successfully finds a goal in the case of *wh*-clitics is unsurprising given that (non-clefted) *wh*-words in the language generally must appear inside vP. With *-ke*, we could imagine two possible reasons why L fails to find a goal: either the *-ke* clitic could be located syntactically outside of vP or it could simply not be a suitable goal for L.

Van der Spuy (1993) and Buell (2005) discussed elements such as vocatives and yes/no question particles that are reliable markers of the vP edge: we saw in section 4.2.3 that when these elements appear immediately after the verb, the disjoint form is required, but when something else intervenes between the verb and these elements, the conjoint is required.

(282) a. uSipho   u- *(**ya**-) gijima **Mama**   phandle
       AUG.1Sipho 1s- YA-   run   1mother outside
       'Sipho is running, Mom, outside.'

       b. uSipho   u- (*ya-) dlala ibhola   **Mama**   (phandle)
       AUG.1Sipho 1s- YA-   play AUG.5soccer 1mother (outside)
       'Sipho is playing soccer, Mom, outside.'

If -*ke* is syntactically located outside of *v*P, we might expect a similar distribution, with the presence of -*ke* on the verb requiring following elements to be dislocated. Unlike the vocatives and question particles, however, -*ke* does *not* require the dislocation.[14] In (283), we see that -*ke* can appear on a matrix verb in the conjoint form, while the question particle *yini* requires the disjoint form in an analogous construction in (283c).[15]

(283) a. Si- bong- e- **ke** ukuthi abantu   ba- zi- phath- e   kahle
       1PL- thank- PFV- KE that   AUG.2people 2s- REFL- care- PFV well
       'We are grateful that people took good care of themselves.'[16]

       b. *u- bong- e **yini** ukuthi abantu   ba- zi- phath- e   kahle
       1s- thank- PFV Q   that   AUG.2people 2s- REFL- care- PFV well
       intended: 'Was he thankful that people took good care of themselves?'

       c. u- bong- **ile yini** ukuthi abantu   ba- zi- phath- e   kahle
       1s- thank- PFV Q   that   AUG.2people 2s- REFL- care- PFV well
       'Was he thankful that people took good care of themselves?'

Similarly, in (284), -*ke* may appear on the verb followed by a non-agreeing, non-dislocated object, while the question particle *yini* requires that the following object agree with the verb:[17]

14. Most contexts in which the clitic -*ke* is appropriate tend to be contexts in which postverbal elements, such as objects, are old information and therefore dislocate for independent reasons. The constructions reported here involve less-common contexts where non-dislocation was permitted.

15. Recall that in the near past/perfective construction, -*ile* is the disjoint form, while -*e* is the conjoint. Buell (2005) discusses this parallelism in detail.

16. Source: <http://mapholoba.blogspot.com>, accessed April 10, 2012, confirmed by direct elicitation.

17. In these constructions, we cannot observe a contrast between conjoint and disjoint morphology because the morphological contrast disappears in the presence of negation. Instead, the only cues for object placement come from object agreement and relative position.

(284) a. a- ngi- thand- i- **ke** imifino
           NEG- 1SG- like- NEG- KE AUG.4vegetables
           'OK, so I don't like vegetables!'

       b. *a- wu- thand- i **yini** imifino?
           NEG- 2SG- like- NEG what AUG.4vegetables
           intended: 'Don't you like vegetables?'

       c. a- wu- yi- thand- i yini imifino?
           NEG- 2SG- 4O- like NEG what AUG.4vegetables
           'Don't you like vegetables?'

These constructions show that -*ke* does not demarcate a syntactic boundary in the same way that question particles and vocatives do. Instead, in these constructions, the choice between conjoint or disjoint form does not seem to take -*ke* into account. As I mentioned above, we could either interpret this fact as evidence that the clitic is syntactically present inside *v*P when L probes, but that it is not a potential goal for L, or that it is not syntactically located in *v*P.

The function of -*ke* seems to be discourse related, modifying the speaker's attitude rather than anything specific about the predicate. In addition, Doke (1997 [1927]) notes that the placement of the clitic is predictable, independent of meaning. It can attach to any part of speech, but it typically attaches to the highest element in the relevant clause or to the predicate. This predictable placement is compatible with an analysis where the clitic is located high in the structure, outside of the probing domain of L, during the syntax, but cliticizes to the predicate to form a single prosodic word late in the derivation.

4.4.4 Summary

In this section, I examined the behavior of non-nominal elements with respect to the conjoint/disjoint alternation and to the structural licensing effects that I propose are related to the alternation. While it seems that nearly every element in the language—including CPs, adverbials, and locatives—are involved in the conjoint/disjoint alternation, I presented evidence here that these elements do share crucial properties with nominals. It is therefore reasonable to assume that while L does not display any morphological evidence of phi-agreement (unlike subject and object agreement in the language), it is nevertheless probing for nominal elements.

4.5 MOVEMENT AND THE TIMING OF THE DERIVATION

In section 4.3, we saw that both the conjoint/disjoint alternation and the distribution of augmentless nominals are sensitive to syntactic movement. In particular, elements that move out of *v*P are treated as *v*P-external for the conjoint/disjoint alternation. In the same way, augmentless nominals that move out of *v*P do not receive structural licensing, while augmentless nominals that move from a *v*P-external position to a *higher* *v*P-internal position *do* receive structural licensing. A common factor in both of these processes, then, is that movement of an element bleeds probing of that element, yielding a pattern that appears to hold only on the surface.

The profile of these operations is similar to the pattern discussed by Holmberg and Hróarsdóttir (2004) for raising constructions that involve dative experiencer arguments in Icelandic. They show first that these dative arguments act as interveners for object agreement when they remain in situ after the verb:

(285) **Icelandic dative experiencers in situ block object agreement**

    a. það finnst einhverjum stúdent   tölvurnar   ljótar
        EXPL findSG some   studentDAT the computersNOM uglyNOM
        'Some student finds the computers ugly.'

    b. *það finnast einhverjum stúdent   tölvurnar   ljótar
        EXPL findPL some   studentDAT the computersNOM uglyNOM
                                    (Holmberg and Hróarsdóttir, 2004, ex. (14))

When the dative arguments undergo A-movement, however, number agreement with the lower object becomes possible:

(286) **Icelandic raised dative experiencers do not block object agreement**

    a. einhverjum stúdent   finnst tölvurnar   ljótar
      some   studentDAT findSG the computersNOM uglyNOM
      'Some student finds the computers ugly.'

    b. einhverjum stúdent   finnast tölvurnar   ljótar
      some   studentDAT findPL the computersNOM uglyNOM
      'Some student finds the computers ugly.'

                                  (Holmberg and Hróarsdóttir 2004, ex. (9))

As Holmberg and Hróarsdóttir (2004) point out, given that dative experiencers act as interveners for agreement, illustrated in (285), the grammatical construction in (286b) must involve A-movement of the dative *before* the agreement operation takes place.

(287)   **Icelandic dative A-traces are not interveners**

Step 1: DAT Raising

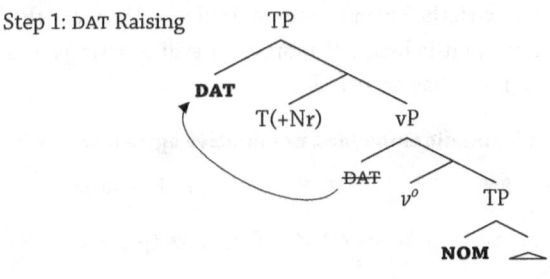

Step 2: Number Agreement

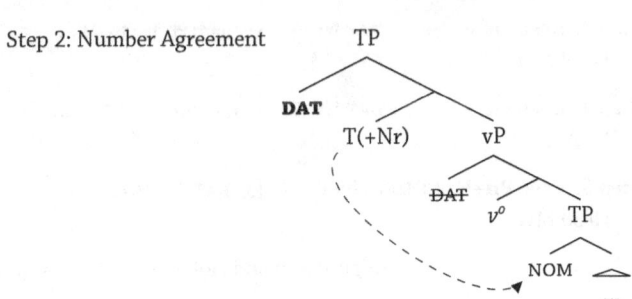

The derivation of (286b) illustrated in (287) has the same character as my analysis of Zulu nominal licensing by L: for both the conjoint/disjoint alternation and the licensing of augmentless nominals, Zulu seems to require any A-movement of arguments out of vP to occur before L probes into that vP.

Sigurðsson and Holmberg (2008) note a similar timing pattern in one variety of Icelandic for matrix agreement with a nominative embedded argument across an intervening dative:

(288)   **Icelandic optional dative intervention**
það þótti/   þóttu   einum málfræðingi [þessi rök
EXPL thoughtSG/ thoughtPL one   linguistDAT   these argumentsNOM
sterk   ]
strong

'One linguist thought these arguments to be strong.' (Sigurðsson and Holmberg, 2008, ex. (22))

Sigurðsson and Holmberg analyze the possibility of plural agreement in (288) as the result of probing *following* A-movement: they claim the intervening dative argument undergoes low subject raising from Spec,vP to a position above the matrix T and that this low subject movement is movement *around* the initial position of the Number probe to a position that is below the Person probe. The derivation of a construction like (288) involving nominative number agreement is one in which the dative argument moves *before* Number probes, and thus does not block agreement with the lower argument. Note that Person agreement with the lower argument is blocked because the landing site for the dative argument is below Person, so it still functions as a Person intervenor after movement has occurred.

(289) **Derivation of Icelandic embedded nominative agreement**

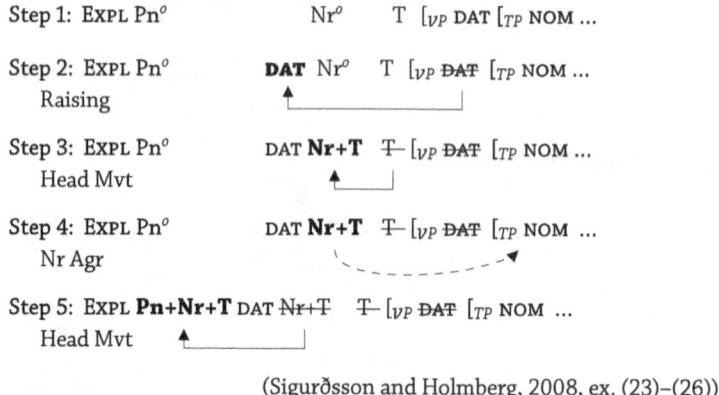

Step 1: EXPL Pn^o · · · · · · · · · · · · · Nr^o · · · T [$_{vP}$ DAT [$_{TP}$ NOM ...

Step 2: EXPL Pn^o · · · · · · **DAT** Nr^o · · · T [$_{vP}$ ~~DAT~~ [$_{TP}$ NOM ...
Raising

Step 3: EXPL Pn^o · · · · · · DAT **Nr+T** ~~T~~ [$_{vP}$ ~~DAT~~ [$_{TP}$ NOM ...
Head Mvt

Step 4: EXPL Pn^o · · · · · · DAT **Nr+T** ~~T~~ [$_{vP}$ ~~DAT~~ [$_{TP}$ NOM ...
Nr Agr

Step 5: EXPL **Pn+Nr+T** DAT ~~Nr+T~~ ~~T~~ [$_{vP}$ ~~DAT~~ [$_{TP}$ NOM ...
Head Mvt

(Sigurðsson and Holmberg, 2008, ex. (23)–(26))

With the opposite ordering of operations, with Number probing preceding movement, the dative argument acts as an intervenor for *both* Number and Person, yielding default agreement.

(290) **Derivation of Icelandic embedded nominative agreement**

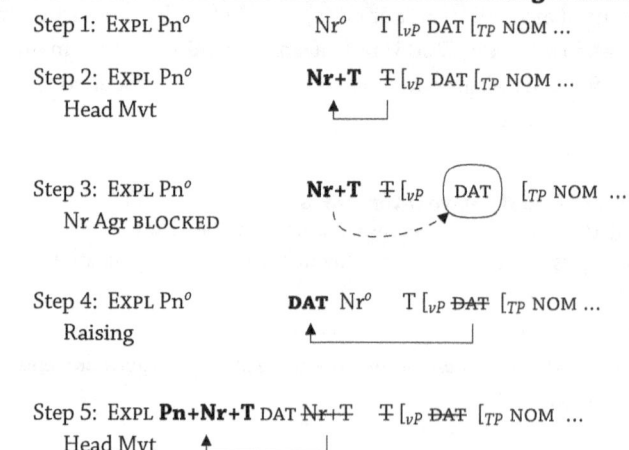

Step 1: EXPL Pn^o · · · · · · · · · · · · Nr^o · · · T [$_{vP}$ DAT [$_{TP}$ NOM ...

Step 2: EXPL Pn^o · · · · · · **Nr+T** ~~T~~ [$_{vP}$ DAT [$_{TP}$ NOM ...
Head Mvt

Step 3: EXPL Pn^o · · · · · · **Nr+T** ~~T~~ [$_{vP}$ (DAT) [$_{TP}$ NOM ...
Nr Agr BLOCKED

Step 4: EXPL Pn^o · · · · · · **DAT** Nr^o · · · T [$_{vP}$ ~~DAT~~ [$_{TP}$ NOM ...
Raising

Step 5: EXPL **Pn+Nr+T** DAT ~~Nr+T~~ ~~T~~ [$_{vP}$ ~~DAT~~ [$_{TP}$ NOM ...
Head Mvt

Asarina (2011) extends this type of analysis to optional agreement with quirky dative subjects in Faroese, making explicit reference to the relative timing of case assignment and movement. What all of these proposals have in common is an appeal to the (phase-internal) free ordering of operations where one process would bleed another, backed up by an optionality in the resulting agreement morphology.

The two processes in Zulu that I have focused on in this chapter—case-licensing and the conjoint/disjoint alternation—can similarly be bled by A-movement. In this sense, they fall into the same category as the Icelandic facts: movement around a head can bleed an operation in which that head would probe the moved element. In Zulu, we can understand the "late" timing of case-licensing and the conjoint/disjoint alternation if vP-internal nominals move around L before L probes the vP.[18] The result of this ordering is a lack of licensing on the A-moved nominals and disjoint morphology whenever A-movement leaves the vP empty. As we saw in chapter 2, movement out of vP always correlates with phi-agreement, so I will assume here that the movement operation that is relevant is the one triggered by the phi-probe T.[19]

The "bleeding" derivations for the conjoint/disjoint alternation and licensing of augmentless nominals are given below. First, as we saw, nominals that vacate vP are never visible for the conjoint/disjoint alternation:

(291) **Nominals that leave vP trigger disjoint morphology**

    a. uSipho$_i$ u- **ya**- pheka t$_i$ $_{v}$P]
       AUG.1Sipho 1s- YA- cook
       'Sipho is cooking.'

    b. iqanda$_k$ uSipho$_i$ u- **ya**- li- pheka t$_i$ t$_k$ $_{v}$P]
       AUG.5egg AUG.1Sipho 1s- YA- 5o- cook
       'As for the egg, Sipho is cooking it.'

(292) **Appearance of disjoint morphology**

    Step 1: SUBJ moves   Step 2: L probes and fails to find a target

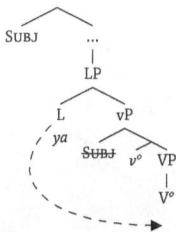

18. Zeller (2015) makes some similar observations about timing in Zulu, specifically focusing on the fact that the subject agreement operation appears to obligatorily precede other processes in the phase and proposing that T must probe before all other vP-external heads.

19. A consequence of this assumption is that T and L are located in the same phase. At this time I am unaware of any evidence against such a conclusion. In chapter 6, I will argue that the effects of phases for A-agreement in Zulu arise only when a dominating category is an *intervenor*—that is, as an instance of the A-over-A condition (following Rackowski and Richards, 2005). Based on this notion of phase boundaries, the lack of phases in the relevant domain here is expected.

Second, augmentless nominals, which must be probed by L in order to be licensed, are unlicensed if they undergo movement to preverbal, *v*P-external position. As we saw in (240), this is not a prohibition on augmentless nominals appearing outside of their original position, since raising-to-object that results in a *v*P-internal object in the higher clause does permit augmentless nominals. Rather, as with the conjoint/disjoint pattern, we can capture this distribution if movement out of *v*P must precede probing by L, as illustrated below in the examples repeated in (242):

(242)   **Nominals that leave *v*P are not case-licensed**

    a.   ngeke ku- fundis- e   **muntu** ₍*v*P₎]
           never 17s- teach- SJC 1person
           'Nobody will ever teach.'

    b.   *ngeke **muntu**$_i$ a-   fundis- e   t$_i$ ₍*v*P₎]
           never 1person 1SJC- teach- SJC

Just as in Icelandic, where the moved dative allows Number to probe a lower nominative, when a subject moves to a *v*P-external position in Zulu, the lower object becomes available as a goal for L. The result of this ordering allows an object to be augmentless just in case the subject has moved to a preverbal position, as illustrated in the derivation in (293):

(293)   **Licensing of augmentless objects**

    Step 1: SUBJ moves   Step 2: L probes and licenses [−aug] OBJ

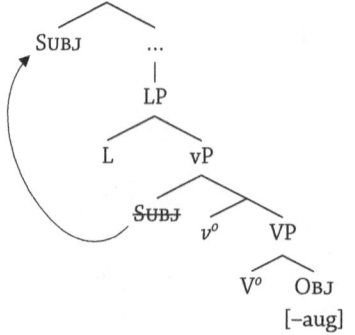 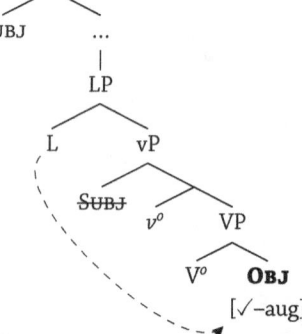

To summarize, we can understand the Zulu conjoint/disjoint alternation and nominal-licensing patterns as the result of A-movement occurring *before* L probes, just as can occur in Icelandic and Faroese. In principle, however, the *opposite* ordering should also be available, with probing by L preceding A-movement, yielding optionality of the type exhibited by Icelandic. As we have seen, this is not the case. Instead, Zulu appears to *only* allow the bleeding order of operations. In the next subsection, I propose that the absence of the unattested order arises naturally as a consequence of the Activity Condition (Chomsky, 2000, 2001).

4.5.1 Activity and the Lack of Optionality

Faroese and Icelandic, in which we saw similar evidence for movement around a probe preceding probing, exhibit *optionality* in the agreement possibilities involving potential dative interveners. As Holmberg and Hroársdóttir (2004) and Jónsson (2009) show, though default Number agreement must occur when the dative subject remains low, Number morphology on the predicate can either be default *or* can agree with the nominative object when the dative subject has moved to a preverbal position, as in (294).

(294) **Optional number agreement in Icelandic**

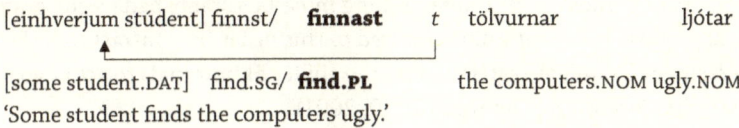

[einhverjum stúdent] finnst/ **finnast**   *t*   tölvurnar   ljótar

[some student.DAT] find.SG/ **find.PL**   the computers.NOM ugly.NOM
'Some student finds the computers ugly.'

If we assume that operations are freely ordered within a phase, along the lines of Chomsky (2008), then this optionality is an expected result as long as both of the relevant operations take place inside the same phase.[20] As Asarina (2011) discusses, this is a fairly natural assumption to make for the Icelandic data above in (294) since the relevant movements all take place within the inflectional domain. That is, until Spell-out forces a portion of the derivation to be finalized, operations can in principle happen in any order. If L and the phi-probes in Zulu are in the same phase, then the ability of movement within LP to precede probing by L would fall into the same domain as the Icelandic facts: movement of the subject to preverbal, *v*P-external position would be followed by L probing the now-evacuated *v*P.[21]

As (294) illustrates, the optionality in agreement possibilities in Icelandic indicates that both orderings of operations are possible. When Number probes before movement, the dative subject intervenes, yielding default agreement.

20. Holmberg and Hróarsdóttir (2004) and Sigurðsson and Holmberg (2008) also discuss the fact that *wh*-movement of dative experiencers also appears to take place around a probe, which is a different type of evidence for a counter-cyclic derivation, though they provide an alternate explanation for why *wh*-phrases do not act as interveners in that instance.

21. As I will discuss in chapter 7, there are a number of facts about Zulu that suggest that it might be missing a 'lower' phase boundary—associated with *v*P—including the possibility for TECs and ditransitive expletives and the lack of 'accusative' type licensing.

When the dative moves before Number probing, nominative agreement can hold.

In contrast to Icelandic, we saw that Zulu does not exhibit this type of optionality. In every acceptable Zulu derivation presented in the previous section, movement precedes probing by L. The other order of operations, where L probes before movement, is problematic.

If L could probe *vP* *before* movement of arguments occurs, we would expect to see two unattested patterns. First, such an ordering of operations would yield conjoint morphology even in constructions in which all arguments have moved to *v*P-external positions during the derivation. On such a derivation, at the time when L probes, these eventually moved arguments would still be *v*P-internal and accessible to L. Second, this ordering would yield the option for an augmentless nominal to be licensed by L *before* it moves to a *v*P-external position. In this chapter and the previous one, I have established that neither of these patterns occurs and we can conclude that the Zulu data thus show that the order of movement *before* probing must be established by the grammar. I will propose here that Zulu is limited to this order (in contrast to Icelandic) as a result of a familiar restriction on the ability of nominals to act as goals—the Activity Condition (Chomsky, 2000, 2001).

With the Activity Condition, Chomsky posits that an element is only available as a potential goal if it has an unvalued uninterpretable feature:

(295) **Activity Condition:** A goal is accessible for Agree iff it has at least one unvalued uninterpretable feature. (Chomsky, 2001)

For Chomsky, the relevant feature on which Activity hinges for nominals is case: this principle was designed to capture the fact that nominals cannot undergo further A-movement or agreement after being case-licensed in languages like English. Once the uninterpretable case of a nominal has been checked, that nominal is "inactive"—and thus inaccessible for further Agree operations. We saw in chapters 2 and 3 that English disallows raising from a case position (Spec,TP in a finite clause) to another case position (Spec,TP in a finite clause), a derivation that would be ruled out by the Activity Condition. Zulu, by contrast, allows this type of raising from an agreeing finite clause to another agreeing finite clause and indeed allows a single nominal to control multiple instances of phi-agreement on a verb. As we saw, the ability of Bantu nominals to move from agreement position to agreement position was one of the original arguments against the existence of syntactic case in the language family. What happens to the Activity Condition in a language without case? Carstens (2005, 2011) and Carstens and Diercks (2013) argue that just as case appears to be absent in the Bantu family, so too is Activity. Carstens (2011) proposes that the relevant requirement for Activity is that a goal have at least one *unchecked*—rather than *unvalued*—uninterpretable feature. She then argues that the noun class (gender) features of nominals in Bantu are uninterpretable but are also *intrinsically* valued—and therefore never get *checked* over the course of the derivation. Because nominals retain these unchecked, uninterpretable noun class features, they remain Active regardless of the number of Agree relations they enter into.

Given my proposal that Bantu nominals are subject to case-licensing requirements, we can return to the original idea that Activity of nominals is linked to case. We've seen ample evidence that phi-agreement does not track case in Zulu, so the lack of evidence for the role of the Activity Condition in subject phi-agreement in Zulu is unsurprising. Instead, I argue that the behavior of augmentless nominals is a straightforward consequence of the Activity Condition with respect to *licensing*. In a construction where augmentless nominals first undergo movement, they are not licensed by L and therefore must be licensed later in the derivation, through raising-to-object to put them in range of a higher L. In a construction where L probes before the augmentless nominal moves, probing by L licenses case on the nominal and renders it *inactive* for all further movement. In other words, once L probes the augmentless nominal, that nominal is "frozen" inside *v*P and therefore cannot act as a goal for higher probes.

The status of *augmented* nominals with respect to this licensing-based Activity is less straightforward. While both augmentless nominal licensing patterns and the conjoint/disjoint alternation indicate that augmented nominals are goals for L, it is also clear that, unlike augmentless nominals, they do not *require* L to license them. If augmentless nominals are not dependent on L for case-licensing, it is not immediately clear whether L would render these nominals inactive. Indeed, we might wonder why augmented nominals, which appear to have their case licensed by virtue of the augment itself, are active at any point in the derivation, if the elimination of unvalued case generally yields inactivity. I propose that augmented and augmentless nominals are indistinguishable at the point in the derivation when L probes. I will argue in the next chapter that case morphology, including the augment, enters the derivation very late in Zulu, after A-agreement processes have taken place. On this view, we expect the behavior of augmented and augmentless nominals to be the same with respect to Activity and probing by L. The augment enters the derivation later—either to license otherwise unlicensed nominals, or to yield interpretive effects on already-licensed nominals in the manner I discussed in chapter 3, and to which I will return in section 5.4 of the next chapter.

Returning to the issue of hyperactivity in Zulu, we now have a different answer for why nominals in the language can enter multiple phi-agreement relationships than the one proposed by Carstens (2011). As noted above, Carstens eliminates Activity effects in Bantu by proposing that Activity is relativized to phi-agreement, and not case, in the Bantu language family and that noun class features can never be checked and rendered inactive. I have proposed here that Activity in Zulu is sensitive to case-licensing, which is independent from phi-agreement. I further proposed that the order of phi-agreement and licensing by L is interchangeable: when L probes first, the licensed nominal is immediately inactivated and remains in *v*P. When T probes first, the nominal leaves *v*P, controls phi-agreement and remains unlicensed and active—and therefore able to enter subsequent phi-agreement relationships. Licensing in this second scenario is satisfied late in the derivation by case morphology, as I will discuss in the next chapter.

It is crucial to my analysis that when L probes a nominal, that nominal goal becomes inactive not only for subsequent licensing processes, but also for subsequent phi-agreement processes, which we have seen do *not* involve case-licensing in Zulu (contra Carstens, 2011, a.o.). In other words, while phi-agreement does not inactivate a goal in Zulu, case-licensed nominals cannot undergo subsequent phi-agreement processes. This view of Activity as relativized to different processes—and specifically linked to case-licensing processes—is argued for by Bhatt and Walkow (2013). Bhatt and Walkow (2013) show that coordinated DPs in Hindi behave differently with respect to T agreement when they are subjects than they do when they are objects. Specifically, they show that when T agrees with conjoined subjects, *resolved* agreement—a syntactic process—results, but when T agrees with conjoined objects, only the closest NP in the conjunction may agree, which they argue reflects a post-syntactic process.

(296) **Hindi conjoined subjects: resolved agreement**

    Ram   aur   Ramesh   gaa   {rahe   hãĩ   / *rahaa   hai}

    Ram.M and Ramesh.M sing PROG.MPL be.PRES.PL / *PROG.MSG be.PRES.SG

    'Ram and Ramesh are singing.'   (Bhatt and Walkow, 2013, ex. (6a))

(297) **Hindi conjoined objects: closest conjunct agreement**

    a. Ram-ne   ek thailii aur ek baksaa (aaj)   uṭhaa {-yaa   / *-yii   /

       Ram-ERG a bag.F and a box.M (today) lift   {-PFV.M.SG / *-PFV.F /

       ???-ye}

       ???-PFV.M.PL

       'Ram lifted a small bag and a box (today).'

    b. us-ne   kharid-ii   kursii   aur sofa

       he-ERG buy.PERF-F.SG chair.F.SG and sofa.M.SG

       'He bought the chair and the sofa.'   (Bhatt and Walkow, 2013, ex. (8a),

       (12a))

Bhatt and Walkow (2013) argue that this difference arises from the differences in how case is assigned to subjects and objects in Hindi. Their account builds on Bhatt (2005), who argues that agreeing subjects in Hindi are case-licensed through the same operation that yields T agreement, while agreeing objects are already case-licensed before T agreement happens. This difference in case assignment means that while the conjoined subjects in Hindi are still Active as syntactic goals, the conjoined objects are not. Even though T agreement is not a case-licensing operation for objects in the language, the fact they they have been case-licensed renders them inactive for all future Agree relations—including phi-agreement. The result is that T agreement is valued through a *post-syntactic* process (closest conjunct agreement) with objects, since the syntactic agreement process (resolved agreement) is not possible. This type of behavior with respect to the Activity Condition matches what we find in the Zulu cases as well—case-licensing from L renders a nominal inactive for *all* further Agree relations, even if they do not involve case.

While the account that I have developed rules out A-movement by case-licensed augmentless nominals, it does not in principle disallow A-bar movement. In languages like English, nominals that have been case-licensed and thus rendered inactive are still available as goals for A-bar processes, such as *wh*-movement or topicalization. However, as we saw in the case of topicalized objects in Zulu, as in (208), nominals in these A-bar positions behave like those found in A-positions: they have the properties of elements that have moved before L probes vP. Following Buell's (2005) observation that phi-agreement must accompany both A- and A-bar movement in Zulu, I suggest that *all* moved arguments—subjects and objects—first undergo a step of A-movement that yields phi-agreement, even if they subsequently dislocate to an A-bar position.[22] If A-movement is a prerequisite for all dislocation in Zulu, then we do not expect A-bar nominals to be exempt from the Activity effects that require movement to occur before L probes. The question remains, however, of whether there are any elements that can escape vP *after* L has probed them.

In principle, this account predicts that goals of L could appear outside of vP as long as the movement or linearization involved does not depend on the A-movement step that I have argued underpins A-bar processes in Zulu. Recall that we in fact saw one striking instance of an unpredicted conjoint verb form that was not followed by any vP-internal element: the object-sharing VP-coordination construction that I introduced in section 4.2.4. The construction involved conjoined predicates sharing a single overt (non-agreeing) object. The object appears in the vP of the second verb, while the verb in the first conjunct receives phrase-final prosody and a conjoint verb form—a combination that is otherwise unattested in the language:

---

22. An alternate analysis of dislocated nominals would be that they do not undergo A-bar movement to dislocated positions but are rather generated in these positions and co-referential with an agreement-controlling *pro* in A-position (along the lines of Bresnan and Mchombo, 1987). Either approach would yield the same result: the element that controls agreement A-moves before L probes.

(236) **Shared object: prosodic boundary in first conjunct, conjoint required**

ngi-buk-**e**:la   ) futhi (ngi-phinde) ngi-dlal-e   ibho:la   )
1SG-watch-APPL) and 1SG-again   1SG.SJC-play-SJC AUG.5soccer
'I watch and I (also) play soccer.'

I presented this construction as evidence that the conjoint/disjoint alternation does not have the same distribution as vP-edge prosodic markers. In light of the account I have developed for the conjoint/disjoint alternation—that it reflects the outcome of probing by L—we can further understand this construction as evidence that L in the first conjunct has probed successfully, even though its goal *ibhola* does not surface in the position where it was probed. This construction does not involve object agreement and thus is exactly the type of construction where we would expect the nominal to be successfully manipulated after agreement with L. Since no A-movement is involved, the nominal may be linearized in or moved to a position outside of the first conjunct even though L has probed it, as the conjoint morphology indicates.

4.6 INVESTIGATING L AND CASE: CLUES FROM OTJIHERERO

In this chapter, I continued my investigation of case effects in Zulu by linking the augmentless nominal distribution patterns from chapter 3 to another syntactic process: the conjoint/disjoint alternation. I showed that the conjoint/disjoint alternation, which marks verbal predicates, shows the same structural sensitivities as the licensing of augmentless nominals: both involve vP-internal elements and both show the same sensitivities to A-movement. I proposed that both phenomena involve the same syntactic head L, which spells out as Ø when it successfully finds a goal and *ya* when it fails to find a goal within vP. An element that is probed by L is structurally licensed and becomes inactive. Augmentless nominals and the complementizer *sengathi* appear in positions local to L in order to receive licensing. Elements that are not probed by L are grammatical if they bear an augment (or the appropriate complementizer). I further proposed that the apparent surface-oriented effects that we get with both the conjoint/disjoint alternation and nominal licensing—both seem to apply before A-movement—are the result of the Activity Condition.

One property of this system in Zulu is that while conjoint/disjoint morphology marks whether the head L has licensed a goal, goals themselves are unmarked. In particular, the augment is capable of appearing on nominals whether or not they are structurally licensed and I have argued that a variety of other elements that have no augment contrasts—including CPs, adverbs, and locatives—can also receive structural licensing. While the lack of dependent-marking in Zulu means that we cannot see a consistent morphological marker on goals of L, recent work on Otjiherero suggests that we find exactly this pattern elsewhere in Bantu.

Recall from the previous chapter that while Otjiherero nominals are almost uniformly augmented, nominal morphology varies with respect to the tonal melody on the augment and noun class prefix in different syntactic environments:

(178) **Otjiherero nominal tone patterns** (Kavari et al., 2012, ex. (2)–(5))

    a. **òtjì**- hávérò tj-á   ù
       7D- chair 7s-PST fall.down
       'The chair fell down.'   *Default:* LL

    b. vé   múná **òtjí**- hávérò
       2s.HAB see   7C- chair
       'They usually see the chair.'   *Complement:* LH

    c. **ótjì**- hávérò
       7P- chair
       'It's a chair.'   *Copulative/predicative:* HL

    d. **tjì**- hávérò
       7V- chair
       'O chair!'   *Vocative:* ØL

Setting aside the copulative and vocative environments,[23] the difference between the complement and default distributions bears a striking resemblance to Zulu licensing patterns: the complement tone pattern appears only on elements that are highest in *v*P, in certain tenses, while the default appears elsewhere.

As we saw above, the LH complement pattern appears on a non-agreeing direct object. Just as in Zulu, however, when the object controls agreement and is in a dislocated *v*P-external position, the pattern changes: in Zulu, the augment becomes obligatory, while in Otjiherero the LL default tone pattern is used:

(298) mb-é   vé-mún-ù, òvà-nátjè
      1SG-PAST 2o-see-FV 2D-children
      'I saw them, the children.'   (Kavari et al., 2012, ex. (48))

---

23. Note, though, that for a number of Bantu languages discussed in the previous chapter, both copular and vocative constructions triggered alternative augment behavior.

Similarly, while an agreeing pre-verbal subject receives the LL default, a non-agreeing vP-internal post-verbal subject receives a LH complement pattern:

(299)   a. **òvà-** ndù   v-á   hìt-í   mò-n-gándà
            2D- people 2s-PST enter-FV 18-9C-house
            'People entered into the house.'

         b. (mò-n-gàndà) mw-á   hìt-í   **ová-** ndù
            18-9D-house 18s-PST enter-FV 2C- people
            'Into the house entered people.'   (Kavari et al., 2012, ex. (40), (44))

The contrast in tonal patterns on the subject in (299) shows that, just like in Zulu, the entire vP seems to be the domain for complement tone assignment. The examples in (299) also illustrate another similarity to Zulu: the locative phrase *monganda* receives the complement tone pattern inside vP, as in (299a), but the default pattern in preverbal position, as in (299b), suggesting that locatives are also susceptible to this type of licensing.

If we look more closely at non-arguments, we also find evidence that complement tone assignment truly targets the highest element in vP: when a time adverbial follows a vP-internal object, it receives the default tone pattern, but when there is no object it receives the complement pattern, as (300) illustrates.

(300)   a. mbì   ryá ò-nyámà **ò-ngùróvà**
            1SG.HAB eat 9C-meat 9D-evening
            'I usually eat meat in the evening.'

         b. mbì   ryá **ò-ngúróvà**
            1SG.HAB eat 9C-evening
            'I usually eat in the evening.'   (Kavari et al., 2012, ex. (35), (37))

Finally, Kavari et al. (2012) show that as with Zulu augmentless nominal licensing, raising-to-object in Otjiherero can feed assignment of complement tone pattern on the raised object:[24]

(301)   a. mb-á   tjíw-à   [kùtjá **òvà-** éndá v-á   rì mò-ngándà]
            1SG-PST know-FV that   2D- guests 2s-PST be 18-9C-home
            'I knew that the guests were in the house.'

24. It is not clear from Kavari et al. (2012) whether CPs themselves participate in the complement tonal melody process or not. While the complementizer *kùtjá* seems to have a LH tonal pattern, that pattern appears to stay even when the embedded subject raises to matrix object position. I set aside the issue of CP status with respect to tonal licensing in Otjiherero in the absence of evidence on CP behavior.

b. mb-á   tjíw-à   **òvá-** éndá [kùtjá v-á   rì mò-ngándà]
1SG-PST know-FV 2C- guests that   2S-PST be 18-9C-home
'I knew that the guests were in the house.'

(Kavari et al., 2012, ex. (28), (30))

Kavari et al. (2012) note that while Otjiherero does not have a morphological conjoint/disjoint distinction, the environments in which the complement tone pattern is assigned are exactly the environments in which other Bantu languages, such as Tswana, use a conjoint verb form. They suggest, along the lines of what I have proposed for Zulu, that the tonal melodies in Otjiherero are case markers—and that Otjiherero has a case that is specifically restricted to the distribution of the conjoint/disjoint alternation.

This parallel between Zulu and Otjiherero strengthens the proposal I have developed in this chapter. Taken together, the two languages illustrate that there can be variation in whether L licensing is head-marked or dependent-marked in a given language. At the same time, given that in Otjiherero, licensing by L is always marked on the goal, we can return to the question of what role the augment morpheme plays in a language like Zulu. Thus far, I have simply assumed that an augment vowel—or appropriate complementizer— exempts an element from structural licensing requirements, while still being compatible with licensed positions. In chapter 5, I turn to these intrinsically licensing morphemes to account more precisely for their role in the syntax.

Case Morphology in Zulu and Beyond

The previous two chapters developed the argument that structural case plays a crucial role in governing the distribution of Zulu nominals. I proposed that nominals in Zulu can be structurally licensed in *v*P-internal positions by entering into a local relationship with a Licensing head or a CAUS or APPL head. I argued that all nominals are capable of entering a relationship with L. However, as the Zulu data in the previous chapters makes clear, only *augmentless* nominals are subject to these structural restrictions. As I noted in chapter 3, our discussion so far has left open the precise reason why augmented nominals do not need to be licensed externally. In this chapter I return to the issue of augmented nominals to determine what the morphosyntactic properties of the augment are such that augmented nominals do not need to receive structural case through the mechanisms argued for in the previous chapters.

Cross-linguistically, it appears that we need to distinguish between three different types of case morphology in case-marking languages: *structural*, *quirky*, and *inherent* (e.g., Schütze, 1997; Woolford, 2006). Building on these existing typologies of case morphology, I propose that we can understand the relationship between morphological and structural case in terms of two parameters, which I call [±Intrinsic] and [±Agreeable]. I then demonstrate that Zulu attests all four possible combinations of [±Intrinsic] and [±Agreeable] in how nominals are marked. The augment is merely one of these possibilities, the full range of which is illustrated in table 5.1.

In section 5.1, I discuss some previous accounts of the relationship between morphological case and structural licensing and show how this relationship can be understood in terms of table 5.1. I demonstrate that the discussion of structural case in Zulu from the previous two chapters fits into this picture in section 5.2. In section 5.3, I expand the discussion of Zulu to show that the

Table 5.1. LICENSING STRATEGIES
AND NOMINAL MORPHOLOGY

+ intrinsic + agreeable ("*augment*")	− intrinsic + agreeable ("*structural*")
+ intrinsic − agreeable ("*inherent*")	− intrinsic − agreeable ("*quirky*")

augment interacts differently with two different types of oblique morphology in Zulu and that these interactions have consequences for nominal licensing. In particular, I argue that oblique morphology in Zulu in some instances corresponds to *quirky* case, which morphologically marks but does not license nominals, and in others to *inherent* case, which morphologically marks *and* structurally licenses nominals. The augment is in complementary distribution with the inherent oblique morphology but behaves differently from it with respect to agreement. In section 5.4, I return to the question of interpretation with respect to these different nominals in Zulu. I show that in a variety of languages, interpretive properties of nominals can depend on the interaction between structural and morphological case in a similar way to what we see in Zulu. Section 5.5 turns to the relationship between case morphology and agreement. I show that the timing of case and agreement is the reverse of what has been argued to hold in languages like Icelandic and discuss the consequences of this discovery. Finally, in section 5.6 I examine DP-internal factors that affect the distribution of the augment to see how we can understand them in light of this analysis.

5.1 CASE CLASSIFICATION

The original insight behind the theory of abstract, or structural, case as a system that governs the syntactic distribution of nominals is the observation that in some languages *morphological* case marking correlates with specific syntactic positions in which nominals are licensed (Vergnaud, 2006 [1976]). In a language with overt case morphology like Icelandic, for example, nominal licensing associated with T typically corresponds to "nominative" case while licensing associated with v^o typically corresponds to "accusative", as in example (99) below, repeated from chapter 3:

(99) **Icelandic NOM–ACC pattern**

    a. Við   kusum   **stelpuna**
        We.NOM elected.1PL the.girl.ACC
        'We elected the girl.'

    b. **Stelpan**   var   kosin
        the.girl.NOM was.3SG elected
        'The girl was elected.'   (Sigurdsson, 1992, ex. (1))

As (99) shows, nominals in object position receive one type of morphology, while nominals in subject position of a finite clause receive different morphology. This morphology is connected to structural position, rather than grammatical function, as the behavior of the passivized internal argument shows.

This correlation between morphological case and structural licensing is imperfect, however. In Icelandic, nominals that appear in the structurally-licensed positions that correspond to nominative and accusative sometimes receive unexpected case morphology (e.g., Andrews, 1982; Thráinsson, 1979; Zaenen et al., 1985; Sigurðsson, 1989; Holland, 1993; Jonas, 1996; Schütze, 1997; Fanselow, 2000; Jónsson, 2003; Woolford, 2006). In (302a), the subject receives *dative* case, while the object is *nominative*. In (302b), the subject is *genitive*.

(302) **Icelandic "quirky" pattern**

    a. Henni líkuðu hestarnir.
       her.DAT liked   horses.NOM
       'She liked the horses.'

    b. Hennar var saknað.
       her.GEN was missed
       'She was missed (by someone).'   (Sigurðsson, 2004, ex. (7d,i))

In order to capture this imperfect relationship between morphological case marking and positions in which nominals seem to be structurally licensed, researchers have developed a more fine-grained typology of case that addresses the different types of relationships that may hold between case morphology and structural licensing. In general, these types of distinctions have led researchers to conclude that morphological case is a distinct phenomenon from the type of structural licensing that I have discussed so far in this book. Nevertheless, the clear points of contact between structural licensing and nominal morphology have remained a major focus. A common way to address this issue is in terms of a three-way distinction among types of case (e.g.,

Schütze, 1997; Woolford, 2006). While terminology varies slightly, I follow Schütze (1997) in referring to these types as *structural*, *quirky*, and *inherent*.

The term *structural case* refers to nominal licensing via a structural relationship. This is the type of case that arises in Zulu via local relationships with L, APPL, and CAUS, if the results reported in the previous chapters are correct. We can say that a particular morphological case reflects structural case insofar as it predictably arises on nominals licensed in a particular structural configuration.

Certain nominals display an identical syntactic distribution to nominals that receive predictable morphological case in specific structurally-licensed positions, yet they are not marked with predictable case morphology and instead must be marked with specific case morphology that seems to be lexically determined. This type of nominal morphology has been labelled as *quirky case*. As we can see in example (303) below, the internal argument of the transitive predicate *luku* 'finished' requires dative case, instead of the expected accusative. When the predicate is passivized, the internal argument retains the dative case even when it moves to preverbal subject position, which would typically go along with a shift to nominative case, as we saw in (99).

(303) **Icelandic quirky DAT: limited to structurally licensed positions**

    a. þeir   luku   kirkjunni
       they.NOM finished church.DAT
       'They finished the church.'

    b. Kirkjunni*i* var lokið   t*i*
       church.DAT was finished
       'The church was finished.'   (Andrews, 1982)

While the predictable morphology associated with structural case correlates with the manner in which the nominal is licensed, quirky case is independently selected by specific predicates and serves to obscure the structural licensing relationship.

Finally, some researchers further distinguish a third category: *inherent case*. This type of morphological case can appear on nominals in particular semantic relationships, where the elements they mark can appear outside of structurally licensed positions. This type of morphological case, then, can be taken as a direct signal of nominal licensing that is independent of the larger clause (the result of some local case-assigning P or perhaps driven purely by meaning—i.e., "semantic case"—as discussed in detail by Schütze, 1997). Schütze considers genitive-marked nominals in possessive constructions in languages like English to be an example of this type of inherent case, as well as instances of "semantic DAT of duration" in Icelandic, as illustrated in (304) on the following page.

(304) **Icelandic inherent case**
  dögum saman
  days.DAT together
  'for days at a time'   (Schütze, 1997, p. 43)

In addition to the differing behavior of these types of morphological case with respect to structural licensing, they also display different properties with respect to other aspects of the syntax. Schütze (1997) argues that while nominals marked with structural case are able to agree with a predicate, nominals that are marked with quirky or inherent case are unable to agree, as in the contrast in (305) below.

(305) a. **strákunum**   leidd- **ist** / *ust
         the.boys.DAT.PL bored- 3SG / *3PL
         'The boys were bored.'

     b. **strákarnir**   leidd-   **ust** / *ist
         the.boys.NOM.PL walked.hand.in.hand- 3PL / *3SG
         'The boys walked hand in hand.'[1]   (Sigurðsson, 1996, ex. (1), (2))

Based on these patterns, we can capture these different types of case in terms of two points of variation: [± Intrinsic] and [± Agreeable].

The property [± Intrinsic] addresses whether a nominal is dependent on the clausal structure for licensing. Nominals with [+Intrinsic] case, such as the *inherent* case discussed above, are independently licensed and not restricted to structurally licensed positions. Nominals with [−Inherent] case, such as the *structural* and *quirky* case discussed above, must be licensed via the standard clausal licensing mechanisms.

The [± Agreeable] property addresses whether a particular case allows a nominal that it marks to agree in phi-features with a verb. Nominals with [+Agreeable] case, such as *structural* case, can agree with a verb, while nominals with [−Agreeable] case, such as *quirky* and *inherent*, cannot. The fact that case seems to interact with agreement in this way raises the question of what the causality of the restrictions on certain cases coinciding with phi-agreement is, particularly in light of the discussion of Activity from chapter 4. I will construe [± Agreeable] as a *surface* restriction. As we will see in section 5.3.3, while Zulu observes the same restriction as found in Icelandic, it is realized in a slightly different fashion. In section 5.5, I return to this question of the timing relationship between case and phi-agreement.

Though Schütze (1997) and others argue for three different types of case, if these two defining points of variation are allowed to combine freely, we

---

1. The two verbs in these constructions are homonyms, distinguished by the fact that one assigns quirky dative to the subject, while the other does not.

Table 5.2. LICENSING STRATEGIES
AND NOMINAL MORPHOLOGY

+ **intrinsic** + **agreeable**	– intrinsic + agreeable ("*structural*")
+ intrinsic – agreeable ("*inherent*")	– intrinsic – agreeable ("*quirky*")

might expect them to yield *four* possibilities for case morphology. In addition to the types described above, a [+Intrinsic, +Agreeable] case would both locally license nominals to which it attaches and would allow these nominals to agree. These possibilities are illustrated in table 5.2, repeated from above.

Building on my analysis of structural case licensing from the previous chapters, I argue in this chapter that Zulu illustrates *all* of these possible types of case licensing and nominal morphology. As I discussed in chapter 3, this conclusion is remarkable because in the Bantu language family, it has long been assumed that *none* of these categories exists. In addition to the research arguing against the existence of case effects in Bantu (e.g., Harford Perez, 1985; Ndayiragije, 1999; Alsina, 2001; Baker, 2003b; Carstens and Diercks, 2013; Diercks, 2012), it has been taken for granted that the uniform appearance of augmented nominals in different structural positions means that Bantu languages also lack *morphological* case, as we saw in example (98), repeated below:

(98) **Lack of structural case morphology in Zulu**

    a. **u-mntwana** u- cul- e i-ngoma
      AUG-1child   1s- sing- PFV AUG-9song
      'The child sang a song.'

    b. u-Mfundo   u- nik- e **u-mntwana** u-jeqe
      AUG-1Mfundo 1s- give- PFV AUG-1child   AUG-1steamed.bread
      'Mfundo gave the child steamed bread.'

    c. u-Mfundo   u- nik- e u-gogo   **u-mntwana**
      AUG-1Mfundo 1s- give- PFV AUG-1granny AUG-1child
      'Mfundo gave granny the child.'

In this chapter, I will argue that the *augment* is in fact part of the morphological case system of Zulu and is an instantiation of the fourth type of case: [+Intrinsic,+Agreeable]. Augmented nominals thus are not subject to structural licensing effects, since the augment signals local, or *intrinsic*, licensing, but they are nevertheless able to agree. I will compare the behavior of the augment with the behavior of other nominal prefixes in the language that fill out Zulu's case paradigm.

5.2 STRUCTURAL LICENSING: RECAP

In the previous two chapters, we saw structural restrictions on augmentless nominals in Zulu that cannot be explained by independent factors. Specifically, we saw that augmentless nominals are licensed only as the highest element inside *v*P, licensed by L°, or by an added APPL or CAUS head, which attaches at the VP level and is thus local to the theme.

(132) **Licensing via L**

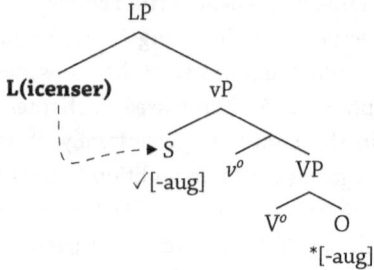

(133) **Licensing via extra 'external' arguments**

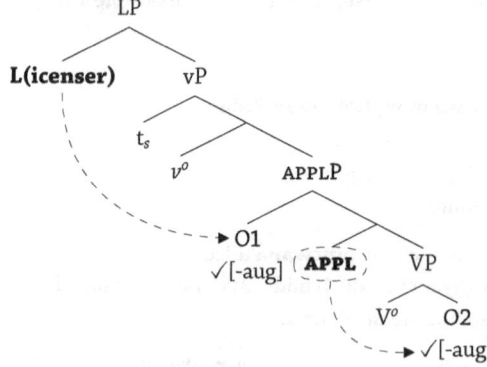

While these positions of structural licensing are different from those of the familiar case languages discussed in the previous section, I argued that this type of structural licensing process is exactly parallel to these familiar patterns of case licensing.

We also saw in chapter 3 that though augmentless nominals must be licensed in *v*P-internal—and thus non-agreeing—positions, they can nevertheless control agreement on a verb. Evidence for this conclusion comes from raising-to-object constructions in which an augmentless nominal raises from an embedded agreeing subject position to *v*P-internal position in the matrix clause:

(240a) angifuni **muntu** [ukuthi **a-** phek- e (i)-qanda]
       NEG-1SG-want 1person that 1SJC- cook- SJC (AUG)-5egg
       'I don't want anyone to cook an egg.'

If we evaluate this type of licensing in terms of the distinctions made in the previous section, augmentless nominals are [−Intrinsic,+Agreeable]. That is, these nominals are dependent on structural case-licensing and are able to agree with a verb—exactly like nominals that receive *structural* case in a language like Icelandic. The fact that these nominals are distinguished by a lack of morphology means that structural case has no morphological correlate in Zulu.

As the previous two chapters discuss, two factors help to obscure the existence of structural case in Zulu. First, the fact that the positions in which nominals are licensed differ from those observed in languages like English or Icelandic—for example, the lack of licensing through finite Tense—gives nominals in Zulu a different distributional profile than we have come to expect from more familiar case languages. Second, the fact that these structural case effects are only observable with augmentless nominals gives us many fewer opportunities to see it in the first place. In the next section, I'll look more closely at the behavior of the augment and other pieces of Zulu nominal morphology to argue that the augment serves as a local ([+Intrinsic]) licenser.

5.3 ZULU NOMINAL PREFIXES AND LICENSING

So far, I have focused mainly on the differences between augmented and augmentless nominals in Zulu. We have seen that while augmentless nominals require structural licensing, augmented nominals do not. In this section, I will compare the behavior of augmented nominals to nominals with oblique morphology. I will show that while certain oblique morphemes are in complementary distribution with the augment, others are not. I will argue that these two types of oblique morphology are equivalent to inherent and quirky case.

5.3.1 Classification of Oblique Prefixes

Zulu has a number of prefixes that mark oblique nominals, some of which we saw briefly in section 4.4.2 in the previous chapter. I focus on a set of prefixes that fall into the two distinct classes discussed below, which I will refer to as *augment-replacing* and *augment-permitting* prefixes.

Augment-replacing prefixes include the oblique markers *ku-* and *kwa-*, which typically mark locatives but can also be used for benefactives (especially when not introduced by applicative *-el-* morphology), as in (306b,d). These prefixes uniformly take an augmentless complement, as the examples in (306) below show.

(306) **Augment-replacing prefixes: augmentless complement**

a. u-   buy-   is-   el-   e   ifowuni   y-akho   en-dala
2SG.SJC- return- CAUS- APPL- SJC AUG.9phone 9ASSOC-2SG 9REL-old
kwa-MTN   Service Provider
KWA-5MTN Service Provider
'Return your old phone to the MTN Service Provider.'[2]

b. u-Sipho   u- zo- pheka ukudla   **kwa**- zingane
AUG-1Sipho 1s- FUT- cook   AUG.15food KWA- 10child
'Sipho will cook food for the children.'

c. u-Sipho   u- zo- thum- ela imali   **ku**- mama
AUG-1Sipho 1s- FUT- send- APPL AUG.9money KU- 1mother
'Sipho will send money to mother.'

d. u-Sipho   u- zo- thumela imali   **ku**- bantwana
AUG-1Sipho 1s- FUT- send.APPL AUG.9money KU- 2child
'Sipho will send money to the children.'

The examples in (306) show that regardless of the noun class these prefixes attach to, they always surface with the same form and show no evidence of an augment vowel. By contrast, the typical pattern when a vowel-final prefix attaches to an augmented nominal is for the two vowels to predictably coalesce to resolve hiatus (Doke, 1997 [1927]). We will observe this process below in the behavior of augment-permitting prefixes in (308) and (309), but example (307) below shows that the augment cannot appear with the augment-replacing prefixes:

(307) **Augment-replacing: augment ungrammatical**

a. *u-Sipho   u- zo- pheka inyama   **kwe**-   zingane
AUG-1Sipho 1s- FUT- cook   AUG.9meat KWA.AUG- 10child
intended: 'Sipho will cook meat for the children.'

2. Google, accessed November 18, 2011.

b. * u-Sipho   u- zo- thumela imali   **ko**-   bantwana
AUG-1Sipho 1s- FUT- send.APPL AUG.9money KU.AUG- 2child
intended: 'Sipho will send money to the children.'

The augment-permitting oblique-marking prefixes that I focus on here are *nga-*, and *na-*, though a third prefix—the so-called associative marker—shows similar behavior. The prefix *nga-* is used to mark a variety of oblique arguments, typically instrumentals or certain temporal adverbials:

(308) **Augment-permitting** *nga-*: **augmented complement**

a. uMlungisi   u- zo- fika **ngo**-   ten   (= nga+u-ten)
AUG.1Mlungisi 1s- FUT- arrive NGA.AUG- 1.ten
'Mlungisi will arrive at ten o'clock.'

b. uMlungisi   u- zo- fika **nge**-   sonto   (= nga+isonto)
AUG.1Mlungisi 1s- FUT- arrive NGA.AUG- 5Sunday
'Mlungisi will arrive on Sunday.'

c. ngi- bhala **nge**-   peni   (= nga+ipeni)
1SG- write NGA.AUG- 5pen
'I write with a pen.'

d. ngi- bhala **nga**-   mapeni   (= nga+amapeni)
1SG- write NGA.AUG- 6pen
'I write with pens.'

We can observe the presence of the augment vowel in the examples in (308) through the process of coalescence. The *a* vowel of the prefixes predictably lowers the vowel height of the augment, with *u* lowering to *o*, *i* lowering to *e*, and *a* remaining unchanged.

This same process occurs in constructions involving the *na-* prefix, which means 'with' and is used in both comitative constructions and in certain types of existential and possessive predication (Buell and de Dreu, 2013). I focus on the comitative use of *na-* here, since the more flexible word order that it permits will better allow us to observe distributional restrictions.

(309) **Augment-permitting** *na-*: **augmented complement**

a. uXolani u- dlala **no**-   mfana   (= na+umfana)
1Xolani 1s- play NA.AUG- 1boy
'Xolani is playing with a boy.'

b. uXolani u- dlala **ne**-   ntombazane   (= na+intombazane)
1Xolani 1s- play NA.AUG- 9girl
'Xolani is playing with a girl.'

c. ngi- **na-**   bangane abaningi   (= na+abangane)
   1SG- NA.AUG- 2bangane 2REL.many
   'I have many friends.'

d. nge-   NXA   yeholide   ku- **ne-**   siminyaminya
   NGA.AUG- 9cause 9ASSOC.AUG.5holiday 17S- NA.AUG- 7crowd
   sezimoto
   7ASSOC.AUG10cars
   'Because of the holiday, there's a lot of traffic.'   (=na+isiminyaminya)

A final instance of this type of augment-preserving oblique prefix is the so-called associative marker, which marks the possessor in possessive constructions and appears in a number of other nominal modifying contexts that roughly correspond to the distribution of English *of* (Sabelo, 1990). As with *na-* and *nga-*, the associative prefix ends in an *a* vowel that predictably coalesces with the augment of the following nominal; unlike the other augment-permitting prefixes, it also shows noun class concord with the preceding nominal. In (310), we see evidence for both of these characteristics:

(310) **Augment-permitting associative marker: augmented complement**

a. inja   **yo-**   mfana   (= ya + umfana)
   AUG.9dog 9ASSOC.AUG- 1boy
   'the boy's dog.'

b. indlu   **yo-**   tshani   (= ya + utshani)
   AUG.9house 9ASSOC.AUG- 14grass
   'grass hut'

c. isiminyaminya **sa-**   maphela   (= sa + amaphela)
   AUG.7crowd   7ASSOC.AUG- 6cockroaches
   'a swarm of cockroaches'

d. nge-   nxa   **yo-**   laka   luka-   Sipho, a- ngi-
   NGA.AUG 9cause 9ASSOC.AUG- 11temper 11ASSOC.AUG- 1Sipho NEG- 1SG-
   thand- i   uku- khuluma na- ye
   like- NEG INF- talk   NA- 1PRO
   'Because of Sipho's temper, I don't like to talk to him.'

The examples in (308), (309), and (310) show that the augment is possible with these prefixes, where it was not with the augment-replacing prefixes. While the augment-replacing prefixes (306) always require an augmentless nominal, the augment-permitting prefixes do not always require the augment. Instead, the augment-permitting prefixes *preserve* the distribution of the augment that we observed with core arguments in chapter 3. In example (311) below, we can see that the augment is in fact required with augment-permitting prefixes in these particular environments:

(311) **Augment-permitting: augment required in non-licensed environment**

    a.   * uXolani u- dlala **na**- mfana
            1Xolani 1s- play NA- 1boy
            intended: 'Xolani is playing with a boy.'

    b.   * nge-   nxa   yeholide   ku- **na**- siminyaminya
            NGA.AUG- 9cause 9ASSOC.AUG.5holiday 17s- NA- 7crowd
            sezimoto
            7ASSOC.AUG10cars
            intended: 'Because of the holiday, there's a lot of traffic.'

    c.   * indlu   **ya**-   tshani
            AUG.9house 9ASSOC- 14grass
            intended: 'grass hut'

The environment in (311) is an environment where a core argument, such as a subject or direct object, would also be required to bear an augment: though the nominal is within *v*P, the construction does not meet the nonveridicality requirement established in chapter 3. By contrast, if we place nominals with augment-permitting prefixes in negated sentences, as in (312) below, the augment may now be dropped. Here I focus the discussion only on *nga-* and *na-*, since the associative marker marks nominals that are DP-internal. As I will discuss in section 5.5.4, though, we do find circumstances in which an associative-marked nominal may lose its augment, illustrated below in (312d).[3]

(312) **Augment-permitting prefixes: augment contrasts preserved**

    a. a- ngi- bhal- i   **nga**- peni
       NEG- 1sg- write- NEG NGA- 5pen
       'I don't write with any pen.'

    b. uXolani   a-   ka- dlal- i   **na**- mfana
       AUG.1Xolani NEG- 1s- play- NEG NA- 1boy
       'Xolani isn't playing with any boy.'

    c. a-   ku- **na**- siminyaminya sezimoto
       NEG- 17s- NA- 7crowd   7ASSOC.AUG10cars
       'There's no traffic.'

3. Many speakers of Durban Zulu find the construction in (312c) to be marked and prefer an alternative involving the existential predicate *kho(na)*:

    (i) a-   ku -kho (i)siminyaminya se-   zimoto
        NEG- 17s- exist (AUG)7.crowd   7ASSOC.AUG- 10cars
        'There's no traffic.'

d. a-   ngi- bon- anga sigqoko **sa-**   muntu
   NEG- 1SG- see- NEG 7hat   7ASSOC- 1person
   'I didn't see anybody's hat.'

In short, the examples in (312) illustrate that the nominals under these prefixes may lose their augments roughly where we would expect a non-prefixed nominal to be able to lose an augment.

5.3.2 Structural Restrictions on Obliques

So far in this section, we have seen a split in the behavior of the oblique prefixes in Zulu. Augment-replacing prefixes always take an augmentless complement, even when the nominal appears in environments (and with interpretations) that do not permit non-oblique arguments to be augmentless, as in (306). Augment-permitting prefixes, by contrast, preserve the basic augment contrasts that hold for non-obliques. The augment-permitting prefixes combine with an augmented nominal in non-negative contexts but can combine with an augmentless NPI nominal in downward-entailing environments, as in (312).

In this subsection, I will show that this pattern extends to the structural licensing restrictions on non-obliques discussed in the previous two chapters. Specifically, nominals with augment-replacing prefixes do not seem to require structural licensing, while nominals with an augment-permitting prefix do show sensitivities—in the absence of an augment.

Recall that (in the absence of CAUS or APPL) structural licensing comes from a Licensing head above vP, as repeated in (132) below:

(132)   **Licensing via L**

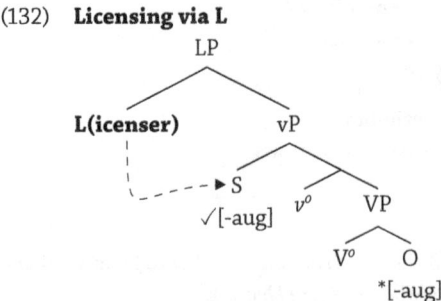

In these constructions, L targets the highest element in vP, which means that nominals that are not local to L cannot receive licensing. If oblique nominals require structural licensing, we would expect them to only be grammatical in a position that is local to L.

First, as (313) shows, augment-replacing prefixed nominals may appear in positions that are *not* maximally local to L. We saw nominals with augment-replacing prefixes in this position in the non-negative environments in (306), but in example (313) we can see the absence of restriction even in a downward-entailing context with an NPI interpretation. The *kwa*-marked augmentless nominal appears after the direct object, in a position that is not local to L.

(313) **Augment-replacing prefix: second object non-local to L**

u-Sipho a- ka- zu- pheka u-kudla **kwa**- zingane
AUG-1Sipho NEG- 1S- FUT- cook AUG-15food KWA- 10child
'Sipho will not cook food for any children.'

Similarly, augmented nominals that are marked with an augment-permitting prefix may also appear following a direct object, in a position that is non-local to L. In (314), as in (313), the augmented obliques with augment-permitting prefixes can appear in a position following the direct object.

(314) **Augment-permitting prefix +AUG: non-local to L**

a. u-Mfundo u- dlala i-bhola **no**- muntu (na+umuntu)
AUG-1Mfundo 1S- play AUG-5ball NA.AUG- 1person
'Mfundo is playing soccer with someone/the person.'

b. u-Mfundo u- bhala i-zincwadi **nge**- peni (nga+ipeni)
AUG-1Mfundo 1S- write AUG-10letter NGA.AUG- 5pen
'Mfundo writes letters with a pen.'

When an augment-permitting prefix combines with an *augmentless* nominal, however, we find a structural restriction in exactly the environment that I showed in section 4.4.2 of chapter 4. The nominal in these cases is sensitive to the same structural restrictions as plain arguments. In (315a), an augmentless oblique with an augment-permitting prefix is ungrammatical when it follows the direct object. This ungrammaticality contrasts with the grammatical augmented oblique in this same position in (314a) or (315b). While speakers do judge an NPI interpretation to be felicitous with the augmented oblique in (315b), exactly as they did for augmented *v*P-internal arguments that did not receive licensing in chapter 3, (315c) shows that speakers also employ a *syntactic* repair to the ungrammatical sentence in (315a). In (315c), the oblique nominal has been shifted to a position above the direct object, where it can be licensed.

(315) **Augment-permitting prefix –AUG: restricted to highest in vP**

a. * u-Mfundo   a-   ka- dlal- i   i-bhola   na- muntu
AUG-1Mfundo NEG- 1s- play- NEG AUG-5ball NA- 1person

b. u-Mfundo   a-   ka- dlal- i   i-bhola   **no-**   muntu
AUG-1Mfundo NEG- 1s- play- NEG AUG-5ball NA.AUG- 1person
'Mfundo isn't playing soccer with the person/anyone.'

c. u-Mfundo   a-   ka- dlal- i   **na- muntu** i-bhola
AUG-1Mfundo NEG- 1s- play- NEG NA- 1person AUG-5ball
'Mfundo isn't playing soccer with anyone.'

Recall from chapter 2 that Buell (2005, 2009) demonstrates that this type of adjunct/oblique shift is available when the adjunct receives focus and the core arguments do not. Interestingly, the construction in (315c), where the augmentless augment-permitting oblique precedes the direct object, is strongly dispreferred with an *augmented* augment-permitting oblique, as (316) shows. This contrast is perhaps expected given the tendency for a generic interpretation of augmented *umuntu*, which would rule out the availability of the shift.

(316) ?? u-Mfundo   a-   ka- dlal- i   **no-**   **muntu** i-bhola
AUG-1Mfundo NEG- 1s- play- NEG NA.AUG- 1person AUG-5ball
'Mfundo isn't playing soccer with the person/someone.'

Even without establishing a precise derivation for (315c),[4] we can see that as with the core arguments, augment-permitting obliques with an augmentless complement seem to be restricted to being the highest element in vP, or most local to L.[5]

---

4. See Lechner (2003) and Csirmaz (2006) for discussion of similar c-command relationships between arguments and case-marked adjuncts in unrelated languages.

5. Note that this type of movement, with the nominal requiring licensing shifting around a non-agreeing in situ argument, is not possible for a non-oblique argument. For internal and external arguments, including those introduced by APPL or CAUS, the only way to become local to L is if a *higher* argument undergoes A-movement out of vP. Though I will not pursue a full account of this contrast here, note that this seems to be a more general property of adjuncts vs. arguments in Zulu. Again, as I showed in chapter 2, while vP-internal arguments display rigid word order with respect to each other, Buell (2005) demonstrates that certain adjuncts can have variable word order with respect to a vP-internal subject:

(i) a. ng- a-   ya lapho ku-   17PRT-hlala **uSipho**   khona
1SG- PST- go where 17PRT- stay   AUG.1Sipho there

b. ng- a-   ya lapho ku-   17PRT-hlala (khona) **uSipho**
1SG- PST- go where 17PRT- stay   (there) AUG.1Sipho
'I went to where Sipho lives.'   (Buell, 2005, ex. (282))

The pattern that we see with the augment-permitting obliques is reminiscent of the quirky case pattern in Icelandic, where nominals that require a particular morpheme are still limited to structurally licensed positions:

(303) **Icelandic quirky DAT: limited to structurally licensed positions**

    a. þeir   luku   kirkjunni
       they.NOM finished church.DAT
       'They finished the church.'

    b. Kirkjunni var lokið
       church.DAT was finished
       'The church was finished.'   (Andrews, 1982)

Notably, just as in Icelandic, Zulu *augment-permitting* morphology is required by these oblique nominals but does not serve to license them. Instead, they are limited to structurally licensed positions—or to appearing with an augment. As I will discuss in more detail in section 5.3.3, these remarkable similarities will be essential to our understanding of Zulu's case system.

The final aspect of oblique behavior that is relevant to our understanding of their case-type properties concerns the behavior of these nominals with respect to movement and agreement. As (315c) showed, nominals with augment-permitting morphology that undergo a syntactic shift into a structurally licensed position maintain their augment-permitting prefix. Both augment-replacing and augment-permitting obliques are also able to dislocate with their prefixes intact:

(317) a. abantu   ba- phuza umqombothi   [**kwa**- Zulu]
         AUG.2people 2s- drink AUG.3traditional.beer KWA- 5Zulu

      b. [**kwa**- Zulu] abantu   ba- phuza umqombothi
         KWA- 5Zulu AUG.2people 2s- drink AUG.3traditional.beer
         'People drink sorghum beer in Zululand.'

      c. uXolani   u- gunda utshani   [**nge**-   sigundatshani]
         AUG.1Xolani 1s- cut   AUG.12grass NGA.AUG- 7lawn.mower

I will assume that the inability of arguments to move within *v*P prevents a construction like (315c) from being a grammatical option in constructions where a lower nominal requires licensing but a higher nominal intervenes. An alternative possibility, suggested by Michael Diercks, would be that the obliques in these constructions are not actually undergoing movement within *v*P, but instead are flexible in their possible attachment sites and can simply attach in a position local to L when structural licensing is required. On this account, the inability of arguments to "move" within *v*P would reduce to the fact that arguments only have one possible attachment site within *v*P. In the absence of strong evidence to distinguish these possible accounts, I set them aside here and simply note that this difference will need to be dealt with by any theory of licensing in Zulu.

d. [**nge-** sigundatshani] uXolani u- gunda utshani
NGA.AUG- 7lawn.mower AUG.1Xolani 1s- cut AUG.12grass
'Xolani cuts the grass with a lawn mower.'

This behavior contrasts starkly with what happens when augment-replacing *or* augment-permitting obliques move to an *agreeing vP-external* position. In chapter 2, I showed that Zulu allows certain oblique arguments, such as locatives or instrumentals, to appear in Spec,TP, while the subject remains inside *v*P (Buell, 2007; Zeller, 2010). In (318) and (319), I show that while the non-inverted versions of these constructions *require* augment-replacing or augment-permitting morphology, the inversion constructions *prohibit* it. That is, when oblique nominals move to preverbal agreeing positions, they retain their oblique interpretation while losing their oblique morphology. The agreement we find in these situations, as discussed in chapter 2, is agreement with the noun class of the oblique nominal (and not with the thematic subject or with the oblique morphology itself).

(318) **Locative inversion: no augment-replacing morphology**

a. abantu aba-dala ba-hlala *(**ku**)- lezi zindlu
AUG.2people 2REL-old 2s-stay KU- 10these 10houses
'Old people live in these houses.'

b. (*ku-) lezi zindlu zi- hlala abantu aba-dala
KU- 10these 10houses 10s- stay AUG.2people 2REL-old
'Old people live in these houses.' (Buell 2007, ex. (7), adapted)

(319) **Instrument inversion: no augment-permitting morphology**

a. u- John u- dla *(**nge**)- sipuni
AUG- 1John 1s- eat NGA.AUG- 7spoon
'John is eating with a spoon.'

b. (*nga-) i- sipuni si- dla u- John.
NGA AUG- 7spoon 7s- eat AUG- 1John
'John is eating with a spoon.' (Lit. 'The spoon is eating John.')

(Zeller 2010, ex. (50), adapted)

In chapter 3, we saw that though augmentless nominals were incapable of surfacing in agreeing positions, they were capable of controlling agreement if they further raised to a non-agreeing position. Here we see that while oblique nominals are capable of agreeing and appearing in an agreeing positions, they do so at the expense of their oblique morphology. Example (320) below is further illustration that the ungrammaticality of the oblique morphology on agreeing subjects in (318) and (319) is the result of agreement, rather than surface position. In this construction, when an inverted oblique further raises to a *v*P-internal position in the matrix clause—where we know that oblique morphology may surface—it still must appear without an augment-replacing morpheme:

(320) a. ngi- funa (ukuthi) (*ku-) lezi   zindlu   zi-   hlal- e   abantu
          1SG- want (that)   KU-   10these 10houses 10SJC- stay- SJC AUG.2people
          aba-dala
          2REL-old
          'I want old people to live in these houses.'

      b. ngi- funa (*ku-) lezi   zindlu   ukuthi zi-   hlal- e   abantu
          1SG- want KU-   10these 10houses that   10SJC- stay- SJC AUG.2people
          aba-dala
          2REL-old
          'I want old people to live in these houses.'

I return to the issue of the disappearing oblique morphology in section 5.5.2, where I will compare the relationship between agreement and case in Zulu and Icelandic.

5.3.3 Case Morphology in Zulu

To summarize what we've seen so far, in this chapter I have shown that there are four types of nominal in Zulu that differ from each other in their behavior. First, as the previous chapters had already established, we find a distinction between augmentless nominals, which require structural licensing, and augmented nominals, which do not. Second, we saw a similar distinction among the oblique nominals. Nominals with augment-replacing morphology did not require independent licensing. The augment-replacing prefixes appear to be in complementary distribution with the augment—augment-replacing morphology uniformly attaches to augmentless nominals—but at the same time nominals with augment-replacing morphology showed no sensitivity to structural restrictions. Nominals with augment-permitting morphology, by contrast, did require independent licensing, in the form of either an augment or structural licensing in vP. I propose here that these four types of nominals correspond to the case-licensing and nominal morphology paradigm introduced when I discussed languages like Icelandic earlier in this chapter. As I will discuss in this subsection, these nominal types map onto the paradigm as shown in table 5.3.

The intrinsic parameter

Recall that Icelandic showed a distinction between case morphology that signals that a nominal is licensed locally (independent of structural licensing mechanisms), and case morphology that does not. This distinction was represented by the feature [±Intrinsic]. In Zulu, two types of nominal morphology

Table 5.3. LICENSING STRATEGIES AND
NOMINAL MORPHOLOGY IN ZULU

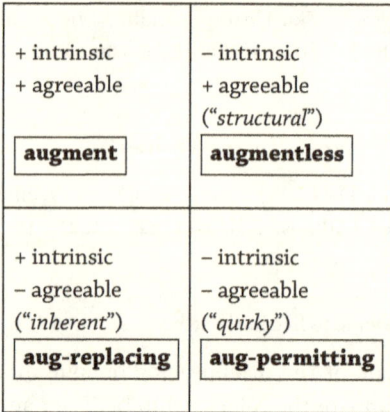

+ intrinsic + agreeable **augment**	− intrinsic + agreeable (*"structural"*) **augmentless**
+ intrinsic − agreeable (*"inherent"*) **aug-replacing**	− intrinsic − agreeable (*"quirky"*) **aug-permitting**

do not show sensitivity to structural licensing effects: the *augment* and *augment-replacing prefixes*. While these [+Intrinsic] nominals in Zulu do not require structural licensing, they are nevertheless capable of appearing in licensed positions, as chapter 4 established (contra Schütze, 1997). We can understand the complementarity of the augment and the augment-replacing prefixes in terms of their [+Intrinsic] property: either morpheme is capable of licensing the nominal, but augment-replacing morphology is more highly specified than the augment, since it correlates with oblique meaning, so when augment-replacing morphology is appropriate it will take precedence. In other words, while I have argued that the augment vowel is essentially a morphosyntactic default that does not correspond to any particular mean- ing or syntactic configuration, augment-replacing morphology is selected for in certain constructions and carries some semantic content. Selection of augment-replacing morphology eliminates the need for an augment. In section 5.5.3 I return to the fact that these two morphemes never combine and contrast it with the behavior of the augment and augment-permitting, which do combine.

As I discussed in section 5.2, structural [−Intrinsic,+Agreeable] case in Zulu does not correspond to a particular morpheme or class of morphemes. Rather, this type of case is what we observe with augmentless nominals. Similarly, augment-permitting morphology also has [−Intrinsic] properties: nominals marked with this morphology require independent licensing, just like quirky cased nominals in Icelandic. While in Icelandic the only solution to licensing quirky nominals is for them to receive structural licensing, augment- permitting obliques have two potential solutions to the licensing dilemma. They may appear in structurally licensed positions, just as in Icelandic, but they may also combine with a [+Intrinsic] augment morpheme, as we saw in the previous subsection.

The agreeable parameter

The second split that we've observed in this chapter has been represented with the feature [±Agreeable]. In Icelandic, we saw that nominals marked with quirky and inherent case are unable to control agreement, while nominals marked with structural case are able to agree. We find this same type of pattern in Zulu. We have seen throughout this book that both augmented and augmentless nominals are capable of controlling subject agreement in preverbal position. With augmentless nominals, this agreement pattern can only be observed if the augmentless nominal further raises to a structurally licensed position, as repeated in (240a) below:

(240a) a-ngi-fun-i   **muntu** [ukuthi a-   phek-e (i)qanda]
        NEG-1SG-want-NEG 1person that   1SJC- cook   (AUG)5egg
        'I don't want anyone to cook an egg.'

These augmented and augmentless nominals are therefore [+Agreeable], in that they permit agreement with a verb.

Nominals with augment-replacing or augment-permitting morphology, by contrast, cannot control subject agreement, as we saw in the previous subsection. In inversion constructions, oblique nominals may control agreement, but in doing so, they lose their oblique morphology. Just as in Icelandic, then, we find that the categories in Zulu that correspond to quirky and inherent case are unable to agree. In section 5.5.2, I return to a notable but systematic difference between the two languages: that while Icelandic obliques keep their case morphology at the expense of agreement, Zulu obliques undergo agreement at the expense of their case morphology.

5.4 THE AUGMENT AND THE ROLE OF CASE MORPHOLOGY IN ZULU

In this chapter, I have returned to a question first raised in chapter 3: what properties must be attributed to the augment to explain why augmented nominals do not require structural licensing? As I discussed in that chapter, it is difficult to understand the Zulu augment as making any particular reliable semantic contribution: I have shown that the augment can mark nominals that are definite, indefinite, specific, nonspecific, high- or low-scope. If the augment is merely a case marker, as I have argued in this chapter, then this lack of a specific semantic contribution becomes less surprising; when we consider the role of case morphemes that mark "nominative" or "accusative", we typically do not discuss them in semantic terms.

At the same time, if we compare the Zulu system of case morphology to the one described for Icelandic at the beginning of this chapter, we do find differences in the apparent extra-syntactic roles the different types of nominal morphology play. All of the non-structural morphology that we saw in Icelandic is constrained to particular semantic or structural configurations. Quirky case is idiosyncratically assigned by verbs to particular arguments. Inherent case corresponds to particular types of oblique semantics. While the augment-replacing and augment-permitting obliques follow this familiar pattern—corresponding to particular meanings, including locative, bene-factive, comitative, and instrumental (with the choice between "quirky" augment-permitting and "inherent" augment-replacing apparently sometimes idiosyncratic)—the augment does not. In Zulu, the augment vowel is not restricted in its distribution in any observable way—by structure, idiosyn-cratic selection, or semantics.

One way to characterize this free distribution of the augment would be as a "default" case marker that can license a nominal in any structural position. This sense of "default" is reminiscent of proposals that certain languages employ a default case marker that can license nominals that are not otherwise structurally licensed, as McCloskey (1985) and Chung and McCloskey (1987) argued for accusative subjects of nonfinite clauses in Irish, and as Kang (1988) argued for nominative subjects of certain small clauses in Korean. This view is a departure from more recent discussions of default case (including Schütze, 1997, 2001; McFadden, 2004), which take default case to simply be the unmarked morphological marker applied to nominals that are assumed to not require structural licensing in the first place. Crucially, as Schütze (2001, p. 208) discusses, on these theories default case does *not* serve to license nominals because if such a case were available, it "would render the Case Filter vacuous." This result is not, in fact, unwelcome in Zulu: as we have seen, the availability of the augment *does* obscure the effects of the Case Filter throughout much of Zulu grammar. It is only when we focus on the distribution of nominals without the augment that any structural effects are detectable.

While augmented nominals do not appear to have any reliable semantic correlates, neither are they completely freely available. In particular, as we saw in chapter 3, in environments where an augmentless nominal is possible, an augmented nominal is interpreted as necessarily specific:

(124) **Reported meaning contrast with augment**
    a. a-   ka- limaz- i   **a-**   **bantwana**
       NEG- 1S- hurt- NEG AUG- 2children
       'He doesn't hurt (some particular) children.'

b. a- ka- limaz- i **bantwana**
NEG- 1S- hurt- NEG 2children
'He doesn't hurt any children.'

(de Dreu, 2008, p. 18, ex. (2b), (3b), adapted)

We can understand this contrast as the result of the semantic (and additional structural) restrictions that *augmentless* nominals have in Zulu: they must occur in downward-entailing environments and carry certain (typically NPI or *wh-*) interpretations. In an environment in which a more highly specified element, the augmentless nominal, is available, the choice to use the less specified augmented version indicates a contrast. In other words, we can think of the more specified augmentless nominal as blocking the augmented version in contexts where both are possible. In this sense, the semantic and distributional properties of augmented and augmentless nominals seem to be the reverse of what we expect: under this analysis, *structural* case in Zulu correlates with a limited distribution and restricted semantics, while an *intrinsic* case does not.

While it may seem odd for structural case to have interpretive consequences, this type of pattern is in fact well-attested cross-linguistically (see de Hoop, 1996, for an overview of several of these cases). In a number of languages, an alternation between two case morphemes (either both structural, or one structural and one not) in a particular structural position can have the same sort of interpretive consequences observed in Zulu.

One such case alternation with interpretive restrictions and consequences occurs with the distribution of the Finnish partitive (Brattico and Leinonen, 2009; Csirmaz, 2012; Heinämäki, 1984; de Hoop, 1996; Kiparsky, 1998, 2001; Thomas, 2003; Vainikka, 1989, 1993, and others). Certain nominals in Finnish can alternate between partitive and non-partitive case, with corresponding interpretive differences. The two main functions of partitive case, among several others, have been described as *aspectual* and *NP-related* (Kiparsky, 1998). These functions yield the definiteness contrast illustrated in (321), with partitive signaling indefinite interpretation, and a telicity contrast, with partitive signaling an atelic predicate as in (322).

(321)   a. Anne tapaa vieraita
Anne meets guests.PART
'Anne meets some guests.'

b. Anne tapaa vieraat
Anne meets guests.ACC
'Anne meets the guests.'   (de Hoop, 1996, ex. (20), (21))

(322)   a. Ammu- i-   n   karhu- a
shoot- PST- 1SG bear- PART
'I shot at the (a) bear.' (atelic)

b. Ammu- i-   n   karhu- n
   shoot PST- 1SG bear- ACC
   'I shot the (a) bear.' (telic)   (Kiparsky, 1998, ex. (1))

These alternations are restricted to particular structural positions: while
internal arguments can participate in either the definiteness or telicity alternation, as illustrated in (321) and (322) above, the highest arguments of the
predicate, even the sole argument of an unaccusative, never receive partitive
case to signal atelicity, but can receive partitive case as indefinites, as (323)
shows:

(323) Sitä   käsikirjoitusta oli   sängy- n   alla- kin
       that.PART manuscript.PART be.PST3SG bed-   GEN under- even
       '(Parts of) that manuscript were even under the bed.'
                                                              (Kiparsky, 1998, ex. (54))

This interaction between morphological case alternations, structural position, and interpretation in Finnish has a similar character to the patterns we
find in Zulu. In a recent analysis, Csirmaz (2012) argues that the distribution
of partitive case in Finish can be unified by the notion of *divisibility*, where
"a predicate P is divisible if and only if for every argument of the predicate,
all proper parts of the argument are parts of arguments of P" (Csirmaz, 2012,
p. 3). A bare plural or a mass noun is divisible, therefore, because all parts of
these nouns, including individual elements and parts of individual elements,
are parts of (a part of) the original set.

Assuming that case morphology is inserted post-syntactically, Csirmaz
claims that a nominal spells out with partitive case if it is minimally contained
within a divisible Spell-out domain. That is, if either the nominal itself *or*
the entire vP that contains it is divisible, the nominal will bear partitive
morphology. With a divisible vP, such as the atelic predicate in (322a), the
object of that vP will be marked with partitive because it spells out inside the
divisible vP phase. The subject of such a predicate would not bear partitive,
because it is outside of the divisible Spell-out domain. If a DP itself is divisible
(either subject or object), as in (323) or (321a), it will also spell out with
partitive case.

On this analysis, despite the fact that partitive case appears in a wider
variety of environments than accusative case, it is characterized as the
non-default case. The more restricted accusative case is in fact the default
morphological realization of structural case. In this sense, this analysis of
Finnish is also in line with my analysis of Zulu, since I argue that the
more restricted augmentless nominals are the true reflection of structural
licensing.

We find another interesting interaction between partitive constructions, interpretation, and structural licensing in French.[6] As we saw in chapter 3, French shares with Zulu an apparent subject/object asymmetry in NPI licensing. In particular, an embedded bare indefinite in French can be licensed by matrix negation in object position, but not in subject position, as repeated below:

(324) a. ? Je n' ai exigé qu' ils arrêtent **personne**
       I NEG have required that they arrest nobody
       'I didn't require that they arrest anyone.'

     b. * Je n' ai exigé que **personne** soit arrêté
       I NEG have required that nobody be arrested
       intended: 'I didn't require that anyone be arrested.'

(Kayne, 1981, ex. (3)–(4))

While I concluded in chapter 3 that the general properties of the French constructions differ enough from Zulu that a unified account is not desirable, if we focus in particular on the behavior of the partitive article in these constructions, we see that a similar logic emerges to the Zulu augment distribution, suggesting that while the mechanisms governing both processes may be different, the realization of case may function similarly.

In particular, the so-called partitive article in French, which marks indefinite non-count and plural count nouns, is typically compatible with both specific and nonspecific readings (Miestamo, 2014). Under negation, the partitive article seems to require a specific interpretation, while the bare *de* form yields the nonspecific indefinite/NPI reading:

(325) a. je bois **du** lait
      1SG.NOM drink.1SG PART.M milk
      'I'm drinking (some) milk.'

     b. je ne bois pas **de** lait
      1SG.NOM NEG drink.1SG NEG DET milk
      'I'm not drinking (any) milk.'

     c. je ne bois pas **du** lait qu' il m' offre
      1SG.NOM NEG drink.1SG NEG PART.M milk that 3SG.NOM 1SG.DAT offer
      'I'm not drinking (any of) the milk that he's offering me.'

(Miestamo, 2014, ex. (5e-f), (6a))

This requirement that the partitive article scope above negation (yielding specificity) goes away in exactly the environment where a bare nominal/bare *de* form is ungrammatical, as in the following examples:

6. Thanks to an anonymous reviewer for pointing out these facts.

(326) a. Je   n' ai   pas exigé qu' ils   achètent **du**
    1SG.NOM NEG have.1SG NEG required that 3PL.NOM buy.3PL PART.M
    lait
    milk
    'I didn't require that they buy some milk.'

    b. Je   n' ai   pas exigé qu' ils   achètent **de** lait
    1SG.NOM NEG have.1SG NEG required that 3PL.NOM buy.3PL DET milk
    'I didn't require that they buy any milk.'

    c. Je   n' ai   pas exigé que **du** lait soit   acheté
    1SG.NOM NEG have.1SG NEG required that PART.M lait be.3SG bought
    'I didn't require that some/any milk be bought.'

    d. * Je   n' ai   pas exigé que **de** lait soit   acheté
    1SG.NOM NEG have.1SG NEG required that DET milk be.3SG bought
    intended: 'I didn't require that any milk be bought.'

                                    (Jean-Philippe Marcotte, p.c.)

Just as in Zulu, then, the more general use of the partitive article is blocked by the more highly specified *de* form; when a partitive article is used in a construction were a *de* form is possible, the result is interpreted as meaningful. In this way, the meanings of the augment in Zulu and the partitive article in French are similar: we can say that neither one has a particular meaning with respect to definiteness, specificity, or scope. Rather, it is the augmentless or bare form that is licensed only in a specific set of interpretive (and structural) conditions. When these conditions are met, the use of the less specific form creates a meaning contrast.

Beyond the partitive patterns in Finnish and French, we find other languages where morphological case alternations have semantic consequences. Another well-described alternation is the genitive of negation in Russian, where genitive case alternates with structural case in negative contexts to yield a weak indefinite interpretation (though with complications, as discussed by Partee and Borschev, 2004). In Turkish as well, the distribution of accusative case has interpretive consequences (Dede, 1986; Enc, 1991; Kornfilt, 1997; among others). On objects in immediately preverbal position, the presence of the accusative morpheme signals specificity. As the examples in (327) show, the accusative morpheme can co-occur with the indefinite article *bir*; since Turkish lacks a definite article, accusatives without an article are typically interpreted as definite:

(327) **Turkish distribution of ACC in preverbal position**
    a. (Ben) kitap oku-du-m
       I   book read-PST-1SG
       'I was book-reading.'

b. (Ben) bu kitab-ı   oku-du-m
   I   this book-ACC read-PST-1SG
   'I read this book.'

c. (Ben) kitab-ı   oku-du-m
   I   book-ACC read-PST-1SG
   'I read the book.'

d. (Ben) bir kitap oku-du-m
   I   a book read-PST-1SG
   'I read certain book.'

e. (Ben) bir kitab-ı   oku-du-m
   I   a book-ACC read-PST-1SG
   'I read a certain book.'   (von Heusinger and Kornfilt, 2005, ex. (1))

When the object does not appear immediately before the verb, accusative case is required. While these non-adjacent accusative-marked objects typically receive a specific interpretation, they do not always, as von Heusinger and Kornfilt (2005) show:

(328) a.   Bizim ev-de   çay-ı   her zaman Aytül yap-ar
           our   house-LOC tea-ACC always   Aytül make-AOR
           'Aytül always makes the tea in our family.'

      b. *Bizim ev-de   çay her zaman Aytül yap-ar
           our   house-LOC tea always   Aytül make-AOR
           intended: 'Aytül always makes the tea in our family.'
                                    (von Heusinger and Kornfilt, 2005, ex. (10))

As von Heusinger and Kornfilt (2005, p. 3) conclude: "the accusative case marker can indicate the referential property of the direct object (such as specificity) in clearly defined morphological environments in a reliable fashion; in other contexts, it is not a reliable indicator of properties like specificity." While the precise environments and conditioning factors for the alternation differ from Zulu and some of the others we have observed, we again find a similar pattern where structural case morphology becomes entangled in semantic effects.

In all of these constructions, the relevant case alternation and its interpretive consequences are limited to a particular syntactic domain. In these environments, a more widely available morpheme that typically does not convey particular values for specificity and/or definiteness takes on a more specified interpretation in contrast to the meaning conveyed by the restricted alternative. Outside of the correct structural environment, the case alternation is impossible and cannot be employed to mark the interpretive difference. Strikingly, the restricted value in Finnish was the structural accusative. For

Turkish objects, the restricted value was the unmarked form—the same form in which nominative subjects appear. In light of these facts, my analysis of Zulu nominal marking appears to be in good company: the emergence of structural case—augmentless nominals—in a limited set of environments and linked to specific interpretations is part of a broader cross-linguistic picture. While a unification of the semantics of the augmented/augmentless alternation with the syntax I have proposed here is beyond the scope of this work, this collection of similar cross-linguistic patterns suggests an ideal starting point for such research.

5.5 CASE AND AGREEMENT INTERACTIONS

In this section I return to some of the issues surrounding the case system proposed in this chapter. First, I return to the property of [±Agreeable] to argue that we can predict whether a particular morpheme will be [+Agreeable] in Zulu based on its morphological relationship to the noun class marker: the augment allows agreement because it itself "agrees" in noun class with the stem, while augment-replacing and augment-permitting prefixes do not. Next, I relate the prohibition on agreeing obliques in Zulu to the similar prohibition we find in languages like Icelandic. A comparison of the two suggests that different timing relationships between agreement and morphological case assignment are necessary in the two different languages. With these differences in mind, I return briefly to the discussion of Activity from section 4.5.1 in the previous chapter. I then address the question of why certain nominal morphemes—the augment and the augment-permitting prefixes— may combine with each other on a single nominal while others cannot. I propose that the augment-permitting prefixes are prepositional, while the augment and augment-replacing prefixes are not. Finally, I discuss a few additional facts about the distribution of the augment within certain complex DP structures and suggest that the unexpected appearance of augmentless nominals within these structures can be understood as a form of case concord.

5.5.1 On Agreeableness

Perhaps the main distinguishing feature of the augment, in the context of the analysis developed in this chapter, is the fact that though it is intrinsically licensing, it permits nominals that it marks to agree. While Schütze (1997) proposed that only nominals marked with structural case are capable of agreement, the fact that the augment permits agreement requires a different generalization for Zulu.

I propose that in Zulu, what determines whether a particular type of nominal morphology will allow or prevent agreement is not the abstract category of that morphology, but rather the nature of the morpheme itself. Crucially, the fact that the augment vowel *reflects the noun class* of the nominal it combines with makes the phi-features of that nominal available for outside agreement process. By contrast, augment-replacing and augment-permitting morphology does not "agree" with the noun class of the nominal it marks and thus prevents those phi-features from being accessed. Rezác (2008) makes a similar proposal for PPs in certain Basque dialects, arguing that prepositions that agree with their complements become "transparent" for Agree and can therefore participate in outside agreement processes in the same manner as plain nominals.

Simply by looking at the shape of these morphemes, then, we can determine whether they will allow or disallow agreement: augment-replacing and augment-permitting morphology *does not* reflect the noun class of the complement and thus is opaque for outside agreement. The augment *does* reflect noun class and thus permits agreement, but the augmentless nominals receive their licensing from higher in the clause—and thus presumably have no need for the intervening level of structure present in the other three categories.

(329)   a. **Agreeing KP**   b. **Non-agreeing KP**[7]   c. **Augmentless**

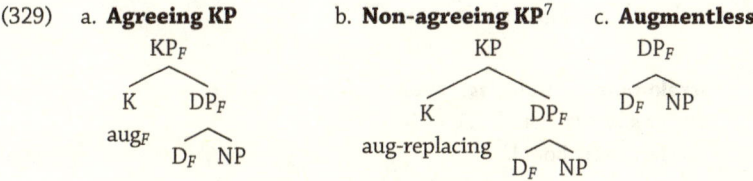

The structures in (329) are one possible way to represent this difference: the phi-features of the noun class marker make the entire DP available for agreement. When the augment "agrees" with the DP, the entire KP is now available. When the case marker does not agree, those features are not visible at the KP-level (see Baker, 2008, and Taraldsen, 2010, for a similar take on on noun class agreement with determiners in Bantu, and in Zulu in particular). In section 5.5.3 I address a possible alternative analysis for the augment-permitting prefixes, but one that is still compatible with this view of Agreeableness.

---

7. In section 5.5.3, I return to the syntactic status of the augment-permitting prefixes. I argue that, based on systematic differences between these prefixes and the augment and augment-replacing morphology, the augment-permitting prefixes are better classified as true prepositions, rather than case heads, as represented here. The observations about their non-agreeing status—and the consequences that follow—that I make in this section remain valid.

5.5.2 Timing of Agreement and Case

As mentioned in this and preceding sections, one property that Zulu shares with a language like Icelandic is the inability of oblique case-marked nominals to agree with the verb. In Zulu, as we saw, this prohibition on agreeing obliques results in omission of oblique morphology when the oblique argument appears in an agreeing position:

(318) **Locative inversion: no augment-replacing oblique morphology**

    a. abantu   abadala   ba-hlala *(**ku**)- lezi   zindlu
       AUG.2people 2REL.old 2s-stay KU-   10these 10houses
       'Old people live in these houses.'

    b. (*ku-) lezi   zindlu   zi- hlala abantu   abadala
       KU-   10these 10houses 10s- stay AUG.2people 2REL.old
       'Old people live in these houses.'   (Buell 2007, ex. (7), adapted)

By contrast, as we saw in Icelandic in chapter 4, when oblique nominals occupy a position that would normally trigger agreement, they keep their oblique morphology and instead cause a change in verbal agreement patterns. In a simple intransitive with a quirky subject, default 3SG agreement appears on the verb as in (305a), in contrast to an intransitive with a nominative subject, which requires agreement, as in (305b).

(305)   a. **strákunum**   leidd- **ist** / *ust
        the.boys.DAT.PL bored- 3SG / *3PL
        'The boys were bored.'

      b. **strákarnir**   leidd-   **ust** / *ist
        the.boys.NOM.PL walked.hand.in.hand- 3PL / *3SG
        'The boys walked hand in hand.'   (Sigurðsson, 1996, ex. (1),(2))

When the subject is marked with quirky case, the verb can sometimes agree with certain (third person) non-subject arguments, such as nominative objects, as in (330), or embedded arguments (I discussed the circumstances under which this type of agreement is permitted in chapter 4), as in (331).

(330)   honum   lík- **a þeir**
       him.DAT.SG like- 3PL they.NOM.PL
       'He likes them.'   (Sigurðsson, 1996, ex. (7c))

(331)   henni   virð- **ast myndirnar**   vera ljótar
       her.DAT.SG seem- 3PL the.paintings.NOM.PL be   ugly
       'It seems to her that the paintings are ugly.'
                     (Sigurðsson and Holmberg, 2008, ex. (4a))

Thus, while it seems that Zulu and Icelandic have the same surface ban on agreeing obliques, they achieve a grammatical output in different ways. In Zulu, oblique case morphology is lost and agreement appears, while in Icelandic agreement is sacrificed (at least in constructions where the oblique nominal acts as an intervenor, as discussed in detail in chapter 4) but the oblique case morphology is retained.

This difference has consequences for our understanding of the timing of different grammatical processes. Bobaljik (2008) takes the dependence of verbal agreement in Icelandic on morphological case to be evidence for treating phi-agreement as a post-syntactic process. He argues that because morphological case in Icelandic can be determined via post-syntactic insertion rules, any operations that are dependent on morphological case are therefore also post-syntactic. In Zulu, by contrast, we appear to have the opposite dependency: agreement with a nominal appears to prevent it from bearing (otherwise obligatory) oblique morphology. This reverse order of operations suggests that agreement has to be able to precede morphological case in Zulu. Furthermore, the strict correspondence between agreement and syntactic movement in Zulu suggests that agreement is more closely entangled with syntactic processes in the language, rather than post-syntactic ones.

A related issue to the question of the relative timing of case and agreement is the role of the Activity Condition, as discussed in section 4.5.1 of chapter 4. In that chapter, I proposed that when nominals are case-licensed by L, they are rendered inactive for all further agreement processes—including phi-agreement with T. Since I have proposed in this chapter that the augment and the augment-replacing prefixes also license nominals, we might ask whether the nominals they mark are rendered inactive by virtue of this licensing process. If so, then we would expect all nominals to be unable to agree *after* they are case-marked. In this section, I have suggested for oblique nominals, on the basis of the contrasts between Zulu and Icelandic, that case morphology is introduced very late in Zulu—after phi-agreement. If this relatively late insertion holds not just for the oblique markers, but also for the augment itself, then inactivity will not arise until late in the derivation. If the augment is inserted *after* all movement and agreement has taken place, then its presence on a nominal at the end of the derivation is essentially irrelevant to the Activity of a nominal throughout the derivation. In other words, regardless of the case morphology that a nominal bears at the end of the derivation, we will only see the effects of Activity that arise through structural licensing: if a nominal is probed by L it will become inactive and if it moves before probing it will remain active. In chapter 4, I showed that augmented nominals behave as though they can receive licensing from L, even though they don't seem to need it. Under this view, even nominals that surface with an augment are in fact augmentless at the point in the derivation where L probes.[8]

One remaining issue is the question of what allows the the oblique morphology—and the meaning it conveys—to disappear in inversion constructions. A possible factor in the availability of these constructions is their rather limited distribution. Unlike in Bantu languages that have locative inversion constructions that retain—and agree with—locative noun class morphology on the inverted locative (as shown, for example, by Bresnan and Kanerva, 1989; Bresnan, 1994; Marten, 2006; Diercks, 2011), the Zulu locative inversion of the type discussed here has a more limited distribution. The example in (332) from Otjiherero below show that, at least in some languages, locative inversion of this type can occur with a transitive predicate (though as Marten, 2006, shows, the availability of this construction varies even across Bantu languages that have full locative agreement in inversion):

(332) pò- ndjúwó pé-   tjáng- èr-   à òvá- nàtjè   ò- mbàpírà
       16- 9house 16s.HAB- write- APPL- FV 2-   children 9- letter
       'At the house write (the) children a letter.' (Marten, 2006, ex. (36)) *Otjiherero*

In Zulu, the construction is restricted, roughly, to middle-type contexts and certain other unaccusatives, as illustrated below:

(333) a. lezi   zindlu   zi- hlala abantu abadala
          10these 10houses 10s- stay 2people 2old
          'Old people live in these houses.'   (Buell, 2007, ex. (7))

       b. lesi   silonda si- phuma ubovu
          7this 7sore 7s- exit   AUG.11pus
          'Pus is coming out of this sore.'   (Nkabinde, 1985, p. 47)

In other environments, the alternation is simply not possible:

(334) a.   abangane   ba- cula **ku**- le-   ndlu
            AUG.2children 2s- sing KU- 9DEM- 9house
            'Children sing in this house.'

---

8. An alternative to this view of the augment as always being inserted late in the derivation would be to assume that while the insertion of the augment *does* inactivate the DP it licenses, the entire KP that it heads is still active, following (Carstens, 2005, 2011), who argues that elements with uninterpretable phi-features become inactive only when they have been probed. The fact that the KP contains phi-features would be crucial to its ability to enter into phi-agreement processes with higher heads, again in contrast to the augment-replacing morphology.

b. # le-   ndlu   i- cula abangane
9DEM- 9house 9s- sing AUG.2children
'The house sings children.'
*'Children sing in this house.'

The distribution of the instrument inversion is even more restricted, as Zeller (2010) notes. In particular, it appears to be grammatical for only the most archetypal instances of instruments for specific actions. In (335), we can see that while the inversion is permitted with the predicate *dla* 'eat' if *isipunu* 'spoon,' the typical Zulu eating utensil, is used, it is ungrammatical when other utensils are substituted. The example in (336) shows the same pattern with *bhala* 'write' and *ipeni* 'pen':

(335) a.   isipuni   si- dla uJohn
AUG.7spoon 7s- eat AUG.1John
'John is eating with a spoon.'   (Zeller, 2010, ex. (50))

b. *imfoloko/ ama-chopsticks i-/a-   dla uJohn
AUG.9fork/ AUG.6-chopsticks 9s-/6s- eat AUG.1John

(336) a.   ipeni   li- bhala uSipho
AUG.5pen 5s- write AUG.1Sipho
'Sipho wrties with a pen.'

b. *ipenseli/   ikhompyutha li- bhala uSipho
AUG.5pencil/ AUG.5computer 5s- write AUG.1Sipho

It seems likely that what unites these environments in which augment-replacing or augment-permitting oblique morphology may be omitted—thus permitting the inversion and agreement—are those in which there is a certain degree of predictability to the meanings, which allows for recoverability.

5.5.3 The Status of Augment-permitting Prefixes

To return to the issue of the internal structure and Agreeableness of the different categories of nominal case morphology, in this subsection I focus on the interaction of the augment and augment-permitting morphology. As I discussed in the previous sections, while the augment is in complementary distribution with augment-replacing morphology, it can appear in conjunction with augment-permitting morphology:

(306a) **Augment-replacing morphology**
u-buy-is-el-e   i-fowuni   y-akho   en-dala
2SG-return-CAUS-APPL-SJC AUG-9phone 9ASSOC-your 9REL-old
kwa-MTN   Service Provider
KWA-5MTN Service Provider
'Return your old phone to the MTN Service Provider.'

(309a) **Augment-permitting morphology**

uXolani u- dlala **no-**   mfana   (= na+umfana)
1Xolani 1s- play NA.AUG- 1boy
'Xolani is playing with a boy.'

If the augment and the augment-permitting prefixes are both case heads, it is perhaps mysterious why they can combine on a single nominal—and why the augment and the augment-replacing prefixes cannot. One possible explanation for this difference would be to analyze augment-permitting morphology—but not augment replacing morphology—as prepositional, rather than as a case marker. With such an analysis, Zulu begins to look more uniform in certain respects. First, we can understand why the augment can combine with augment-permitting morphology, which attaches as a P outside of KP, but not with augment-replacing morphology, which is itself a K:

(337) **Augment-permitting morphology**

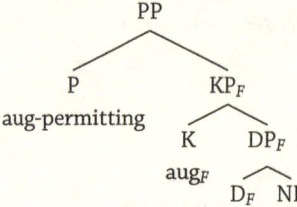

For comparison, the structures proposed for the other categories— augment, augment-replacing, and augmentless—are repeated below:

(329)   a. **Agreeing KP**   b. **Non-agreeing KP**   c. **Augmentless**

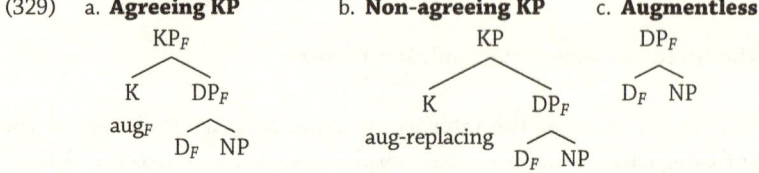

Second, if only the augment and augment-replacing morphology correspond to a level of KP structure, then all K heads in Zulu are nominal licensers. Nominals that require structural licensing—both 'plain' augmentless nominals and those marked with augment-permitting prefixes—are missing this layer of structure. On this analysis, P would not be a nominal licenser in Zulu—in the same way that T and v^o are not licensers. This type of analysis may perhaps also shed light on the differences between augment-permitting morphology and quirky case in languages like Icelandic. Though the two have the same profile with respect to the Intrinsic and Agreeable properties discussed earlier in this chapter, quirky case in Icelandic is typically selected for by certain predicates. Zulu does not display that type of selection for augment-permitting morphology.

There are several additional respects in which augment-permitting morphology differs from augment-replacing morphology which might support an analysis of the augment-permitting prefixes as prepositions. First, as I noted in section 5.3.1, the augment-permitting prefix *na-* is involved in possessive and certain existential predication constructions (see Buell and de Dreu, 2013, for discussion).

(338) a. ngi- **na**-   bangane abaningi   (= na+abangane)
          1SG- NA.AUG- 2friend 2REL.many
          'I have many friends.'

      b. ngenxa   yeholide   ku- **ne**- siminyaminya sezimoto
          because.of 9ASSOC.AUG.5holiday 17S- NA.AUG- 7crowd   7.AUG.10cars
          'Because of the holiday, there's a lot of traffic.'
                                                      (=na+isiminyaminya)

Neither the augment nor any augment-replacing morphemes I am aware of play any similar role. The use of augment-permitting morphology—and not of augment-replacing morphology—in these types of predication is expected if the augment-permitting prefixes are true prepositions as opposed to simply case markers, following claims by Freeze (1992), Harley (2003), and others, who argue that exactly these constructions involve a prepositional element.

Another factor that suggests that augment-permitting morphology differs from augment-replacing morphology and the augment concerns tone patterns.[9] As Mzolo (1968) describes, Zulu augments are high-toned. When they combine with a low-toned stem, their high tone can spread into the stem. This tone pattern contrasts with an augmentless nominal, which remains fully low-toned:

(339) a. A- ngi- m- bon- i   **úmúntù**
          NEG- 1SG- 2O- see- NEG AUG.1person
          'I don't see the person.'

      b. A- ngi- bon- i   **mùntù**
          NEG- 1SG- see- NEG 1person
          'I don't see anyone.'   (Mzolo, 1968, p. 204)

The augment-replacing prefixes that I have examined contribute a high tone, just like the augment:

9. Thanks to Leston Buell for raising this issue.

(340) u-Sipho   u- zo- thum- ela   imali   **kú- múntú**
AUG-1Sipho 1s- FUT- send- APPL AUG.9money KU- 1person
'Sipho will send money to the person.'

This tone pattern persists even in environments where an augmentless
nominal would be expected, which suggests that the high tone is coming from
the prefix itself, rather than from a 'hidden augment' that contributes only
tone, but not vowel quality:

(341) u-Sipho   a- ka- zu- thum- ela imali   **kú- múntù**
AUG-1Sipho NEG- 1s- FUT- send- APPL AUG.9money KU- 1person
'Sipho will not send money to anyone.'

The augment-permitting prefixes, by contrast, do not contribute a high
tone. As the contrast in (342) illustrates, when augment-permitting prefixes
combine with a low-tone stem without an augment, the whole word remains
low-toned:

(342)   a. ngi- khuluma **nó-   múntù**
1SG- speak   NA.AUG- 1person
'I'm speaking with a/the person.'

b. a-   ngi- khulum- i   **nà- mùntù**
NEG- 1SG- speak-   NEG NA- 1person
'I'm not speaking to anyone.'

By treating augment-permitting morphology as true prepositions, as
opposed to K⁰ heads, we therefore not only gain an explanation for why they
are able to combine with the augment, but we also gain new understanding on
why the augment and augment-replacing prefixes share certain properties to
the exclusion of the augment-permitting prefixes.

5.5.4 Case Concord?

A final issue that I will briefly address in this section concerns the distribution
of the augment inside complex DPs that contain relative clauses, possessors,
and other types of adnominal dependents. So far we have seen that only
the nominal that is most local to a licensing head may appear without its
augment in Zulu. When we consider nominals in DP-internal positions,
the picture changes slightly. Recall that in (312d), an associative-marked
possessor nominal could appear without its augment under negation, though
an augment was required otherwise. This contrast is illustrated again in (343):

(343) a. ngi- si- bon- ile isigqoko **so-** muntu
   1SG- 7O- see- PFV AUG.7hat 7ASSOC.AUG- 1person
   'I saw the person's hat.'

   b. a- ngi- bon- anga sigqoko **sa-** muntu
   NEG- 1SG- see- NEG 7hat 7ASSOC- 1person
   'I didn't see anybody's hat.'

In (343a), the associative prefix *sa-* combines with the augment *u-* to yield *so-*. In (343b), the augment is absent, leaving the possessive to surface as *sa-*. As we saw in chapter 3 constructions like those in (343) contain a single structural licenser, and so should only be able to license one augmentless nominal, raising the question of what the source of licensing for *muntu* is.

We find a similar situation in adjectival and relative clauses. For some speakers of Zulu,[10] the initial vowel on certain adjectival modifiers or relative clauses can be omitted when the noun that they modify is also augmentless:[11]

(344) a. a- ngi- bon- i abantu **a- ba- dala** /*badala
   NEG- 1SG- see- NEG AUG.2people AUG.REL- 2- old /*2.old
   'I don't see the old people.'

   b. a- ngi- bon- i bantu (a-) **badala**
   NEG- 1SG- see- NEG 2people (AUG.REL) 2.old
   'I don't see any old people.'

(345) a. a- ngi- bon- i abantu abagqoka izigqoko ezibomvu
   NEG- 1SG- see- NEG AUG.2people AUG.REL.2.wear AUG.8hat AUG.REL.8.red
   'I don't see the people wearing red hats.'

   b. a- ngi- bon- i bantu bagqoka zigqoko zibomvu
   NEG- 1SG- see- NEG 2people 2.wear 8hat 8.red
   'I don't see any people wearing any red hats.'

In (344), the initial vowel of the modifying adjective is required when the head noun is augmented, but is optional when the nominal is augmentless. In (345b), we can see that this process can even carry over to elements inside a relative clause (see Visser, 2008, for similar findings in Xhosa).

The environments in which this unexpected augment drop is possible all share a common property: the head noun of their containing DP must itself

---

10. This construction was generally used and accepted more by older speakers of Durban Zulu than by younger speakers.

11. Roughly, it appears that the elements that allow the vowel to be omitted are those that have an overt prefix signaling noun class, separate from the vowel, such as class 2 (*a- ba-* → *ba-*), while those that do not permit the vowel drop lack this prefix, such as class 1 (**o-* → Ø).

be augmentless. When the head noun appears with an augment, internal elements must also bear an augment, even if the clause-level licensing conditions have not changed, as the ungrammatical sentences in (346) illustrate:

(346) a. *a- ngi- bon- i **a**bantu **ba**- dala
 NEG- 1SG- see- NEG AUG.2people 2- old
 'I don't see the old people.'

 b. *a- ngi- bon- anga **i**sigqoko **sa**- muntu
 NEG- 1SG- see- NEG AUG.7hat 7ASSOC- 1person
 'I didn't see anybody's hat.'

While the distribution of these augmentless DP-internal elements may be surprising from a syntactic licensing point of view, we can understand them as a form of case concord (Norris, 2012, 2014). That is, the ability of a nominal (other than the head) inside a DP to appear without its augment is dependent on matching of the case value of the entire DP to elements within the DP. Norris (2014) formalizes case concord as follows:

(347) **Case Concord** (Norris, 2014, ex. (264))
 a. Let X and Y be two nodes in a single extended projection, Y immediately dominating X.
 b. If Y has a valued case feature [CASE:α] (but X does not), then copy Y's case feature to X.

On this view, if a DP receives structural licensing via L, then that case value (which is morphologically realized as the ability to be augmentless in nonveridical environments) can be copied down onto its dependents, licensing them as augmentless nominals as well. The trickle-down effect imposed by the process in (347) also appears to be evident in Zulu. As (348) below illustrates, when a DP-internal constituent appears *with* its augment, dependents of that constituent must also have an augment:

(348) a. a- ngi- bon- i bantu bagqoka zigqoko zibomvu
 NEG- 1SG- see- NEG 2people 2.wear 8hat 8.red
 'I don't see any people wearing any red hats.'

 b. *a- ngi- bon- i bantu **a**bagqoka zigqoko (e)-
 NEG- 1SG- see- NEG AUG.2people AUG.2REL.wear 8hat (AUG.REL)-
 zibomvu
 8.red
 'I don't see any people wearing any red hats.'

 c. *a- ngi- bon- i bantu bagqoka **i**zigqoko zibomvu
 NEG- 1SG- see- NEG 2people 2.old AUG.8hat 8.red
 'I don't see any people wearing any red hats.'

d. a- ngi- bon- i bantu bagqoka **i**zigqoko **e-** zibomvu
    NEG- 1SG- see- NEG 2people 2.old AUG.8hat AUG.REL- 8.red
    'I don't see any people wearing any red hats.'

When the relative clause in (348b) appears with an augment, elements inside the relative clause must also be augmented. In (348c), the relative clause is augmentless, but the head noun of its object bears an augment, which means that the object's modifier must also bear an augment, as the grammatical version in (348d) illustrates.

For Norris (2014), this copying process can only occur if the recipient is not already valued for case. This requirement fits the patterns we've seen in Zulu: as discussed in section 5.5.2, it appears that the augment—and other intrinsic case-licensing morphology—enters into the derivation late, perhaps after all A-movement and agreement. These case concord constructions would therefore involve spread of L-licensing downward onto dependents inside the DP. While we can adopt this understanding of case concord to account for the basics of the Zulu pattern, the Zulu constructions have a number of other properties that complicate the picture compared to the languages in Norris' sample. First, as Norris (2014) notes, concord processes in Estonian, Icelandic, and many other languages he discusses are obligatory: concord must occur in the entire available domain. As examples like (348) illustrate, the Zulu process appears to be optional. Norris recognizes the existence of optional concord, pointing to constructions in Nez Perce where case morphology is optionally copied onto adjectives and numerals:

(349) **Nez Perce optional concord**

a. 'e-pewi-tx   yoosyoos wixsilikeecet'es-**ne**
   3OBJ-look.for-IMPER.PL blue   chair-OBJ
   'Look for the blue chair!'

b. 'e-pewi-se   yoosyoos-**na** wixsilikeecet'es-**ne**
   3OBJ-look.for-IMPV blue-OBJ   chair-OBJ
   'I am looking at the blue chair.' (Norris, 2014, ex. (427), citing Deak, 2010)

Norris suggests that this type of optional concord in Nez Perce may be due to post-syntactic optionality: specifically, in his system the morphological realization of syntactic concord is due to insertion of Agr^o nodes, so he concludes that perhaps Nez Perce allows for this insertion step to be skipped. As (349) illustrates, the relevant concord processes in Nez Perce involve the *addition* of morphology in the concord construction and the *absence* of morphology when concord does not occur. In the Zulu augment drop cases, we essentially find the reverse: concord involves the *absence* of morphology, while the lack of concord involves the insertion of an augment.

Zulu also presents an additional complication: in all other instances of structural licensing that we have observed, subsequent insertion of an augment morpheme on a licensed nominal has been possible – and indeed is obligatory in some contexts. If we consider the ungrammatical examples in (348), for example, we might wonder what rules out the following derivation: first, concord occurs throughout the entire DP, licensing augment drop on every element; second, optional augment insertion occurs on the head nominal, but not other elements inside DP. The unavailability of this hypothetical derivation, as indicated by (348), suggests that these instances of concord have a more restricted distribution of the augment than other constructions.

We can rule out this unattested combination due to the interpretive requirements on augmentless nominals discussed in chapter 3 and in section 5.4 of this chapter: in addition to being licensed by L, Zulu augmentless nominals must also be licensed as NPIs. In particular, we saw that outside of case-licensed positions, the augment contributes no particular meaning; augmented nominals in these positions are compatible with definite, specific indefinite, or nonspecific indefinite readings. In nonveridical case-licensed positions, where the conditions for NPI licensing have been met, the use of an augment becomes meaningful, signaling specificity:

(350) **Reported meaning contrast with augment**

a. a- ka- limaz- i **a- bantwana**
NEG- 1s- hurt- NEG AUG- 2children
'He doesn't hurt (some particular) children.'

b. a- ka- limaz- i **bantwana**
NEG- 1s- hurt- NEG 2children
'He doesn't hurt any children.'   (de Dreu, 2008, ex. (2b), (3b), adapted)

Specific nominals act as islands for NPI licensing (Ladusaw, 1980; Progovac, 1993b; Han and Siegel, 1996), as the English complex NP data in (351) shows:

(351) a. Nobody heard [*a* rumor that Mary **ever** kissed John].

     b. * Nobody heard [*the* rumor that Mary **ever** kissed John].
              (Han and Siegel, 1996, fn 5, ex. (43a))

The inability of the head nominal to bear an augment while its dependents are augmentless is therefore expected due to NPI licensing conditions: while the addition of the augment may not matter from the perspective of case-licensing or concord, it rules out the availability of the augment on DP-internal elements due to its island-inducing specificity.

With this understanding of the restriction on adding an augment to higher elements in a DP with case concord, we can adopt a fairly simple account for the apparent optionality of the Zulu concord process. We can suppose, as Norris

(2014) does for Nez Perce, that the syntactic copying operation involved in concord is obligatory throughout the entire DP domain. The availability of the augment on lower elements inside the DP is exactly parallel to the general availability of augments on L-licensed nominals elsewhere in the language. The only restrictions on the late addition of an augment are those that would create problems for NPI licensing.

5.6 EXAMINING THE AUGMENT INSIDE DP

So far in this chapter, I have argued that we can consider the augment vowel to be an instantiation of a case head (K°) in Zulu. At the clause level, nominals with this morphology are licensed by the augment itself, while those without require some other form of structural licensing. Recall from chapter 3 that there are a variety of other environments, internal to DP, in which nominals can or must appear without an augment vowel. In contrast to the DP-internal augment concord processes discussed in the previous section, in which concerned elements are dependent to the head nominal inside DP, these environments involve the head noun itself, either at a level below DP or as part of a more complex DP. In this section, I will examine these environments in more detail. The full summary of augmentless nominal distribution, as reported by Mzolo (1968), von Staden (1973), and Buell (2011), is given in table 5.4. The table compares the previously described distributions of the augment in particular environments with my own findings for Durban Zulu.

As we look at the NP-level and DP-level environments in which we find augmentless nominals, we will see that these patterns are generally compatible with a case analysis of the augment vowel.

5.6.1 Augmentless nominals at the NP level

As table 5.4 shows, augment vowels are omitted from nouns in a variety of derivational processes. These derivational patterns appear to be robust: Durban Zulu speakers replicate the judgments reported in the literature.

First, a noun that is the second member of a compound must appear without its augment vowel, regardless of the category of the first member of the compound, as in (352) below:

(352) **Compounds: second member loses augment**

    a. -veza + **indlebe** → iveza**ndlebe**
       reveal AUG.9ear   AUG.5illegitimate.child
       'illegitimate child'

    b. imbuzi + **amawa** → imbuzi**mawa**
       AUG.9goat AUG.6cliff   AUG.9baboon
       'baboon'

Table 5.4. COMPARATIVE DISTRIBUTION OF AUGMENTLESS NOMINALS

	ENVIRONMENT	AUGMENT STATUS	
		Reported in Buell (2011)	Durban Zulu
NP-level:	2nd member of compound	omitted (352)	omitted
	noun class transposition	omitted (354)	omitted
	denominal adjectives	omitted (355a)	omitted
	denominal adverbs	omitted (355b).	omitted
DP-level:	following a demonstrative pronoun	omitted (356)	omitted
	following an 'absolute' pronoun	optional (360)	optional/preferred (361), (362)
	proper names after titles	strongly dispreferred (363)	strongly dispreferred
	before -*ni* 'what kind/amount'	omitted (364a), (365a)	dispreferred (364), (365)
	before -*phi* 'which'	omitted (366)	preferred (construction dispreferred) (367)
	before numeral quantifiers and 'all'	optional (369), (370)	required (371), (372)
Vocatives:		omitted	omitted
Clause-level:	*wh*-words	no discussion	optional
	Negative Polarity Items	omitted	omitted (within *v*P)/optional

In (352), we can see that the second member of the compound is not merely a root: the *n* of *indlebe* 'ear' and the *ma* of *amawa* 'cliffs' are noun class prefixes, separate from the root. The fact that these morphemes remain through compounding shows that only the augment is omitted, while the other noun class morphology remains. In addition, while Zulu often deletes one vowel in a V + V sequence to resolve hiatus (Doke, 1997 [1927]), it is not the case that the second vowel is routinely deleted in compounding. Compare the compounds in (352) above with the [verb + locative] compound in (353) below:

(353) -bhonga + e- ndlu- ini → ibhong**endlini**
      roar LOC- 9home- LOC AUG.5coward
      'coward'

In particular, just as we see in (353) above, word-final *a* vowels can generally be deleted to resolve hiatus throughout the language. Other hiatus resolution processes, including the vowel coalescence that we saw earlier in this chapter are also available. The contrast between (352a) and (353) thus suggests that the absence of the augment in these compounds is a morphosyntactic fact.

In addition to compounding, the augment associated with a particular *root + noun class* combination also disappears in noun class transposition, where a noun is shifted from one noun class to another, typically as a way of making proper names (class 1a) out of nouns from other classes.[12] In (354), we can see that the class 7 prefix *si* remains on the stem while class 1a augment morphology is added on top:[13]

(354) isimaku → u**Simaku**
      AUG.7small.white.fluffy.dog AUG1.7small.white.fluffy.dog
      'small, white, fluffy dog' name appropriate for a small, white, fluffy dog

12. This process is distinct from the process through which a single noun root may be realized in several different noun classes, as with the stem *-ntu*: *umuntu* (class 1) 'person', *isintu* (class 7) 'mankind', *ubuntu* (class 14) 'humanity/ human nature.' While these cases place the morphology for each different noun class directly on the root, the transposition process results in the new noun class morphology on top of the noun class prefix of the base word.

13. The most common noun classes that result from this type of transposition are class 1a/2a, which do not have an overt noun class prefix—only an augment. It is difficult, therefore, to determine whether this process involves the noun class prefix of the resulting nominal or only its augment.

We find the same process when adjectives and adverbs are derived from nouns: the noun class prefix remains as part of the adjectival or adverbial stem, but the augment is omitted:

(355) **Denominal derivations: augment omitted**

    a. amanzi   → -**manzi**
       AUG.6water   wet

    b. ubuhlungu → ka**buhlungu**
       AUG.14pain   painfully

(Buell, 2011, ex. (10) & (11))

All of these processes apply to nouns that lack full NP/DP structure. In the compounding and transposition cases, the noun stem becomes part of a larger nominal that itself must bear an augment. In the cases of adjectival and adverbial derivation, the resulting category change creates a non-nominal output. If the augment is a means of licensing DPs, it is unsurprising that these environments all prohibit an augment vowel, since there is no need for case under these circumstances.

5.6.2 DP-level processes

When we turn to environments in which an augment may be omitted on the head of a DP due to other DP-internal factors, we begin to find differences between the judgments reported in the literature and those of my Durban Zulu consultants. While I focus on how we can understand the patterns found in Durban Zulu, I will present the judgments reported in the literature for comparison.

Turning first to demonstratives, Durban Zulu speakers confirm the general reported pattern. Specifically, nominals that follow demonstrative pronouns lack the augment, as in (356) below, while those that precede the demonstrative require the augment, as in (357):

(356) **Prenominal demonstrative: augment omitted**

    lo   **mntwana** u- ya- ganga
    1DEM 1child   1s- YA- misbehave
    'This child is misbehaving.'

(357) **Postnominal demonstrative: augment required**

    u-   **mntwana** lo   u- ya- ganga
    AUG- 1child   1DEM 1s- YA- misbehave
    'This child is misbehaving.'

As we examine these constructions more closely, however, it is not clear that we in fact want to categorize a structure like *lo mntwana* in (356) as lacking an augment. If we look across noun classes, the proximal demonstrative series involves an invariant *la-* morpheme that combines using vowel coalescence with the augment, and sometimes also the noun class prefix, of the head noun:[14]

(358) a. la + u   → lo   mntwana
          DEM 1AUG   1DEM 1child
          'this child'

      b. la + i   → le   ncwadi
          DEM 9AUG   9DEM 9book
          'this book'

      c. la + izi → lezi   zipho
          DEM AUG.8   8DEM 8gift
          'these gifts'

Given (358), it seems that we want to consider the prenominal demonstrative construction one that contains an augment, even though the augment is realized on the demonstrative and not the noun stem itself. Just like a prefixal augment, the demonstrative comes with a high tone that can spread onto a toneless noun stem in predictable fashion:

(359) a. mùntù 'anyone'

      b. úmúntù 'person'

      c. ló múntù 'this person'

We can think of these prenominal demonstratives, then, as ones in which case is realized on the demonstrative rather than the head noun.[15]

If this analysis is correct, then we in fact find two augment vowels in the postnominal demonstrative construction: one on the nominal itself and one on the demonstrative. As de Dreu (2008) discusses for Zulu, and Carstens (2008) and Giusti (2008) discuss for closely related languages, the

---

14. The medial and distal demonstrative series also follow this general pattern, beginning with *la* followed by an augment. They differ from the proximal demonstrative in what follows the augment, e.g. *lowo mntwana* 'that child', *lowaya mntwana* 'yonder child.' Since my focus here is on the augment, I will set aside these differences and consider only the proximal series.

15. Tarald Taraldsen (personal correspondence) reports that nominals that follow the demonstrative pronoun in Zulu *can* bear an augment if is a clear prosodic break between the pronoun and the following noun. Similarly, Visser (2008) reports that the augment on nouns following demonstratives is optional in Xhosa. Given the different prosody reported for this type of construction, I believe that these are likely appositive structures where the demonstrative and nominal are adjoined, rather than part of the same basic extended DP.

postnominal demonstrative construction appears to involve movement of the noun to a high position at the edge of the DP, above the demonstrative, where it presumably once again becomes the attachment site for the augment. Here we might think of the augment on the demonstrative as an instance of concord, exactly as we saw for relative clauses and other modifiers in the previous section.

We find a somewhat similar situation with nominals that follow full pronouns, though here the judgments of Durban Zulu speakers begin to differ from those reported in the literature. Pronouns themselves seem to uniformly lack an augment in Zulu.[16] The reported pattern is that nominals that follow pronouns retain the augment when the nominal functions as an appositive but omit it when the nominal functions as an "extension" of the pronoun:

(360) **Contrast in augment following absolute pronoun**

    a. na- mi, **umfundi**,   be-   ngi- bona
       and- 1SG AUG.1student PST.IMP- 1SG- see
       'I, a student, was also seeing.'

    b. na- mi **mfundi** be-   ngi- bona
       and- 1SG 1student PST.IMP- 1SG- see
       'I (in my capacity as) a student was also seeing.' (von Staden, 1973, p. 168)

The contrast that von Staden (1973) describes is not one of definiteness; rather, he seems to be proposing that specificity is the distinguishing factor between the examples in (360) above, with (360a) yielding a specific reading of *umfundi* 'student', while (360b) implies that the subject is acting generically in the manner of a student.

For some speakers of Durban Zulu, the augmentless nominal in these constructions is completely ruled out, even when it would yield the type of generic reading that von Staden describes. For these speakers, the augmented version is required regardless of interpretation:

(361) **Variation: augmentless nominal dispreferred after pronoun**

    a.   thina **amadoda** si-   thanda inyama
       we   AUG.6men 1PL- like   AUG.9meat
       'We men like meat.' / 'We, the men, like meat.'

    b. % thina **madoda** si-   thanda inyama
       we   6men   1PL- like   AUG.9meat
       'We men like meat.'

16. The only exception I'm aware of is when they function as nominal predicates. Zulu has two copulas, whose distribution depends on the quality of the following vowel: *y-* precedes high front vowels, and *ng-* precedes everything else. When a pronoun follows a copular, a vowel that matches the expected augment, even if it differs from the vowels in the pronoun, is inserted: *y-imina* 'it's me' vs. *ng-uyena* 'it's him (class 1)'.

A number of speakers do allow augmentless nominals to appear after pronouns in these constructions. For these speakers, the interpretation of these constructions is clearly as a generic:

(362) **Augmentless nominals with generic interpretation**

iNdebe   yo-   Mhlaba a- yi- si-   siz- anga   nga-
AUG.9cup 9ASSOC.AUG- 3world NEG- 9S- 1PL.O- help- PST.NEG NGA-
lutho [thina **bantu** abampofu na- ba- hlala emijondolo]
11thing we   2people REL2.poor and- REL2- live LOC-4slum
eNingizimu Afrikha
LOC.5South 5Africa
'The World Cup didn't help us poor slum dwellers of South Africa at all.'

(Magagula, 2010)

We find similar variation in judgments inside of proper names, for example when a title precedes a name. Buell (2011) reports an overwhelming preference for for augmentless forms in this context, as in (363a) and (363c) below. Durban Zulu speakers show such a preference as well, though they also accept the augmented form, with no discernible difference in meaning:

(363) **Augmentless nouns preferred after titles**

a. uMongameli **Zuma** 'President Zuma' (preferred)

b. uMongameli **uZuma** 'President Zuma'

c. uNkosikazi **Sibiya** 'Mrs. Sibiya' (preferred)

d. uNkosikazi **uSibiya** 'Mrs. Sibiya'

We can perhaps think of both of these cases as involving different preferences in concord of the augment on subparts of the nominal.

Another class of DP-level constructions that have been reported to lack an augment involve complex *wh*-phrases. Given that we saw in chapter 3 that simple *wh*-words themselves may be augmentless in structurally licensed positions, it is perhaps unsurprising that the augment may be omitted in this domain as well.

First, in some cases the *wh*-clitic *-ni* 'what' can cliticize directly onto a nominal, typically yielding a meaning like 'how much' or 'what kind'. Buell (2011) observers that these constructions involve an augmentless nominal, as in (364a) and (365a). Durban Zulu speakers duplicate this judgment, though they also accept the augmented version of these nominals as well:

(364) **Augmentless nominal preferred with clitic** *-ni*

    a.   ku- biza **mali-** ni?
        17s- cost 9money- what

    b. (?) ku- biza **imali-** ni?
          17s- cost AUG.9money- what
          'How much does it cost?'

(365) a.   u- zo- fika nga- **sikhathi** si- ni?
          1s- FUT- arrive NGA- 8time   8- what

    b. (?) u- zo- fika **nge-** **sikhathi** si- ni?
          1s- FUT- arrive NGA.AUG- 8time   8- what
          'What time will you arrive?'

We can think of these nominals as being exactly equivalent to other *wh*-aruguments: an augment is optional in licensed, *v*P-internal positions, but required outside of them. In a somewhat similar construction, Buell (2011) notes that nominals that precede agreeing *-phi* 'which' have been reported to omit the augment, as shown in (366a), while those that follow *-phi* retain the augment, as in (366c):

(366) **Literature: nominals preceding 'which' omit augment**

    a.   w- a- bona **muntu** mu- phi?
        1s- PST- see 1person 1- which
        'Which person did you see?' (Buell, 2011, ex. (28), citing Poulos and Msimang (1998))

    b. * w- a- bona muphi **muntu**?
          1s- PST- see 1.which 1person

    c.   w- a- bona muphi **umuntu**?
        1s- PST- see 1.which AUG.1person
        'Which person did you see?'

For speakers of Durban Zulu, however, the construction in (366a) is largely ungrammatical. While some speakers will marginally accept the construction, most reject it. For these speakers, adding an augment to the nominal improves the construction slightly, though all speakers have a strong preference for the construction in (366c), where the nominal follows *-phi* and bears the augment, as illustrated in (367d):

(367) **Variation: Durban Zulu use of 'which'**

    a. */?? w- a- bona **muntu** mu- phi?
          1s- PST- see 1person 1- which

    b. */?? w- a- bona **umuntu** mu- phi?
          1s- PST- see AUG.1person 1- which
          'Which person do you see?'

c. * w- a- bona muphi **muntu**?
    1s- PST- see 1.which 1person

d. w- a- bona muphi **umuntu**?
    1s- PST- see 1.which AUG.1person
    'Which person did you see?'

While these constructions also create *wh*-phrases, they differ from the -*ni* constructions in being slightly more complex: here, the *wh*-element is separate from the head noun. Interestingly, the *wh*-element *muphi* itself is an augmentless form. Indeed, if we place this type of construction in a position without clause-level structural licensing, we find that an augment is required, as (368) illustrates:

(368) a. Uma u-funa   ukw-azi   ukuthi **umuphi**   umsakazi
          if   2sg-want INF-know that   AUG.1which AUG.1broadcaster
          o-zo-hlukanisa   unyaka   ngo-mhlaka   31 December 2014, thenga
          1REL-FUT-divide AUG.3year NGA.AUG-3date 31 December 2014 buy
          iphephandaba   iBayede   Newspaper namhlanje!
          AUG.5newspaper AUG.5Bayede Newspaper today
          'If you want to know which DJ will be closing out the year on December 31, 2014, buy Bayede[17] Newspaper today!'
                                              (Twitter, @ukhozi_fm, December 12, 2014)[18]

       b. * A-ng-azi   ukuthi **muphi** umsakazi   o-zo-hlukanisa
          NEG-1sg-know that   1which AUG.1broadcaster 1REL-FUT-divide
          unyaka.
          AUG.3year
          intended: 'I don't know which DJ will be closing out the year.'

The contrast in (368) suggests that we should treat this construction as yet another variation on the generalization that *wh*-elements can lose their augment in structurally licensed positions. The variation in judgments suggests that there are perhaps differing preferences regarding how concord works inside these DPs.

Finally, the literature on augmentless nominals claims that the augment can be omitted on nominals that are modified by certain quantifiers, including -*nke* 'all' and -*nye* 'one, another.' Von Staden (1973) claims that the presence or absence of the augment in these constructions affects the meaning, as reflected in the translations in (369) and (370) below:

---

17. *Bayede* is an interjection that is typically used to salute Zulu royalty.
18. https://twitter.com/ukhozi_fm/status/543330509481574400, accessed January 8, 2015.

(369)   **Literature: Augmentless nominals permitted before** *-nke*

    a. Ng- a- qala uku- qalaza   **izindawo**   zonke
       1SG- PST- start INF- look.around AUG.10places 10.all
       'I started to watch all the (particular, individual) places.'

    b. Ng- a- qala uku- qalaza   **zindawo** zonke
       1SG- PST- start INF- look.around 10places 10.all
       'I started to watch all places (every place).'   (von Staden, 1973, p. 168)

(370)   **Literature: Augmentless nominals permitted before** *-nye*

    a. zi- bik- e **izwi**   linye
       10s- report- PFV AUG.5statement 5.one
       'They have reported one (particular, individual) *message*.'

    b. zi- bik- e **zwi**   linye
       10s- report- PFV 5statement 5.one
       'They have reported *one* (particular, individual) message.'   (von Staden,
       1973, p. 169-70)

In (369), von Staden (1973) seems to be describing the difference in terms of specificity: the augmented nominal in (369a) receives a specific interpretation, while the augmented version in (369b) is nonspecific. In (370), the glosses suggest that although both versions are interpreted as specific, the augmented version in (370a) puts focus on the nominal, while the augmentless version in (370b) focuses the quantifier.

    Durban Zulu speakers, by contrast, reject the augmentless versions of these constructions in (369a) and (370a) above. For these speakers, only the augmented version of the nominal is grammatical, whether it precedes or follows the nominal:

(371)   **Variation: Durban Zulu requires augment with** *-nke*

    a. *ng- a- vakasha **zindawo** zonke
       1SG- PST- visit   10places 10.all

    b. ng- a- vakasha **izindawo**   zonke
       1SG- PST- visit   AUG.10places 10.all
       'I visited all of the places / every place.'

    c. *ng- a- vakasha zonke **zindawo**
       1SG- PST- visit   10.all 10places

    d. ng- a- vakasha zonke **izindawo**
       1SG- PST- visit   10.all AUG.10places
       'I visited all of the places / every place.'

(372)   **Variation: Durban Zulu requires augment with** *-nye*

    a. *ng- a- bona **muntu** (o)munye
       1SG- PST- see   1person 1REL.one

b. ng- a- bona **umuntu** omunye
   1SG- PST- see AUG.1person 1REL.one
   'I saw a (specific) person / I saw another person.'

c. *ng- a- bona (o)munye **muntu**
   1SG- PST- see 1REL.one 1person

d. ng- a- bona omunye **umuntu**
   1SG- PST- see 1REL.one AUG.1person
   'I saw another person / I saw a (specific) person.'

As (371) and (372) show, the augment is required in these constructions for Durban Zulu speakers. The different meanings that von Staden (1973) ascribed to the augmented and augmentless constructions involving -*nke* are both available for the augmented construction. Durban Zulu speakers interpret phrases with -*nye* somewhat differently from von Staden, so it is difficult to directly compare the range of interpretations, but they do not seem to attribute any particular focus structure to the constructions in (372).[19]

As we saw in chapter 3, augmentless nominal licensing at the clause level can apply only to nominals that receive a negative indefinite or *wh*-interpretation in the first place. We also saw in chapter 3 that Bantu languages exhibit some variation in interpretive properties of augmentless nominals, even when they show similarity in the structural conditions that govern them. As the facts in (370) and (372) show, the interpretation of the modifier -*nye* seems to have shifted in Durban Zulu to require a specific meaning, so it is perhaps unremarkable that these phrases now uniformly require an augment. In the case of -*nke*, the interpretations that von Staden (1973) identified are still available, though they now require an augment. It seems likely to me that this is a fact about the interpretive properties of augmentless nominals, rather than the morphosyntactic licensing conditions. In particular, it is clear that augmentless nominals are more marked to Durban Zulu speakers than they are in previously reported varieties of Zulu. The loss of this particular environment is in line with the observation that augmentless nominals are licensed as indefinites in nonveridical environments, as discussed in chapter 3.

19. While von Staden (1973) reports the use of -*nye* simply as an enumerative, meaning 'one,' Durban Zulu speakers do not typically use it in this sense. For these speakers, -*nye* as a modifier either means 'a specific' or 'another.' Speakers use the stem -*dwa* 'alone' to convey 'one' as a numeral quantifier:

i. ng- a- bona umuntu oye**dwa**
   1SG- PST- see AUG.1person 1REL.alone
   'I saw one person.'

The picture that emerges from these licensing processes, then, is that at the DP-level, we find that the distribution of the augment matches what we have come to expect: we find an augment marking the DP when it is not in a licensed environment, as with the prenominal demonstratives, but omission of the augment when the DP is turned into a *wh*-element and appears inside *v*P. Inside these more complex DPs, the picture gets a bit more complicated: we find variation in whether subparts of a complex noun permit or require an augment. This type of variation contrasts with the N/NP-level processes we saw at the beginning of the section, where an augment is uniformly omitted when a bare noun combines with additional structure.

5.7 CONCLUSION

Building on the previous two chapters, this chapter has expanded the case system of Zulu. I argued that structural case licensing via L (or APPL/CAUS) is simply one way for a nominal to be licensed in Zulu. In addition to this mechanism, Zulu has a system of nominal case morphology akin to that of more familiar languages. As we have seen, structural case licensing in Zulu lacks an overt morphological exponent; case morphology in Zulu instead bears one of two relationships to licensing. First, some case morphology can locally license the nominal, independent of broader syntactic structure, along the lines of *intrinsic* case that has been proposed for other languages. Second, other case morphemes seem to be required in particular circumstances but do not serve as an independent means of licensing, similar to *quirky* case effects in other languages. I defined the properties of case in terms of two parameters, [±Intrinsic] and [±Agreeable], where the [±Agreeable] parameter further distinguishes between case morphology that can occur on nominals that control phi-agreement and case morphology that cannot. Unlike previously described case systems, I argued that the augment in Zulu is a novel category of case, [+Intrinsic,+Agreeable], in that it intrinsically licenses nominals—along the lines of oblique or intrinsic cases in other languages—but also allows those nominals to agree.

I then showed that this analysis of the augment and other nominal morphology in Zulu as case marking leads to a number of other parallels with case behavior in other languages, including in the interpretive properties that can emerge with structural case marking, the relationship between oblique cases and agreement, and the existence of phenomena like case concord. By treating the nominal marking system of Zulu in this way, we thus gain insight on a number of other properties beyond the original augment distribution puzzles introduced in chapter 3.

CHAPTER 6
Optional Agreement and Other Consequences

The focus of this book so far has been on the nature of structural case and its relationship to case morphology. While we initially saw evidence that Zulu and other Bantu languages lack the standard hallmarks of syntactic case, I have argued that Zulu in fact does have a system of case-licensing that is comparable to those found in many other languages. At the same time, the account of Zulu case developed in this book is notable in that it is not dependent on phi-agreement processes. In particular, we have seen ample evidence that T in Zulu does not appear to assign case. In this chapter, I return to this part of the picture and explore some of the implications of my proposed separation of phi-agreement and case effects in the language.

This investigation will center around some novel patterns of subject agreement in Zulu. As I discussed in chapter 2, and as we have seen throughout this book, subject agreement in Zulu strongly correlates with movement out of *v*P: *v*P-internal subjects cannot agree with the verb, while *v*P-external subjects must agree. In this chapter, I discuss two exceptions to this pattern: complex NPs and raising-to-subject constructions. Both of these constructions allow what appears to be *optional* agreement. The verb can agree with the head noun of the complex NP or the raised subject when they are in Spec,TP, but another possibility is *ku*- agreement—even in the presence of a preverbal subject:

(373)   **Complex NPs: optional subject agreement**

    a. [**indaba**   y-okuthi   w- a-   thatha umhlala phansi] **y**- a-   ngi-
         AUG.9news 9ASSOC-that 1s- PST- take   AUG.3sit down   9s- PST- 1SG.O-
         mangaza
         surprise
         'The news that he retired surprised me.'

b. [**indaba** y-okuthi w- a- thatha umhlala phansi] **kw**- a- ngi-
AUG.9news 9ASSOC-that 1S- PST- take AUG.3sit down 17S- PST- 1SG.O-
mangaza
surprise
'The news that he retired surprised me.'

(374) **Raised subject: optional subject agreement**

a. **uZinhle** **u**- bonakala [ukuthi **u**- zo- xova ujeqe]
AUG.1Zinhle 1S- seem that 1S- FUT- make AUG.1steamed.bread
'It seems that Zinhle will make steamed bread.'

b. **uZinhle** **ku**- bonakala [ukuthi **u**- zo- xova ujeqe]
AUG.1Zinhle 17S- seem that 1S- FUT- make AUG.1steamed.bread
'It seems that Zinhle will make steamed bread.'

I will refer to this type of variability as "optional agreement." There are two senses of "optional" that are relevant here. One sense construes the choice of subject agreement morphology and *ku-* as a choice between full phi-agreement with the subject and no agreement at all, leading to the appearance of *ku-* as a default morpheme, as we saw in chapter 2 (see also Buell, 2012, for a discussion of both expletive and non-expletive uses of class 17 agreement in Zulu). In the other sense, "optional agreement" reflects the choice between two potential targets of Agree—with *ku-* reflecting true agreement with some element other than the preverbal subject. I will argue that this second sense of "optional"—reflecting a choice between two different Agreement targets—is the correct understanding of the optional agreement constructions in (373) and (374) above. I first establish that in both of these constructions, the preverbal non-agreeing subject occupies the same Spec,TP position that in other constructions requires it to control subject agreement. I then argue that the *ku-* morphology alternative does in fact involve phi-agreement—with a CP. I propose that the reason that these two constructions allow both of these agreement patterns is because both involve a CP that is close enough to the verb to serve as an alternative target for agreement. In the case of complex NPs, the nominal and its CP complement are equally close to the verb and thus are equally good targets for agreement. In the case of raising-to-subject, I propose that the *ku-* agreement pattern reflects the fact that T has agreed with the entire embedded CP. Only once this agreement takes place can the embedded subject be accessed by the matrix predicate (Rackowski and Richards, 2005). In the raising constructions, the matrix verb agrees with both the embedded CP and the embedded subject, and as a result, either agreement can be spelled out on the verb.

These phenomena are closely linked to the analysis of case and agreement in Zulu that I have been developing in previous chapters. As I will argue in this chapter, the optional agreement effect for complex NPs is predicted by my claim that Zulu lacks structural case associated with Spec,TP. If nominals were dependent on Spec,TP for licensing, optional CP agreement would be ungrammatical, since without agreement with T, the nominal would remain unlicensed. In addition, the analysis of optional agreement in raising-to-subject constructions that I develop here can shed light on a puzzle that emerged from the discussion of raising-to-subject constructions in chapter 2: why is raising permitted at all out of an agreeing, finite clause—a domain that typically prohibits such movement? While proposals that Bantu lacks case provide an account for the lack of Activity effects on the moving nominal, they have less to say about the apparent lack of phase effects in raising out of finite clauses (e.g., Zeller, 2006; Diercks, 2012; Carstens and Diercks, 2013). On this analysis, the agreement with CP is what permits the subsequent raising to subject: I extend the results of Rackowski and Richards (2005), who claim that agreement with an entire phase allows elements within the phase to be visible for subsequent agreement operations, from A-bar processes to the A-movement that we find in Zulu raising. The existence of this optional raising construction also gives us insight on the relationship between agreement and the EPP in Zulu, as I discuss in section 6.3.

6.1 SUBJECT AGREEMENT: RULE AND EXCEPTIONS

We saw in chapter 2 that subject agreement in Zulu correlates with movement of the subject out of *v*P. In the following example, when the subject is preverbal and the *v*P is empty, signaled by the appearance of disjoint morphology, agreement with the preverbal subject is required:

(375) **Preverbal subjects: agreement is required**

    a.   uZinhle   u- ya- pheka
            AUG.1Zinhle 1s- YA- cook
            'Zinhle is cooking.'

    b. *uZinhle   ku- ya- pheka
            AUG.1Zinhle 17s- YA- cook

When the subject remains in its *v*P-internal position, as the conjoint verb form indicates, agreement with the subject is ungrammatical and class 17 *ku-* agreement appears instead:

(376) ***v*P-internal subjects: agreement prohibited**

    a. *u- pheka uZinhle
        1s- cook AUG.1Zinhle
        *'Zinhle is cooking.' (OK: 'He is cooking/grilling Zinhle.')

    b.   ku- pheka uZinhle
        17s- cook AUG.1Zinhle
        'Zinhle is cooking.'

The two exceptions to this pattern are *complex NP subjects* and *subjects of raising predicates*, repeated from above. With these exceptions, subject agreement with the preverbal subject is optional: either full agreement or default agreement is allowed. In the examples in (373), we can see that the predicate *mangaza* 'surprise' either allows class 9 agreement with the head of the complex NP *indaba* 'news' or *ku-* agreement.[1] In (374), the matrix predicate may either agree with the class 1 raised subject *Zinhle* or may bear *ku-* agreement.

(373) **Complex NPs: optional subject agreement**

    a. [**indaba**   y-okuthi   w- a-   thatha umhlala phansi] **y**- a-   ngi-
       AUG.9news 9ASSOC-that 1s- PST- take   AUG.3sit down   9s- PST- 1SG.O-
       mangaza
       surprise
       'The news that he retired surprised me.'

    b. [**indaba**   y-okuthi   w- a-   thatha umhlala phansi] **kw**- a-   ngi-
       AUG.9news 9ASSOC-that 1s- PST- take   AUG.3sit down   17s- PST- 1SG.O-
       mangaza
       surprise
       'The news that he retired surprised me.'

(374) **Raised subject: optional subject agreement**

    a. **uZinhle**   **u**- bonakala [ukuthi **u**- zo- xova ujeqe   ]
       AUG.1Zinhle 1s- seem   that   1s- FUT- make AUG.1steamed.bread
       'It seems that Zinhle will make steamed bread.'

    b. **uZinhle**   **ku**- bonakala [ukuthi **u**- zo- xova ujeqe   ]
       AUG.1Zinhle 17s- seem   that   1s- FUT- make AUG.1steamed.bread
       'It seems that Zinhle will make steamed bread.'

In this section, I will show that the preverbal nouns in both constructions are in the same structural position that requires subject agreement in other constructions and that these constructions thus pose a true puzzle for our understanding of agreement patterns in Zulu.

6.1.1 Complex NP Subjects

It is fairly straightforward to see that complex NP subjects are a true exception to the generalization that preverbal subjects must agree. We can compare their behavior to simple NPs in the same environment and observe the contrast:

---

1. Note that the CP in these constructions bears an associative controlled by the NP component, which we saw in chapter 3. I return to this fact in section 6.2.2.

(377) **Complex NP: optional subject agreement**

a. [**indaba** y-okuthi w- a- thatha umhlala phansi] **y**- a- ngi-
AUG.9news 9ASSOC-that 1s- PST- take AUG.3sit down 9s- PST- 1SG.O-
mangaza
surprise
'The news that he retired surprised me.'

b. [**indaba** y-okuthi w- a- thatha umhlala phansi] **kw**- a- ngi-
AUG.9news 9ASSOC-that 1s- PST- take AUG.3sit down 17s- PST- 1SG.O-
mangaza
surprise
'The news that he retired surprised me.'

(378) **Simple NP: agreement required**

a. [leyo ndaba] **y**- a- ngi- mangaza
9DEM 9news 9s- PST- 1SG.O- surprise
'That news surprised me.'

b. * [leyo ndaba] **kw**- a- ngi- mangaza
9DEM 9news 17s- PST- 1SG.O- surprise

While the unexpected *ku-* agreement is grammatical with the complex NP subject in (377b), this type of agreement is ungrammatical with a simple NP, as in (378b). In (379) below, I show that the length or general complexity of the complex NP in (377) cannot account for this difference. The example in (379) involves a complex and lengthy relative clause, which contains a similar structure—a head noun followed by a large clause—to the complex NP in (377), but the non-agreeing version in (379b) is ungrammatical.

(379) **Relative clause: default agreement prohibited**

a. [**indaba** e- wu- yi- bhal- e phansi izolo
AUG.9news REL- 2SG- 9O- write- PST down AUG.5yesterday
ekuseni esikoleni] **y**- a- ngi- mangaza
LOC.15morning LOC.7school 9s- PST- 1SG.O- surprise
'The news that you wrote down yesterday morning at school surprised me.'

b. * [**indaba** e- wu- yi- bhal- e phansi izolo
AUG.9news REL- 2SG- 9O- write- PST down AUG.5yesterday
ekuseni esikoleni] **kw**- a- ngi- mangaza
LOC.15morning LOC.7school 17s- PST- 1SG.O- surprise
intended: 'The news that you wrote down yesterday morning at school surprised me.'

I conclude from these contrasts above that there is something specific about the complex NP construction that allows the optional agreement pattern shown in (377).

6.1.2 Raised Subjects

As I showed in chapter 2, Zulu has optional subject-to-subject raising out of
finite subjunctive and indicative clauses (Zeller, 2006; Halpert, 2012b):

(380) **Raising out of subjunctives**

    a. ku- fanele   [ukuthi **uZinhle**   **a-**   xov- e
       17s- be.necessary that   AUG.1Zinhle 1SJC- make- SJC
       ujeqe   manje]
       AUG.1steamed.bread now
       'Zinhle must make steamed bread now.'

    b. **uZinhle**   **u-** fanele   [ukuthi **a-**   xov- e
       AUG.1Zinhle 1s- be.necessary that   1SJC- make- SJC
       ujeqe   manje]
       AUG.1steamed.bread now
       'Zinhle must make steamed bread now.'

(381) **Raising out of indicatives**

    a. ku- bonakala [ukuthi **uZinhle**   **u-** zo- xova ujeqe
       17s- seem   that   AUG.1Zinhle 1s- FUT- make AUG.1steamed.bread
       manje]
       now
       'It seems that Zinhle will make steamed bread.'

    b. **uZinhle**   **u-** bonakala [ukuthi **u-** xova ujeqe   manje]
       AUG.1Zinhle 1s- seem   that   1s- make AUG.1steamed.bread now
       'Zinhle seems to be making steamed bread now.'

In chapter 2, we saw that in the non-raised version of these constructions,
(380a) and (381a), the subject remains in the embedded clause and only
agrees with the embedded verb. In the raised version, (380b) and (381b), the
raised subject controls subject agreement on both the matrix and embedded
verbs. In this chapter, I introduced a third option for raising-to-subject
predicates: the subject can appear in the higher clause *without* agreeing with
the matrix predicate, as illustrated in (382) for both subjunctive and indicative
complements.

(382) **Raised subject: non-agreeing matrix predicate**

    a. **uZinhle**   **ku-** fanele   [ukuthi **a-**   xov- e
       AUG.1Zinhle 17s- be.necessary that   1SJC- make- SJC
       ujeqe   manje]
       AUG.1steamed.bread now
       'Zinhle must make steamed bread now.'

b. **uZinhle** <u>**ku-**</u> bonakala [ukuthi **u-** zo- xova ujeqe
AUG.1Zinhle 17s- seem that 1s- FUT- make AUG.1steamed.bread
manje]
now
'It seems that Zinhle will make steamed bread now.'

The constructions in (382) add further puzzles to the general issues surrounding raising constructions in Zulu. In this section, I will argue that the subjects in these constructions occupy Spec,TP, just as in the agreeing raising constructions—and not some other position at the left periphery. This analysis requires some argumentation because while these non-agreeing raised subjects appear to be in the same position as the preverbal agreeing subjects in (380a) and (381a), Zulu also allows long-distance dislocation from embedded predicates, as shown in (383b) below:

(383) a. ngi- cela ukuthi [**uZinhle** **a-** xov- e ujeqe namhlanje]
1SG- request that AUG.1Zinhle 1SJC- make- SJC AUG.1bread today
'I ask that Zinhle make bread today.'

b. **uZinhle**$_i$ ngi- cela [ukuthi t$_i$ **a-** xov- e ujeqe
AUG.1Zinhle$_i$ 1SG- request that t$_i$ 1SJC- make- SJC AUG.1bread
namhlanje]
today
'(As for) Zinhle, I ask that she make bread today.'

In (383b), the subject from the embedded predicate fronts to a preverbal position in the matrix clause, where it receives a topic interpretation. In this construction, the fronted embedded subject triggers agreement only in the embedded clause. The existence of this construction means that there are two possible structures that could account for the constructions in (382): long-distance dislocation or subject-to-subject raising.

These two possible structures are distinguishable by a number of independent factors. If the long-distance dislocation construction is the correct structure for the appearance of *ku-* agreement with a preverbal subject, then the fronted subject should reliably behave like a dislocated topic. If the raising analysis is correct, the fronted subject should reliably pattern with agreeing subjects. Though the non-agreeing subjects in (382) may look more like dislocated topics on the basis of the agreement facts alone, on a variety of other measures, the fronted embedded subjects in (382) behave like a non-dislocated agreeing subject, and not like a dislocated element.[2]

2. It is also possible for non-agreeing fronted subjects to behave like dislocated elements, but I will not focus on this pattern here. Since such behavior could either arise through long-distance dislocation *or* through subsequent dislocation after the subject has first raised, these patterns do not give us new insight on the construction. I

Evidence from information structure

As we saw in chapter 2, preverbal dislocated nominals require a topic reading. This same topic requirement holds of long-distance dislocation, but not of subject-to-subject raising, as we can see in (384), where the agreeing raising-to-subject construction permits a new-information context for the raised subject, while a long-distance dislocation construction does not.

(384) Q: kw- enzeka- ni?
　　　　 17s- happen- 9what
　　　　 'What's happening?'

　　　 A1:　**uZinhle**　　**u**- fanele　　　ukuthi **a**-　xov-　e
　　　　　　 AUG.1Zinhle 1s- be.necessary that　1sJC- make- SJC
　　　　　　 ujeqe　　　　　　　manje
　　　　　　 AUG.1steamed.bread now
　　　　　　 'Zinhle must make steamed bread now.'

　　　 A2:　**uZinhle**　　**u**- bonakala ukuthi **u**- xova ujeqe　　　　　 manje
　　　　　　 AUG.1Zinhle 1s- seem　　that　1s- make AUG.1steamed.bread now
　　　　　　 'Zinhle seems to be making steamed bread now.'

　　　 A3:　# **uZinhle**　　ngi- cabanga ukuthi **u**- xova ujeqe　　　　　 manje
　　　　　　 AUG.1Zinhle 1sG- think　　that　1s- make AUG.1steamed.bread now
　　　　　　 '(As for) Zinhle, I think that she's making steamed bread now.'

Similarly, (385) shows that while idiomatic subjects are felicitous in subject-to-subject raising constructions, they cannot preserve their idiomatic interpretation under long-distance dislocation:

(385)　a.　**iqhina**　　　**li**- bonakala ukuthi **li**- phuma embizeni
　　　　　　 AUG.5steinbok 5s- seem　　that　5s- exit　LOC.9cooking.pot
　　　　　　 'The secret seems to be coming out.'

　　　 b.　# **iqhina**　　　ngi- cabanga ukuthi **li**- phuma embizeni
　　　　　　 AUG.5steinbok 1sG- think　　that　5s- exit　LOC.9cooking.pot
　　　　　　 '(As for) the steinbok, I think that it's coming out of the cooking pot.'

We can use these contrasts to test the non-agreeing fronted subjects in constructions like (382). In both of these environments, the fronted subject behaves like the agreeing subjects in the raising constructions in (384) and (385)—and not like the long-distance dislocations:

therefore ignore these patterns and focus instead on the existence of a non-dislocated parse for the non-agreeing subjects—in contrast to the absence of such a parse for clearly dislocated elements—which crucially tells us that a non-dislocated A-position is at least an option for these non-agreeing subjects.

(386) Q: kw- enzeka- ni?
       17s- happen- 9what
       'What's happening?'

   A1: **uZinhle**   **ku**- fanele   ukuthi **a**-   xov- e
       AUG.1Zinhle 1s- be.necessary that   1sJC- make- SJC
       ujeqe   manje
       AUG.1steamed.bread now
       'Zinhle must make steamed bread now.'

   A2: **uZinhle**   **ku**- bonakala ukuthi **u**- xova ujeqe   manje
       AUG.1Zinhle 1s- seem   that   1s- make AUG.1steamed.bread now
       'Zinhle seems to be making steamed bread now.'

(387) a. **iqhina**   **ku**- bonakala ukuthi **li**- phuma embizeni
         AUG.5steinbok 5s- seem   that   5s- exit   LOC.9cooking.pot
         'The secret seems to be coming out.'

   b. **iqhina**   **ku**- fanele   ukuthi **li**- phum- e   embizeni
      AUG.5steinbok 5s- be.necessary that   5sJC- exit- SJC LOC.9cooking.pot
      'The secret seems to be coming out.'

The fronted subjects in (386) are felicitous in a new information context,
just like the agreeing raised subjects. In (387), the non-agreeing fronted
idiomatic subject still receives an idiomatic interpretation. In sum, the
interpretive evidence suggests that the fronted subjects do not require a
dislocated interpretation and are compatible with a non-dislocated subject
interpretation.

Prosodic evidence

We saw in chapters 2 and 4 that Zulu marks the right edges of certain syntactic
domains with a prosodic boundary, realized by penultimate lengthening and
a pause (Cheng and Downing, 2009). While the focus in those chapters was
on the use of prosodic boundaries to identify *v*P edges, here we will consider
the prosodic differences between dislocated and non-dislocated elements in
preverbal positions. As Cheng and Downing (2009) show, preverbal topics
require a prosodic boundary at their right edge, while preverbal non-dislocated
subjects need not have one.

The constructions in (382), like the agreeing raising constructions, may be
pronounced without a prosodic break after the subject, as (388) shows:

(388) **Raising verb with fronted embedded subject: no pause**

   a. **amantombazane a**- fanele   **a**-   fund- e isiZulu
      AUG.6girl   6s- be.necessary 6sJC- study- SJC AUG.7Zulu
      namhla:nje)
      today
      'The girls must study Zulu today.'

b. **amantombazane** ku- fanele   **a-**   fund- e   isiZulu
    AUG.6girl   17s- be.necessary 6SJC- study- SJC AUG.7Zulu
    namhla:nje)
    today
    'The girls must study Zulu today.'

By contrast, with a long-distance dislocated topic, as in (389), the boundary must appear:

(389)   **Long-distance topic fronting: obligatory pause**

    amantombaza:ne) ngi- cabanga ukuthi a- funda isiZulu   namhla:nje)
    AUG.6girl   1SG- think   that   6s- study AUG.7Zulu today
    '(As for) the girls, I think that they are studying Zulu today.'

Since the fronted non-agreeing subjects do not require topic phrasing, this evidence also suggests that their structure is more in line with the agreeing raised subjects.

Syntactic evidence 1: multiple raising constructions

One piece of syntactic evidence that suggests that the non-agreeing constructions involve raising and not dislocation comes from the behavior of stacked raising predicates. If optional agreement morphology in raising constructions signals that the fronted subject is an an A-bar position, then we expect further A-movement of the subject to be impossible (Chomsky, 1973, 1981; May, 1979).

With two raising predicates in a single construction, then, a topic dislocation analysis would predict that if the subject agrees with the matrix raising predicate, it must also agree with intermediate predicates: *ku-* agreement on the intermediate raising predicate rule out further raising into the matrix clause. By contrast, the raising analysis would not rule out an intermediate *ku-* agreement: if the preverbal subject of a non-agreeing raising predicate is in an A position, then it should be available for further A-movement into the matrix clause, even if *ku-* agreement appears in the intermediate position.

As (390b) shows, the embedded subject can raise to preverbal position in the matrix clause *and* agree with the matrix predicate even if there is *ku-* agreement on the intermediate predicate:

(390)   **Multiple raising: ku- on intermediate predicate**

    a. **uThemba**$_i$ **u-** bonakala ukuthi t$_i$ **u-** fanele   ukuthi t$_i$ **a-**   y-
      AUG.1Themba 1s- seem   that   1s- be.necessary that   1SJC- go-
      e   esikoleni   manje
      SJC LOC.7school now
      'Themba seems to have to go to school now.'

b. **uThemba**$_i$ **u-** bonakala ukuthi t$_i$ **ku-** fanele   ukuthi t$_i$ **a-**   y-
AUG.1Themba 1s- seem   that   17s- be.necessary that   1sJC- go-
e esikoleni   manje
SJC LOC.7school now
'Themba seems to have to go to school now.'

This evidence thus suggests that the fronted subjects undergo A-movement, rather than A-bar movement.

Syntactic evidence 2: indicative clause extraction patterns

An additional piece of syntactic evidence for the A-movement analysis comes from a point of variation in the speech of some Durban Zulu speakers that yields another diagnostic for long-distance dislocation and raising. For many speakers of Durban Zulu, long-distance topic dislocation is only permitted out of *subjunctive* complements, and not out of indicative complements.[3] I'll refer to this pattern as Durban B, where Durban A speakers permit dislocation out of both types of complements. As (391) shows, for these speakers, long-distance dislocation from an indicative complement is ungrammatical:

(391)   **Durban B prohibits long-distance dislocation out of indicatives**

   a. ✓**Subjunctive extraction**

   uZinhle   ngi- cela   [ukuthi **a-**   xov- e ujeqe
   AUG.1Zinhle 1sG- request that   1sJC- make- SJC AUG.1steamed.bread
   namhlanje]
   today
   '(As for) Zinhle, I ask that she make steamed bread today.'

   b. *****Indicative extraction**

   * **uZinhle**   ngi- cabanga [ukuthi **u-** zo- xova ujeqe
   AUG.1Zinhle 1sG- think   that   1s- FUT- make AUG.1steamed.bread
   namhlanje]
   today
   intended: '(As for) Zinhle, I think that she will make steamed bread today.'

Speakers of Durban B Zulu restrict indicative complements in other ways as well. For these speakers, cross-clausal licensing of NPIs in the embedded clause by matrix negation—which we saw was possible in chapter 3—is permitted only in subjunctive complements, and not in indicatives, as (392) shows.

---

3. 12 out of 30 speakers for whom I have comprehensive data on this phenomenon are unable to do long-distance dislocation out of indicatives.

(392) **Durban B prohibits cross-clausal NPI licensing into indicatives**

    a. √**Subjunctive NPI licensing**

        A-   ngi- fun- i   ukuthi uZinhle   a-   phek- e   **lutho**

        NEG- 1SG- want- NEG   that   AUG.1Zinhle 1SJC- cook- SJC 11thing

        'I don't want Zinhle to cook anything.'

    b. *****Indicative NPI licensing**

        * A-   ngi- cabang- i   ukuthi uZinhle   u- pheka **lutho**

        NEG- 1SG- think- NEG that   AUG.1Zinhle 1s- cook 11thing

        intended: 'I don't think that Zinhle is cooking anything.'

The restrictions on indicative complement clauses shown by Durban B speakers also extend to the indicative complement of the raising verb *bonakala*. The examples in (393) and (394) show that long-distance dislocation and cross-clausal NPI licensing are both impossible with the matrix predicate *bonakala* for these speakers.

(393) **Durban B: long-distance topic extraction prohibited with** *bonakala*

    * ujeqe   ku- bonakala ukuthi uZinhle   u- ya- wu- xova

    AUG.1steamed.bread 17s- seem   that   AUG.1Zinhle 1s- YA- 1aO- make

    manje

    now

    intended: '(As for) steamed bread, Zinhle seems to be making it now.'

(394) **Durban B: cross-clausal licensing of NPIs prohibited with** *bonakala*

    * a-   ku- bonakal- i   ukuthi uZinhle   u- pheka lutho

    NEG- 17s- seem- NEG that   AUG.1Zinhle 1s- cook 14thing

    intended: 'It doesn't seem that Zinhle is cooking anything.'

These same speakers of the Durban B variety *do* allow the embedded subject of a *bonakala* complement to be fronted *without* agreeing in the matrix clause:

(395) √**Durban B: fronting of embedded subject with** *bonakala*

    a. **uZinhle**   **u**- bonakala ukuthi **u**- xova ujeqe   manje

        AUG.1Zinhle 1s- seem   that   1s- make AUG.1steamed.bread now

        'Zinhle seems to be making steamed bread now.'

    b. **uZinhle**   **ku**- bonakala ukuthi **u**- xova ujeqe   manje

        AUG.1Zinhle 17s- seems   that   1s- make AUG.1steamed.bread now

        'Zinhle seems to be making steamed bread now.'

Since Durban B speakers otherwise treat raising complements like other indicative complements with respect to A-bar movement and NPI licensing, the fact that (395b) is possible cannot simply be because it involves a raising verb. Rather, this pattern can be understood as evidence that the fronted subject is not sensitive to restrictions on long-distance dislocation shown by these speakers.

Syntactic evidence 3: relativization

The final piece of evidence that I discuss concerns relativization.[4] In object relatives in Zulu, the subject of the relativized predicate can intervene between the head of the relative clause and the verb, as in (396), where the subject *Zama* intervenes between the head *indoda* 'man' and the verb.

(396) **Object relative: subject can intervene between head and verb**
　　　[indoda　**uZama**　a-yi-bon-ile]　　i-gqoka isikipa　　esibomvu
　　　AUG.9man AUG.1Zama REL.1S-9O-see-PFV 9s-wear AUG.7tshirt REL.7-red
　　　'The man who Zama saw is wearing a red T-shirt.'

By contrast, a dislocated topic cannot intervene. The example in (397a) shows that long-distance dislocation is permitted for this particular predicate. Example (397b) shows that an object relative clause can be built around the same predicate. Example (397c) shows that it is ungrammatical to combine long-distance dislocation with the object relative.

(397)　**Object relative: topic cannot intervene between head and verb**
　　a.　**uMpho**　　ngi- cabanga ukuthi **u**- zo-　yi- thenga inyama
　　　　AUG.1Mpho 1SG- think　　that　1s- FUT- 9O- buy　　AUG.9meat
　　　　'(As for) Mpho, I think that she will buy the meat.'

　　b.　[inyama　engi-　cabanga ukuthi **uMpho**　　**u**- zo- yi- thenga]
　　　　AUG.9meat REL1SG- think　　that　AUG.1Mpho 1s- FUT- 9O- buy
　　　　i-zo-biza　imali　　　enkulu
　　　　9s-FUT-cost AUG.9money REL9big
　　　　'The meat that I think Mpho will buy will be expensive.'

　　c.　*[inyama　**uMpho**　engi-　cabanga ukuthi **u**-zo-yi-thenga]
　　　　AUG.9meat AUG.1Mpho REL1SG- think　　that　1s-FUT-9O-buy
　　　　i-zo-biza　imali　　　enkulu
　　　　9s-FUT-cost AUG.9money REL9big

We can use this pattern to test the status of the non-agreeing subject in a raising construction. If the fronted subject is dislocated, it should be unable to intervene between the head and the verb, but if it is in a subject position, it should be able to intervene. In (398b), we see that it is able to intervene, just like the agreeing version in (398a).

4. Thanks to Jochen Zeller for suggesting these constructions.

(398) **Object relative: non-agreeing fronted subject can intervene between head and verb**

  a. inyama   uMpho   **a-**   fanele a-   yi- phek- e   i-si-thengiwe
     AUG.9meat AUG.1Mpho REL.1s- must 1SJC- 9O- cook- SJC 9s-now-bought
     'The meat that Mpho must cook has now been bought.'

  b. inyama   uMpho   e-   **ku-** fanele a- yi- phek- e   i-si-thengiwe
     AUG.9meat AUG.1Mpho REL- 17s- must 1s- 9O- cook- SJC 9s-now-bought
     'The meat that Mpho must cook has now been bought.'

Again, the non-agreeing fronted subject behaves like a non-dislocated subject, and is not sensitive to restrictions on topic placement in relative clauses.

6.1.3 Tallying the Score

This section presented evidence that the the optional agreement constructions introduced in this chapter in fact involve non-agreeing subjects in non-dislocated Spec,TP positions. While this conclusion was fairly straightforward in the case of complex NPs, the subject-to-subject constructions were amenable to two potential analyses: as long-distance dislocated topics or raised, non-dislocated subjects. Although the agreement facts were compatible with an analysis of this construction as long-distance dislocation, a variety of interpretive, prosodic, and syntactic tests allow us to distinguish between preverbal subjects in A-positions (both in monoclausal and agreeing raised constructions) and elements that have undergone A-bar movement to a preverbal position. Despite the surprising agreement pattern, the overwhelming result of these diagnostics is that the non-agreeing preverbal nouns in the constructions in (382) pattern with A-position subjects—and not with dislocated A-bar elements.

The conclusion of this section is therefore that these two optional agreement constructions are true exceptions to the typical agreement pattern in Zulu. Given this conclusion, we must now take seriously the question of why this type of exceptional agreement pattern is permitted in these environments.

6.2 UNDERSTANDING OPTIONAL AGREEMENT

The complex nominal and raising constructions in this chapter are exceptions to the general pattern of obligatory agreement with preverbal subjects in Zulu. In this section, I propose that these optional agreement constructions involve CPs that are accessible as alternative targets for the agreement operation—and not merely a default agreement morpheme. The *ku-* agreement morphology that we see in these constructions results when CP agreement is realized on the verb. To reach this conclusion, I first show that Zulu allows clausal agreement in general and that this agreement is realized as *ku-*. Then I argue that both complex NPs and subject-to-subject raising involve CPs that are local to T and thus can be targets for agreement.

6.2.1 Clausal Agreement

Throughout this book, I have referred to class 17 *ku-* agreement marker as a "default" agreement marker. As we first saw in chapter 2, this is the agreement morpheme that appears in constructions where the subject is *v*P-internal, as in (399), in constructions that have no thematic subjects, such as the weather predicate in (400), and in the non-raised version of raising predicates, as in (401):

(399) **vP-internal subject with *ku-* agreement**
        ku- pheka uZinhle
        17s- cook AUG.1Zinhle
        'Zinhle is cooking.'

(400) **Weather predicate with *ku-* agreement**
        ku- ya- banda
        17s- YA- be.cold
        'It's cold.'

(401) **Raising predicate with non-raised subject**
        ku- bonakala [ukuthi uZinhle   u- zo- xova ujeqe   ]
        17s- seem   that   AUG.1Zinhle 1s- FUT- make AUG.1steamed.bread
        'It seems that Zinhle will make steamed bread.'

In addition to these constructions where we might expect to find default agreement because no nominal is available to agree, *ku-* agreement also appears with CPs. It is easiest to see *ku-* signaling agreement with CPs in the context of object agreement. As I showed in chapter 4, CP complements may optionally agree with the verb. These agreeing CPs must appear *outside* *v*P, just as we saw with the subject agreement patterns, as (402) shows. In (402), we can use the presence or absence of the morpheme *-ya-* to tell whether the CP complement is dislocated—as we saw in chapter 4, agreeing CP complements must be dislocated, and therefore *-ya-* must appear on the verb.

(402) a. ngi- ya- **ku-** cabanga [ukuthi uMlungisi   u- ya- bhukuda manje]
           1sG- YA- 17o- think   that   AUG.1Mlungisi 1s- YA- swim   now
           'I think that Mlungisi is swimming now.'

b. *ngi- **ku-** cabanga [ukuthi uMlungisi   u- ya- bhukuda manje]
   1SG- 17O- think   that   AUG.1Mlungisi 1s- YA- swim   now

In chapter 2 we saw that a subject agreement morpheme is always present on the verb in Zulu—which is why *ku-* agreement appears in the absence of phi-agreement with an accessible nominal. Object agreement, by contrast, *only* appears when it is controlled by a true thematic object. When there is no agreeing object, object agreement morphology is simply missing and no default morpheme appears in its place.[5] The example in (403) shows that *ku-* agreement is ungrammatical with an unergative predicate that lacks an accessible object for agreement:

(403) *ngi- ya- **ku-** gijima
      1SG- YA- 17O- run

On the basis of these patterns, I conclude that the *ku-* agreement we find with dislocated CPs is true phi-agreement[6] with those CPs. Some further evidence the object *ku-* in (402) is actual agreement—perhaps with the complementizer itself—comes from the fact that object agreement with a CP depends on the presence of a complementizer, as we saw in chapter 4. When the complementizer is dropped, agreement is impossible, though the CP can still dislocate:

(404) a. ngi- ya- **ku-** funa [**ukuthi** uXolani   a-   win- e   umjaho]
           1SG- YA- 17O- want that   AUG.1Xolani 1sJC- win- SJC AUG.3race
           'I (do) want Xolani to win the race.'

       b. *ngi- ya- **ku-** funa [uXolani   a-   win- e   umjaho]
           1SG- YA- 17O- want AUG.1Xolani 1sJC- win- SJC AUG.3race

       c. ngi- (ya-) funa [uXolani   a-   win- e   umjaho]
           1SG- YA-   want AUG.1Xolani 1sJC- win- SJC AUG.3race
           'I (do) want Xolani to win the race.'

---

5. Following the diagnostics developed by (Preminger, 2009a) discussed in chapter 2, this absence of object agreement morphology when no object agreement occurs suggests that object agreement in Zulu may in fact be a clitic, rather than a true agreement morpheme, though as Riedel (2009) demonstrates, there is no set of clear diagnostics that can distinguish agreement vs. clitic status for object markers across the Bantu languages. Along similar lines, Zeller (2012), shows that the status of the object marker in Zulu is somewhat unclear, since it exhibits both clitic-like and agreement-like behavior across a variety of diagnostics. While this is certainly an important issue, for the analysis in this chapter, what is most relevant is simply the fact that the object marker is able to track the phi-features of the CP that it depends on. I will thus set aside the question of the nature of this morpheme to focus on what it can tell us about the nature of CPs.

6. Or at least a true reflection of the phi-features of a CP.

Now note a consequence of this reasoning: if *ku-* agreement can be true phi-agreement with a CP object, it is also possible that *ku-* subject agreement could sometimes reflect true agreement with a CP, and not merely function as a default. Unlike a language like English, however, which permits CPs as sentential subjects, CPs in Zulu are resistant to occupying preverbal positions in Zulu. Speakers generally reject agreeing sentential subjects,[7] as the example in (405) shows:

(405) * [ukuthi uMpho   u- zo- thenga inyama]   **ku-** zo- jabulisa
           that   AUG.1Mpho 1s- FUT- buy   AUG.9meat 17s- FUT- be.happy-CAUS
         umama
         AUG.1mother
         'That Mpho will buy meat will make mother happy.'

It is important, therefore, to separate the issue of whether CPs are potential targets for phi-agreement from the issue of whether they can appear in a particular agreeing position. The object agreement examples in (402) clearly show that CPs have accessible phi-features in Zulu. I will assume that these features are accessible for subject agreement as well as object agreement. The independent ban on CPs in preverbal subject position will have crucial consequences for the derivation of raising constructions, as I will show in section 6.2.3.

6.2.2 Complex NP Subjects

Complex NPs, as repeated in (406) below, involve a noun component and a clausal component, as in the English sentence in (407).

(406) **Complex NPs: optional subject agreement**
        a. [**indaba**   y-okuthi   w- a-   thatha umhlala phansi] **y**- a- ngi-
           AUG.9news 9ASSOC-that 1s- PST- take   AUG.3sit down   9s- PST- 1SG.O-
           mangaza
           surprise
           'The news that he retired surprised me.'
        b. [**indaba**   y-okuthi   w- a-   thatha umhlala phansi] **kw**- a- ngi-
           AUG.9news 9ASSOC-that 1s- PST- take   AUG.3sit down   17s- PST- 1SG.O-
           mangaza
           surprise
           'The news that he retired surprised me.'

7. They tend to "fix" such examples by adding a head noun and turning it into a complex NP, though for a few speakers the CP subject construction is apparently marginally acceptable.

(407) The rumors that he retired surprise me.

One notable feature of this construction is that it involves the associative marker that we saw in chapter 3: the head noun controls associative morphology on the CP, exactly as possessees do on their possessors in Zulu:

(408) **Possessive concord**

    a. inja   **yo**-   mfana   (= ya + umfana)
       AUG.9dog 9ASSOC.AUG- 1boy
       'the boy's dog.'

    b. isithuthuthu   **se**-   nkosikazi   (= sa + inkosikazi)
       AUG.7motorcycle 7ASSOC.AUG- 9woman
       'the woman's motorcycle'

As we saw in chapter 3, in addition to the use of this construction in possessives, it appears in a range of other environments that roughly correspond to the distribution of the English preposition *of*, as Sabelo (1990) documents:

(409) **Associative concord distribution**

    a. indlu   yami   **ya**-   matshe
       AUG.9house 9POSS.my 9ASSOC.AUG- 6stones
       'my stone house'   (Sabelo, 1990, p. 19)

    b. isiminyaminya **sa**-   maphela
       AUG.7crowd   7ASSOC.AUG- 6cockroaches
       'a swarm of cockroaches'

    c. (i)ngenxa **yo**-   laka   luka-   Sipho, a- ngi- thand-
       because.of 9ASSOC.AUG- 11temper 11ASSOC.AUG- 1Sipho NEG- 1SG- like-
       i   uku- khuluma na- ye
       NEG INF- talk   NA- 1PRO
       'Because of Sipho's temper, I don't like to talk to him.'

The parallel between complex NP structures and associative structures in Zulu bears a striking resemblance to the *N of an N* construction in English and other languages (e.g., Bennis et al., 1998; Dikken, 1998; Matushansky, 2002):

(410) a. You whining coward of a vampire!

    b. my dear fool of a mother   (Matushansky, 2002, ex. (1))

Matushansky argues that these constructions, though they may look similar to possessives in some languages or to subordinating structures more generally, in fact involve a modification relationship between the two elements. That this type of construction would appear in Zulu complex NPs is in line with Stowell (1981), who argues that [N CP] structures are best analyzed as appositives, with the clausal component essentially functioning as an appositive modifier to the nominal.[8] In an appositive structure, the two components are equidistant from higher heads in the structure: as de Vries (2006) shows, while the noun and following clause form a constituent, there appears to be no clear c-command relationship between the two components.

If the nominal and clausal components of a complex NP are equally accessible to T, either one should be a potential target for agreement (Fitzpatrick, 2002).[9] I propose that this equidistance is responsible for the optional agreement effect: the verb can either agree with the nominal or the clausal component of the complex NP, as schematized in (411) and (412).

(411) **Agreement with the nominal component:**

[**indaba**   y-okuthi   w- a-   thatha umhlala phansi] **y-** a-   ngi-
AUG.9news 9ASSOC-that 1s- PST- take   AUG.3sit down   9s- PST- 1SG.O-
mangaza
surprise
'The news that he retired surprised me.'

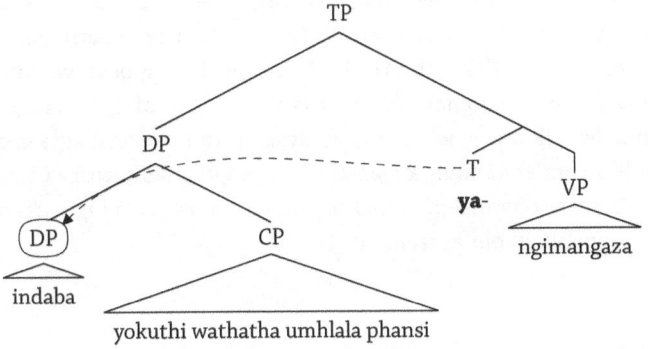

8. It is not clear, however, that all [N CP] structures function as appositives. While the ones discussed in this chapter involve CPs that play a purely modifying role, it is less clear that complex NPs like *The proof that the defendant is guilty* have the same type of appositive structure. In the absence of clear evidence from Zulu, I set aside this possibility for the moment.

9. A possible alternative would be to view the CP as the sole source of agreement in these constructions, with the fact that it bears both the phi-features of a CP and the noun class concord of the "head" leading to the optionality. In other words, we could interpret the optionality in agreement as the result of an optionality in which features "project" from the CP. We can rule out this possibility on the basis that associative constructions in general do not show optional agreement effects, and on the basis of the morphosyntactic and interpretive evidence that suggests that the nominal component is the "head" of this structure—and that the two elements are truly equidistant.

(412) **Agreement with the clausal component:**

[indaba **y-okuthi w- a- thatha umhlala phansi**] **kw-** a-
AUG.9news 9ASSOC-that 1s- PST- take AUG.3sit down 17s- PST-

ngi- mangaza
1SG.O- surprise

'The news that he retired surprised me.'

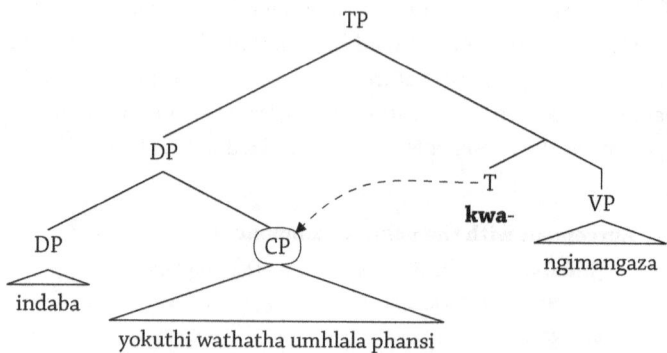

There is independent evidence that this type of analysis for complex NPs in Zulu, where T may target either the nominal or clausal component for agreement, is on the right track. In particular, appositive constructions that involve two nominals show exactly this type of optionality. Unlike in the complex NP cases, where my analysis of the optional agreement effects depends on understanding *ku-* agreement as agreement with a CP, rather than a default, these nominal–nominal appositives show unambiguous evidence for true optionality in phi-agreement:

(413) **Optional agreement with appositives**

a. **intombi yami**,   uThembi,   **i-** thanda ukucula
AUG.9girl 9ASSOC.1SG AUG.1Thembi 9s- like   INF.sing

b. intombi yami,   **uThembi**,   **u-** thanda ukucula
AUG.9girl 9ASSOC.1SG AUG.1Thembi 1s- like   INF.sing
'My girlfriend, Thembi, likes to sing.'

(414) a. **izinkomo zami**,   uSikhonyane   noMvula,   **zi-**
AUG.10cattle 10ASSOC.1SG AUG.1Sikhonyane and.AUG1Mvula 10s-
nhle
beautiful

b. izinkomo zami,   **uSikhonyane   noMvula**,   **ba-** hle
AUG.10cattle 10ASSOC.1SG AUG.1Sikhonyane and.AUG1Mvula 2s- beautiful
'My cattle, Sikhonyane and Mvula, are beautiful.'

(415) a. uMadiba, **iqhawe lami**, **li**- y- indoda
       AUG.1Madiba AUG5.hero 5ASSOC.1SG 5S- COP- AUG.9man
       e-qhotho
       9REL-righteous

    b. ?**uMadiba**, iqhawe lami, **u**- y- indoda
       AUG.1Madiba AUG5.hero 5ASSOC.1SG 1S- COP- AUG.9man
       e-qhotho
       9REL-righteous
       'Nelson Mandela, my hero, is a righteous man.'

In the examples above, speakers allow the verb to agree in noun class with either nominal in the appositive subject.[10] The fact that we see two non-default options with this construction is evidence that when two agreeable elements are equidistant from T, either one can control agreement. I have argued in this section that when one of these elements is a CP, *ku*- agreement can result as actual phi-agreement with the CP itself—and not as a default.

This pattern of optional subject agreement in complex NPs in Zulu contrasts with the pattern that we find in a language like English. In English, despite the fact that CP sentential subjects can appear in a preverbal subject position, a complex NP requires agreement with the nominal component:

(416) a. [That John is a murderer] is upsetting his mother.

    b. The claims that John is a murderer **are**/*is upsetting his mother.

10. While the optionality described in these specific examples is robust, the possibility for optional agreement with appositive constructions seems to depend on the specific noun classes involved, and sometimes on the order of the two nouns. For example, (i) below shows that with a different combination of noun classes, speakers tend to reject certain agreement options:

(i) a. ukudla e-ngi-ku-thanda-yo, **inyama ya-ngaphakathi**, i-
         AUG.15food REL-1SG-15O-like-REL AUG.9meat 9ASSOC-NGA.inside 9s-
         mnandi
         nice
         'My favorite food, tripe, is nice.'

    b. ***ukudla e-ngi-ku-thanda-yo**, inyama ya-ngaphakathi, **ku**-
         AUG.15food REL-1SG-15O-like-REL AUG.9meat 9ASSOC-NGA.inside 15s-
         mnandi
         nice
         for: 'My favorite food, tripe, is nice.'

It is not clear to me whether there are systematic patterns that govern the agreement options with different noun classes. It is possible that these differences in agreement choice are related to the patterns of agreement resolution with conjoined DPs reported in Bosch (1985).

This difference between English and Zulu is expected given the analysis of structural case in Zulu that I have developed in this book. That is, the fact that the actual subject nominal in a complex NP doesn't have to agree can be seen as a consequence of the lack of structural agreement associated with Spec,TP in Zulu. Since agreement is not linked to case, as it is in English, there is no reason to rule out a structure in which the clausal component of the subject controls agreement.[11]

6.2.3 Raised Subjects

In the previous subsection, I argued that the availability of *ku-* agreement in complex NPs was due to the presence of a CP that was local to T. The subject-to-subject raising constructions with optional agreement share a common element with the complex NPs discussed above: both contain a CP that is local to T:

(417) **Complex NP**

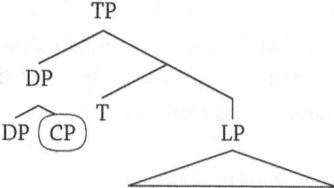

(418) **Subject-to-subject raising**

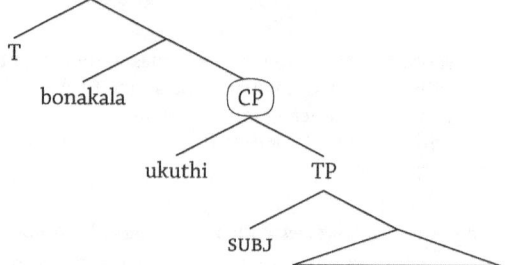

11. This analysis does, however, raise the question of how both nominals in an appositive structure in languages like English get case. One possibility is that the modifying nominal in these constructions is eligible for *default* case, along the lines of Schütze (1997). This possibility is in line with agreement patterns—when the two nominals in an appositive trigger different agreement, speakers tend to prefer agreement with the "subject" and not the modifying component:

(i)   John's committee, his three favorite professors, **is**/*?are late for his defense.

Another possibility is that T in fact agrees with both elements in the appositive structure, which we see overtly in Zulu, but is less easy to detect in a language like English.

As the structure in (417) illustrates, the CP and the nominal in complex NPs are equidistant from T, which I argued resulted in the optional agreement effect. The structure of the raising complement in (418), by contrast, does not involve two equidistant elements. Rather, while the CP itself is local to the matrix T, the embedded subject is *contained within* the CP. If, as I have argued, CPs are goals for phi-agreement, the result of this structure is an A-over-A configuration, where one phi-goal is contained within another (Chomsky, 1964):

(419)   ku- bonakala [*cp* ukuthi **uZinhle**   u- zo- xova ujeqe   ]
        17s- seem   [*cp* that   **AUG.1Zinhle** 1s- FUT- make AUG.1steamed.bread
        'It seems that Zinhle will make steamed bread.'

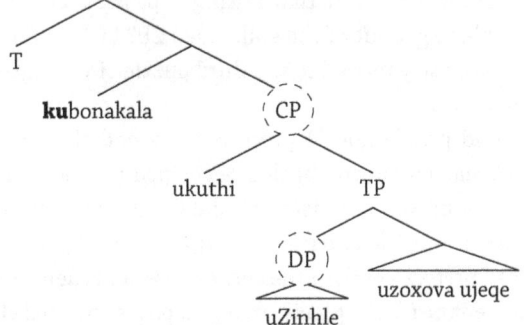

While I have been treating the availability of CP agreement in these subject-to-subject raising constructions as unexpected, now that we have seen that CPs are capable of controlling phi-agreement, it less surprising the *ku-* agreement would be possible in raising constructions. Indeed, such an outcome would be the expected result of T agreeing with the nearest phi-feature-bearing element, the CP. In addition, as I discussed in chapter 2, the fact that raising is possible at all out of these constructions is itself surprising. The Phase Impenetrability Condition (Chomsky, 2000)—which here emerges as a special case of the A-over-A Condition, since CP phases are viable goals for phi-agreement—typically governs such raising constructions cross-linguistically, ruling out raising of material in the complement of a phase head. In Zulu, as we first saw in chapter 2, finite CP complements do not seem to be subject to such restrictions. Thus the full range of raising-to-subject facts, as collected below, presents a puzzle from several angles:

(420)   a. **uZinhle**   u- bonakala [ukuthi **u**- xova ujeqe   ]
           AUG.1Zinhle 1s- seem   that   1s- make AUG.1steamed.bread
           'Zinhle seems to be making steamed bread now.'

        b. **ku**- bonakala [ukuthi **uZinhle**   **u**- xova ujeqe   ]
           17s- seem   that   AUG.1Zinhle 1s- make AUG.1steamed.bread
           'Zinhle seems to be making steamed bread now.'

c. **uZinhle**   **ku-** bonakala [ukuthi **u-** xova ujeqe   ]
AUG.1Zinhle 17s- seem   that   1s- make AUG.1steamed.bread
'Zinhle seems to be making steamed bread now.'

The first puzzle is why the raising construction is optional in the first place. We have already seen part of the answer earlier—the lack of case assignment associated with subject positions and the ability of the augment to license any nominal, combined with the absence of Activity effects in non-licensed positions, allowed nominals to either raise or remain in situ. In the next section, I will discuss how the EPP might also play a role as a factor in this optionality of movement.

The second puzzle concerns the fact that raising is possible at all: why is the embedded subject able to get out of the embedded CP? I will argue in this section that this puzzle is closely related to the third puzzle of why agreement is optional in this construction.

Turning to this second puzzle now, I propose to extend the analysis of PIC obviation for A-bar movement in Tagalog developed by Rackowski and Richards (2005) to these A-movement cases in Zulu. On the basis of evidence from Tagalog, Rackowski and Richards (2005) argue that PIC effects are obviated if a higher head first agrees with the *entire phase*, and then continues on to agree with an element *inside* the phase. That is, a phase-internal element is made available for outside processes if the entire phase first enters into an agreement relationship. The core proposals that they make about Agree are given below, the first four of which will be relevant to our understanding of the Zulu constructions:

(421)   **Rackowski & Richards (2005) Mechanics of Agree:**

   Relevant to Zulu:

   a. A probe must Agree with the *closest* goal α that *can move*.

   b. A goal α *can move* if it is a phase.

   c. A goal α is the *closest* one to a probe if there is no distinct goal β such that for some X (X a head or maximal projection), X c-commands α but not β.

   d. Once a probe P is related by Agree with a goal G, P can ignore G for the rest of the derivation (Richards, 1998; Hiraiwa, 2001).[12]

12. Evidence for this claim comes from multiple *wh*-questions, where the higher *wh*-phrase (or its copy) does not act as an intervenor for the lower *wh*-phase.

Not relevant to Zulu:

e. v^o has a Case feature that is checked via Agree. It can also bear EPP-features that move active phrases to its edge.

f. [+wh] C has a [+wh] feature that is checked via Agree (and sometimes Move).
(Rackowski and Richards, 2005, ex. (35))

The conclusion they reach from combining these principles is that only CPs and DPs that themselves undergo Agree for independent reasons will be transparent for extraction. The extraction that Rackowski and Richards focus on is *wh*-movement. They show that in cases of long-distance *wh*-extraction in Tagalog, the matrix v^o, which typically agrees with an element that has shifted to its specifier, must agree with the embedded CP. This agreement is realized as a morpheme on the predicate that tracks the case of the agreed-with argument. In the following examples from Tagalog, we can see that the required case on the matrix predicate with long-distance *wh*-extraction is always the case of the entire embedded CP—and cannot be the case of another argument, like the subject:[13]

(422) a. Kailan [sa-sabih-**in** ng sundalo [*na* Ø-u-uwi *ang pangulo e*]]?
when ASP-say-ACC CS soldier that NOM-ASP-go.home ANG president
'When will the soldier say *that the president will go home*?'

b. * Kailan [**m**-agsa-sabi *ang sundalo* [na Ø-u-uwi ang
when NOM-ASP-say ANG soldier that NOM-ASP-go.home ANG
pangulo *e*]]?
president
'When will *the soldier* say that the president will go home?'

(Rackowski and Richards, 2005, ex. (48))*Tagalog*

(423) a. Kailan [**i**-p-inangako ng sundalo [*na* Ø-u-uwi *ang*
when OBL-ASP-promise ANG soldier that NOM-ASP-go.home ANG
pangulo e]]?
president
When did the soldier promise *that the president will go home*?'

b. * Kailan [**n**-angako *ang sundalo* [na Ø-u-uwi ang
when NOM.ASP-promise ANG soldier that NOM-ASP-go.home ANG
pangulo *e*]]?
president
'When did *the soldier* promise that the president will go home?'

(Rackowski and Richards, 2005, ex. (49)) *Tagalog*

13. I follow the convention in (Rackowski and Richards, 2005) of indicating the case agreement on the predicate in boldface and the agreed-with constituent in italics.

(424) a. Kailan [p-in-aniwala-**an** ng sundalo [*na Ø-u-uwi*   *ang*
        when -ASP-believe-DAT CS soldier that NOM-ASP-go.home ANG
        pangulo e]]?
        president
        'When did the soldier believe *that the president would go home?*'

    b. * Kailan [**n**-aniwala   *ang sundalo* [na Ø-u-uwi   ang
        when NOM.ASP-believe ANG soldier that NOM-ASP-go.home ANG
        pangulo e]]?
        president
        'When did *the soldier* believe that the president would go home?'
                         (Rackowski and Richards, 2005, ex. (50)) *Tagalog*

In examples (422)–(424), it is the fact that v^o agrees with the embedded CP that allows the CP to become transparent for *wh*-extraction. After v^o agrees with CP, it can then agree with the embedded *wh*-phrase inside CP and raise that *wh*-phrase to its specifier. From its position as a specifier of the matrix v^o, the *wh*-phrase is ultimately accessible to Agree with the matrix C, which enables it to move to its scope position.

Rackowski and Richards (2005) explore their proposal in the context of A-bar extraction phenomena such as *wh*-extraction, but there is nothing in the principles they build from that suggests that this logic should not extend to A-movement phenomena as well. Indeed, as stated, the basic principles in (421) predict that the same considerations should apply to A-movement (and Agreement) phenomena such as the raising process that I have focused on in this chapter. I therefore propose that this same type of process accounts for both the ability of nominals to raise out of finite complements in Zulu *and* the optional agreement effects that result.[14] The optional agreement with raised subjects reflects the fact that the matrix T Agrees *twice*: first with the entire embedded CP and then with the embedded subject.

This process is outlined in the trees in (425) and (426) below. First, T probes and finds the CP as the closest bearer of phi-features. It agrees with the embedded CP, which remains in situ. Then, T probes again, for reasons I will discuss in section 6.3; this time it is able to ignore the already-agreed-with CP and agree with the embedded subject, which raises to matrix Spec,TP as a result.

14. By the same token, we might wonder the extent to which their proposal applies to A-bar movement processes in Zulu as well. I will not address this question at all here, but I will note that if elements that undergo long-distance A-bar extractions in Zulu first move to the edge of an embedded CP, then the CP itself (or perhaps the relevant C head) would not act as an intervenor and thus the question would not arise.

(425)　**Step 1: T Agrees with embedded CP**

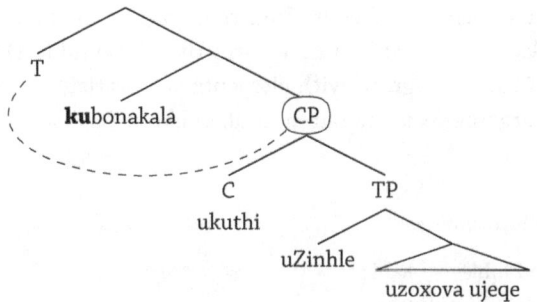

(426)　**Step 2: T Agrees with and fronts embedded subject**

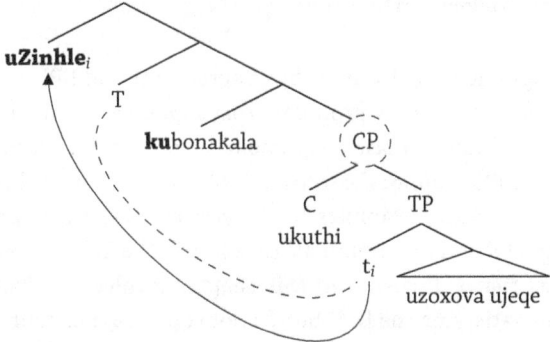

Because T has Agreed twice, first with the CP and then with the embedded subject, it can optionally realize the morphology of *either* Agree operation. The non-agreeing raised subjects we saw in (382) are the result of T spelling out the morphology from the first agreement operation with CP.

On this analysis, the choice of *ku-* or agreement with the raised subject in any particular raising predicate would have no impact on the agreement morphology possible for subsequent Agree operations: with any raising predicate T would Agree with both the embedded CP and the raised DP. The choice of morphological spell-out for any particular instance of T would be unrelated to any other instance. This result is necessary given the multiple raising data in (390).

To summarize the proposal given in this section, the optional agreement involving subject-to-subject raising results from T Agreeing *twice*, first with CP and then with DP. I argued that this type of multiple agreement can not only account for the optional agreement effect, but is what allows the embedded subject DP to raise at all. The fact that this analysis depends on T agreeing twice raises the question of why this type of multiple agreement happens in Zulu. In the next section, I address this issue and propose that the multiple agreement process results from the way the EPP works in the language.

6.3 EPP INSIGHTS

In the straightforward agreement cases in Zulu that we saw in chapter 2, agreement always tracks the element (not necessarily the logical subject) that surfaces in Spec,TP.[15] Crucially, agreed-with elements *must* satisfy the EPP: agreement with *in situ* arguments is ungrammatical, unlike in English:

(427) a. * **u**- pheka uZinhle   kahle
           1s- cook   AUG.1Zinhle well

       b. **ku**- pheka uZinhle   kahle
           17s- cook   AUG.1Zinhle well
           'Zinhle cooks well.'

(428) a. There *are* two bunnies in the garden.

       b. * There *is* two bunnies in the garden.

This direct correspondence between subject agreement and EPP effects in Bantu has been a focus of various proposals that argue that while in some languages agreement is linked to case assignment, in Bantu it is only linked to the EPP (e.g., Baker, 2003b, 2008; Carstens, 2005). In this chapter, however, I have explored some counter-examples to the generalization that agreeing nominals satisfy the EPP and that nominals that satisfy the EPP always agree.

The basic puzzles that I discussed in this chapter involve nominals that occupy Spec,TP, thus satisfying the EPP, but do not control agreement:

(373b) [**indaba**   y-okuthi   w- a-   thatha umhlala phansi] **kw**- a-   ngi-
        AUG.9news 9ASSOC-that 1s- PST- take   AUG.1sit down   17s- PST- 1SG.O-
        mangaza
        surprise
        'The news that he retired surprised me.'

(374b) **uZinhle**   **ku**- bonakala [ukuthi **u**- zo- xova ujeqe   ]
        AUG.1Zinhle 17s- seem   that   1s- FUT- make AUG.1steamed.bread
        'It seems that Zinhle will make steamed bread.'

With appositive structures, including complex NPs I focused on, either element in the complex subject may agree, so agreement is merely targeting a subpart of the complex entity that fulfills the EPP.[16] With subject-to-subject raising constructions, the pattern is more mysterious: here we get a situation

---

15. Recall that this element can be *pro* if the argument is *pro*-dropped.

16. A similar thing may be happening in some cases of conjoined subjects. Bosch (1985) discusses the range of agreement patterns that result in these constructions; some of which involve only one element of the conjunction.

where the preverbal (raised) element that satisfies the EPP is not connected to the *ku-* agreement morphology at all.

I proposed in the previous section that these raising constructions result from multiple Agreement: T Agrees with CP *and* the embedded subject. This proposal left open the question of why multiple Agreement can occur in these cases. In this section I will argue that phi-agreement in Zulu is driven purely by the EPP and will show how such a proposal will account for the multiple Agree pattern.

First, imagine that the EPP in Zulu simply states that the specifier of TP must be occupied, either by an overt nominal or by *pro*.[17] Any nominal that enters Spec,TP through movement can only do so if that nominal Agrees with T. In every Zulu construction, T can satisfy the EPP in one of two ways: by movement or via an expletive *pro* that can be freely inserted in non-theta positions.

(429) **Two ways to satisfy the EPP in Zulu:**

    a. Insert pro_{EXPL} directly in Spec,TP

    b. Search for an argument of the verb and move it to Spec,TP

If the first option is chosen, T does not probe and instead default *ku-* agreement appears instead. When the second option is chosen, T probes the structure to find the closest element with phi-features, Agrees with that element, and raises it to Spec,TP.

What happens in a construction where the closest phi-bearing element is CP? While we saw in section 6.2.1 that CPs are able to serve as targets for agreement, I also showed that Zulu speakers reject CPs in preverbal subject position. I will not attempt to explain this restriction here, but I will simply take it as an independent prohibition that prevents CPs from raising to Spec,TP. In a raising construction, then, if T chooses to fulfill the EPP by probing the structure, it will first encounter the embedded CP and Agree with

---

17. The account that I develop here is compatible with instantiations of the EPP as a *syntactic* phenomenon (e.g., Chomsky, 1995; Bobaljik and Jones, 1996; Alexiadou and Anagnostopoulou, 1998; Richards, 2011; and others) since, as we will see below, it is crucial for me that the EPP can drive (agreement-yielding) movement operations in the syntax that would otherwise not be necessary. By contrast, theories that conceive of the EPP as a purely phonological mechanism (e.g., Landau, 2007) fail to allow for the EPP to be the engine of syntactic movement and additionally incorrectly predict that *pro* will not satisfy the EPP. The account—as well as the empirical patterns—discussed in this chapter is also incompatible with "reverse Agree" approaches that seek to reduce the EPP to the requirement that goals c-command their probes in order for valuation to take place (e.g., Bošković, 2007; Wurmbrand, 2011, 2012; Zeijlstra, 2012). Such approaches fall short because they also disallow the possibility of the EPP as an engine in the syntax. More significantly, if the analysis of optional agreement as agreement with the embedded CP is correct, these Zulu constructions stand as a counterexample to reverse agree: the embedded CP Agrees with matrix T but *cannot* raise to c-command it.

it. Even though agreement has taken place, the independent prohibition will prevent CP from raising to fulfill the EPP. Now T has Agreed with the CP but still has not satisfied its EPP requirement. At this point it starts the process again, choosing between insertion of a pro_{EXPL} and probing for a phi-goal (see, for example, Nomura, 2005; Ussery, 2013, on this type of optional Sequential Agree process). If it chooses to probe for a second time, it can now access the embedded subject, Agree with it, and raise it to matrix Spec,TP to satisfy the EPP. Since Agree has happened twice, either agreement morpheme may surface. It is crucial to the derivation, therefore, that the EPP is perseverant: an initial failure to satisfy it leads to a second attempt, rather than global failure (or accommodation). Since on this view phi-agreement with T is essentially a by-product of the EPP, it is perhaps unsurprising that T Agrees multiple times only in cases where the EPP is not satisfied on the initial attempt.

An account in which subject-to-subject raising is brought about by an EPP requirement for T can perhaps help us to understand a gap in the Zulu raising data. Subjects can in general occupy either Spec,vP or Spec,TP in Zulu. In raising, as I noted in chapter 2, the subject can occupy one of three positions, despite the fact that two clauses are involved: embedded Spec,vP, embedded Spec,TP, or matrix Spec,TP:

(430) **Three subject positions with raising predicates**

    a. ku- bonakala [ukuthi **ku**- zo- xova **uZinhle**   ujeqe
       17s- seem   that   17s- FUT- make AUG.1Zinhle AUG.1steamed.bread
       manje]
       now
       'It seems that Zinhle will make steamed bread.'

    b. ku- bonakala [ukuthi **uZinhle**   u- zo- xova ujeqe
       17s- seem   that   AUG.1Zinhle 1s- FUT- make AUG.1steamed.bread
       manje]
       now
       'It seems that Zinhle will make steamed bread.'

    c. **uZinhle**   **u**- bonakala [ukuthi **u**- xova ujeqe   manje]
       AUG.1Zinhle 1s- seem   that   1s- make AUG.1steamed.bread now
       'Zinhle seems to be making steamed bread now.'

The 'missing' position in which raised subjects generally cannot appear is matrix Spec,vP:

(431)   *ku- bonakala **uZinhle**   [ukuthi **u**- zo- xova ujeqe
       17s- seem   AUG.1Zinhle that   1s- FUT- make AUG.1steamed.bread
       manje]
       now
       intended: 'It seems that Zinhle will make steamed bread.'

This gap is predicted on an account where raising-to-subject is driven purely by the EPP needs of the matrix T: since the embedded subject is licensed by the augment, it does not depend on the matrix L for licensing and its only impetus to raise will be matrix T.

In addition, this notion of EPP-driven raising also gives us some insight into the apparent true optionality of the process. As we saw in chapter 2 and throughout this book, subjects in Zulu are grammatical either in situ inside vP or in Spec,TP. While both of these constructions are syntactically viable, the choice of subject position has interpretive consequences: subjects in vP are interpreted as (part of the) focus, while pre-verbal subjects cannot receive narrow focus. Raising constructions differ from monoclausal constructions in that the subject has a choice between two Spec,TP positions—a choice that has no consequence for the basic interpretive properties of the subject. Given these conditions, the resulting optionality is unsurprising.

6.3.1 Exotic Cases of Raising: English and Greek

In this section, I have argued that raising out of finite clauses in Zulu is possible for two reasons. First, as we've seen throughout this book, there is no case-licensing associated with Spec,TP in Zulu. Consequently, nominals in these positions remain Active for further agreement and are licensed by an augment after all A-movement has occurred. Second, the matrix T first agrees with the entire embedded CP, which obviates PIC effects and allows the embedded subject to be targed by subsequent agreement with T. I argued that these properties of Zulu raising followed straightforwardly from treating the PIC as a specialized case of the A-over-A Condition, as proposed by Rackowski and Richards (2005). One might ask, however, why the Zulu pattern is not more widely attested outside of Bantu (as we have seen in this book, Harford Perez, 1985; Diercks, 2012; and Carstens and Diercks, 2013, all show that raising out of finite clauses seems to be fairly common within the Bantu family). In this subsection, I briefly examine how this theory interacts with some better-known patterns of raising, including English, which systematically lacks raising out of finite clauses, and Greek, which, as noted by Zeller (2006), shares with Zulu the possibility of raising out of an agreeing embedded clause.

In English, as we have seen, raising is required out of a nonfinite complement but prohibited out of a finite, agreeing complement:

(432) a. Sipho$_i$ seems [t$_i$ to be making bread].

  b. * It seems [Sipho to be making bread].

  c. * Sipho$_i$ seems [that t$_i$ is making bread].

  d. It seems [that Sipho is making bread].

It is standardly assumed that the contrasts in (432) result from nonfinite CP lacking nominitive case on its subject *and* lacking phasehood, while finite CP has both of these properties. In other words, (432a) occurs because the embedded clause is not a phase—so the embedded subject is thus accessible to the matrix T—and the embedded subject remains Active due to a lack of case assignment in the embedded clause, which rules out the construction in (432b). The example in (432c), on this view, is doubly ruled out—by both Activity and the PIC.

The major difference that we have seen throughout this book between English and Zulu is that English displays distributional properties in line with nominal licensing in finite Spec,TP, while Zulu does not. If in English, as I have argued for Zulu, the Activity Condition prevents further A-movement of nominals in licensed positions, then whether or not the phasehood of finite and nonfinite CPs in fact differs, the subject of a finite clause will be unable to undergo further A-movement. The reason to posit that certain nonfinite clauses are not phasal in English is to account for why nominals may raise out of these constituents. If the same CP-agreement process that I argued for in Zulu occurs in English, then this distinction may not be necessary. In other words, if the matrix T first Agrees with the embedded CP in English, then the only factor determining whether the embedded subject will raise is Activity.

Another way in which English differs from Zulu is that it allows CPs in what appears to be preverbal subject position. And indeed, while *seem* does not allow a CP complement to fulfill the EPP, *be likely* does:

(433)   a.   * [That Sipho is making bread]$_i$ seems t$_i$.

      b.   [That Sipho is making bread]$_i$ is likely t$_i$.

      c.   [That Sipho is making bread] and [that he is sleeping] are equally likely.

We could imagine that this same CP agreement is occurring with infinitival clauses, but that in these cases, the second instance of Agreement—with the embedded subject—is what surfaces due to the case needs of that subject.

One reason to be skeptical of such an approach, however, is work on the nature of CPs that suggests that these elements cannot function as true subjects. For example, Koster (1978) and Adger (2003) argue that CPs do not in fact occupy Spec,TP and Iatridou and Embick (1997) argue that CPs lack the phi-features necessary for agreement (contrary to what I have claimed in this chapter). If in addition to differing from Zulu in the structural configurations associated with licensing, English also differs from Zulu in whether CPs bear phi-features, then it is possible that English embedded CPs do not instantiate the A-over-A Condition in the first place. While Rackowski and Richards (2005) assume that all CPs are potential goals (in the *wh*-constructions they focus on) simply because they have the ability to move, we could imagine relativizing the goal-hood of CPs in a raising construction to whether or not they have phi-features—the specific features targeted by T. That is, perhaps CPs are never barriers to raising (though theoretically they could be barriers to other Agree processes) because CPs in English lack the relevant features.

To summarize the situation for English, the analysis that I propose here for Zulu is at least minimally compatible with current views of English, which assume a systematic difference in phasehood between finite and nonfinite clauses to account for the raising facts. Perhaps more interestingly, the analysis that I develop contains two avenues through which we could simplify the account of English by eliminating this difference in phasehood—either by agreement with CPs as in Zulu or by relativizing the notion of a barrier to specific sets of features and probing operations.

In Greek, the situation is rather different than in English. As Iatridou (1993) and Alexiadou and Anagnostopoulou (1999) have noted, Greek appears to lack truly nonfinite clauses, though it does have raising constructions. Iatridou (1993) first notes that all embedded clauses appear to agree with their subjects, regardless of whether those subjects receive case in the matrix clause:

(434) a. vlepo **ton Kosta**   na **tiganizi** psaria
        see.1SG DET Kosta.ACC C fries.3SG fish
        'I see Kostas fry fish.'

      b. elpizo **o**   **Kostas**   na **tiganizi** psaria
        hope.1SG DET Kosta.NOM C fries.3SG fish
        'I hope Kostas fries fish.'   (Iatridou, 1993, ex. (1), (4))

In (434), the ACC case is assumed to come from the matrix clause, while NOM is assumed to be assigned within the embedded clause. Iatridou shows that this difference in case assignment corresponds with the ability of the embedded verb to bear (past) tense. The non-case assigning predicates, as in (434a) are incompatible with past, as (435a) shows, while the case assigning predicates, as in (434b) allow it (435b):

(435) a. *idha/   vlepo ton Kosta   na tighanize psaria
         saw.1SG/ see.1SG DET Kosta.ACC C fried.3SG fish

      b. elpizo o Kostas   na tiganise psaria
         hope.1SG DET Kosta.NOM C fried.3SG fish
         'I hope Kostas fried fish.'   (Iatridou, 1993, ex. (1′), (4′))

Extending this contrast in (435), Alexiadou and Anagnostopoulou (1999) argue that the primary difference between the matrix predicates in the "a" and "b" examples above is that the complements of the "b" predicate always contain semantic tense, while the complements of the "a" predicate do not. They argue that it is this property of semantic tense (following Martin, 1996; Varlokosta,

1994) that is linked to case assignment and show that like the "a" predicates above, the complements of raising verbs in Greek lack semantic tense:

(436) a. ta pedhia   arxisan   na trexoun
           DET children.NOM started.3PL C run.3PL
           'The children started to run.'

       b. *o eaftos tu   arxizi   na ton   anisixise
           DET self   his.NOM begin.3SG C CLITIC.ACC worry.3SG.PAST
           'He started being worried about himself.'
                          (Alexiadou and Anagnostopoulou, 1999, ex. (11), (30a))

Given that there is an independent way to predict whether an embedded predicate will assign nominative case (the presence of semantic tense), we can understand the difference in whether an embedded subject raises or not as one of whether it has received case in the lower clause. With respect to the PIC, the choices for how to understand its relevance are essentially the same as in English above. Since much of the evidence against CPs bearing phi-features that Iatridou and Embick (1997) give comes from Greek, it is perhaps more desirable to take the approach that the PIC is globally irrelevant for CPs when higher phi-agreement is involved, because CPs lack the relevant features altogether and thus do not intervene. To summarize, while Greek shared with Zulu the superficial property of allowing raising out of agreeing clauses, independent evidence suggests that agreeing embedded clauses contrast in Greek with respect to licensing properties—with raising only occurring out of those clauses that do not assign nominative.

This comparison of English, Greek, and Zulu suggests that the case-assigning property of T varies quite a bit across languages. In English, it appears that all agreeing T heads appear to assign case; in Greek, only some T heads that agree are case-assigners; and in Zulu, *none* of the agreeing T heads assign case. In this regard, we can perhaps consider Zulu to be the natural endpoint of a continuum if T's case-assigning properties.

6.4 CONCLUSION

In this chapter, I moved beyond the focus on case assignment to focus on the *absence* of case: in particular, I examined the effects of purely EPP-driven phi-agreement in Spec,TP in Zulu. I presented novel data on Zulu optional subject agreement constructions. I showed that Zulu allows optional agreement with preverbal subjects in constructions that involve complex NP subjects and raised subjects. I presented some diagnostics that differentiate between preverbal subjects and preverbal topics in these constructions and proposed that the restriction of optional agreement to these environments is due to the availability of CP goals for T in both constructions.

The result of agreement with a CP goal is the same *ku-* agreement that we find in cases where we expect default agreement. In complex NP constructions, the clausal and nominal components of the subject are equidistant from T, and so either may be a target for agreement. In raising constructions, the matrix T first agrees with the entire embedded CP. Subsequent agreement with the embedded subject causes the subject to raise to preverbal position in the matrix clause, but the verb may spell out either agreement relationship.

This analysis provides a unified explanation for these two exceptions to the requirement that preverbal subjects agree in Zulu. It also sheds some light on why subjects may raise out of finite (phasal) CPs in Zulu and gives us new insights on the relationship between agreement and the EPP in the language. An understanding of these Zulu constructions our understanding of cross-linguistic variation in case assignment in important ways: Zulu differs from a number of better-studied case languages in lacking a nominative effect. In this chapter, I have illustrated that other surprising properties of Zulu syntax are directly related to this difference in case assignment.

CHAPTER 7

Variation in the Syntactic Landscape

This book has explored the issue of cross-linguistic variation in the syntactic domains of case-licensing and agreement. The point of departure for this investigation was the question of what makes Zulu, and its many Bantu relatives, look so different from what we have come to expect based on the case and agreement systems of more familiar languages. Put another way: what sort of variation in the grammar leads to the Zulu's more exotic-looking properties, including the combination of robust phi-agreement with an absence of apparent case effects governing the distribution of nominals?

I have argued that this type of variation does not arise at the macro-level—both case and agreement are intact in the grammar of Zulu—but is rather due to a few specific points of variation: association of case-licensing with novel heads, independence of case-assignment from phi-agreement, and availability of certain intrinsic case-licensing morphology. By combining the familiar mechanisms of case and agreement in these novel ways, Zulu reveals the aspects of the grammar that are deeply similar despite surface differences, particularly as we saw for Zulu and Icelandic throughout the book. At the same time, these novel instantiations of familiar properties give us insight on the nature of syntactic variation and on the organization of the grammar, most notably with respect to the independence of case and agreement. In this concluding chapter, I summarize what we have learned by comparing Zulu to other languages within and outside of the Bantu family and discuss some ways in which we can use these discoveries to learn more about core properties of syntax.

7.1 ACCOUNTING FOR ZULU

I argued in the previous chapters that there are two syntactic operations in Zulu that occur in the derivation of every clause and that are behind many of the patterns we observed. The first is a familiar one: T probes for phi-features in every derivation. The second was novel: the Licenser head, located above vP and below T, also probes every derivation and can case-license the highest goal. We thus immediately find a point of variation between Zulu and languages like English or Icelandic, for which phi-agreement and case seem to involve a single head:

(437) **Case and phi in a NOM–ACC language**

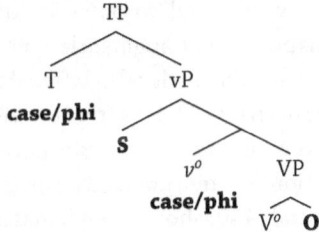

(438) **Case and phi in Zulu**

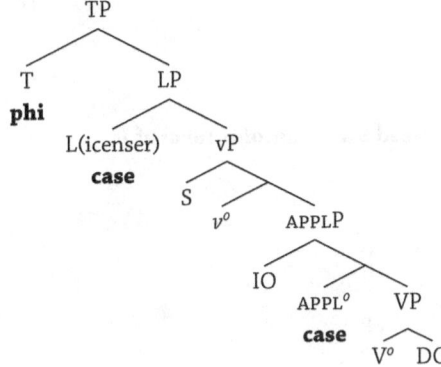

This section summarizes the evidence for this view of Zulu.

Chapter 2 established the basics of Zulu phi-agreement. We saw that phi-agreement in Zulu correlates with syntactic position: subjects in Spec,TP—and more generally those that are vP-external—must control phi-agreement while vP-internal subjects cannot control agreement. This pattern—that vP-internal elements cannot agree while vP-external elements must agree—also held for objects in Zulu. We also saw that in general, while both vP-internal and vP-external positions are available for the subject, the choice of position has consequences for interpretation. At the same time, I showed a particularly puzzling instance of syntactic optionality in Zulu syntax: raising predicates permit *optional* A-movement of the subject out of an agreeing position in an embedded finite clause into an agreeing position in the matrix clause. This puzzle raised the question of whether notions such as case and the PIC, which are commonly assumed to play a role in ruling out such raising constructions, play any role in Zulu syntax. In the following chapters, I investigated these questions.

Chapters 3–5 focused on the case piece of the puzzle, examining the patterns of relatively unrestricted nominal distribution raised initially in chapter 2. I argued that Zulu has a system of structural licensing and case morphology parallel to that of more familiar case languages like Icelandic. Evidence for structural licensing came from the behavior of *augmentless* nominals, which I showed display restrictions to specific syntactic positions that go beyond the known licensing conditions previously assumed to account for their distribution. In particular, I argued in chapter 3 that augmentless nominals are licensed in two ways: either through a maximally local relationship to a licensing head L or to a CAUS or APPL head. In chapter 4, I tied this distribution to the morphosyntactic phenomenon of the *conjoint/disjoint* alternation and argued that the conjoint/disjoint alternation is a morphological spell-out of the licensing process. As the trees in (439) and (440) show, when L successfully finds a goal, that goal is structurally licensed and a conjoint form is used. When L does not find a goal, the outcome is grammatical, but L's failure is marked by a disjoint morpheme, *ya*:

(439) **Successful probing: Licensed S and conjoint form of L**

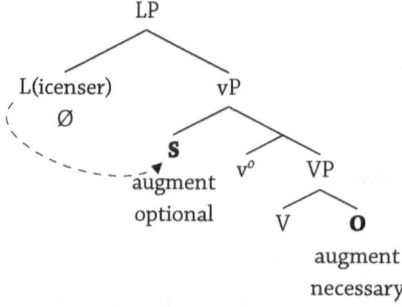

(440) **Unsuccessful probing: disjoint form of L**

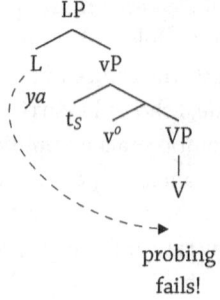

Table 7.1. LICENSING STRATEGIES
AND NOMINAL MORPHOLOGY IN
ZULU

+ intrinsic + agreeable **augment**	− intrinsic + agreeable (*"structural"*) **augmentless**
+ intrinsic − agreeable (*"inherent"*) **aug-replacing**	− intrinsic − agreeable (*"quirky"*) **aug-permitting**

Both of these processes—the licensing of augmentless nominals and the conjoint/disjoint alternation—have the unusual property that they appear to be sensitive to the *surface* position of arguments. I established in chapters 3 and 4 that we can in fact distinguish these processes from truly surface-oriented ones and argue that they should therefore be captured in the syntax. I proposed that their apparent surface-oriented properties arise from the ability of the licensing relationship to be freely ordered with respect to A-movement, which allows arguments to move before they can be structurally licensed. I attributed the absence of the opposite order of operations—in which arguments would first be licensed by L and subsequently move—to the Activity Condition (Chomsky, 2001). I argued that once a nominal is licensed by L, it is inactive for all further A-processes. Phi-agreement alone, by contrast, following Carstens (2011), does not inactivate nominals.

In chapter 5, I returned to the question of why many nominals in Zulu do not appear to require structural case-licensing. I argued that the *augment* vowel that marks most nominals functions as an intrinsic case licenser, allowing nominals that it marks to appear in unlicensed positions—as well as licensed ones. By comparing the augment vowel to oblique morphology in Zulu, I showed that Zulu has a familiar system of case morphology that corresponds to the *structural*, *quirky*, and *inherent* cases found in languages like Icelandic (e.g., Schütze, 1997). At the same time, I argued that the augment itself was evidence of a new type of case—one that inherently licenses nominals but is able to agree with the verb—that is a logical combination of the two parameters that seem to delineate the typology of case [±Intrinsic] and [±Agreeable] as shown in table 7.1 above.

Finally, in chapter 6 I investigated some consequences for this proposed system of agreement and licensing, addressing two novel constructions in Zulu that involve *optional* agreement of T with the nominal in its specifier: *complex NP* subject constructions and *raising-to-subject* constructions. I showed that both of these constructions are true exceptions to the pattern established in chapter 2, that preverbal nominals must control phi-agreement on T. I argued that the "default" agreement option in these constructions does not result from an absence of agreement with T. Rather, I proposed that both of these constructions involve a configuration where T can either spell out the result of a phi-agreement relationship with a CP or with the expected nominal.

(441) **Agreement possibilities with a complex NP**

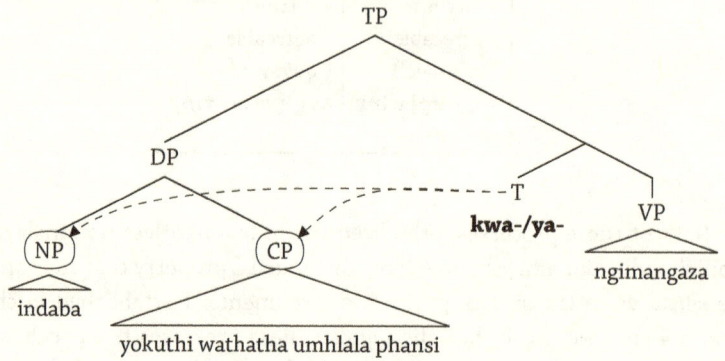

(442) **Multiple agreement operations in a raising construction**

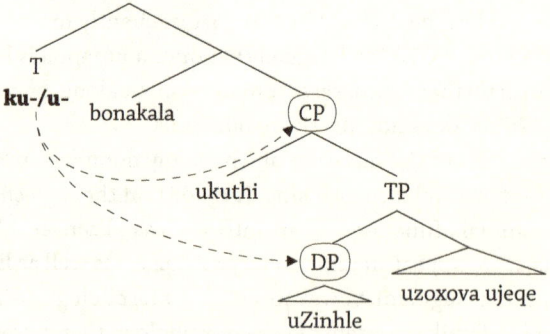

This analysis relies on the ability of CPs to control phi-agreement, which I motivated in chapters 4 and 5. In complex NP constructions, I argued that the CP complement and the nominal head are *equidistant* from T and thus either can serve as a goal. In raising-to-subject constructions, I argued that CP agreement results from agreement with the embedded CP itself and that this step of agreement is necessary in order to obviate the PIC (following Rackowski and Richards, 2005) and to therefore enable the matrix T to access the embedded subject. After T Agrees with the CP, which cannot raise for independent reasons, it may continue on to Agree with the embedded subject in order to satisfy the EPP. As a result of this second Agreement operation, the embedded subject must raise, but the result of either agreement operation may be spelled out. In this way, I was able to account for both the unusual agreement pattern and the outstanding puzzle of what permitted the raising construction out of a finite clause in the first place.

7.2 MORALS FOR SYNTACTIC THEORY

Throughout this book, we have seen ways in which the proposed analysis of Zulu relates to our current understanding of syntactic theory and the nature of syntactic variation. Here I collect some of these observations and comment on how we might further use Zulu as a tool to understand syntactic patterns and to explore the syntax of other languages.

7.2.1 Zulu and the Organization of the Grammar

The grammatical phenomena that are the focus of this book involve the relationship between nominals and predicates. Because of this focus, the grammatical components that commonly mediate these relationships—case, agreement, and the EPP—were at the center of the investigation. As the previous section has made clear, the proposed account for Zulu contains all of these familiar ingredients, though sometimes in novel combinations. By considering these novelties and comparing them to more familiar patterns, we gain new insights into these core components of syntactic theory.

Case

Perhaps one of the most surprising conclusions of this work is the discovery that case plays an active role in Zulu morphosyntax. In particular, I argued that Zulu not only has a system of structural case-licensing via syntactic heads but that it also expresses case via morphological marking on nominals. This conclusion goes against the prevailing view that case is not relevant in the grammar of most Bantu languages, either because it is completely absent or because its assignment has no visible effect on the distribution of nominals (Harford Perez, 1985; Baker, 2003a, 2008; Carstens and Diercks, 2013; Diercks, 2012; and others). While the system developed in chapters 3–5 has a familiar profile in terms of of its global patterns, it also displays a number of interesting differences when compared to the more familiar systems of languages like Icelandic and English.

A first point of difference, as the trees in (439) and (440) illustrated, is that the positions in which structural case-licensing occur in Zulu are *not* the ones familiar from standard accounts of nominative–accusative languages. Strikingly, the heads that we associate with structural licensing in a language like English—T and v^o—are not licensers in Zulu. First, while finite T is *not* a case licenser in Zulu, I introduced a lower L(icensing) head—above vP but below T—that is a licenser. The existence of a head in this position that probes the entire vP was confirmed by the conjoint/disjoint alternation, which seems to be a head-marking morphological reflection of this probing process. While this type of head is unfamiliar outside of the Bantu language family, conjoint/disjoint alternations are common within Bantu (e.g., Hyman and van der Wal, in preparation). The link between conjoint/disjoint processes and case-licensing in Zulu suggests a point of similarity to nominative assignment in other languages: in both processes, the assignment of case is linked to some other functional process in the language (in the case of nominative, the link is to tense). The behavior of the conjoint/disjoint alternation indeed seems to suggest that case-assignment in Zulu is secondary to the conjoint/disjoint process: failure to find a goal to case-license does not induce a crash.

If comparing L-licensing in Zulu to T-licensing in nominative languages sheds light on the behavior of "higher" case assignment, we can also examine what we learn from the other position in which nominals may be structurally licensed in Zulu—as in situ direct objects. While this position is familiar as the location of accusative case in NOM–ACC case systems, the circumstances under which direct objects are licensed in Zulu are somewhat different. Specifically, if the direct object is highest in vP, it can be licensed by L directly. If it is not the highest in vP, the only circumstance in which it can be licensed is in the presence of an APPL or CAUS head. While this seems like a novel condition on object licensing, it is in fact similar to a familiar one: Burzio's Generalization. Burzio's Generalization ties the ability of an object to be structurally licensed to the specifier-taking property of v^o. When v^o does not take a specifier, the object cannot be licensed. In Zulu, while the status of v^o itself seems to be irrelevant, what APPL and CAUS share with transitive v^o is that they too take a specifier argument.

In chapter 3 I described the ability of CAUS and APPL to license "accusative" case as a Burzio-type effect—in that something beyond a simple transitive v^o was needed to license a direct object. It is possible that the fact that licensing is independent from v^o is systematically connected to other aspects of Zulu syntax. In particular, one thing that we have seen throughout the book is that Zulu is perhaps unusually permissive in allowing multiple arguments—up to three in a ditransitive expletive or "triple object" structure—to remain in vP. This type of behavior is typologically unusual, and unexpected on syntactic accounts that prohibit multiple DPs within a single phase (e.g., Alexiadou and Anagnostopoulou, 2001, 2006; Richards, 2010). At the same time, the account of the timing patterns involved in licensing that I proposed for Zulu in chapters 3 and 4 exploited the ability of T to probe vP-internal goals before L does—a logic that depends on the operations taking place within a single phase. If vP is simply never a phase in Zulu, then we can understand the properties of timing, the absence of standard "accusative", and the grammaticality of multiple vP-internal arguments as part of a larger pattern.

This book also explored some interesting properties that emerge in the domain of morphological case in Zulu. In particular, I argued that the augment vowel in Zulu functions as a freely-applying intrinsic licenser, which can "rescue" a nominal in any position but does not impinge on the nominal's ability to agree. Exactly this type of freely-applying case has been ruled out by various theories (e.g., Schütze, 2001) on the grounds that it would render the Case Filter vacuous. That particular worry seems to justify such an analysis of the augment, since my investigation began with the observation that it is difficult to find any evidence of case with augmented nominals in Zulu. The investigation into nominal morphology also yielded some interesting conclusions about oblique prefixes, whose distribution closely matches that of prepositions in languages like English or oblique case morphology in languages like Icelandic. Unlike in in English, where P heads seem to function as case licensers, we saw that in Zulu nominals inside PPs in Zulu are subject to the same broader licensing conditions as 'plain' nominals, as the behavior of augment-permitting prefixes showed.

Zulu also showed evidence for a novel interaction between case and agreement. While Zulu shows the same surface ban on oblique-marked nominals controlling agreement that we find in languages like Icelandic, it resolves potential violations in a different way—by simply removing the oblique morphology. I return to this difference in the discussion of Icelandic in section 7.2.2 below.

Finally, the discussion in this book touched on the intersection between case and semantic effects at several points. As we first saw in chapter 3, the augmentless nominals that I argued were structurally case-licensed are subject to a number of interpretive and licensing requirements beyond simple licensing by L. I argued in chapter 5 that this type of interdependence of structural case and meaning is not unique to Zulu; we found similarities between the restrictions on augmentless nominals and the distribution of partitives in Finnish and French and accusatives in Turkish. In all of these constructions, the relevant case morphology alternates with a more generally-available case morpheme in licensed positions only, yielding a strict mapping of each case marker onto a particular meaning. Outside of these positions, the restricted case—like the augmentless nominals—is unavailable and the more general one is compatible with both meanings, suggesting that the more general morpheme itself does not convey any specific semantics. These parallels suggest that the NPI-type restrictions that we find for augmentless nominals in Zulu, and other Bantu languages, are part of a much larger picture relating case and meaning effects.

Agreement

As was clear from the very beginning, agreement truly seems to be at the heart of Zulu syntax. Phi-agreement is entangled in virtually all movement processes in the language and concord with the full phi-features of nominals is pervasive in all sorts of constructions. One thing that is clearly illustrated in this book is that phi-agreement in Zulu has no syntactic overlap with structural licensing. We saw in chapters 3 and 4 that the outcome of structural licensing does not involve any visible phi-agreement. As I argued in chapter 4, structural licensing prevents nominals from engaging in higher phi-agreement operations due to the Activity Condition—though phi-agreement does not render a nominal inactive for future licensing operations. While the idea that case and agreement are not linked to each other in Bantu has been proposed by Baker (2003a, 2008) and others, this observation rested on the assumption that case was playing little to no role in these languages in the first place. While Zulu points to the same higher-level conclusion, it does so by showing that case and agreement can both be active in the language yet not overlap or show any dependencies. In this sense, Zulu appears to be more like the languages Baker (2008) discusses that have overt evidence for separate systems of agreement and case, including Burushaski, Georgian, and Warlpiri. In these languages, all of which show ergative alignment in at least some environments, morphological case is present but does not interact with agreement in the way that it does in a language like Icelandic: subject agreement tracks ergative arguments in the same way as nominative or absolutive arguments. In his discussion of these languages, Baker notes that they have no EPP requirement on agreeing subjects, unlike in Bantu. He posits that in a language like Burushaski, agreement is simply determined by the closest (pre-movement) goal in the c-command domain of the probe (p. 170, fn. 14). Despite the strong role that the EPP plays in Zulu syntax, I have argued in this book that the same type of downward agree configuration governs both agreement and licensing in the language. As I'll discuss next, this conclusion requires a somewhat more nuanced understanding of the relationship between subject agreement and the EPP in Zulu.

EPP

In chapter 2, we saw that when T agrees with a nominal in Zulu, that nominal must raise to Spec,TP (sometimes moving further to a dislocated position). When T does not agree, no nominal occupies Spec,TP. Baker (2008) captures this type of pattern as a precondition on agreement: T only agrees with a DP that asymmetrically c-commands it (The Directionality of Agreement Parameter). In a similar vein, type of pattern is exactly what proponents of "reverse agree" theories have used to argue that the EPP is an artifact of the agreement process (e.g., Bošković, 2007; Wurmbrand, 2014; Zeijlstra, 2012). These theories propose that all valuation of unvalued features—such as the phi-features on a head like T—must be accomplished in a downward fashion, with the source of the features c-commanding the unvalued element. To achieve this downward relationship, therefore, agreeing elements must move to c-command their probe, yielding obligatory spec–head agreement. This type of configuration also achieves an EPP effect: if a head must always have its features valued by a c-commanding element, then there will always be some element in a local c-commanding position.

In chapter 6, however, we saw evidence that makes such an approach to Zulu untenable and indeed suggests that the directionality of agreement in the language is not as clear cut as we might have thought. While T can successfully agree with an embedded CP in Zulu, that CP *cannot* raise—in other words, unlike agreeing nominals in Zulu, which always surface above the probe T, agreeing CP goals can remain in situ below T. Moreover, I argued that in these constructions, T can probe a *second* time—something we do not see elsewhere in the language—to find the embedded subject. I argued that this second instance of probing is driven purely by the EPP, since T's phi needs are satisfied by the first instance of agreement. In fact, in this way of looking at Zulu, it perhaps does not make sense to say that phi-agreement on T is necessary— rather we could consider it to be merely a by-product of the EPP, arising only when the EPP is satisfied through movement (and not, say, through an expletive). Thus, a more accurate way to describe a dependency between the EPP and agreement in Zulu would be to have agreement arise as a consequence of the EPP rather than the other way around.

On this view, the behavior of the two probes that are central to the discussion of Zulu—T and L—begins to look more similar. As the discussion of case effects above makes clear, the failure or success of the L probe in finding a goal has no impact on the grammaticality of a construction; both successful and unsuccessful operations allow a grammatical output. By contrast, I have characterized phi-probing by T differently: the phi-probe appears to require success in Zulu. However, as the CP-agreement cases teach us, success of the phi-probe is, in a sense, also irrelevant to grammaticality: the EPP seems to be the "needy" component in the derivation, motivating multiple phi-agreement operations if necessary. As I discussed in chapter 6, another upshot of the EPP behavior that we see in the optional agreement constructions is that the EPP in Zulu cannot be a post-syntactic PF phenomenon—rather, it appears to be capable of driving syntactic movement. Moreover, while PF theories of the EPP (such as Landau, 2007) tend to require that the EPP be satisfied by *phonologically overt* material, Zulu appears to allow *pro* to satisfy the

Table 7.2. CASE AND AGREEMENT IN ICELANDIC AND ZULU

Icelandic	Zulu
NOM in Spec,TP	no NOM in Spec,TP licensing within complement of L^o
ACC from transitive v^o	"ACC" from CAUS or APPL
DAT can move around phi-probe	S or O can move around L probe
structural, quirky, and inherent case	structural, quirky, inherent, and *augment*
no agreement with quirky/inherent oblique acts as intervenor	no agreement with quirky/inherent oblique morphology is dropped

EPP—something that is in line with syntactic theories (and is especially predicated by theories such as Richards, 2011) but incompatible with the PF approach.

7.2.2 Some Final Thoughts: Zulu and the Nature of Syntactic Variation

While the previous subsection reviews some of the general insights we gain on case, agreement, and the EPP from this investigation of Zulu grammar, I will close this book by examining these issues from the point of view of direct comparison between languages to see what might be gained in terms of knowledge of syntactic variation and avenues for future research.

Zulu vs. Icelandic

Throughout the book, a main foil to Zulu and its patterns of nominal and licenser behavior was Icelandic. Icelandic is a striking counterpoint to Zulu because while both share properties of rich phi-agreement, their surface case properties diverge sharply: Icelandic wears its complex and robust case system on its sleeve, while at first glance Zulu appears to lack case. Nevertheless, closer investigation revealed numerous points of similarity between the languages. Both languages have a system of structural licensing that intersects with a system of morphological case, yielding surface patterns that can obscure the source of licensing. The availability of certain case morphemes in both languages depends on properties beyond the basic clause structure. Both languages have restrictions on the types of morphological case that can undergo agreement. Table 7.2 above compares the case and agreement properties of Icelandic to those that this book establishes for Zulu.

Many of the differences between Zulu and Icelandic listed in table 7.2 amount to fairly superficial variation—differences in the location of case-licensing heads, a gap in the typology of morphological case. One difference that is worth highlighting here due to the theoretical conclusion is prompts is the "resolution" of oblique nominals in agreeing positions. As I showed in chapter 5, both Zulu and Icelandic prohibit subject agreement with oblique-marked nominals. While the unattested agreement pattern does not surface in either language, the output of a structure where an oblique nominal is located in a position that would otherwise yield agreement is interestingly different. In Icelandic, agreement simply does not occur, and the oblique nominal acts as an intervenor for lower potential goals. On the basis of this fact Bobaljik (2008) argued that phi-agreement is necessarily post-syntactic: he claimed that morphological case in Icelandic can be captured as a post-syntactic process and that phi-agreement clearly follows the realization of oblique case, which places phi-agreement outside of narrow syntax. In Zulu, by contrast, oblique nominals in agreeing positions *do* agree, but omit their oblique morphology. This reordering of agreement *before* morphological realization of case suggests that both of these processes are best dealt with in syntax, exactly as argued by Preminger (2011, 2014) on the basis of similar ordering variations.

Zulu and the rest of Bantu: known and unknown

In this book, I have developed a specific view of how nominal licensing and agreement operate in Zulu and compared that picture to what we know of case and agreement in more familiar languages. We've also seen numerous points of comparison to other languages in the Bantu family, which share many of the broad properties regarding agreement and case documented here for Zulu. These broad similarities suggest that the Bantu language family will be an important testing ground for the proposals in this book. At the same time, many of the Zulu constructions I have investigated here have not been systematically approached in other Bantu languages in great detail, if they have been documented at all. In this final section, I will discuss what we have already learned from the cross-Bantu patterns and what we might wish to know. Even with all of the similarities we find between Bantu languages, the amount of variation present in the family suggests that investigating the ways in which Zulu differs from other Bantu languages will further refine our understanding of the relevant syntactic mechanisms driving the Zulu constructions.

A good starting point for this comparison is phi-agreement and the EPP. As we've seen throughout the book, many Bantu languages have rich phi-agreement and require agreeing subjects to appear in moved positions. This correlation between EPP and agreement is behind a number of proposals that formalize a direct link between the two operations in the Bantu language family (e.g., Baker, 2003a, 2008; Carstens, 2005; Collins, 2004). The Bantu languages also show widespread evidence for the existence of the so-called hyperagreement and relatively unbounded A-movement that led to proposals that case is not active in the language family (e.g., Harford Perez, 1985; Carstens, 2005, 2011; Carstens and Diercks, 2013; Diercks, 2012). The conclusions in this book about the relationship between agreement and the EPP are directly in line with this previous work, though my conclusion about structural case is very different. Moreover, I have provided a different answer to the puzzle of Bantu hyperactivity than what is suggested by, e.g., Carstens (2005, 2011). I suggested that just as in more familiar languages, the Activity Condition is directly linked to case assignment—and not to phi-agreement. I proposed that while structural case-licensing inactivates a nominal for any further processes, including phi-agreement, case-licensing by the augment vowel and other licensing morphology happens very late, which allows unlicensed nominals to A-move freely.

Despite the broad similarities in movement and agreement patterns across Bantu, we did see one notable point of variation. As Van der Wal (2012) demonstrates, Bantu languages like Matengo, Makwe, and Matuumbi allow for subject phi-agreement with vP-internal subjects. In other words, contrary to the general pattern, these languages have phi-agreement without the EPP. Van der Wal (2012) points out that the absence of the EPP as the driving force behind subject phi-agreement raises the question of whether phi-agreement is tied to some other syntactic process; in particular, on the proposals of Carstens (2005) and Baker (2003a, 2008), if phi-agreement is not tied to the EPP, then it is tied to case-licensing. Van der Wal (2012) suggests that a possible conclusion about this Bantu-internal variation, then, is that there is variation between Bantu languages that have case and Bantu languages that do not. Given the conclusion of this book—that at least one Bantu language with EPP-linked subject agreement has syntactic case—we might consider some different interpretations of this variation. A minimal modification of Van der Wal's suggestion would be to categorize the difference between Matengo-type languages and Zulu-type languages is simply one regarding the *location* of syntactic case, where Matengo shows the more familiar T-associated nominative effect. Another would be to investigate evidence for any possible lower L-associated case effects in these languages; if present, then the correct interpretation of the Matengo pattern may simply be that phi-agreement is untethered from either case or the EPP.

Exploring the behavior of subject phi-agreement across the Bantu languages gives us some insight on the nature of nominal licensing in the family. Another area to investigate is the behavior of nominals lower in the clause—in particular the distribution of vP-internal subjects, which varies across the Bantu languages. As this book documents, Zulu is quite permissive of vP-internal subjects: they can appear in a variety of constructions and can co-occupy the vP with multiple other arguments. At the same time, Zulu is rather conservative with its inversion constructions, allowing only very limited cases of locative and instrument inversion and disallowing all types of object inversion. In many other Bantu languages, the pattern is different: low subjects require inversion of other arguments to Spec,TP position, where they control subject agreement (e.g., Marten, 2006; Marten et al., 2007; Ndayiragije, 1999). In the previous section, I suggested that the ability of multiple arguments to crowd into vP in Zulu might be related to the phasehood properties of v^o and perhaps also to the case-licensing patterns involving the direct object. If other Bantu languages display different patterns with respect to the grammaticality of multiple vP-internal arguments then we might expect some of these other properties to co-vary. One way to view the variation that we find both in terms of subject agreement/EPP properties and vP-internal argument distribution is as variation on intervention effects. I suggested in chapter 5 that vP-internal subjects are inactive for phi-agreement because they have first been case-licensed by L. In a language with inversion, T appears to be able to probe a lower argument—somehow going *around* the low subject. The account for hyperraising presented in chapter 6 suggests a new possible account for these constructions: inversion languages could potentially employ the same multiple Agree strategy that Zulu main clauses employ in hyperraising, with T first probing the inactive subject—which cannot move to satisfy the EPP—and then undergoing a second probing operation.

The other side of the licensing puzzle in Zulu involved case morphology— and in particular, the augment vowel. Variation in the augment vowel is well-documented in the Bantu family, as we saw in chapter 3, so any application of theory proposed here for Zulu to other Bantu languages will have to be flexible enough to accommodate this variation. Chapter 3 showed a number of points of variation in augment patterns across the Bantu family. First, we saw that some languages lack a segmental augment altogether, like Swahili (Katamba, 2003) or Matengo (Yoneda, 2011) and some require an augment in nearly all syntactic environments, as Otjiherero does (Elderkin, 2003). In other languages, as we saw for Bulu, the distribution of the augment vowel seems to be purely driven by semantics (Barlew and Clem, 2014). In a number of languages that have active augment contrasts, however, we find several points of similarity to Zulu. Notably, much of the variation that we observe appears to be limited to the types of properties that I propose are *separate* from case-licensing in Zulu. In particular, we find variation in the particular interpretive correlation and licensing environments for augmentless nominals, though some common themes seem to hold. As we saw in languages like Kinande and Xhosa, augmentless nominals appear to be some sort of indefinite; in both languages, NPIs and *wh-* words may be augmentless, while Kinande also allows some augmentless indefinites that outside of NPI and *wh-* contexts (Carstens and Mletshe, 2013a,b). In Luganda, in addition to these indefinite environments, focus also licenses augmentless nominals. In all of these languages, though, augmentless nominals were licit only in vP-internal positions—exactly as in Zulu—which suggests that the low structural licensing that I propose for Zulu is adaptable to these other processes. While Carstens and Mletshe (2013a,b) argue that the Xhosa patterns are purely the result of syntactic negative indefinite licensing, we saw that this approach does not cover the full range of Xhosa (and Zulu) facts; the differences that they point to between Zulu and Xhosa suggest that there is perhaps small-scale variation in licensing—and whether or not it requires a step of movement—between the two languages. In general, the account of Zulu proposed here provides a targeted blueprint for investigation of augment distribution patterns that will allow us to go beyond the basic descriptions that currently exist in other Bantu languages.

As we saw in chapter 4, Otjiherero suggests another way in which licensing effects may emerge in Bantu languages. As noted above, Otjiherero does not seem to have active augment contrasts. At the same time, as Kavari et al. (2012) demonstrate, Otjiherero nominals *do* show different morphological marking in the form of tonal melodies, which they show are associated with particular syntactic environments. Two of these "tone cases" were particularly relevant to our understanding of Zulu: the so-called default tone pattern, which emerged as a sort of elsewhere marking, and the so-called complement tone pattern, which marked only the highest element in vP. I suggested in chapter 4 that this tone pattern was the realization of licensing by L in Otjiherero; as Kavari et al. (2012) note, while Otjiherero lacks a morphological conjoint/disjoint alternation, the distribution of the complement pattern seems to mirror the expected distribution of the conjoint/disjoint as it appears in other languages. This point raises yet another area of investigation for future research: I have proposed that in Zulu, the conjoint/disjoint alternation is the locus of the higher structural case-licenser; whether this correlation holds in other Bantu languages—particularly those without a morphological conjoint/disjoint alternation—remains to be seen. The initial evidence from Otjiherero that the vP as a relevant domain of licensing is present even in the absence of conjoint/disjoint marking is promising, suggesting ways in which we can look for such effects even when the morphology is absent.

While the fuzzy picture of the Bantu family thus looks inviting to the proposals in this book in a number of respects, it remains to be seen what picture of variation will emerge as the many missing details are filled in. By targeting these areas of known variation for future research, we stand to gain a much more nuanced understanding of the theory that I have proposed here.

BIBLIOGRAPHY

Adams, Nikki. 2008. Object (a)symmetry in Zulu: Object marking, NPIs and wh-word licensing. LSA talk handout.

Adams, Nikki. 2010. The Zulu ditransitive verb phrase. Doctoral dissertation, University of Chicago.

Adams, Nikki. 2011. Multiple focused objects in Zulu. Presentation at B4ntu, Berlin, April 2011.

Adger, David. 2003. *Core Syntax*. Oxford: Oxford University Press.

Alexiadou, Artemis, and Elena Anagnostopoulou. 1998. Parametrizing Agr: Word order, V-movement and EPP-checking. *Natural Language and Linguistic Theory* 16:491–539.

Alexiadou, Artemis, and Elena Anagnostopoulou. 1999. Raising without infinitives and the nature of agreement. In *Proceedings of WCCFL 18*, ed. Sonya Bird, Andrew Carnie, Jason Haugen, and Peter Norquest, 15–25. Somerville, MA: Cascadilla Press.

Alexiadou, Artemis, and Elena Anagnostopoulou. 2001. The subject-in-situ generalization and the role of case in driving computations. *Linguistic Inquiry* 32:193–231.

Alexiadou, Artemis, and Elena Anagnostopoulou. 2006. The subject-in-situ generalization revisited. In *Proceedings of the Workshop on Interfaces + Recursion = Language?*, ed. Hans-Martin Gärtner and Uli Sauerland. Berlin: Mouton de Gruyter.

Alsina, Alex. 2001. Is case another name for grammatical function? Evidence from object asymmetries. In *Objects and Other Subjects*, ed. William D. Davies and Stanley Dubinsky, 77–102. Dordrecht, The Netherlands: Kluwer Academic Publishers.

Alsina, Alex, and Sam Mchombo. 1993. Object asymmetries and the Chichewa applicative construction. In *Theoretical Approaches to Bantu Grammar*, ed. Sam Mchombo, volume 1, 17–45. Stanford University, Stanford, CA: CSLI Publications.

An, Duk-Ho. 2007. Clauses in noncanonical positions at the syntax-phonology interface. *Syntax* 10:38–79.

Andrews, Avery D. 1982. A note on the constituent structure of adverbials and auxiliaries. *Linguistic Inquiry* 13:313–317.

Asarina, Alya. 2011. Case in Uyghur and beyond. Doctoral dissertation, Massachusetts Institute of Technology, Cambridge, MA.

Asudeh, Ash. 2002. Richard III. In *CLS 38: The Main Session*, ed. Mary Andronis, Erin Debenport, Anne Pycha, and Keiko Yoshimura, volume 1, 31–46.

Asudeh, Ash, and Ida Toivonen. 2012. Copy raising and perception. *Natural Language and Linguistic Theory* 30:321–380.

Baker, Mark. 1988. Theta theory and the syntax of applicatives in Chichewa. *Natural Language and Linguistic Theory* 16:353–390.

Baker, Mark. 1996. *The Polysynthesis Parameter*. Oxford: Oxford University Press.

Baker, Mark. 2003a. Agreement, dislocation, and partial configurationality. In *Formal Approaches to Function in Grammar*, ed. Andrew Carnie et al., 107–132. Amsterdam: John Benjamins.

Baker, Mark. 2003b. *Lexical Categories*. Cambridge: Cambridge University Press.

Baker, Mark. 2008. *The Syntax of Agreement and Concord*. Cambridge, United Kingdom: Cambridge University Press.

Baker, Mark. 2014. Pseudo-noun incorporation as covert noun incorporation: Linearization and crosslinguistic variation. *Language and Linguistics* 15:5–46.

Barlew, Jefferson, and Emily Clem. 2014. The augment in Bulu. LSA presentation, January 2014.

Béjar, Susana, and Milan Rezác. 2003. Person licensing and the derivation of PCC effects. In *Romance Linguistics: Theory and Acquisition*, ed. Ana Teresa Pérez-Leroux and Yves Roberge, 49–62. Amsterdam: John Benjamins.

Bennis, Hans, Norbert Corver, and Marcel Den Dikken. 1998. Predication in nominal phrases. *The Journal of Comparative Germanic Linguistics* 1:85–117.

Bhatt, Rajesh. 2005. Long distance agreementi in Hindi-Urdu. *Natural Language and Linguistic Theory* 23:757–807.

Bhatt, Rajesh, and Martin Walkow. 2013. Locating agreement in grammar: An argument from agreement in conjunctions. *Natural Language and Linguistic Theory* 31:951–1013.

Bittner, Maria. 1994. Cross-linguistic semantics. *Linguistics and Philosophy* 17:53–108.

Bjorkman, Bronwyn. 2011. Be-ing default: The morphosyntax of auxiliaries. Doctoral dissertation, Massachusetts Institute of Technology, Cambridge, MA.

Bobaljik, Jonathan David. 2008. Where's Phi? Agreement as a postsyntactic operation. In *Phi Theory*, ed. Daniel Harbour, David Adger, and Susana Béjar, 295–328. Oxford: Oxford University Press.

Bobaljik, Jonathan David, and Dianne Jonas. 1996. Subject positions and the roles of TP. *Linguistic Inquiry* 27:195–236.

Bosch, Sonja E. 1985. Subject and object agreement in Zulu. Master's thesis, University of Pretoria, Pretoria, South Africa.

Bošković, Željko. 2007. On the locality and motivation of Move and Agree: An even more minimal theory. *Linguistic Inquiry* 38:589–644.

Branigan, Philip. 1992. Subjects and complementizers. Doctoral dissertation, Massachusetts Institute of Technology, Cambridge, MA.

Brattico, Pauli, and Alina Leinonen. 2009. Case distribution and nominalization: Evidence from Finnish. *Syntax* 12:1–31.

Bresnan, Joan. 1994. Locative inversion and the architecture of Universal Grammar. *Language* 70:72–131.

Bresnan, Joan, and Jonni M. Kanerva. 1989. Locative inversion in Chichewa: A case study of factorization in grammar. *Linguistic Inquiry* 20:1–50.

Bresnan, Joan, and Sam Mchombo. 1987. Topic, pronoun, and agreement in Chicheŵa. *Language* 63:741–782.

Bresnan, Joan, and Lioba Moshi. 1990. Object asymmetries in comparative Bantu syntax. *Linguistic Inquiry* 22:147–186.

Buell, Leston. 2005. Issues in Zulu morphosyntax. Doctoral dissertation, UCLA, Los Angeles, CA.

Buell, Leston. 2006. The Zulu conjoint/disjoint verb alternation: Focus or constituency? *ZAS Papers in Linguistics* 43:9–30.

Buell, Leston. 2007. Semantic and formal locatives: Implications for the Bantu locative inversion typology. *SOAS Working Papers in Linguistics* 15:105–120.

Buell, Leston. 2008. VP-internal DPs and right dislocation in Zulu. In *Linguistics in the Netherlands*, ed. Marjo van Koppen and Bert Botma, 37–49. John Benjamins Publishing Company.

Buell, Leston. 2009. Evaluating the immediate postverbal position as a focus position in Zulu. In *Selected Proceedings of the 38th Annual Conference on African Linguistics*, ed. Masangu Matondo et al., 166–172. Somerville, MA: Cascadilla Proceedings Project.

Buell, Leston. 2011. The Nguni augment from a syntactic perspective. Talk handout, B4ntu, April 2011.

Buell, Leston. 2012. Class 17 as a non-locative noun class in Zulu. Journal of African Languages and Linguistics 33:1–35.

Buell, Leston, and Merijn de Dreu. 2013. Subject raising in Zulu and the nature of PredP. *The Linguistic Review* 30:423–466.

Burzio, Luigi. 1986. *Italian Syntax*. Dordrecht: Reidel Publishers.

Carstens, Vicki. 2001. Multiple agreement and case deletion: Against *phi*-(in)completeness. *Syntax* 4:147–163.

Carstens, Vicki. 2005. Agree and EPP in Bantu. *Natural Language and Linguistic Theory* 23:219–279.

Carstens, Vicki. 2008. DP in Bantu and Romance. In *The Bantu-Romance Connection*, ed. Katherine Demuth and Cécile de Cat, 131–166. Amsterdam: John Benjamins.

Carstens, Vicki. 2011. Hyperactivity and hyperagreement in Bantu. *Lingua* 121:721–741.

Carstens, Vicki, and Michael Diercks. 2013. Parameterizing case and activity: Hyper-raising in Bantu. In *Proceedings of the 40th Annual Meeting of the North East Linguistic Society*, ed. Seda Kan, Claire Moore-Cantwell, and Robert Staubs, 99–118. Amherst, MA: GLSA.

Carstens, Vicki, and K. K. W. Kinyalolo. 1989. On IP structure: Tense, aspect and agreement. Manuscript, Cornell University and UCLA.

Carstens, Vicki, and Loyiso Mletshe. 2013a. Implications of Xhosa expletive constructions. LingBuzz/001750.

Carstens, Vicki, and Loyiso Mletshe. 2013b. N-words in disguise: a negative concord approach to augmentless NPIs in Xhosa and Zulu. Lingbuzz/001938, October 2013.

Chen, Tingchun. 2012. Restructuring in Mayrinax Atayal. Handout, AFLA 19, June 2012.

Cheng, Lisa, and Laura J. Downing. 2012. Against FocusP: Arguments from Zulu. In *Contrasts and Positions in Information Structure*, ed. Ivona Kucerova and Ad Neeleman, 247–266. Cambridge: Cambridge University Press.

Cheng, Lisa Lai-Shen, and Laura J. Downing. 2009. Where's the topic in Zulu? *The Linguistic Review* 26:207–238.

Chomsky, Noam. 1964. *Current Issues in Linguistic Theory*. The Hague: Mouton & Company.

Chomsky, Noam. 1973. Conditions on transformations. In *A Festschrift for Morris Halle*, ed. Stephen R. Anderson and Paul Kiparsky, 232–286. New York: Holt, Reinhart and Winston.

Chomsky, Noam. 1980. On binding. *Linguistic Inquiry* 11:1–46.

Chomsky, Noam. 1981. *Lectures on Government and Binding*. Dordrecht, The Netherlands: Foris Publications.

Chomsky, Noam. 1995. *The Minimalist Program*. Cambridge, Massachusetts: MIT Press.

Chomsky, Noam. 2000. Minimalist inquiries: The framework. In *Step by Step: Essays on Minimalist Syntax in Honor of Howard Lasnik*, ed. Roger Martin, David Michaels, and Juan Uriagereka, 89–156. MIT Press.

Chomsky, Noam. 2001. Derivation by phase. In *Ken Hale: A Life in Linguistics*, ed. Michael Kenstowicz, 1–52. Cambridge, Massachusetts: MIT Press.

Chomsky, Noam. 2008. On phases. In *Foundational Issues in Linguistic Theory*, ed. Robert Freidin, Carlos Otero, and Maria Luisa Zubizarreta, 133–166. Cambridge, MA: MIT Press.

Chomsky, Noam, and Howard Lasnik. 1977. Filters and control. *Linguistic Inquiry* 8:425–504.

Chung, Sandra, and James McCloskey. 1987. Government, barriers, and small clauses in Modern Irish. *Linguistic Inquiry* 18:173–237.

Cinque, Guglielmo. 2004. "Restructuring" and functional structure. In *Structures and Beyond: The Cartography of Syntactic Structures*, ed. Adriana Belletti, volume 3, 132–191. Oxford: Oxford University Press.

Cinque, Guglielmo. 2006. "Restructuring" and the order of aspectual and root modal heads. In *Restructuring and Functional Heads*, ed. Guglielmo Cinque, volume 4 of *The Cartography of Syntactic Structures*, 81–98. New York, New York: Oxford University Press.

Clem, Emily. 2014. The interaction of lexical and grammatical tone in the Bulu verb system. BA thesis, The Ohio State University.

Collins, Chris. 2004. The agreement parameter. In *Triggers*, ed. Anne Breitbarth and Henk van Riemsdijk, 115–136. Mouton de Gruyter.

Collins, Chris. 2005. A smuggling approach to raising in English. *Linguistic Inquiry* 36:289–298.

Collins, Chris, and Phil Branigan. 1997. Quotative inversion. *Natural Language and Linguistic Theory* 15:1–41.

Corbett, Greville G. 2006. *Agreement*. Cambridge: Cambridge University Press.

Creissels, Denis. 1996. Conjunctive and disjunctive verb forms in Tswana. *South African Journal of African Languages* 16:109–115.

Csirmaz, Aniko. 2006. Interface interactions: A and case. Handout, 8th Seoul International Conference on Generative Grammar, August 2006.

Csirmaz, Aniko. 2012. The case of the divisible phase: Licensing partitive case in Finnish. *Syntax* 15(3):215–252.

Day. 2003. Bare nominals: non-specific and contrastive readings under scrambling. In *Word Order and Scrambling*, ed. Simin Karimi, 67–90. Blackwell Publishers.

Dayal, Veneeta. 1999. Bare NPs, reference to kinds, and incorporation. In *Proceedings of Semantics and Linguistic Theory 9*, ed. Tanya Matthews and Devon Stolovitch, 35–51. Ithaca, NY: CLC Publications.

Dayal, Veneeta. 2011. Hindi pseudo-incorporation. *Natural Language and Linguistic Theory* 29:123–167.

Deal, Amy Rose. 2010. Ergative case and the transitive subject: A view from Nez Perce. *Natural Language and Linguistic Theory* 28:73–120.

Dede, Müşerref. 1986. Definiteness and referentiality in Turkish verbal sentences. In *Studies in Turkish linguistics*, ed. Slobin D. I. and K. Zimmer, 147–164. Amsterdam: Benjamins.

Dewees, John. 1971. The role of syntax in the occurrence of the initial vowel in Luganda and some other Bantu languages. Doctoral dissertation, University of Wisconsin.

Diercks, Michael. 2010. Agreement with subjects in Lubukusu. Doctoral dissertation, Georgetown University.

Diercks, Michael. 2011. The morphosyntax of Lubukusu locative inversion and the parameterization of Agree. *Lingua* 5:702–720.

Diercks, Michael. 2012. Parameterizing case: Evidence from Bantu. *Syntax* 15: 253–286.

Dikken, Marcel den. 1998. Predicate inversion in DP. In *Possessors, Predicates and Movement in the Determiner Phrase*, ed. Artemis Alexiadou and Chris Wilder, 177–214. Amsterdam: John Benjamins Publishing Company.

Doke, Clement. 1997 [1927]. *Textbook of Zulu Grammar*. Cape Town: Longman, sixth edition.

de Dreu, Merijn. 2008. The internal structure of the Zulu DP. Master's thesis, Universiteit Leiden.

Elderkin, Edward D. 2003. Herero (R31). In *The Bantu languages*. Routledge.

Enç, Mürvet. 1991. The semantics of specificity. *Linguistic Inquiry* 22:1–27.

Fanselow, Gisbert. 2000. Optimal exceptions. In *The Lexicon in Focus*, ed. Barbara Stiebels and Dieter Wunderlich, 173–209. Berlin: Akademie Verlag.

Farkas, Donka, and Henriëtte de Swart. 2003. *The Semantics of Incorporation*. Stanford Monographs in Linguistics. Stanford, CA: CSLI Publications.

Fitzpatrick, Justin M. 2002. On Minimalist approaches to the locality of movement. *Linguistic Inquiry* 33:443–463.

Fortune, George. 1977. Shona grammatical constructions. Doctoral dissertation, University of Zimbabwe, Harare, Zimbabwe.

Freeze, Ray. 1992. Existentials and other locatives. *Language* 68:553–595.

van Geenhoven, Veerle. 1998. *Semantic Incorporation and Indefinite Descriptions: Semantic and Syntactic Aspects of Noun in Corporation in West Greenlandic*. Stanford University, Stanford, CA: CSLI Publications.

Geenhoven, Veerle van. 2002. Raised possessors and noun incorporation in West Greenlandic. *Natural Language and Linguistic Theory* 20:759–821.

Giannakidou, Anastasia. 2000. Negative...concord? *Natural Language and Linguistic Theory* 18:457–523.

Giannakidou, Anastasia. 2011. Negative and positive polarity items: Variation, licensing, and compositionality, 1660–1712. In *Semantics: An International Handbook of Language Meaning*, ed. Claudia Maienborn, Klaus von Heusinger, and Paul Portner. Mouton de Gruyter, second edition.

Giusti, Giuliana. 2008. Agreement and concord in nominal expressions. In *The Bantu-Romance Connection*, ed. Katherine Demuth and Cécile de Cat, 201–237. Amsterdam: John Benjamins.

Givón, Talmy. 1976. Topic, pronoun and grammatical agreement. In *Subject and Topic*, ed. Charles Li, 149–188. Academic Press.

Grimes, B.F., ed. 2000. *Ethnologue: Languages of the World*. Dallas, TX: SIL International, 13 edition.

Güldemann, Tom. 2003. Present progressive vis-à-vis predication focus in Bantu: A verbal category between semantics and pragmatics. *Studies in Language* 27: 323–360.

Haegeman, Liliane. 1995. Root infinitives, tense, and truncated structures in Dutch. *Language Acquisition* 4:205–255.

Haegeman, Liliane. 1997. *Elements of Grammar: Handbook in Generative Syntax*. Dordrecht: Kluwer Academic Publishers.

Haegeman, Liliane, and Terje Lohndal. 2010. Negative concord and (multiple) Agree: A case study of West Flemish. *Linguistic Inquiry* 41:181–211.

Halpert, Claire. 2011. Low subjects in Zulu and the prosody–syntax interface. Handout, Annual Conference on African Linguistics 42, University of Maryland, June 2011.

Halpert, Claire. 2012a. Argument licensing and agreement in Zulu. Doctoral dissertation, MIT.

Halpert, Claire. 2012b. Case, agreement, EPP and information structure: A quadruple-dissociation in Zulu. In *Proceedings of WCCFL 29*, ed. Jaehoon Choi, E. Alan Hogue, Jeffrey Punske, Deniz Tat, Jessamyn Schertz, and Alex Trueman, 90–98. Somerville, MA: Cascadilla Proceedings Project.

Han, Chung-Hye, and Laura Siegel. 1996. Syntactic and semantic conditions on NPI licensing in questions. In *Proceedings of WCCFL 15*, ed. Brian Agbayani and Sze-Wing Tang, 177–191. Stanford, CA: CSLI Publications.

Harford Perez, Carolyn. 1985. Aspects of complementation in three Bantu languages. Doctoral dissertation, University of Wisconsin-Madison, Madison, WI.

Harley, Heidi. 2003. Possession and the double object construction. In *Yearbook of Linguistic Variation*, ed. Pierre Pica and Johan Rooryck, 29–62. Amsterdam: Benjamins.

Harley, Heidi. 2013. External arguments and the Mirror Principle: On the distinctness of Voice and v. *Lingua* 125:34–57.

Heinämäki, Orvokki. 1984. Aspect in Finnish. In *Aspect Bound: A Voyage into the Realm of Germanic, Slavonic, and Finno-Ugrian Aspectology*, ed. C. de Groot and H. Tommola, 179–198. Dordrecht: Foris.

Henderson, Brent. 2006a. Multiple agreement and inversion in Bantu. *Syntax* 9:275–289.

Henderson, Brent. 2006b. Multiple agreement, concord, and case-checking in Bantu. In *Selected Proceedings of the 36th Annual Conference on African Linguistics*, ed. Olaoba F. Arasanyin and Michael A. Pemberton, 60–65. Somerville, MA: Cascadilla Proceedings Project.

von Heusinger, Klaus, and Jaklin Kornfilt. 2005. The case of the direct object in Turkish: Semantics, syntax and morphology. *Turkic languages* 9:3–44.

Hiraiwa, Ken. 2001. Multiple Agree and the defective intervention constraint in Japanese. In *The proceedings of HUMIT 2000*, ed. Ora Matushansky, Albert Costa, Javier Martín-González, Lance Nathan, and Adam Szczegielniak, 67–80. Cambridge, MA: MITWPL.

Holland, Gary. 1993. Transitivity, causativity, and surface case in Old Norse. *Arkiv för Nordisk Filogi* 108:19–37.

Holmberg, Anders, and Thorbjörg Hróarsdóttir. 2004. Agreement and movement in Icelandic raising constructions. *Lingua* 114:651–673.

Hombert, Jean-Marie. 1980. Noun Classes of the Beboid languages. In *Noun Classes in the Grassfields Bantu Borderland*, ed. Larry M. Hyman, volume 8:83–98. Southern California Occasional Papers in Linguistics.

de Hoop, Helen. 1996. *Case configuration and noun phrase interpretation*. New York: Garland Publishing, Inc.

Hyman, Larry, and Jenneke van der Wal, ed. In preparation. *The Conjoint/Disjoint Alternation in Bantu*. Trends in Linguistics. Berlin: Mouton de Gruyter.

Hyman, Larry M. 2003. Suffix ordering in Bantu: A morphocentric approach. In *Yearbook of Morphology 2002*, ed. Geert Booij and Jaap van Marle, 245–281. Dordrecht: Kluwer Academic Publishers.

Hyman, Larry M. 2005. Initial vowel and prefix tone in Kom: Related to the Bantu augment? In *Studies in African Comparative Linguistics with Special Focus on Bantu and Mande: Essays in Honor of Y. Bastin and C. Gregoire*, ed. Koen Bostoen and Jacky Maniacky, 313–341. Rüdiger Köppe Verlag.

Hyman, Larry M., and Francis X. Katamba. 1991. Cyclicity and suffix doubling in the Bantu verb stem. In *Proceedings of Berkeley Linguistics Society 17*, 134–144.

Hyman, Larry M., and Francis X. Katamba. 1993. The augment in Luganda: Syntax or pragmatics? In *Theoretical Aspects of Bantu Grammar 1*, ed. Sam Mchombo, 209–259. CSLI Publications.

Iatridou, Sabine. 1993. On nominative case assignment and a few related things. In *Papers on Case and Agreement II*, ed. Colin Phillips, volume 19, 175–196. MIT Working Papers in Linguistics.

Iatridou, Sabine, and David Embick. 1997. Apropos pro. *Language* 73:58–78.

Ishihara, Shinichiro. 2007. Major phrase, focus intonation, multiple spell-out. *The Linguistic Review* 24:137–167.

Jonas, Dianne. 1996. Clause structure and verb syntax in Scandinavian and English. Doctoral dissertation, Harvard University.

Jónsson, Jóhannes Gísli. 2003. Not so quirky: On subject case in Icelandic. *Nordlyd* 36:142–164.

Jónsson, Jóhannes Gísli. 2009. Covert nominative and dative subjects in Faroese. *Nordlyd* 36:142–164.

Julien, Marit. 2002. *Syntactic Heads and Word Formation*. New York: Oxford University Press.

Kahnemuyipour, Arsalan. 2004. The syntax of sentential stress. Doctoral dissertation, University of Toronto, Toronto, Canada.

Kang, Myung-Yoon. 1988. Topics in Korean syntax. Doctoral dissertation, MIT, Cambridge, MA.

Katamba, Francis X. 2003. Bantu nominal morphology. In *The Bantu Languages*, ed. Derek Nurse and Gérard Philippson, 103–120. Routledge.

Kavari, Jukura, Lutz Marten, and Jenneke van der Wal. 2012. Tone cases in Otjiherero: Head–complement relations, linear order, and information structure. *Africana Linguistica* XVIII:315–353.

Kayne, Richard. 1981. Two notes on the NIC. In *Theory of Markedness in Generative Grammar*, ed. Adriana Belletti, Luciana Brandi, and Luigi Rizzi, Proceedings of the 1979 GLOW conference, 317–347. GLOW, Pisa: Scuola Normale Superiore.

Khumalo, J.S.M. 1981. Zulu tonology, part 1. *African Studies* 40:53–130.

Khumalo, J.S.M. 1982. Zulu tonology, part 2. *African Studies* 41:3–125.

Kinyalolo, Kasangati. 1991. Syntactic dependencies and the spec–head hypothesis in KiLega. Doctoral dissertation, UCLA, Los Angeles, CA.

Kiparsky, Paul. 1998. Partitive case and aspect. In *The Projection of Arguments: Lexical and Compositional Factors*, ed. Miriam Butt and Wilhelm Geuder, 265–308. Stanford, CA: CSLI Publications.

Kiparsky, Paul. 2001. Structural case in Finnish. *Lingua* 111:315–376.

Kiss, Katalin É. 1998. Idendificational focus versus information focus. *Language* 74:245–273.

Koopman, Hilda. 1996. The spec head configuration. In *Syntax at Sunset: UCLA Working Papers in Syntax and Semantics*, volume 1, 37–65. Los Angeles, CA: UCLA Working Papers in Linguistics.

Kornfilt, Jaklin. 1997. *Turkish*. London: Routledge.

Koster, Jan. 1978. Why subject sentences don't exist. In *Recent Transformational Studies in European Languages*, ed. Samuel Jay Keyser, 53–64. Cambridge, Massachusetts: MIT Press.

Kratzer, Angelika, and Elisabeth Selkirk. 2007. Phase theory and prosodic spellout: The case of verbs. *The Linguistic Review* 24:93–135.

Ladusaw, William. 1980. *Polarity Sensitivity as Inherent Scope Relations*. New York: Garland Publishing, Inc.

Landau, Idan. 2007. Constraints on partial VP-fronting. *Syntax* 10:127–164.

Landau, Idan. 2011. Predication vs. aboutness in copy raising. *Natural Language and Linguistic Theory* 29:779–813.

Lechner, Winfried. 2003. Phrase structure paradoxes, movement, and ellipsis. In *The Interfaces*, ed. Kerstin Schwabe and Susanne Winkler, 177–205. Amsterdam: John Benjamins.

Legate, Julie Anne. 2005. Split absolutive. Manuscript, University of Delaware.

Longobardi, Giuseppe. 1994. Reference and proper names. *Linguistic Inquiry* 25:609–666.

Longobardi, Giuseppe. 2000. "Postverbal" subjects and the mapping hypothesis. *Linguistic Inquiry* 31:691–702.

Magagula, Constance. 2010. INdebe yoMhlaba ayisisizanga ngalutho thina bantu abampofu nabahlala emijondolo eNingizimu Afrikha [The World Cup didn't help us poor slum dwellers of South Africa at all]. <http://www.abahlali.org/node/7297>, speech given at Rhodes University on behalf of Abahlali baseMjondolo [Durban Shack Dwellers' Movement], September 2010.

Maho, Jouni. 2003. A classification of the Bantu languages: An update of Guthrie's referential system. In *The Bantu Languages*, ed. Derek Nurse and Gérard Phillipson. New York: Routledge.

Marten, Lutz. 2006. Locative inversion in Otjiherero: More on morpho-syntactic variation in Bantu. *ZAS Working Papers in Linguistics* 43:97–122.

Marten, Lutz, Nancy Kula, and Nhlanhla Thwala. 2007. Parameters of morpho-syntactic variation in Bantu. *Transactions of the Philological Society* 105:253–338.

Martin, Roger. 1996. A Minimalist theory of PRO and control. Doctoral dissertation, University of Connecticut, Storrs, CT.

Massam, Diane. 2001. Pseudo noun incorporation in Niuean. *Natural Language and Linguistic Theory* 19:153–197.

Matushansky, Ora. 2002. A beauty of a construction. In *Proceedings of the 21st West Coast Conference on Formal Linguistics*, ed. Line Mikkelsen and Christopher Potts, 264–277. Somerville, MA: Cascadilla Press.

May, Robert. 1979. Must COMP-to-COMP movement be stipulated? *Linguistic Inquiry* 10:719–725.

McCloskey, James. 1985. Case, movement and raising in modern Irish. In *Proceedings of WCCFL 4*, ed. Jeffrey Goldberg, Susannah MacKaye, and Michael T. Wescoat, 190–205. Stanford, CA: CSLI Publications.

McFadden, Thomas. 2004. The position of morphological case in the derivation: A study on the syntax–morphology interface. Doctoral dissertation, University of Pennsylvania, Philadelphia, PA.

McGinnis, Martha. 2001. Phases and the syntax of applicatives. In *North East Linguistic Society*, ed. Minjoo Kim and Uri Strauss, 333–349. University of Massachusetts, Amherst: GLSA.

Meeussen, A.E. 1959. Essai de grammaire Rundi. In *Annales du Musée Royal du Congo Belge*, number 24 in Série Sciences Humaines. Musée Royal du Congo Belge.

Miestamo, Matti. 2014. Partitives and negation: A cross-linguistic survey. In *Partitive cases and related categories*, ed. Silvia Luraghi and Tuomas Huumo, number 54 in Empirical Approaches to Language Typology, 63–86. Berlin: Mouton de Gruyter.

Mithun, Marianne. 1984. The evolution of noun incorporation. *Language* 60:847–894.

Mzolo, D. 1968. The Zulu noun without the initial vowel. *African Studies* 27:195–210.

Ndayiragije, Juvénal. 1999. Checking economy. *Linguistic Inquiry* 30:399–444.

Nkabinde, A.C. 1985. *An Introduction to Zulu Syntax*. Pretoria, South Africa: Acacia Books.

Nomura, Masashi. 2005. Nominative case and agree(ment). Doctoral dissertation, University of Connecticut, Storrs, CT.

Norris, Mark. 2012. Toward an analysis of concord (in Icelandic). In *Proceedings of WCCFL 29*, ed. Jaehoon Choi, Alan Hogue, Jeffrey Punske, Deniz Tat, Jessamyn Schertz, and Alex Trueman, 205–213. Somerville, MA: Cascadilla Proceedings Project.

Norris, Mark. 2014. A theory of nominal concord. Doctoral dissertation, UC Santa Cruz, Santa Cruz, CA.

Nurse, Derek, and Gérard Philippson, ed. 2003. *The Bantu Languages*. New York: Routledge.

Nyembezi, C.L. Sibusiso. 1991. *Uhlelo lwesiZulu*. Pietermaritzburg, South Africa: Shuter & Shooter Publishers Ltd., fifth edition.

Nyembezi, Sibusiso. 1963. *Zulu Proverbs*. Johannesburg, South Africa: Witwatersrand University Press.

Öztürk, Balkız. 2003. Pseudo incorporation in Turkish. *Harvard Working Papers in Linguistics* 8:139–158.

Partee, Barbara H., and Vladimir Borschev. 2004. The semantics of Russian genitive of negation: The nature and role of perspectival structure. In *Proceedings of SALT XIV*, ed. Kazuha Watanabe and Robert B. Young, 212–234. CLC Publications.

Polinsky, Maria, and Eric Potsdam. 2006. Expanding the scope of control and raising. *Syntax* 9:171–192.

Postal, Paul. 1974. *On Raising*. Cambridge, Massachusetts: MIT Press.

Potsdam, Eric, and Jeffrey T. Runner. 2001. Richard returns: Copy Raising and its implications. In *Proceedings of CLS*.

Poulos, George, and Christian Msimang. 1998. *A Linguistic Analysis of Zulu*. Cape Town: Via Afrika.

Preminger, Omer. 2009a. Breaking agreements: Distinguishing agreement and clitic doubling by their failures. *Linguistic Inquiry* 40:618–666.

Preminger, Omer. 2009b. Long-distance agreement without *probe–goal* relations. In *Towards a Purely Derivational Syntax: Survive-minimalism*, ed. Michael T. Putnam, 41–56. Amsterdam: John Benjamins.

Preminger, Omer. 2010. Failure to agree is not a failure: Phi-agreement with post-verbal subjects in Hebrew. *Linguistic Variation Yearbook* 9(1):241–278.

Preminger, Omer. 2011. Agreement as a falliable operation. Doctoral dissertation, Massachusetts Institute of Technology.

Preminger, Omer. 2014. *Agreement and its failures*. Number 68 in Linguistic Inquiry Monograph. Cambridge, MA: MIT Press.

Progovac, Ljiljana. 1993a. Long-distance reflexives: Movement-to-Infl versus relativized subject. *Linguistic Inquiry* 24:755–772.

Progovac, Ljiljana. 1993b. Negative polarity: Entailment and binding. *Linguistics and Philosophy* 16:149–180.

Puech, Gilbert. 1988. Augment et préfixe nominal en ngubi. *Pholia* 3:247–256.

Pylkkänen, Liina. 2002. Introducing arguments. Doctoral dissertation, Massachusetts Institute of Technology.

Pylkkänen, Liina. 2008. *Introducing Arguments*. Linguistic Inquiry Monograph. Cambridge, MA: MIT Press.

Rackowski, Andrea, and Norvin Richards. 2005. Phase edge and extraction: A Tagalog case study. *Linguistic Inquiry* 36:565–599.

Rezác, Milan. 2008. Phi-Agree and Theta-related Case. In *Phi theory*, ed. Daniel Harbour, David Adger, and Susana Béjar, 83–129. Oxford: Oxford University Press.

Richards, Norvin. 1998. The principle of minimal compliance. *Linguistic Inquiry* 29:599–629.

Richards, Norvin. 2010. *Uttering Trees*. Linguistic Inquiry Monograph. Cambridge, MA: MIT Press.

Richards, Norvin. 2011. Uttering theory. Manuscript, MIT.

Riedel, Kristina. 2009. The syntax of object marking in Sambaa: A comparative Bantu perspective. Doctoral dissertation, Universiteit Leiden.

Rizzi, Luigi. 1986. On chain formation. In *The Grammar of Pronominal Clitics(19)*, ed. Hagit Borer. New York, New York: Academic Press.

Sabel, Joachim, and Jochen Zeller. 2006. *Wh*-question formation in Nguni. In *Selected Proceedings of the 35th Annual Conference on African Linguistics*, ed. John et al Mugane, 271–283. Somerville, MA: Cascadilla Proceedings Project.

Sabelo, Nonhlanhla O. 1990. The possessive in Zulu. Master's thesis, University of Zululand, KwaDlangezwa, South Africa.

Schneider-Zioga, Patricia. 2007. Anti-agreement, anti-locality and minimality. *Natural Language and Linguistic Theory* 25:403–446.

Schütze, Carson. 1997. INFL in child and adult language: Agreement, case and licensing. Doctoral dissertation, Massachusetts Institute of Technology, Cambridge, MA.

Schütze, Carson T. 2001. On the nature of default case. *Syntax* 4:205–238.

Sigurðsson, Halldór Ármann. 1989. Verbal syntax and Case in Icelandic. Doctoral dissertation, Department of Scandinavian Languages, University of Lund.

Sigurðsson, Halldór Ármann. 1992. The case of quirky subjects. *Working Papers in Scandinavian Syntax* 49:1–26.

Sigurðsson, Halldór Ármann. 1996. Icelandic finite verb agreement. *Working Papers in Scandinavian Syntax* 57:1–46.

Sigurðsson, Halldór Ármann. 2004. Icelandic non-nominative subjects: Facts and implications. In *Non-nominative subjects*, ed. Peri Bhaskararao and K.V. Subbarao, volume 2, 137–159. John Benjamins.

Sigurðsson, Halldór Ármann, and Anders Holmberg. 2008. Icelandic dative intervention: Person and Number are separate probes. In *Agreement Restrictions*, ed. Roberta D'Alessandro, Gunnar Hrafn Hrafnbjargarson, and Susann Fischer, 251–280. Berlin: Mouton de Gruyter.

Slattery, H. 1981. *Auxiliary Verbs in Zulu*. Occasional Papers, Department of African Languages. Rhodes University, Grahamstown, South Africa: Department of African Languages.

Van der Spuy, Andrew. 1993. Dislocated noun phrases in Nguni. *Lingua* 90:335–355.

Van der Spuy, Andrew. 2001. Grammatical structure and Zulu morphology. Doctoral dissertation, University of the Witwatersrand.

von Staden, P.M.S. 1973. The initial vowel of the noun in Zulu. *African Studies* 32:163–181.

Stowell, Timothy. 1981. Origins of phrase structure. Doctoral dissertation, Massachusetts Institute of Technology, Cambridge, MA.

Taraldsen, Tarald. 2010. The nanosyntax of Nguni noun class prefixes and concords. *Lingua* 120:1522–1548.

Thomas, Rose. 2003. The partitive in Finnish and its relation to weak quantifiers. Doctoral dissertation, University of Westminster, Westminster, UK.

Thráinsson, Höskuldur. 1979. *On Complementation in Icelandic*. New York: Garland Press.

Thwala, Nhlanhla. 2006a. On the subject–predicate relation and subject agreement in SiSwati. *Southern African Linguistics and Applied Language Studies* 24:331–359.

Thwala, Nhlanhla. 2006b. A unified analysis of questions in Nguni languages. Manuscript, School of Oriental and African Studies.

Ura, Hiroyuki. 1994. Varieties of raising and the feature-based bare phrase structure theory. Doctoral dissertation, Massachusetts Institute of Technology, Cambridge, MA.

Ussery, Cherlon. 2013. The syntax of optional agreement in Icelandic. Manuscript, Carleton College, draft 2/20/13, February 2013.

Vainikka, Anne. 1989. Deriving syntactic representations in Finnish. Doctoral dissertation, University of Massachusetts, Amherst, MA.

Vainikka, Anne. 1993. The three structural cases in Finnish. In *Case and Other Functional Categories in Finnish*, ed. Anders Holmberg and Urpo Nikanne, 129–159. Berlin: Mouton de Gruyter.

Varlokosta, Spyridoula. 1994. Issues on Modern Greek sentential complementation. Doctoral dissertation, University of Maryland, College Park, MD.

Vergnaud, Jean-Roger. 2006 [1976]. Letter to Noam Chomsky and Howard Lasnik. In *Syntax: Critical Concepts in Linguistics*, ed. Robert Friedin and Howard Lasnik, volume 5, 21–34. London: Routledge.

Visser, Marianne. 2008. Definiteness and specificity in the isiXhosa determiner phrase. *South African Journal of African Languages* 11–29.

Voeltz, F.K. Erhard. 2004. Long and short verb forms in Zulu. University of Cologne.

de Vries, Mark. 2006. The syntax of appositive relativization: On specifying coordination, false free relatives, and promotion. *Linguistic Inquiry* 37:229–270.

Van der Wal, Jenneke. 2009. Word order and information structure in Makhuwa-Enahara. Doctoral dissertation, Universiteit Leiden.

Van der Wal, Jenneke. 2011. Focus excluding alternatives: Conjoint/disjoint marking in Makhuwa. *Lingua* 212:1734–1750.

Van der Wal, Jenneke. 2012. Subject agreement and the EPP in Bantu agreeing inversion. *Cambridge Occasional Papers in Linguistics* 6:201–236.

Woolford, Ellen. 2006. Lexical case, inherent case, and argument structure. *Linguistic Inquiry* 37:111–130.

Wurmbrand, Susi. 2001. *Infinitives: Restructuring and Clause Structure*. Mouton de Gruyter.

Wurmbrand, Susi. 2007. How complex are complex predicates. *Syntax* 10:243–288.

Wurmbrand, Susi. 2011. On Agree and Merge. Manuscript, University of Connecticut. Storrs.

Wurmbrand, Susi. 2012. Agree(ment): Looking up or looking down? Handout, MIT, March 2012.

Wurmbrand, Susi. 2014. The Merge Condition: A syntactic approach to selection. In *Minimalism and Beyond: Radicalizing the Interfaces*, ed. Peter Kosta, Lilia Schürcks, Steven Franks, and Teodora Radev-Bork, 139–177. Amsterdam: John Benjamins.

Yoneda, Nobuko. 2011. Word order in Matengo: Topicality and information roles. *Lingua* 121:754–771.

Zaenen, Annie, Joan Maling, and Hoskuldur Thráinsson. 1985. Case and grammatical functions: The Icelandic passive. *Natural Language and Linguistic Theory* 3:441–483.

Zeijlstra, Hedde. 2004. *Sentential Negation and Negative Concord*. Utrecht: LOT.

Zeijlstra, Hedde. 2008. Negative concord is syntactic agreement. Manuscript, University of Amsterdam, April 2008.

Zeijlstra, Hedde. 2012a. There is only one way to agree. *The Linguistic Review* 29:491–539.

Zeller, Jochen. 2006. Raising out of finite CP in Nguni: the case of *fanele*. *Southern African Linguistics and Applied Language Studies* 24:255–275.

Zeller, Jochen. 2008. The subject marker in Bantu as an antifocus marker. *Stellenbosch Papers in Linguistics* 38:221–254.

Zeller, Jochen. 2010. Semantic locative inversion and predication in Zulu. Manuscript, UKZN, December 2010.

Zeller, Jochen. 2012. Object marking in Zulu. *Southern African Linguistics and Applied Language Studies* 30:219–325.

Zeller, Jochen. 2013. In defence of head movement: Evidence from Bantu. In *Diagnosing Syntax*, ed. Lisa Cheng and Norbert Corver, Studies in Theoretical Linguistics, 87–111. Oxford: Oxford University Press.

Zeller, Jochen. 2015. Argument prominence and agreement: Explaining an unexpected object asymmetry in Zulu. *Lingua* 156:17–39.

Zeller, Jochen, Sabine Zerbian, and Toni Cook. In preparation. Prosodic evidence for syntactic phrasing in Zulu. In *The Conjoint/Disjoint Alternation in Bantu*, ed. Larry Hyman and Jenneke van der Wal, Trends in Linguistics. Berlin: Mouton de Gruyter.

INDEX